PAUL NEWMAN

PAUL NEWMAN

DANIEL O'BRIEN

faber and faber

First published in 2004
by Faber and Faber Limited
Bloomsbury House, 74–77 Great Russell Street,
London WC1B 3DA

This paperback edition first published in 2005

Typeset by Faber and Faber Ltd
Printed in England by CPI Bookmarque, Croydon

A CIP record for this book is available from the British Library

ISBN 978-0-571-21987-2

10 9 8 7 6 5 4 3

Contents

List of Illustrations

Acknowledgements

My thanks to Jacqueline Bisset, Joan Collins, Walter Donohue, Anthony Harvey, Gary Kramer, Mark Lonsdale, David O'Leary, Beth Richards and Robert Wise.

Illustrations

Stills from *The Silver Chalice*, *Somebody Up There Likes Me*, *The Long Hot Summer*, *Exodus*, *Hud* and *Nobody's Fool* courtesy of BFI collections. Copyright is held by the following organizations:

Warner Brothers (*The Silver Chalice*, *The Helen Morgan Story*, *The Left-Handed Gun*, *Harper*, *Cool Hand Luke*, *Rachel, Rachel*, *Pocket Money*, *The Life and Times of Judge Roy Bean*, *The Towering Inferno*, *The Drowning Pool*, *Fort Apache, The Bronx*, *The Hudsucker Proxy*);

Columbia (*Count Three and Pray*, *Absence of Malice*, *The Glass Menagerie*);

Metro-Goldwyn-Mayer (*The Rack*, *Somebody Up There Likes Me*, *Cat on a Hot Tin Roof*, *Sweet Bird of Youth*, *The Prize*, *The Outrage*, *Lady L*);

Twentieth Century Fox (*The Three Faces of Eve*, *The Long Hot Summer*, *Rally 'Round the Flag, Boys!*, *The Hustler*, *Hemingway's Adventures of a Young Man*, *Hombre*, *Butch Cassidy and the Sundance Kid*, *The Effect of Gamma Rays on Man-in-the-Moon Marigolds*, *Quintet*, *The Verdict*, *Road to Perdition*);

United Artists (*Exodus*, *Buffalo Bill and the Indians, or Sitting Bull's History Lesson*);

Paramount (*Hud*, *A New Kind of Love*, *WUSA*, *Fat Man and Little Boy*, *Nobody's Fool*);

Universal (*Torn Curtain*, *The Secret War of Harry Frigg*, *Winning*, *Sometimes a Great Notion*, *The Sting*, *Slap Shot*);

Touchstone Pictures (*The Color of Money*, *Blaze*);

Miramax (*Mr and Mrs Bridge*).

Introduction

Acting is like letting your pants down – you're exposed.
Paul Newman

Paul Newman once defined a star as 'someone who cannot live up to his legend'. Ironically, he himself has proved the exception to the rule: superstar, philanthropist, model husband, world-class racing driver and icon. A successful, respected leading man for over fifty years, he is one of the last living links between Hollywood's 'Golden Age' and the post-studio era. His best known films, notably *The Hustler* (1961), *Cool Hand Luke* (1967), *Butch Cassidy and the Sundance Kid* (1969) and *The Sting* (1973), have become a part of popular culture. Newman is also a successful producer and director, and is one of Hollywood's most prominent liberal activists. His many and varied acting roles include boxer, outlaw, lawyer, pool hustler, jazz musician, private detective, double agent, convict, lumberjack, hanging judge, conman, architect, ice-hockey coach, beat cop and crime boss. Director John Huston, who worked with Newman on *The Life and Times of Judge Roy Bean* (1972), praised him as an adventurous actor, always looking for new characters rather than sticking to a fixed, audience-friendly screen persona.

Newman got off to a bad start in Hollywood, making a disastrous film début in *The Silver Chalice* (1954), a risible biblical epic. An Actors Studio graduate, he didn't click onscreen until he toned down the heavy 'Method' style. Blessed with classic good looks and an athletic build, Newman found his niche playing intelligent, articulate outsiders, often with a non-conformist attitude. In his book on Lee Marvin, showbusiness biographer Donald Zec characterized the Newman magic as 'tanned virility and undiluted charm'. While this suggests a largely superficial approach, Newman is in fact an actor of considerable depth and, like Marlon Brando, a contemporary and rival, he had the rare ability of appearing both strong and vulnerable. Impertinent rather than hostile, Newman injects warmth and humour into his characters, making the occasional hints of cruelty all the more disturbing. Huston regarded him as the ideal film actor: 'graceful, stylish, with an inborn rhythm'.

Thrown to the lions as a Warner Brothers contract actor, Newman prospered in a different arena, playing boxer Rocky Graziano in Metro-Goldwyn-Mayer's *Somebody Up There Likes Me* (1956). This sentimental biopic demonstrated Newman's film potential, though full-fledged stardom took another five years. His deal with Warner produced only one notable film, *The Left-Handed Gun* (1958), a psychological spin on the Billy the Kid legend. Loaned out from Warner, Newman became established in heavyweight, sometimes heavy-handed, melodramas, such as *Cat on a Hot Tin Roof* (1958).

Buying out his Warner contract, Newman turned freelance star with *Exodus* (1960). While Newman despised this modern epic, the film's commercial success boosted his industry standing, and the 1960s would go on to bring Newman career-defining roles in *The Hustler* and *Hud* (1963). Offering emotional depth rather than melodramatic posturing, he turned a pair of cocky, selfish, amoral losers into two of cinema's most memorable characters. Following the critical and commercial failures of *The Outrage* (1964) and *Lady L* (1965), Newman re-established his star status with a trio of popular genre pieces: the private-eye movie *Harper* (1966), the prison drama *Cool Hand Luke* and the western *Butch Cassidy and the Sundance Kid*. Newman's directing début, *Rachel, Rachel* (1968), starring his second wife, Joanne Woodward, succeeded as a low-key character study and at this point Newman looked capable of becoming an important film-maker, as well as a major star. However, for various reasons, his directing career would prove intermittent.

As the 1960s came to an end, Newman responded to the era's social unrest with the political drama *WUSA* (1970), one of his most personal projects. He fell from box-office favour during the early 1970s, turning out a series of commercial flops. While *Sometimes a Great Notion* (1971) and *The Life and Times of Judge Roy Bean* were offbeat and ambitious, other Newman movies of this era seemed less assured. Approaching fifty, Newman boosted his career by co-starring in *The Sting* and *The Towering Inferno* (1974), two 'high-concept' blockbusters.

The second half of the 1970s proved a period of mixed fortunes. Out of step with mainstream Hollywood, Newman alternated a couple of quirky Robert Altman experiments, *Buffalo Bill and the Indians* (1976) and *Quintet* (1979), with the foul-mouthed comedy *Slap Shot* (1977) and the failed disaster epic *When Time Ran Out* (1980). Dodging earthquakes, tidal waves and volcanic eruptions, Newman had reached the nadir of his career, alienating critics and audiences alike. Once again, Newman rallied with two conventional genre pieces: the cop movie *Fort Apache, The Bronx* (1981) and the courtroom drama *The Verdict* (1982). After several years in the wilderness, this 'comeback' was crucial to Newman's career, the latter film winning him an

Oscar nomination. While *The Verdict* is solidly crafted entertainment, lifted by Newman's heartfelt performance, his work during the early 1980s is uneven. Neither *Absence of Malice* (1981) nor *Harry and Son* (1984) sees the star on top form. Handed an ominous honorary Academy Award in 1986, Newman finally took the Best Actor trophy a year later for *The Color of Money* (1986), a belated sequel to *The Hustler*. Frustrated by a lack of good roles, Newman made few films after *Mr and Mrs Bridge* (1990), a Merchant–Ivory showcase for himself and Joanne Woodward. Over the past decade, only *Nobody's Fool* (1994) and *Road to Perdition* (2002) have been successful. That said, Newman's talent and screen presence still shine. Pushing eighty, he is arguably Hollywood's most respected veteran star, working opposite relative newcomers like Bruce Willis, Kevin Costner and Tom Hanks. While *Road to Perdition* will not be Newman's last film appearance, his portrayal of a paternal yet monstrous gang boss is a fitting swansong.

Offscreen, Newman's marriage to Joanne Woodward commands a respect that borders on awe. Their enduring, scandal-free relationship is cited as one of Hollywood's great domestic success stories. That said, Woodward's initially promising film career was rapidly eclipsed by Newman's stardom. Committed to quality work in theatre and television, Woodward admitted that she felt overshadowed by her celebrity husband. Furthermore, few of their joint screen appearances are notable, suggesting that both compromised on quality to work together. They have done better as a director–actor team, following *Rachel, Rachel* with *The Effect of Gamma Rays on Man-in-the-Moon Marigolds* (1972), *The Shadow Box* (1980) and *The Glass Menagerie* (1987). Arguably, Woodward gave her best screen performance in *They Might Be Giants* (1971), a film Newman produced.

While Newman hates discussing his private life, he is widely perceived as a man with little to hide. His personal problems, including bouts of heavy drinking and several arrests, are public knowledge, while rumours of on-location affairs and bisexual tendencies have never been substantiated. On the downside, Newman was not close to his father, who disapproved of Newman's chosen career and died before the actor became successful, let alone famous. The drug-related death of Newman's only son – from his first marriage – has left a permanent sense of guilt. Significantly, Newman became heavily involved with charity fund-raising, through his 'Newman's Own' range of food products.

Most stars acknowledge the element of chance in their careers, yet

Paul Newman genuinely believes in 'Newman's luck'. As he once explained: 'It's allowed me to get close to a lot of edges without falling off.' He is regarded as a star with an unusually strong body of work, whether through sound judgement or good fortune. Critic Ethan Mordden inclines toward the former, citing 'the almost studied diversity of his roles'. Inevitably, this glowing record of achievement is part myth, soon punctured by a glance at Newman's filmography. Leaving aside *The Silver Chalice*, the Newman résumé includes a number of compromises and misfires. He also has his share of what Kirk Douglas termed 'just movies', efficient, bland and forgettable. Critic David Thomson argues that Newman shows little grasp of what makes good cinema. While this is overly harsh, there is a contradiction in Newman's assessment of his abilities as an actor. He has described himself as a limited talent, ill-suited to non-American 'types', yet at the same time, he yearns for roles far removed from his own personality, enabling him to 'crawl out of my skin'.

In truth, Newman's early film credits are largely undistinguished. Reeling from anti-trust legislation, declining audiences, the rise of television and political witch-hunts, the 1950s Hollywood establishment was conservative and unadventurous. Under contract to Warner Brothers, Newman had little say in his film projects. He often worked with jaded craftsmen nearing the end of their careers, notably Victor Saville (*The Silver Chalice*), Michael Curtiz (*The Helen Morgan Story*), Leo McCarey (*Rally 'Round the Flag, Boys!*) and Vincent Sherman (*The Young Philadelphians*). Only Robert Wise, the director of *Somebody Up There Likes Me*, gave Newman the chance to show his star quality. While Arthur Penn's *The Left-Handed Gun* and Richard Brooks's *Cat on a Hot Tin Roof* have their moments, the films were undermined by creative differences, censorship problems and studio tampering.

At the start of the 1960s, Newman enjoyed an ideal partnership with Robert Rossen, the producer, director and co-writer of *The Hustler*. A gifted, if erratic, film-maker, Rossen helped Newman attain a new level of screen acting. While Newman certainly appreciated Rossen's input, he seemed to mistrust directors who dominated their cast and crew. A strong advocate of equality and democracy, Newman believed these principles should apply to the film set. As he once explained: 'It's very simple. The actor should serve as a trigger for the director, and the director should serve as a trigger for the actor.' A film always worked best as a partnership of equals: 'It doesn't make any difference whether you're the actor asking a director about the way he wants to create a role, or whether you're the director asking the actor.' In the long term, it's arguable whether Newman's wariness of 'star' directors limited his career. He has always dismissed the *auteur* theory. In his opinion, a strong screenplay, with a gripping story and interesting characters, is far more important. As Newman explained at the time of *Cool Hand Luke*, 'Give an actor a good script and he'll move the world.' In fairness, Newman's views were shaped by his experiences with *Exodus* director Otto Preminger, who treated actors as puppets. When Alfred Hitchcock used the same approach on *Torn Curtain*, Newman's prejudices were confirmed. Significantly, Newman turned down Stanley Donen's romantic comedy *Two for the Road* (1967), scripted by Fredric Raphael, on the grounds that the film was a director's picture. Having placed his faith in the script, Newman seemed to undervalue the director's contribution. On too many occasions, he was happy to work with journeymen such as Jack Smight (*Harper*, *The Secret War of Harry Frigg*), Stuart Rosenberg (*Cool Hand Luke*, *WUSA*, *Pocket Money*, *The Drowning Pool*) and James Goldstone (*Winning*, *When Time Ran Out*). While Newman and Rosenberg scored a hit with *Cool Hand Luke*, their subsequent collaborations fell short.

The directors most associated with Newman are Martin Ritt and George Roy Hill. Ritt made six Newman films, of which *Hud* and *Hombre* (1967) hold up best. *Hud* rivals *The Hustler* as Newman's greatest film. George Roy Hill steered Newman through *Butch Cassidy* and *The Sting*, high-calibre entertainments with more style than substance. By the time of *Slap Shot*, Hill felt that Newman had wasted much of his potential. In Hill's view, Newman lost his passion for acting, devoting his energy and enthusiasm to motor racing instead. He is probably the only actor in history to compare Laurence Olivier with Nigel Mansell. While Newman seemed disenchanted with acting for much of the 1970s, later films such as *The Verdict*, *The Color of Money*, *Mr and Mrs Bridge*, *Nobody's Fool* and *Road to Perdition* feature the star at the top of his game.

When he did find two agreeable *auteurs*, John Huston and Robert Altman, the end results were mixed. While *Judge Roy Bean* and *Quintet* feature some of Newman's most unusual work, the films are too idiosyncratic for their own good. Newman's own career as a director never fulfilled the promise of *Rachel, Rachel*. From the start, he didn't want to direct and act in the same film, feeling he wouldn't do either role justice. Unwilling to sell himself as a director–star package, Newman limited his options. A skilful director of actors, Newman found a specialist niche in claustrophobic filmed plays, notably *The Effect of Gamma Rays on Man-in-the-Moon Marigolds* and *The Glass Menagerie*. Neither of Newman's two films as an actor–director was intended that way. He took over the direction of *Sometimes a Great Notion* (1971) midway through production when the original choice of Richard Colla didn't work out, and he felt his pet project *Harry and Son* (1984) suffered because he was obliged to star in the film, as well as produce, direct and co-write.

Newman's career has also been marked by a curious reverse narcissism. Rivalling Frank Sinatra for the most famous blue eyes in show business, Newman regarded his good looks as more of a curse than a blessing. His self-penned epitaph is revealing:

> Here lies
> Paul Newman
> Who died a failure
> Because his eyes
> Turned brown.

In Newman's view, an actor praised for their looks will never be judged on anything else. Tired of fans asking for a glimpse of the famous eyes, often hidden behind sunglasses, Newman usually responded: 'Is that all you think of me?' That said, many colleagues in the film business regarded Newman as extraordinarily handsome. Actress Barbara Rush, a friend and co-star, compared Newman to 'a sculpted Roman statue'. Cameraman Conrad Hall, who worked on *Harper*, *Cool Hand Luke*, *Butch Cassidy and the Sundance Kid* and *Road to Perdition*, considered him beautiful. David Mamet, screenwriter on *The Verdict*, described Newman as 'the most beautiful man ever to grace the screen'. However, uncomfortable with his good looks, Newman was reluctant to exploit this natural asset. His wariness of being 'too handsome' may stem from his experiences on *The Silver Chalice* (1954). Lost in the general ineptitude of that film, Newman looked like just another Hollywood pretty boy. His good looks and charisma also counted against him when he repeated his stage role in *Sweet Bird of Youth* (1962), cast as a hopeless Hollywood wannabe. Rock Hudson, the epitome of studio-manufactured stardom, once remarked, 'I can't play a loser: I don't look like one.' Newman, a vastly more gifted actor, has had the same problem.

For all Newman's ambivalence towards his looks, he's nevertheless worked long and hard to preserve and enhance them. For most of his career, Newman routinely employed Murine eyedrops prior to public appearances. His daily saunas and three-mile runs kept him in great shape, despite a prodigious beer intake. He also had a phase of soaking his face in ice water to keep those jowls firm. As Newman admits,

'There is something very corrupting about being an actor. It places a terrible premium on appearance.' That said, he has aged gracefully, his hair thinning, his skin sagging and wrinkled. In an industry where toupees and facelifts are common, this is a bold move. Once compared to a young Greek god, Newman now looks merely human.

It's been claimed that Newman inspires admiration rather than affection in his Hollywood peers. While Newman and Joanne Woodward are seen as a 'classy' couple, they have never been the greatest social mixers. A self-proclaimed loner, Newman enjoys good company but claims to have few close friends. Academy Award historian Anthony Holden describes him as 'perennially aloof', something he rejects: 'I've been accused of being aloof. I'm not. I'm just wary.' Newman also resents the assumption that his star status makes him public property. As he recently explained: 'If people start to treat you like a piece of meat or a long-lost friend or feel they can become cuddly for the price of a $5 movie ticket, you shut them out.' Interviewed in the 1960s, Newman seemed unhappy with his public image: 'Most people have the idea that actors are very grim and lack a sense of humour. And I always seem to be picked out as a prime example.' Journalists have found him remote and evasive, rarely opening up in a media-friendly fashion. Serious and reserved by nature, Newman has a strong, if quirky, sense of humour, both bawdy and whimsical. In many situations, this has served as a defensive barrier: 'I'm not very good at revealing myself. I cover up for it by telling terribly dirty jokes.'

While Newman has clashed with the right-wing media, he has made few enemies in the film-making community. Steve McQueen, who played a bit part in *Somebody Up There Likes Me*, turned Newman into a symbolic hate figure, the star he would one day surpass. Lee Marvin accused Newman of ego problems, or at least poor judgement, over the final edit of *Pocket Money* (1972), in which they co-starred. According to William Goldman, the screenwriter for *Harper* and *Butch Cassidy*, Newman has one of the strongest reputations in the film business, with no stories of bad behaviour. Goldman also admires Newman's refusal to identify with his screen image: 'I don't think Paul Newman really thinks he is Paul Newman in his head.' Martin Ritt never saw any hint of star ego: 'It's refreshing to find someone who has such a modest estimate of himself as Paul.' Gore Vidal, a friend for fifty years, describes Newman as a genuinely good person: 'He is what you would call a man of conscience – not necessarily of judgement, but of conscience. I don't know any [other] actors like that.'

Famously self-deprecating, Newman rejects his icon status: 'Brando,

Lee J. Cobb, Olivier are. I'm not.' He also makes light of his long career – 'I don't take much of it seriously. I really don't' – and rarely discusses his distinguished body of film work: 'It's out there.' Whether providing a brief DVD commentary for *The Hustler* or appearing on camera to discuss *The Long Hot Summer* (1958), Newman gives the impression of a man eager to be elsewhere. He also seems indifferent to his legacy: 'It's going to be whatever it is.' A notorious perfectionist, Newman rarely watches his films, dislikes interviews and dismisses most of his pre-1980 performances as inadequate. From the start, Paul Newman's harshest critic has always been himself.

1 The Man from Shaker Heights

1950s studio portrait

I wasn't driven to acting by an inner compulsion. I was running away from the sporting goods business.

Paul Newman

Paul Leonard Newman was born on 26 January 1925 in Cleveland Heights, an upmarket Jewish suburb of Cleveland, Cuyahoga County, Ohio, in the Mid-West. He was the second son of Arthur and Theresa Newman, an upper-middle-class couple. Their oldest child, Arthur Newman Jr, had been born the previous year.

Arthur Newman Sr (c. 1894–1950) was a second generation American, born in Cleveland to Simon Newman (c. 1853–95), a Hungarian immigrant, and Hannah Cohn (1857–1913), his Polish–Jewish wife. The family name had been anglicized from the original 'Neuman', a common practice of the time. Simon and Hannah Newman had seven children, all born in Ohio: Minnie (c. 1877–1953), Lillie (c. 1879–?), Aaron (1881–1963), Gertrude (c. 1882–1961), Ottile (1885–1965), Joseph Simon (1891–1960) and Arthur. As the youngest child, Arthur never got to know his father, who died, aged only forty-two, when Arthur was still a baby. He would feel this loss keenly when he became a parent himself.

Theresa Newman (1896–1982), née Fetsko, was born in Hungary, the daughter of Stephen Fetsko (1854–1946) and Mary Polenak (1875–?). At the turn of the twentieth century, when Theresa was four, the Fetsko family immigrated to the US, settling in Ohio.

After graduating from Cleveland's Central High School, Arthur Newman found a job in newspaper advertising. Aged seventeen, he became the youngest ever reporter with the *Cleveland Press*. In 1915, Arthur Newman's older brother Joseph founded Newman-Stern, Cleveland's first radio store. Arthur quit the *Cleveland Press*, with some reluctance, to join the new family business. While Joseph Newman had energy, initiative and imagination, he lacked Arthur's head for figures. With Arthur serving as the secretary-treasurer, Newman-Stern rapidly prospered. However, in 1917, the US government banned private radio broadcasts following the country's entry into the First World War. Undeterred, Newman-Stern made a successful switch to sporting goods.

Shortly after Paul's birth, the family moved to an eleven-room house in Shaker Heights. When the great Depression hit in 1929, Newman-Stern largely weathered the storm. Interestingly, Paul later played down his relatively affluent upbringing: ' . . . we felt the pinch. Sporting goods are a luxury, and the business always suffers in a depression.'

Small for his age, Newman had problems with the local bullies: 'I used to get the bejesus kicked out of me regularly in school.' Unable to fight back, at first, he learned how to numb himself from the inevitable pain. Trauma aside, this deliberate suppression of emotion would prove a stumbling block in his future career for, as Newman later admitted, 'That isn't a very valuable quality for an actor.' There may be an element of exaggeration here. James Stotter, a childhood friend of Newman, recalls Shaker Heights as 'a great place for a kid to grow up'. Newman was encouraged to read widely and took music lessons. He also developed a taste for fishing and showed promise in various sports. According to Stotter, Newman was keen on pool and practical jokes from an early age. Both would play significant roles in his adult life.

By all accounts, Arthur Newman Sr was a remote figure, dedicated to the family business. Working six days a week, he insisted that his sons learn the value of gainful employment from an early age. Following a stint as a newspaper delivery boy, Paul was taken on at the Newman-Stern store, working alongside Arthur Jr. Newman described his relationship with Arthur Jr as 'belligerent', though the brothers, close in age, remained on civil terms most of the time. Determined not to show favouritism, Arthur Sr had his sons work for longer hours and less pay than the other store employees. The message was clear: anything of real value came about only through hard work. According to some sources, Theresa also helped out at the store. Arthur Newman Sr assumed that both Paul and Arthur Jr would work for Newman-Stern on a permanent basis once they completed their education. In one case, at least, he would be disappointed.

Newman has admitted that he was never close to his father. A strong believer in moral values and discipline, Arthur Newman Sr could seem excessively strict. Nevertheless, interviewed in 1969, Newman described his father as 'a good-natured man'. He also credited Arthur Newman with 'a marvellous, whimsical sense of humor', a quality passed from father to son. Having grown up without his own father, Arthur Newman never learned how to show affection to his sons. It's notable that Newman talks about him in terms of respect rather than love: '. . . he survived the Depression because of his reputation for honesty. I learnt something about morality from him.' At least some of Arthur Newman's attitude rubbed off on his youngest son. For all Paul's belief in the 'Newman luck', he later claimed, 'I've had to work hard to achieve everything.'

Newman regarded his mother as materialistic, partly a result of her

impoverished upbringing. Born into a Catholic family, Theresa Newman converted to Christian Science soon after her marriage. While
both Arthur Jr and Paul were raised in the faith, Theresa took a liberal approach to her new religion. If anyone in the family fell ill, she still
relied on orthodox medical treatment rather than the power of prayer.
Paul grew up familiar with Judaism, Catholicism and Christian Science, none of which made a lasting impression. Interviewed in 2002,
at the age of seventy-seven, Newman claimed to have no spiritual
beliefs: 'when it's over, it's over'.

Newman inherited at least two traits from his mother. Theresa was
an excellent cook and, Paul felt, a frustrated performer. She certainly
gave Paul his first taste of theatre-going. At the age of seven, he made
his acting début in a grade-school production of *Robin Hood*. Cast as
a court jester, he had to wear a long dark wig and ruffled collar. He
also performed a song written by his uncle, Joseph Newman. A
respected poet and playwright, Joseph was living proof that artistic
sensibility and sound business sense were not mutually exclusive.
Sadly, his brother Arthur never saw it that way. Paul also enrolled in a
local children's theatre group, the Curtain Pullers. At the age of
twelve, with Theresa's encouragement, he joined the junior division of
the Cleveland Playhouse. He was given the starring role in *Saint
George and the Dragon*. He later remarked: 'I wanted to do the Dragon. It was a much meatier role.'

Interviewed in 1998, Newman looked back on his school days as a
largely wasted opportunity:

> The Shaker Heights school system in those days was the best pub-
> lic school system in the country, if not the world . . . I had the
> opportunity and I just blew it. I was never a good student.

As a teenager, he took part in school plays, working as an actor and
stage manager. He was also keen on baseball and American football,
but lacked the height and weight to make the school teams, coming in
at just one pound under the 100 lb minimum. At this time, he didn't
seem likely to excel as an athlete.

Newman claims to have got through adolescence relatively
unscathed: 'I had a good time as a teen – it wasn't a very difficult period for me.' He already had the looks and intensity that drew attention,
especially from the females. James Stotter recalls the adolescent Newman as utterly unaffected, with 'absolutely no idea whatsoever that he
was good looking'. Whatever the temptations, Newman was not
promiscuous as a teenager. Raised with a strong moral sense, he also
had the ever-present threat of parental wrath to think about.

After leaving Shaker Heights High School, Newman earned a little money selling Colliers Encyclopedias door-to-door. James Stotter recalled Newman as a natural salesman, with an easy charm. Shortly afterwards, Newman enrolled at Ohio University, majoring in Economics to keep his father happy. He also appeared in a student production of *The Milky Way*, a now forgotten play by Lynn Root and Harry Clork. Interestingly, Newman was cast as a boxer, anticipating his career breakthrough in *Somebody Up There Likes Me*. While he enjoyed the experience, he seemed to have no serious commitment to acting as a career. More interested in women than his studies, Newman left Ohio University after only four months. At least there was a valid reason to quit: America had been at war with Japan and Germany since 1941, and Newman received his call-up papers.

In June 1943, Newman joined the Navy Air Corps, enlisting on the V-12 programme based at Yale University. Somewhat ironically given his piercing blue eyes, Newman proved to be colour blind, which ruled him out as a pilot. Instead, the NAC trained him as 'a pretty good radio man, but a terrible gunner'. Newman's instructor was actor Robert Stack, a minor Hollywood leading man seen in Ernst Lubitsch's wartime black comedy *To Be or Not to Be* (1942). A capable actor, Stack had to wait another twenty years for stardom, playing gang-buster Eliot Ness in the hit television series *The Untouchables* (1959–62). By this time, his former pupil Newman was an up-and-coming Hollywood star.

Now a radio operator 3rd Class, Newman served two years in the Pacific, in torpedo planes and submarines. He saw very little action, spending most of his time on standby. Newman described the experience as 'drinking beer and reading everything I could get my hands on, eight, ten, fifteen books a week – while I sat in Hawaii, Guam, Saipan and Okinawa'. He avoided any heavy-duty combat: 'I got through the whole war on two razor blades.' Out on deck one day, Newman encountered the ship's chaplain, who struck up a conversation and then made a pass at him. Years later, discussing the incident with Gore Vidal, Newman claimed to be unfazed by this attention. A strikingly attractive individual, Newman would contend with sexual advances, both female and male, throughout his adult life.

Newman felt that luck was on his side throughout his war service. On one occasion, he found himself grounded when his regular pilot developed an ear problem. The rest of their squadron was transferred to an aircraft carrier, which promptly came under attack from Japanese kamikaze planes. One of the kamikaze pilots scored a direct hit, killing everyone on board. However, Newman's wartime experi-

ences left him with no animosity towards the Japanese, years later
starring in several adverts in Japan.

Released from the Navy Air Corps in 1946, Newman did not feel
he'd undergone any great changes in character or outlook. As he later
explained, 'I came out of the Navy just as dumb as I went in.' A civil-
ian once more, Newman remained 'bourgeois, provincial' and an
'emotional Republican'. The influence of Arthur Newman Sr still
loomed large. Rather than return to Ohio University, Newman
enrolled at Kenyon College, also in Ohio. Affiliated to the Episcopal
Church, this all-male establishment was a hundred miles from Cleveland. Despite the distance, Arthur and Theresa Newman approved of
their son's decision. This time, there would be no women to distract
him from his studies. Partly to please his father, Newman majored in
Economics and Business Administration, useful grounding for a career
at Newman-Stern. Still interested in sports, Newman also qualified for
Kenyon's football team.

If Arthur Newman felt that his son was finally settling down, his
relief proved short-lived. Bored with Economics, Newman switched to
English Literature. Unable to summon any passion for seventeenth-
century lyric poets, he then changed his major subject to Drama. Newman still played down any suggestion that he wanted to pursue an
acting career; he now planned to become a drama teacher at college
level. Interviewed by Robert Peer, Newman admitted: 'I wasn't as
good in college as I should have been. I spent an awful lot of time
drinking beer. When I graduated I was called "Magna cum Lager".'
Newman considered himself to be a slow learner, getting by mainly on
concentration and tenacity.

While Newman proved a useful member of the Kenyon football
team, he attracted more attention off the pitch. Hitting the town with
his fellow players one evening, Newman was involved in a drinking
session that got out of hand. The bar owner called the police and five
of the rowdy football players, Newman among them, spent the night
in Knox County Jail. The Kenyon College authorities took a dim view
of the incident, expelling two of the students involved. Four others,
including Newman, were placed on probation. Needless to say, they
were also thrown off the football team. Back in Shaker Heights, Newman's parents were mortified, especially when the story made the front
page of the *Cleveland Plain Dealer*. In truth, Newman was unhappy at
Kenyon, later claiming to have failed most of his courses. Worse, he
got into too many fights, some serious, and was arrested three more
times, albeit on minor charges.

Barred from the football team, Newman shifted his focus to drama, auditioning for a play. As he put it, 'I had nothing better to do, so I read for it and, much to my amazement, got the lead.' Over the next two years, he acted in around a dozen plays; extremely good-looking, with undeniable stage presence, Newman was a natural leading man. While Newman's looks prompted murmurs about favouritism, few could argue that he wasn't being cast on merit. Growing in confidence, Newman wrote, produced and directed a musical, in which he also starred. One of his drama teachers, J. G. Mitchell, felt he had strong technical skills; if he learned to exercise self-discipline, a career in the theatre was a real possibility. Newman, on the other hand, didn't rate himself as an actor. Raised in a family where feelings were kept in check, he was not comfortable with public displays of emotion. As he later explained, he felt scared by 'the emotional requirement of being an actor'.

Away from the stage, Newman established a small laundry business for his fellow students, offering beer as an incentive to potential customers. Increasingly involved in the theatre, he eventually sold his business venture to another student, making a small profit. Arthur Newman Sr might at least have praised his son's initiative. Instead, he dismissed the venture as both frivolous and irresponsible.

According to his official résumé, Newman graduated from Kenyon College with a BA in Drama in June 1949. Former colleagues dispute this, claiming that Newman was working as a professional actor a year earlier. It's possible that, somewhere along the line, an agent or studio executive decided to shorten Newman's time in stock theatre, thus making his rise to the top seem all the more swift. In the summer of 1948, Newman took a job at the Priscilla Beach Theatre in New England. Surprisingly, he'd secured parental approval for this career move, albeit with some strict conditions. Arthur and Theresa Newman would support their son financially for one year, while he tried his luck in the theatre. When the agreed twelve months were up, Newman would either quit and join the family business, like his older brother, or survive on his own. His theatre colleagues of the time recall that he didn't seem overly bothered by this make-or-break pact.

While Theresa Newman had encouraged her son's interest in dramatics, Arthur thought little of the acting profession. Interviewed by Chrissy Iley, Paul explained: 'It pains me a lot, because I think he thought of me as a ne'er-do-well.' Arthur's disapproval had nothing to do with contempt for the arts. Indeed, Newman recalled his father as 'erudite and cultured'. Arthur does, however, seem to have doubted his son's commitment, staying power, and even talent, especially in such a precarious profession. As Paul says:

I think he thought I didn't show much promise in those days and I tend to agree with him. Acting's just a crap-shoot. He just couldn't see the future in it.

Having abandoned a career in journalism for the family business, it's possible that Arthur Newman resented his younger son for having the career he denied himself.

Over the next twelve months, Newman secured roles in *Dear Brutus*, *The Doughgirls* and Arthur Miller's *All My Sons*. Aware that he could trade on his looks alone, Newman nevertheless rejected this option, determined to establish himself as a more versatile actor. With this in mind, he pushed for character parts. As he later explained, 'I was always a character actor. I just looked like Little Red Riding Hood.'

In 1949, the year Newman officially left Kenyon, he found a summer stock job in Williams Bay, Wisconsin. According to myth, Newman was on the train a mere two hours after graduating. For all this early success, he still lacked confidence in his abilities: 'I was a terrible actor – one of the worst in the entire world.' His employers begged to differ, casting him in numerous productions.

During this period, Newman met aspiring actress Jacqueline Witte, who became his first wife. A native of Wisconsin, Witte had recently graduated from Lawrence University. Tall, blonde and brown-eyed, she made an immediate impression on Newman, and their budding relationship quickly gathered speed. One 1960s profile of Newman described Witte as a 'former classmate', though this seems to be a press invention. When Newman joined the Woodstock Players, in Woodstock, Illinois, for the winter season, he was accompanied by Witte and, in December 1949, they were married. Earning a modest $45 a week, he and his new bride could not afford a lavish lifestyle. When Witte became pregnant, Newman worked as a farmhand to boost the family income.

Back on stage, Newman had roles in sixteen plays, including Tennessee Williams's *The Glass Menagerie* and Thornton Wilder's *Our Town*. Williams's work would play an important part in Newman's later career, with *The Glass Menagerie* assuming particular significance. Newman also returned to Wilder's 1938 hit, appearing in television and stage versions nearly fifty years apart. Performing a new play every week, the Woodstock Players worked long days, often twelve to fifteen hours. In addition to his acting duties, Newman directed at least one production for the company, staged at the

Brecksville Little Theatre. His fellow actors included Tom Bosley, who went on to a successful career in theatre, film and television. Interviewed in 2003, Bosley recalled Newman's fondness for beer and popcorn. He later worked with Newman on *The Secret War of Harry Frigg* (1968), before finding national fame in the hit television comedy *Happy Days* (1974–83).

In early 1950, Newman's budding theatre career was put on abrupt hold. Arthur Newman Sr had fallen seriously ill. Under pressure from his family, Newman returned to Shaker Heights to work for the family store. His father died on 18 May 1950, aged only fifty-six. Still a struggling young actor, with a pregnant wife to support, Newman felt he had been a failure in his father's eyes. Arthur Newman mistrusted show business at the best of times, viewing it as a profession without security or real prospects. Reflecting on his father's premature death years later, Newman admitted to lingering sadness and frustration over their awkward, unresolved relationship:

> I think he always thought of me as pretty much of a lightweight.
> He treated me like he was disappointed in me a lot of the time,
> and he had every right to be. It has been one of the great agonies
> of my life that he could never know. I wanted desperately to show
> him that somehow, somewhere along the line, I could cut the mus-
> tard. And I never got a chance . . .

Arthur Newman died without ever seeing his youngest son act professionally.

On 23 September 1950, four months after Arthur's death, Jacqueline Newman gave birth to a son, Alan Scott Newman, born in New York. At his widowed mother's request, Paul had stayed on at the family store. Loyalty and guilt aside, he needed a steady source of income to support his wife and son. When he bought a house nearby, Theresa Newman hoped that her youngest son was back for good. However, just a few months later, Newman quit the sporting goods business for ever. According to one version of events, the Newman family sold its interest in the store. Newman later made light of the decision, claiming that 'It's easy to give something up when you're no good at it.' In reality, it had been a tough choice and Newman was painfully aware that he was walking away from a secure job. For all his early success in the theatre, he could barely support himself as an actor, let alone a wife and son. If nothing else, Newman seems to have been very successful at Newman-Stern, displaying a natural aptitude as a salesman. In leaving the family business, Newman was going against his late father's wishes, confirming all of Arthur's worst fears. Interviewed fifty years later, Newman seemed to take some pride in Newman-Stern:

> We had a marvellous sporting goods store . . . when it folded it
> was the longest continual seller of radio in the United States and it
> was as highly respected as any retail outlet could be. Yet I could
> never understand the allure or romance of business.

In September 1951, Newman moved his family to New Haven,
Connecticut, where he'd enrolled at Yale University's drama school on
the Master's Programme. As he later explained, 'I was instinctively
pursuing the one thing I'd ever really done well.' Still intent on an
academic career, Newman concentrated on directing rather than acting. He talked of returning to Kenyon College as a teacher. There
wasn't much in the Newmans' bank account, and, to support his family, Newman returned to working part-time as an encyclopaedia salesman. He proved as successful with encyclopaedias as he'd been with
sporting goods, once earning nearly $1,000 over two weeks. With
Scott to look after, Jacqueline Newman was now a full-time housewife
and mother, her acting ambitions more or less forgotten.

Having forged ahead with his chosen career path rather than the
one laid down by his father, Newman also followed his own political
instincts. The former 'emotional Republican' became an active member of the Democrat Party, campaigning for Adlai Stevenson during
the 1952 presidential contest. According to Newman, his contribution
amounted to little more than 'stuffing envelopes'.

Though nominally committed to directing, Newman hadn't lost his
interest in acting. He agreed to appear in a student production of
George Bernard Shaw's *Saint Joan*, only to be overcome by nerves.
Tempted to withdraw from the show, Newman realized that he'd only
be proving his father right. As he put it in a 1982 *Time* profile: 'What
an ass. I drag my family with only $900 in the bank all the way to
Connecticut and then think of all the ways I can to cop out.' Returning to the boarding house where the family lodged, Newman took
hold of the script, went down to the boiler room and got to work on
his part: 'I was in drama school. I'd left a good-paying job and I said,
"Well, kiddo, better do it or go back home."'

Newman also acted at the Little Theatre in a new play about Ludwig
van Beethoven, cast in the small role of the composer's nephew. The
audience for one performance included Audrey Wood, a respected
writer's agent, and her husband William Liebling, an actor's agent.
Wood's clients included Tennessee Williams and William Inge, both
major names in the American theatre at the time. While neither Wood
nor Liebling liked the play, written by a student, they were both

impressed with Newman, who made the most of his insubstantial character. After the show, Liebling approached Newman and suggested the young actor get in touch if he ever hit New York. Many of Newman's Yale colleagues had already suggested this move, feeling that Newman could not realize his potential anywhere else. When Newman did abandon his studies at Yale, he claimed it was out of poverty rather than any burning ambition. Others recall that he already had his first New York theatre job lined up.

In the summer of 1952, with Jacqueline's support, Newman gave himself a year to make it in New York. If he didn't succeed as an actor, he'd return to Yale and finish his Master's degree, embracing the academic life. The Newmans moved to an apartment on Staten Island, where Jacqueline had relatives. Newman soon established a daily routine. Each morning, he took the ferry to Manhattan and did the rounds of casting calls and agents. Returning to Staten Island in the afternoon, he peddled more encyclopaedias, contending with the summer heat. Once again, he proved a successful door-to-door salesman, even during the long school vacation, when demand tended to slump. While Jacqueline looked for work as a model, she was usually fully occupied with motherhood. Now two years old, Scott Newman had become a difficult child, prone to screaming fits. At times, he became uncontrollable, alarming visitors to the Newmans' small apartment. In addition, Jacqueline was pregnant again, adding further urgency to Newman's search for employment. Despite his professional and personal difficulties, he remained encouraged by the thriving theatre scene. He was also interested in New York's growing television industry, which specialized in live dramas: 'I wanted a piece of that action . . . getting into television was the first step, the right kind of break.' Fortunately for Newman, his first big break as an actor was not long in coming.

2 Dixie Duse

Joanne Woodward – 1950s studio portrait

I have been dedicated to acting since I was able to talk.
  Joanne Woodward

Joanne Gignilliat Trimmier Woodward was born on 27 February 1930, in Thomasville, Georgia, a small town ten miles from the Florida state line. She was the second child of Wade and Elinor Woodward, who raised their daughter in the Episcopalian faith. Like Newman, Woodward had an older brother, Wade Jr. Wade Woodward Sr worked in school administration, which didn't bring in much money during the Great Depression. Elinor Woodward loved movies, taking Joanne to the Atlanta première of *Gone with the Wind* (1939). Unlike Newman, Woodward dreamed of being an actor from early childhood.

At the age of fifteen, Woodward moved with her family to Greenville, South Carolina. Elinor encouraged her daughter to enter beauty contests, describing Joanne as 'the prettiest girl in town'. Determined to follow a career in acting, Woodward enrolled on a drama course at Louisiana State University in Baton Rouge. In the event, she never completed her studies, dropping out after two years. Back in South Carolina, Woodward appeared in a production of *The Glass Menagerie*, cast as the introverted Laura Wingfield. Inspired by her success in the Tennessee Williams play, she decided to pursue an acting career in New York. Impressed with his daughter's obvious talent, Wade agreed to support this risky move, providing $60 a month to cover basic expenses. Joanne's parents were now divorced, and Wade's patronage may have been partly motivated by guilt. Like Newman, Joanne had never felt too close to her father, who seemed to favour her brother, Wade Jr. The latter went on to become an architect – the kind of stable, respectable profession approved by Wade Sr. Elinor subsequently remarried, to fellow Greenville resident Robert Carter. Wade Woodward Sr later became a vice-president of Charles Scribner's Sons, the New York publisher.

By 1951, Joanne Woodward had found work at New York's Neighborhood Playhouse. She trained under Sanford Meisner, who promptly got rid of Woodward's pronounced southern accent. Woodward was quickly spotted by a talent scout for the powerful Music Corporation of America (MCA) agency, and put under contract. In 1952, her budding career was placed in the hands of a young

MCA agent named John Foreman, who helped her secure a few television roles. Woodward first met Newman through another MCA employee, Maynard Morris, whose personal discoveries included Barbara Bel Geddes and Gregory Peck. Newman described his initial reaction to Woodward as 'Jeez, what an extraordinarily pretty girl.' While Woodward was taken with the strikingly handsome young actor – 'he was so funny and pretty and neat' – she got little sense of the person underneath. More to the point, Newman was a married man with an ever-growing family.

The year 1952 proved pivotal for Newman, both personally and professionally. Respected theatre director Joshua Logan was casting for the first Broadway production of *Picnic*, a new play by William Inge. Set in a small Kansas town during Labor Day festivities, *Picnic* centres on charismatic drifter Hal Carter, who stirs up sexual tension among the staid, frustrated local women. Hot from the smash hits *South Pacific* and *Mr Roberts*, Logan could do wonders for Newman's career. Agent William Liebling made good his promise to Newman, putting him forward for an audition. At the time, Newman was one of Liebling's most favoured clients, the agent convinced that the young man from Shaker Heights had star potential.

Having read for Logan and Inge, Newman won the supporting role of Joker. In truth, the part was minor, the character not appearing until the third act. As the play stood, Newman would have only a few lines. That said, Logan was impressed by the newcomer: 'Paul was very good. He didn't brag, he was modest, and yet he was this handsome, spectacularly beautiful man.' Newman's contract for *Picnic*, which paid over $100 a week, came at a crucial time: Jacqueline was due to give birth and their bank account was nearly empty.

The lead role in *Picnic* went to Ralph Meeker, who seemed perfect casting for the part. Meeker had understudied Marlon Brando during the original Broadway run of Tennessee Williams's *A Streetcar Named Desire* (1947). When Brando left the production, Meeker took over the role, scoring a major success. Joanne Woodward was also hired for *Picnic*, as the understudy to both Janice Rule, cast as beauty queen Madge Owens, and Kim Stanley, who played the less glamorous Millie Owens.

During rehearsals for *Picnic*, the 'Newman luck' came into force once more. Newman found himself promoted to a major role when the original actor proved unsuitable. He would now play Madge Owens's boyfriend, Alan Benson, the decent, strait-laced man she discards for the more exciting Hal. While Newman was a little young for the character envisaged by Inge, the playwright readily agreed to undertake the necessary rewrites. Openly gay, Inge may have had more than a professional interest in the handsome young actor. According to Newman, the producers were by no means sure about recasting him in a lead part, trying out another actor in the role first. During one rehearsal, playwright Tennessee Williams, actress Dorothy McGuire and director Elia Kazan were in the audience. Newman claims to have been so nervous that his knees shook throughout the performance. Nevertheless, all three liked what they saw and the role of Alan Benson was his.

In addition to playing Benson, Newman understudied the role of Hal Carter. This involved extensive rehearsals with fellow understudy Woodward, including an intimate scene dancing the jitterbug. Logan encouraged Newman to 'dirty up' his performance as Hal, wiggling his backside during the dance. As Logan explained it, Newman was not a 'crotch' actor, like Ralph Meeker, but soon learned to find his 'raw self'. Lacking Meeker's solid build, Newman spent hours in the gymnasium each day, putting on the muscle. In spite of this intense preparation, he rarely got to replace Meeker. When the opportunity arose, he was eager for audiences and fellow cast members to appreciate his abilities as a romantic lead. Just as Meeker had understudied Brando in *Streetcar* before inheriting his role, so Newman hoped to succeed Meeker as Hal. Understudying two roles, Woodward had an advantage over Newman, replacing either Janice Rule or Kim Stanley for around fifty performances. Newman didn't get a real break until Meeker took a week's vacation, leaving Hal in his understudy's hands.

Picnic received its New York première at the Music Box Theatre on 19 February 1953. The play proved an instant hit, with critics singling out Newman for praise. Writing in the *New York Times*, Brooks Atkinson declared that 'Paul Newman knows how to express the sensitive aspect of the character.' Audiences were similarly enthusiastic, and the 1953 *Theatre World* anthology would list Newman as 'one of the most promising personalities' of that year. Eager to promote himself as a serious actor, Newman took to smoking a pipe, which made him look both thoughtful and determined. According to Charlton Heston, many young actors of the time employed the same trick. *Picnic* would run on Broadway for 477 performances, winning a Pulitzer Prize for Inge. Newman hoped that Logan would promote him to the lead role for the play's national tour but, though impressed by Newman finding his 'raw self', Logan felt the young actor lacked the 'sexual threat' necessary for Hal. Interviewed in 1982, Newman still seemed nonplussed by this remark: 'I've been chewing on that one for thirty years.'

There are rumours that Joanne Woodward targeted Newman from their first encounter, telling friends: 'I'm going to get that one.' Joshua Logan offered the cryptic comment 'She was carefully working on her life, I'm sure.' By this time, MCA agent John Foreman represented both Woodward and Newman, comparing the latter to 'a Greek god'. Attending a matinee performance of *Picnic*, which featured his clients in the lead roles, Foreman became convinced they were in love. While the mutual attraction between Newman and Woodward was no secret to the *Picnic* cast, they claim to have fought against these feelings at first. As Woodward put it, she and Newman were 'running away from each other'. To the outside world, they were close friends and nothing more.

Newman now had a baby daughter, Susan, born in 1953, and he'd moved his family from Staten Island to a bigger apartment in Queens. Woodward dated several men during this period, becoming engaged on three occasions. One of her supposed intendeds was writer Gore Vidal. Woodward first met Vidal in 1952, introduced by a mutual friend at a Manhattan party. Immediately taken with Woodward, Vidal nicknamed her 'The Dixie Duse'. While Woodward and Vidal enjoyed a genuinely close friendship, he was openly gay. According to Vidal, the engagement was a blatant ploy on Woodward's part to push Newman into divorcing Jacqueline. Feeling that Newman was hesitating, Woodward raised the stakes a little. She also got engaged to James Costigan, a writer and actor. Like Vidal, Costigan remained on good terms with both Woodward and Newman. Over the years, there have been whispers of an affair between Vidal and Newman. In his autobiography, Vidal dismissed such rumours as absurd: 'Paul has been a friend for close to half a century, proof, in my psychology, that nothing could ever have happened.'

While no one took Woodward's engagement to Gore Vidal seriously, her brief involvement with Marlon Brando seemed calculated to enrage Newman. Since *A Streetcar Named Desire*, Brando had established himself as both the leading exponent of 'Method' acting and a major Hollywood star. He was everything an aspiring New York actor aimed to be. Newman, by comparison, had barely left the starting blocks. In 1953, Woodward and Brando dated for around a month. A notorious womaniser, Brando didn't treat the relationship as anything serious, and it's rumoured that Woodward simply wanted to make Newman jealous. Brando was certainly not her type. Well aware of

Brando's promiscuity, Newman could only wonder how far he'd gone with Woodward. Already fiercely competitive with Brando on a professional level, Newman now had to deal with him as a rival in love. In the event, Woodward and Brando soon went their separate ways. By contrast, Newman and Woodward's professional lives kept them close together, both in the theatre and television. Emotional manipulation aside, Woodward's feelings for Newman were clear: 'Paul was so beautiful and he was a wonderful actor.'

During his fourteen-month stint in *Picnic*, Newman also worked on live television. According to John Foreman, the rising actor rarely failed auditions. For his part, Newman loved performing on the small screen: 'It was the best thrill in town, a totally new experience.' One attraction for Newman was the variety of roles on offer: he wanted to be seen as a character actor rather than typecast as a juvenile lead. Newman made his first television appearance in a 1952 episode of *The Aldrich Family*, a popular series that had been running since 1949. Originating on the radio, the Aldriches were middle-class, all-American folk, living in Elm Street, Centerville. The producers were obviously impressed with Newman, and he was called back for several more episodes.

Both Newman and Woodward were hired to star in *Tales of Tomorrow*, ABC's attempt at a live science-fiction series. A forerunner to *The Twilight Zone* and *The Outer Limits*, *Tales of Tomorrow* employed established genre stars, notably Boris Karloff and Lon Chaney Jr, alongside newcomers such as James Dean. Woodward played a supporting role in an episode called 'The Bitter Storm', transmitted on 26 December 1952, while Newman appeared in the episode 'Ice from Space'. This thirty-minute drama concerns a US spaceship that returns to earth with a mysterious block of ice attached. The alien entity begins to grow at an alarming rate, threatening to engulf the whole world. Unfortunately, the production budget didn't run to showing either the spacecraft or the ice. Cast as Sergeant Wilson, Newman seems ill at ease.

Director Sidney Lumet, a friend of Newman, cast him in two instalments of *You Are There* (1953), a series shown on the CBS network which centred on re-enactments of historical events. The shows were hosted by celebrity journalist Walter Cronkite. Newman played Julius Caesar in 'The Assassination of Julius Caesar (March 15, 44 B.C.)', broadcast on 8 March 1953. He subsequently played the title character in 'The Fate of Nathan Hale (September 22, 1776)', transmitted on 30 August 1953.

Nineteen fifty-three also saw Newman join the Actors Studio. This famous outfit was run by Lee and Paula Strasberg and director Elia Kazan, who later took credit for starting the organization. The Actors Studio is best known for promoting the Method, a naturalistic style of acting that focuses on the actor's emotional memory. While potential students were normally required to undertake two gruelling auditions, Newman claims to have been accepted without a single interview. That said, his ever-increasing body of stage and television work was both well-known and respected. According to one version of events, Newman didn't intend to enrol at the Studio; he was simply helping an actress friend with her audition piece, a scene from Tennessee Williams. Whatever the case, Newman credits the Actors Studio as the major influence on his approach to the craft of acting: 'They've got to take the accolade or the blame for whatever it is I've become as an actor.'

At the time, the Actors Studio roll-call included Marlon Brando, James Dean, Kim Stanley, Julie Harris, Eli Wallach, Anne Jackson, Geraldine Page, Eva Marie Saint, Rod Steiger, Lee Remick and Karl Malden. Several of these distinguished students would later co-star opposite Newman: Harris in *Harper*, Page in both the stage and film versions of *Sweet Bird of Youth*, Saint in *Our Town* and *Exodus*, and Remick in *The Long, Hot Summer* and *Sometimes a Great Notion*. Overwhelmed by this powerhouse of talent, Newman remained a spectator for the first few sessions: 'I just sat back there and watched how people did things and had enough sense not to open my big mouth.' Once he became fully involved, he had to endure harsh criticism. One teacher dismissed his approach to acting as both superficial and self-deceiving: 'You are not thinking. You're just thinking you're thinking.'

Newman's teachers included Martin Ritt, who went on to direct him in six films. A long-time friend of Kazan, Ritt started out as an actor, working with Kazan at New York's Group Theatre during the 1930s. Having interrupted his career for war service, he returned to the stage as a director, making his Broadway début in 1946. Between 1948 and 1951, he found employment in the new medium of television, working as a director and actor on hundreds of live productions. Blacklisted for his left-wing politics during the early 1950s, Ritt took up a post at the Actors Studio, remaining there for six years. Despite his personal circumstances, Ritt found this new environment stimulating: 'It was a very exciting time in the American theatre because all the people were working for something they believed in, which happens very rarely.' Employed as Kazan's assistant, Ritt worked with Newman,

Steiger, Remick and Woodward, among others. Unlike Newman, Woodward had had to audition for her place at the Studio, assessed by resident director Jack Garfein. Garfein got to know both Woodward and Newman well, regarding the latter as good-natured and ambitious, with little time for dishonesty or meanness.

Newman's success in theatre and television made Hollywood interest inevitable. As an established New York actor, he had to consider both the benefits and pitfalls of the motion-picture treadmill. Interviewed in 2003, Joanne Woodward commented: 'Both of us started out with dreams of being actors in a real way, not movie stars.' Many of Newman's New York friends warned him against the film industry. Hollywood was no place for a serious actor who didn't want to compromise his craft. Actor Patrick O'Neal, who first met Newman during this period, felt the rising star's destiny was already out of his hands: 'We all knew Paul was headed for the movies, whether he wanted it or not.' That said, Newman's journey into film would be less than smooth.

The film rights to *Picnic* had been acquired by Columbia Studios, who signed Joshua Logan to direct. When Logan and Columbia began casting, MCA put Newman forward for a leading role. Newman tested with actress Carroll Baker, a fellow MCA client and Actors Studio pupil. At the time, Baker was dating Jack Garfein, whom she subsequently married. Years later, Garfein recalled that Newman sought his permission before asking Baker to test with him. While Newman and Baker were never romantically involved, she considered him 'one of the most attractive guys I know'. In the event, both of them lost out. Hollywood star William Holden wanted the lead role of Hal Carter. He had recently won the Academy Award for Best Actor for his performance in Billy Wilder's *Stalag 17* (1953). He also had a deal with Columbia. Under the circumstances, there was no real contest from either Newman or Ralph Meeker. Newman's stage role, Alan Benson, went to newcomer Cliff Robertson. Of the original *Picnic* cast, only Arthur O'Connell reprised his role in the film version.

Newman got his first shot at film stardom through his Actors Studio associate Elia Kazan, who'd enjoyed major Hollywood success with *Gentleman's Agreement* (1947), the film version of *A Streetcar Named Desire* (1951) and the biopic *Viva Zapata!* (1952). The last two starred Marlon Brando, now one of Hollywood's hottest actors. Newman was fleetingly linked with *On the Waterfront* (1954), filmed during the winter of 1953. Set in Hoboken, New Jersey, this Columbia release dealt with Mob infiltration of dock workers, aided and abetted by corrupt union leader Johnny Friendly (Lee J. Cobb). Kazan wanted

Brando to star as Terry Malloy, the ex-boxer turned union heavy who finds redemption through informing on his criminal employees. Despite their strong professional relationship, Brando was reluctant to take the role, troubled by Kazan's testimony before the 1952 House Un-American Activities Committee hearings. As a 'friendly witness', Kazan had named names, putting careers on the line. *Waterfront* screenwriter Budd Schulberg and co-star Lee J. Cobb had also co-operated with HUAAC.

When Brando declined the role, Kazan offered Newman a screen test, despite his lack of film experience. In a letter to Sam Spiegel, *On the Waterfront*'s producer, Kazan praised Newman as an exciting new talent: 'He's a really wonderful prospect, handsome, rugged, sexy and somehow turbulent inside.' Significantly, the director added: 'He looks quite a lot like Brando.' At Kazan's request, Actors Studio associate Karl Malden helped Newman prepare an audition piece, to be per-formed for Spiegel. Newman chose a scene from Ferenc Molnár's fan-tasy play *Liliom*. In need of a leading lady, Newman settled on Joanne Woodward. Malden recalls Newman explaining that he had a special chemistry with the young actress. Whatever the case, the scene went well, Malden praising both Newman and Woodward as 'absolutely great'. According to Brando biographer Peter Manso, Kazan even told Newman he'd won the part. In all likelihood, Newman was simply part of Kazan's strategy to lure Brando back to the project. Kazan later claimed that Brando's only serious rival for the role was singer-actor Frank Sinatra. A native of Hoboken, Sinatra had recently rein-vented himself as a dramatic actor in *From Here to Eternity* (1953). By the time Newman tested for *On the Waterfront*, Spiegel had already approached Sinatra. While Kazan felt that Sinatra could be 'wonderful' casting for Terry Malloy, Brando had the youth and vul-nerability the part required. More to the point, Columbia were only interested in the project with Brando attached. In the event, Kazan had to play on Brando's sense of loyalty, reminding the actor how he'd fought for him to be cast in the original production of *A Streetcar Named Desire*.

Whatever Newman's disappointment over *On the Waterfront*, Kazan soon came calling with another film project. Warner Brothers, which backed *Streetcar*, had agreed to finance *East of Eden* (1955), based on the novel by John Steinbeck. First published in 1952, Stein-beck's tale of familial angst was a heavily allegorical reworking of the Book of Genesis. Kazan asked Newman and fellow Actors Studio alumnus James Dean to test for the roles of the Trask brothers, Cal and Aron, obvious stand-ins for Cain and Abel. Six years Newman's junior, Dean had already tried his luck in Hollywood, playing bit parts in a handful of films. When the work dried up, he moved to the East Coast. Both were committed to 'serious' acting, though they had little in common otherwise – aside from a love of fast cars. Like Newman, Dean had won a major part in a Broadway production, *The Immoralist*. Written by Ruth and Augustus Goetz, this controversial drama was based on an autobiographical novel by André Gide. Cast in the unlikely role of a gay Arab houseboy, Dean caught the eye of a Warner talent scout and was offered a studio contract.

The black-and-white *East of Eden* screen test was filmed in New York. While Newman turned up in a crisp white shirt and bow tie, Dean opted for more casual dress, wearing an open shirt and jeans. According to one version of events, Dean and Newman worked from a script, alternating the roles of Cal and Aron. The story of a troubled young man, desperate to win his distant father's approval, held some resonance for Newman. The screenplay even featured a favoured brother, willing to toe the family line. Judging from the existing film, the two actors largely improvised their dialogue, Dean playing with a flick-knife to draw attention to himself. As the camera rolls, Dean turns to Newman and says, 'Kiss me.' Bemused, Newman responds with either 'Can't hear' or 'Can't here'. Dean biographer Donald Spoto suggests that the sexually ambivalent Dean was genuinely attracted to Newman, staring deep into his eyes throughout the screen test. Whether or not Newman took Dean's advances seriously, he treated this filmed close encounter as a joke, laughing on camera.

In the event, Kazan decided on Dean for the tortured, misunderstood Cal, whose thwarted love is twisted into hatred. By now in his late twenties, Newman was already a little old for the character. It's been suggested that Kazan only considered Newman for the less showy role of Aron. This part went to another newcomer, Richard Davalos, a former cinema usher. Kazan thought Davalos had better chemistry with Dean, despite his relative inexperience. In fairness, the director may have felt that Newman was too dominant and charismatic an actor for the bland, strait-laced Aron.

Interviewed by Jeff Young in the early 1970s, Kazan offered a rather different version of events. At the time, Dean had a small part in a play at the Royale Theater, New York. Kazan met Dean backstage, talked to the young actor for ten minutes and offered him the role on the spot. As Kazan explained: 'I knew right off the bat. You could just see it.' He later described his choice as 'the most apt piece of casting I've ever done in my life'. For the part of Abra, Cal's love interest, Kazan tested a number of promising newcomers, including Joanne Woodward.

The director eventually cast Julie Harris, an established stage and film actress. Warner sold *East of Eden* as James Dean's film début, which patently wasn't the case. Having shaped and guided Marlon Brando's film career, Kazan would now do the same for Dean. Newman, by contrast, was left out in the cold.

While Elia Kazan had passed on Newman for *East of Eden*, Warner Brothers remained interested in the handsome stage actor. It's likely the studio saw Newman as another potential Montgomery Clift or Marlon Brando, useful insurance if James Dean didn't work out. In 1954, Warner offered Newman a standard seven-year contract, paying $1,000 a week. Newman had reservations about the deal, which meant relocating from New York to Los Angeles. On the other hand, there were economic realities to consider. At a time when the average wage was $50 a week, Newman felt unable to decline. While Jacqueline and the children stayed with her family in Wisconsin, he made the three thousand-mile trip from Broadway to Hollywood. Newman claims to have regretted selling himself to Warners from the start: 'The moment I walked into that studio I had a feeling of personal disaster.' As if to confirm his fears, Warner Brothers cast him in *The Silver Chalice* (1954). Newman would dismiss this $4.5-million production as 'the worst film made in the 1950s'. It's certainly in the decade's bottom ten.

The Silver Chalice – Basil and Deborrah (Pier Angeli) contemplate the title object

The Silver Chalice was inspired by the success of The Robe (1953), a stolid biblical melodrama based on a novel by Lloyd C. Douglas, starring Richard Burton. Produced by Twentieth Century Fox, The Robe has a place in movie history as the first film in Cinemascope, an ultra-wide format intended to lure audiences away from their television sets. Made for $5 million, The Robe grossed an impressive $36 million at the box office. Given the film's popularity, Warner Brothers had a natural interest in biblical bestsellers that could benefit from the epic 'scope treatment. The studio was approached by independent producer–director Victor Saville, who owned the rights to The Silver Chalice, a novel by Thomas B. Costain. While The Robe centred on the garment worn by Christ at his trial, prior to crucifixion, The Silver Chalice highlighted the cup used at the Last Supper. Costain's novel was adapted by former journalist Lesser Samuels, best remembered for Billy Wilder's Ace in the Hole (1951).

The Silver Chalice's central character, Basil the Defender, was a liberated Greek slave. Presumably, Warner Brothers felt that Newman's classical, finely chiselled features made him ideal casting for the part. A dejected Newman failed to share his new employer's enthusiasm. This was not the kind of role that Montgomery Clift or Marlon Brando would play. That said, Brando had been cast in The Egyptian (1954), another Fox epic, following his surprise success as Mark Antony in MGM's Julius Caesar (1953). But Brando had walked off the project after the first rehearsal, citing physical and mental exhaustion. He also had major problems with the script, his role, director Michael Curtiz and co-star Bella Darvi, a 'protégée' of studio boss Darryl Zanuck. As a newcomer to Hollywood, Newman did not have the clout, or sheer nerve, to follow Brando's example.

The Silver Chalice starred Virginia Mayo, who appeared in Warner Brothers' period adventures The Flame and the Arrow (1950), Captain Horatio Hornblower (1951) and King Richard and the Crusaders (1954). In The Silver Chalice, Mayo played fair temptress Helena, an escaped slave burning with ambition. The role of Deborrah, Basil's virtuous true love, went to Italian starlet Pier Angeli. Under contract to MGM, Angeli had made a successful American début in Fred Zinnemann's Teresa (1951), scripted by Stewart Stern. A respected craftsman, Stern later became a close friend of both Newman and Joanne Woodward, providing the screenplay for Rachel, Rachel (1968). Virginia Mayo took first billing, followed by Pier Angeli and then Jack Palance, cast as would-be Messiah Simon the Magician. Newman had to settle for fourth place, albeit with a special 'Introducing' credit.

Newman loathed making *The Silver Chalice*. He worked on the production six days a week, often for ten hours or more. Each day of filming left him in a deep depression. Lesser Samuels's ludicrous script offered nothing in the way of plausible character development or motivation, and director Victor Saville had no interest in discussing the psychology of Newman's role. Given that Newman's background at the Actors Studio focused on the character's inner life to the exclusion of all else, this must have left him feeling stranded. Self-conscious about his supposedly bony legs, he hated his costumes, a succession of knee-revealing tunics. Years later, Newman claimed that he refused to look at the camera, which didn't seem to bother Saville. All in all, the experience proved a harsh introduction to the realities of Hollywood film-making. Interviewed on set, Newman's attempt at modesty sounded more like despair: 'Sometimes when I see the work of really good people I get hopeless and wonder if I should go back to the sporting goods business.'

Ironically, Elia Kazan and James Dean were shooting *East of Eden* on a nearby soundstage. Still friendly with Newman, Dean regularly visited the *Silver Chalice* set. While Newman appreciated a familiar face, Dean's presence served as a bitter reminder of how far he was from what he wanted to do. Newman may not have been the main reason for Dean's visits, however. At some point, Dean had been introduced to Pier Angeli; like most of Dean's brief life, his relationship with Angeli is steeped in hearsay, myth and speculation. According to one story, Warner Brothers set Dean up with Angeli for publicity purposes, keen to sell their new star as a romantic leading man, on- and offscreen. Married with two children, Newman could not be linked to his leading lady. Donald Spoto claims that Dean met Angeli purely by chance while visiting Newman.

Jack Garfein noticed striking differences in Dean's and Newman's attitudes to Hollywood. Newman hated the old studio system and made his feelings known, refusing to be seduced by the mix of glamour and hype. By contrast, Dean proved more than willing to play the game, sucking up to influential gossip columnists such as Hedda Hopper. Elia Kazan felt that stardom had an adverse effect on the neurotic, chronically insecure Dean. The success and power bestowed by Hollywood made him arrogant and abusive. Kazan felt that Newman, on the other hand, retained a 'quirky goodness'.

It is a truth universally acknowledged that famously awful films are never quite as bad as their reputation. *The Silver Chalice* is an exception. Interviewed in 1982, Newman dismissed the film as 'junk', and few viewers will disagree. Lasting a hefty 143 minutes, *The Silver*

Chalice is a major endurance test. The film is very badly staged, with clumsy direction, stilted dialogue and a deadly slow pace. Newman admitted to feeling 'uncomfortable' throughout shooting, and it shows. Most of his dialogue is delivered in a low monotone, accompanied by half-hearted pouts and sulks. He also lacks physical grace, angrily trashing his workshop and kicking a Roman soldier with little conviction; occasionally, he seems to be acting in slow motion. He also appears to have very little screen chemistry with either Virginia Mayo or Pier Angeli.

Realizing that *The Silver Chalice* required a hard sell, Warner's marketing division set to work on flogging Newman. Victor Saville was quoted as saying: 'Here is a young man who is destined for screen greatness. He has an intensity and a strange sense of brooding that comes over on the screen with impact.' Saville went on to compare Newman with Rudolph Valentino, legendary star of the silent movies.

The Silver Chalice received its world première in Saranac Lake, New York State, a step down from the prime movie launch pads of Los Angeles and New York City. Apparently, the town achieved this 'honour' by winning a nationwide sales contest for a Christmas charity. The film went on general release in the US on 20 December 1954, carefully timed to catch the Christmas market at its peak. The reviews were largely hostile, seizing on the movie's glaring inadequacies.

When it came to Newman's performance, most critics found themselves short of seasonal goodwill. *The New Yorker* was not impressed: 'Paul Newman, a lad who resembles Marlon Brando, delivers his lines with the emotional fervor of a Putnam Division conductor announcing local stops.' The *Saturday Review* took a similar view, labelling Newman 'a poor man's Marlon Brando'. While the Brando jibe undoubtedly stung, the *New York Times* questioned Newman's ability to act at all, dismissing him as 'rarely better than wooden'. The *New York World Telegram* couldn't even get Newman's name right: ' . . . a new boy, Jack [*sic*] Newman . . . bears an astonishing resemblance to Marlon Brando, an excessively sullen Marlon'. Perhaps the most damning verdict came from Joanne Woodward: 'He looked like a girl in a skirt.' Adding injury to insult, the British Board of Film Censors demanded cuts before granting the movie a family-friendly 'U' certificate.

The Silver Chalice proved an embarrassing flop for Warner, recovering very little of its $4.5-million production cost. Newman refused to appear in any more epics, biblical or otherwise, dismissing the genre as 'cocktail skirt' movies.

According to Carroll Baker, Newman believed that Warner Brothers had ruined his chances in Hollywood. Certainly, the studio seemed in no hurry to use him again, and he would make only three more films under his Warner contract, beginning with *The Helen Morgan Story* (1957). That said, other big studios were interested in him, enabling Warner to take advantage of lucrative loan-out deals. Embarrassment aside, *The Silver Chalice* probably did no great harm to Newman's career. Had he been a young unknown, plucked from obscurity to star in a big-budget epic, the film's failure would have dragged him down. But as an experienced – and respected – Broadway actor, Newman was simply seen to have struck out on his first Hollywood venture. Billed behind Virginia Mayo, Pier Angeli and Jack Palance, he could hardly be blamed for the ineptitude of Victor Saville and Lesser Samuels, or Warner Brothers' poor judgement.

Time – and success – gave Newman a more objective view of his disastrous film début: 'I used to put that picture down, but to have the honor of being in the worst picture of the fifties and surviving is no mean feat.' Charlton Heston, a specialist in epic roles, argued that Newman had no reason to feel embarrassed: 'Paul has an excuse – he doesn't do period parts.' When *The Silver Chalice* premièred on a Los Angeles television station, Newman took out adverts in the *Los Angeles Times*. Framed by a funereal black border, his announcement read: 'Paul Newman apologizes every night this week – Channel 9.' This public atonement for both the film and his own performance typified his sense of humour. It's unlikely that Warner Brothers saw the funny side. That said, Newman preferred to keep his one and only 'cocktail skirt' movie safely buried. In 1975, both he and Joanne Woodward were honoured by the Film Society of Lincoln Center. Newman requested that a tribute montage of film clips omit any mention of *The Silver Chalice*. A few years later, Newman screened the film at his Westport, Connecticut, home for a group of friends. Hoping for a night of high-camp delight, he quickly lost enthusiasm: 'It was fun for about the first reel and then the awfulness of the thing took over.' Interviewed in 1998, he seemed more relaxed about his time as a Greek slave:

> It adds luster and dimension to the word awful, but it gives me a kind of reverse pride because it gives every young actor hope. No matter how bad your early films are, there's hope for a career.

In the meantime, Joanne Woodward's Hollywood career had got off to a less traumatic start. Under contract to Twentieth Century Fox, Woodward made her film début on loan-out to Columbia for *Count Three and Pray* (1955). This post-Civil War drama starred Van Heflin as Luke Fargo, a pastor with a past, while Raymond Burr played the villainous Yancey Huggins. Cast as Lissy, a tomboy orphan, Woodward more than held her own against these seasoned co-stars, regarding the production as a good experience.

Newman's contract with Warner Brothers permitted him to work between film assignments in New York, both on stage and on television. During production on *The Silver Chalice*, he supposedly sent his East Coast agents a telegram, bearing the desperate plea: 'Get me back on Broadway!' While still shooting the film, he accepted a leading role in a Broadway production. *The Desperate Hours* was a new play by Joseph Hayes, based on his 1954 novel. Newman would co-star as Glenn Griffin, a ruthless escaped convict who takes a family hostage.

Touted as a surefire bestseller, *The Desperate Hours* had already drawn Hollywood interest. The film rights were acquired, prior to publication, by Paramount, who offered the project to veteran producer–director William Wyler. The lead role went to Humphrey Bogart. While Bogart was older than the character envisaged by Hayes, he'd been a major star for fifteen years. Wyler, who'd worked with Bogart on *Dead End* (1937), had no problem with his casting. *The Desperate Hours* would be Bogart's penultimate screen appearance. The film was shot between October and December 1954, before Hayes had finished the stage adaptation. However, under the terms of Hayes' deal, Paramount could not release the film until the stage version completed its initial Broadway run.

The theatrical *Desperate Hours* was directed by Robert Montgomery, a successful Hollywood actor in the 1930s and 1940s. When his movie career began to wane, he successfully switched to television, scoring a hit with *Robert Montgomery Presents* (1950–6). Newman's co-star was Karl Malden, another Actors Studio alumnus, cast as the staid family man who outwits the convict. The supporting cast included character actor James Gregory, who described Newman in typical New York lingo as 'a guy with a really classical puss'.

Newman also returned to live television drama, playing lead roles in a number of productions, including *Thunder of Silence*, transmitted on 21 November 1954. The script for *Thunder of Silence* was by Stewart Stern, who alternated Hollywood assignments such as *Teresa* and *Rebel Without a Cause* (1955) with more offbeat small-screen work. Newman and Stern became close friends during rehearsals for *Thunder of Silence*, a decade before they collaborated on *Rachel, Rachel*.

Rehearsals for *The Desperate Hours* went smoothly. While Newman and Montgomery occasionally argued over his role, their discussions remained civilized. In January 1955, the play received a pre-Broadway try-out in New Haven, Connecticut. Back on his old stamping ground, Newman relaxed, confident in both the production and his own performance. *Daily Variety* certainly liked what it saw: 'Show gets off like a firecracker.' During a second try-out in Philadelphia, James Gregory and several other cast members dragged Newman to a cinema showing *The Silver Chalice*. While Newman squirmed throughout, Gregory felt 'it was not that bad a picture'. Gregory also noticed that Newman seemed very partial to beer, but thought little of it. Given Newman's antipathy towards *The Silver Chalice*, it came as no surprise that he wouldn't watch the film sober. In fact, he had begun drinking heavily, unhappy with his personal life. His marriage to Jacqueline seemed increasingly empty, yet the idea of leaving his family was unacceptable.

The Desperate Hours premièred on Broadway on 18 February 1955, two months after *The Silver Chalice* opened. The first-night audience at the Ethel Barrymore Theatre included Newman's mother, Theresa. The play proved a hit, a welcome antidote to the recent *Silver Chalice* debacle. The reviews were highly favourable, especially for Newman. *New York Times* critic Brooks Atkinson, who had praised Newman's performance in *Picnic*, wrote: 'Paul Newman plays the boss thug with a wildness that one is inclined to respect.' With Jacqueline pregnant once more, Newman needed a reminder that he could succeed as a serious professional actor, since Hollywood pretty boys were likely to come and go in a flash, along with their generous salaries. Stephanie, the couple's second daughter, would be born during *The Desperate Hours*' long run. The ever-sceptical Joshua Logan felt that Newman was miscast in the play. As with *Picnic*, Newman had to really work at his role to make it believable. As Logan put it: 'He grew into that part.' *The Desperate Hours* closed earlier than expected, after a summer heatwave led to audiences deserting Broadway theatres. When Karl Malden announced his intention to quit, Joseph Hayes decided the play had run its course. The much-delayed film version finally opened, to disappointing business.

While acting in *The Desperate Hours*, Newman resumed his classes at the Actors Studio, determined not to stagnate as a performer. He also accepted more television roles, including one of his most famous ones in Philco Television Playhouse's *The Death of Billy the Kid* (1955). Written by Gore Vidal, this drama offered a new slant on the short life and violent times of Henry McCarty (1859–81), better known as William H. Bonney, Billy the Kid. One of the legendary figures of the Old West, Bonney supposedly killed twenty-two men before being gunned down by Sheriff Pat Garrett, a former friend. Vidal saw Bonney as a nineteenth-century juvenile delinquent in desperate need of a guiding father figure. He wanted to depict the outlaw as one of the first media-created celebrities: 'My decision was to show not so much Billy himself as the people who created the myth of Billy the Kid,' explained Vidal. He also intended his play as an attack on the complacent, corrupt corporate America of the mid-1950s. *The Death of Billy the Kid* was supervised by Fred Coe, a senior NBC producer. Looking for a director, Coe settled on Robert Mulligan, a former messenger at CBS who quickly rose up through the ranks. The role of Pat Garrett went to Jason Robards Jr, later a distinguished stage and film actor.

Under contract to Metro-Goldwyn-Mayer, Gore Vidal was busy with the script for *The Catered Affair* (1956), based on a teleplay by Paddy Chayefsky. This prior commitment meant he couldn't be on hand throughout the *Billy the Kid* production. Nevertheless, Newman got on well with Vidal during rehearsals. *The Death of Billy the Kid* was broadcast live from New York on 24 July 1955. Going out on a Sunday evening, the play proved a success, despite mixed reviews. Vidal later singled out *Billy the Kid* as a personal favourite among his teleplays, 'though by no means the most admired'. According to Vidal, he and Newman were already discussing a possible film version. Somewhat naively, Vidal hoped that the big-screen *Billy the Kid* would be 'a movie done my way, just as television and stage plays are done as the writer wants them done'. Very much the driving force behind the project, Vidal persuaded Newman to push the idea at Warner Brothers.

Newman also won a major role in the 1955 television version of *Our Town*, a sentimental tribute to small-town America. Made for Producer's Showcase, this reworking of Thornton Wilder's Pulitzer Prize-winning play starred Frank Sinatra as The Narrator. Sinatra also performed the specially written theme song, 'Love and Marriage'. Aged thirty, Newman played George Gibbs, a sixteen-year-old who learns about love and loss in Grover's Corners, New Hampshire. The cast also included Actors Studio graduate Eva Marie Saint, whose film career had recently taken off with *On the Waterfront*. The actors had two weeks of rehearsal prior to the live transmission. Saint enjoyed the experience, claiming that 'live TV was the best training in the world'. Broadcast on 19 September 1955, *Our Town* proved a hit. Saint regarded Newman's performance as outstanding. Interviewed in 2003 for cable channel A&E's *Biography* series, she recalled: 'Paul was very dear in *Our Town*, very sensitive. He's just such a fine actor. I've been spoiled rotten from those days.'

By mid-1955, Newman had separated from Jacqueline for good. Despite the risk of public exposure – and serious career damage – he moved in with Joanne Woodward. In August 1955, Newman and Woodward were staying at the Chateau Marmont hotel, in Los Angeles. Their fellow guests included Gore Vidal and his lover, Howard Austen. Located on Sunset Boulevard, the Chateau Marmont was a favourite among New York's theatrical and literary circles. An imitation French castle, the Chateau offered a downmarket, rather seedy environment, skipping such luxuries as a lobby, bar and restaurant. Nevertheless, it suited the East Coast exiles unimpressed by the sunny delights of Los Angeles. As Woodward put it, 'Life at the Chateau Marmont was dark and strange.'

Back in New York, producer Fred Coe asked Newman to co-star in *The Battler*, a teleplay based on a story by Ernest Hemingway. The screenwriter, A. E. Hotchner, was a close friend of Hemingway. The story of a punchdrunk boxer, *The Battler* was directed by Arthur Penn as part of NBC's 'Playwrights '56' series. A former member of Joshua Logan's stage company, Penn attended the Actors Studio in Los Angeles before joining NBC-TV in 1951. Initially employed as a floor manager, he soon graduated to script-writing and directing. According to Penn, actors appearing on Broadway liked to work in live television dramas, as it broke the monotony of repeating the same role on stage over hundreds of performances.

The title role of *The Battler* went to James Dean, now a major Hollywood star following the success of *East of Eden*. Newman was cast as Nick Adams, Hemingway's literary alter ego. If Newman had any doubts about playing second fiddle to Dean, he didn't let it show. *The Battler* was scheduled for a live New York broadcast on 18 October 1955. However, on 30 September, less than three weeks before the transmission, Dean was killed in a car crash. Stunned by his tragic, wasteful death, Newman found himself in an awkward position. Fred Coe and NBC intended to go ahead with *The Battler* and wanted him to play Dean's role. Newman's first instinct was to decline, commenting, 'I can't do that emotionally.' He soon changed his mind, perhaps convinced that *The Battler* would stand as a tribute to Dean. Penn felt that Newman had another reason for accepting the role. The part of the Battler required heavy make-up; the character had a damaged eye, as well as the obligatory cauliflower ear. With his face barely recognizable, Newman would be trading on his acting skills alone, silencing the sceptics who saw him as just a pretty face. As Penn explained, 'he suffered a little bit from being so handsome –

people doubted just how well he could act'. Years later, William Goldman made a similar observation: 'He makes it look so easy, and he looks so wonderful, that everybody assumes he isn't acting.' Promoting *The Color of Money* in 1986, Newman still seemed preoccupied by the issue: 'It's difficult when you feel you've made your mark because of something you've no control over . . . It makes you feel superficial.' With *The Battler*, Newman had also proved that he could take on a part intended for James Dean and make it his own.

Back in Hollywood, Newman's budding film career finally moved on from *The Silver Chalice*. Short of suitable vehicles for their new star, Warner Brothers loaned Newman out to Metro-Goldwyn-Mayer for *The Rack* (1956). Based on a television play by Rod Serling, this combination of character study and courtroom drama is an honourable failure. Newman plays traumatized Korean War veteran Captain Edward Worthington Hall Jr, who returns home after two years in a prisoner of war camp. Instead of receiving a hero's welcome, Hall is arrested and put on trial for collaborating with the enemy. His defence rests on persuading the court that he was tortured and then brainwashed by Chinese agents.

Scripted by Stewart Stern, *The Rack* was originally intended as a vehicle for Hollywood star Glenn Ford. For whatever reason, Ford dropped out of *The Rack* shortly before the start of production. MGM quickly reassigned the lead to Newman. The deal with Warners involved MGM buying out part of Newman's original contract. Given the star's feelings towards Warners, this was a mutually agreeable arrangement. Unlike *The Silver Chalice*, *The Rack* at least offered Newman a substantial starring role.

The Rack was directed by Arnold Laven, a former dialogue coach who'd enjoyed a modest success with *Down Three Dark Streets* (1954), a police drama featuring Broderick Crawford and Marisa Pavan, Pier Angeli's twin sister. Newman's co-stars were veteran character actor Walter Pidgeon and MGM contract player Anne Francis, who both appeared in the cult favourite *Forbidden Planet*, also released in 1956. The supporting cast included Edmond O'Brien and Cloris Leachman, who'd recently made a striking film début in Robert Aldrich's *Kiss Me Deadly* (1955). A gifted actress, Leachman would become one of Joanne Woodward's closest friends. MGM also assigned a role to a busy, if little-known, actor named Lee Marvin. A year older than Newman, Marvin had carved a niche in sadistic villains, making a memorable appearance in *The Big Heat* (1953). For *The Rack*, he was cast as one of Newman's fellow officers.

The Rack is one of the forgotten films in the Newman canon, unavailable on video or DVD and rarely screened on television. Rod Serling's biographer Joel Engel claims that the film suffers from 'terminal claustrophobia'. Expanding Serling's teleplay to feature length magnified its flaws, and Arnold Laven's bland direction does nothing to enhance the material. The performances are variable, Newman coming off better than most. Unfortunately, the script fails to establish Captain Edward Hall as a credible character. As the tortures inflicted on Hall are left offscreen, it's hard to judge his 'traitorous' actions. Hall preached anti-war propaganda to his fellow POWs, an unforgivable crime in the US army. Now on trial for treason, Hall must also face his father, Colonel Edward Worthington Hall Sr (Walter Pidgeon), a career officer with an exemplary record. Newman, who knew about paternal disappointment, succeeds in giving these scenes some depth though, overall, he felt he'd overplayed in *The Rack*: 'A fine example of me trying too hard.' On the whole, the issue of brainwashed Korean War veterans was better done in *The Manchurian Candidate* (1962).

In April 1956, MGM put *The Rack* out on limited release in order to test audience reaction. The box-office response proved so poor that the film was quickly withdrawn. It was finally given a general release in the US on 2 November 1956, four months after Newman's next film, *Somebody Up There Likes Me*. The latter's success made little difference to *The Rack*'s fortunes. Newman seemed resigned to the film's poor reception: '[It] really aspired to something, and nobody went to see it.' Newman and Lee Marvin didn't work together again until *Pocket Money* (1972).

MGM retained Newman's services for *Somebody Up There Likes Me* (1956), a biopic of Thomas Rocco Barbella, aka Rocky Graziano, world middleweight boxing champion. Whatever the movie's limitations, it proved an ideal vehicle for Newman, establishing him as both a gifted film actor and a potential star. After the disappointments of *The Silver Chalice* and *The Rack*, *Somebody Up There Likes Me* came along at exactly the right time. Having blown $4.5 million on *The Silver Chalice*, Warner Brothers had shown little interest in promoting Newman's career. Without *Somebody Up There Likes Me*, it's arguable that Newman would have given up on Hollywood – and vice versa – long before *The Hustler* and *Hud*.

3 Heavy Hitter

Somebody Up There Likes Me – Rocky Graziano

rl Can Lift a Fellow to the Skies!
ı̈agline, *Somebody Up There Likes Me*

Somebody Up There Likes Me was produced by Charles Schnee, an accomplished screenwriter whose credits included *Red River* (1948) and *The Bad and the Beautiful* (1952), which netted him an Academy Award. Schnee made the film in partnership with director Robert Wise, a former editor at RKO. Having served his apprenticeship cutting *Citizen Kane* (1941) and *The Magnificent Ambersons* (1942), Wise made his directing début with *Curse of the Cat People* (1944), a low-budget fantasy produced by Val Lewton. While still with RKO, Wise directed *The Set-Up* (1949), a powerful boxing drama which won the Critics Prize at the Cannes Film Festival.

Somebody Up There Likes Me was based on Rocky Graziano's 1955 autobiography. Schnee and Wise assigned the screenplay to Ernest Lehman, who'd scripted *Executive Suite* (1954), which Wise had directed.

Still an unknown quantity in movies, Newman owed his shot at Rocky Graziano to one actor's chronic insecurity and another's untimely death. The role was first offered to Montgomery Clift, who'd boxed with conviction in *From Here to Eternity* (1953). Clift hadn't made a film since and promptly turned down the Graziano project. MGM then approached James Dean, who was under contract to Warner Brothers. The loan-out deal would be straightforward, as MGM had loaned Elizabeth Taylor for Warner's *Giant* (1956), which also featured Dean. According to Wise, Dean liked the original book and gave Charles Schnee a verbal commitment to star in the film version. It's generally believed that Dean would have made *Somebody Up There Likes Me* if he'd lived. Both Wise and writer Ernest Lehman had reservations about Dean's casting, feeling that the slight, unmuscular actor lacked the build of a professional boxer. While Dean could have worked out for a few months, his sensitive features were not those of a seasoned street fighter and pugilist.

Compared to Dean, Newman had little Hollywood status. As Robert Wise put it, Newman 'didn't really have any movie name at all'. Wise had seen *The Silver Chalice*, feeling the end result 'wasn't anything to look at to see what one thought of Newman'. He was more impressed with Newman's performance in *The Rack*, despite the failings of the overall film, and both Schnee and Lehman had seen Newman in *The Battler*, an obvious calling card for *Somebody Up There Likes Me*. Arthur Penn, who directed *The Battler*, believes that Newman's performance in the teleplay secured him the role of Rocky Graziano. If so, this was an uncanny example of history repeating itself, Newman inheriting a pivotal starring role from James Dean.

Having won the lead in *Somebody Up There Likes Me*, Newman trained hard for the role, determined to look like a real boxer. Both Newman and Wise spent time with Graziano in New York. According to Wise, Newman studied the ex-boxer closely, picking up on his walk, mannerisms and vocal idiosyncrasies. That said, Newman didn't want to produce a superficial imitation of Graziano. Wise felt that Newman took from Graziano 'only what [he] could make honest for himself'. It's notable that Newman retained Graziano's habit of spitting in the street. He also blamed the ex-boxer for coarsening his vocabulary.

Montgomery Clift and James Dean apart, it's been claimed that MGM's original choice for Rocky Graziano was Marlon Brando. A keen amateur boxer, Brando had sparred with Graziano at Stillman's gym during the Broadway run of *A Streetcar Named Desire*. Whatever the truth of this, the Brando factor weighed heavily on Newman's mind during pre-production. Still smarting from the 'poor man's Marlon Brando' jibe, Newman vented his frustration to journalist Peter Maas. Brando, it seemed, had incorporated some of Graziano's mannerisms and speech patterns into his stage and screen persona. This left Newman with an almost impossible task: 'Now I've got to play Graziano, and they'll say I'm just like Brando.'

The initial script drafts for *Somebody Up There Likes Me* played Graziano's life story for comedy, with little in the way of character development. Newman strongly resisted this approach, arguing that 'Rocky had to be more than a poor, misunderstood kid. He had to be brutal because his only business was survival.' Fortunately, both Charles Schnee and Robert Wise agreed with Newman's views.

Somewhat ironically, the film reunited Newman with Pier Angeli, his co-star from *The Silver Chalice*. Newman, who had Polish–Jewish and Hungarian ancestry, would be playing an Italian–American. Angeli, an Italian, was cast as Graziano's Jewish girlfriend. With an eye to the youth market, MGM also cast Sal Mineo, a Bronx native from a Sicilian family. Mineo had appeared opposite James Dean and Natalie Wood in the recent hit, *Rebel Without a Cause*. His sensitive performance as the disturbed teenager Plato would earn him an Academy Award nomination, though his Hollywood career subsequently faltered.

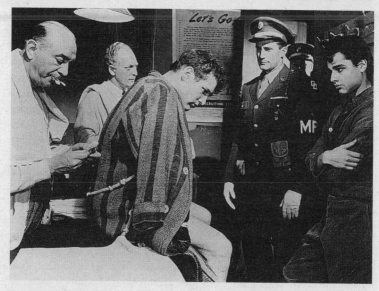

Somebody Up There Likes Me – Irving Cohen (Everett Sloane, left) and Romolo (Sal Mineo, right) look on as the military police arrest Graziano

Somebody Up There Likes Me began production in January 1956, with location shooting in New York. Newman enjoyed making the film, later remarking, '[we] had some fun with that'. Robert Wise recalls Newman being in good spirits on set, commenting that 'He was happy with his role'. The bit players in the film included an Actors Studio hanger-on named Steven McQueen, making his first, unbilled screen appearance as one of Graziano's street gang.

In many ways, *Somebody Up There Likes Me* is nothing more than a standard Hollywood biopic. The film opens with a signed endorsement from Rocky Graziano, who swears it's all true. The banal theme song is performed by Perry Como, another Italian–American made good. Ernest Lehman's script is simplistic and sentimental, and compared to Robert Wise's earlier *The Set-Up*, *Somebody Up There Likes Me* is a very soft-centred movie. Growing up in New York's impoverished East Side, young Rocco Barbella has a cold, abusive father and a doting mother, who suffers a series of breakdowns. Can he climb out of the gutter, channel his inner rage and turn himself into a winner? This is a Hollywood fairy tale, so the happy ending is never in doubt. But on the plus side, the film benefits from the moody black-and-white photography and vivid location work. Wise's direction is as smooth and assured as always.

Sporting curled hair and a convincing New York accent, Newman gives a potent, if mannered, performance that stops just short of caricature. Compared to Eddie Felson in *The Hustler* or Hud Bannon in *Hud*, the dim, head-scratching Graziano has relatively little depth. This is partly due to Newman's overreliance on the Method, which tends to rely on physical mannerisms. In fairness, the script offers limited scope for a rounded character study.

In the early scenes, Newman and his fellow actors look too old for street kids. Newman had just hit thirty-one and Steve McQueen was in his mid-twenties. Only Sal Mineo qualified as a genuine teenager, making the other 'punks' seem even less plausible. But Newman is a believable screen fighter, both in and out of the ring. As Graziano's career progresses, his face becomes increasingly battered. Newman's heavy make-up job, courtesy of William Tuttle, is impressive for its era. As with *The Battler*, Newman welcomed the chance to lose his 'pretty boy' looks, so forcing audiences to judge him as an actor.

Graziano finds salvation through boxing and the love of a good woman, Norma Levine (Pier Angeli). Newman and Angeli make for a likeable screen couple, far removed from their awkward pairing in *The Silver Chalice*. While Norma hates violence *per se*, she learns to accept Graziano's way of life, encouraging him to realize his potential. The movie ends on a triumphant note, with Graziano paraded through his old neighbourhood as Middleweight Champion of the World.

Aware that *Somebody Up There Likes Me* could relaunch his film career, Newman fully co-operated with MGM's publicity machine. Swallowing his dislike of Hollywood's media circus, he agreed to an interview with Hedda Hopper, playing the respectful, modest young hopeful. The strategy paid off, Hopper announcing to her readers: 'Newcomer Newman is Knockout'. *The Silver Chalice* was already fading into the dim and distant past.

Somebody Up There Likes Me opened in the US on 3 July 1956, following a New York première. The reviews for Newman were highly favourable. The *Los Angeles Times* put it simply: 'Newman is excellent'. *Variety* rated his performance as 'superb'. Third time out, Newman had established himself as a forceful, charismatic film actor, and Hollywood insiders were already predicting an Academy Award nomination. Robert Wise felt Newman deserved industry recognition for his 'strong, believable characterization'.

Somebody Up There Likes Me – Graziano and Norma Levine (Pier Angeli)

A few days later, Newman was detained by police in Mineola, Long Island. According to the official report, he had driven under the influence of alcohol, jumped a red light, left the scene of an accident and resisted arrest. Newman later admitted that he'd been on a series of alcohol binges, knocking back the whisky and engaging in gin-drinking contests. While his friends and colleagues were aware of his fondness for beer, few realized that he was on the edge of alcoholism: 'For a while, it really screwed me up.' Torn between his responsibilities to his family and his feelings for Joanne Woodward, Newman felt trapped. Jacqueline had made it clear that she would not give him an easy divorce. Newman was also frustrated with his film career, tied as it was to the Warner Brothers deal. He wanted more serious roles like Rocky Graziano, the kind of parts Marlon Brando played, but Warners treated him as just another handsome leading man. Facing up to his problems, Newman decided to see a psychoanalyst. While he did not remain in analysis, he felt the experience helped him to learn about himself.

At the time, there was no press coverage of Newman's drinking problem. His arrest in Mineola was even turned into favourable publicity for *Somebody Up There Likes Me*. Far from being caught up in his personal demons, Newman had simply acted in character as Rocky Graziano. His only real crime was taking the Method approach one step too far.

Having relaunched his film career with *Somebody Up There Likes Me*, Newman turned his attention back to television. On 3 July 1956, the day *Somebody Up There Likes Me* went on general release, he appeared in the Kaiser Aluminum Hour production *Army Game*. Directed by Franklin J. Schaffner, this downbeat drama cast Newman as Danny, an all-American boy drafted into the army. Unhappy with the rigours of military life, Danny fakes seizures on the firing range, hoping to obtain a release on medical grounds. When the commanding officer discovers this subterfuge, the other soldiers are instructed to torment Danny until he suffers a genuine breakdown. Interestingly, the buzz around *Somebody Up There Likes Me* made little impression on the *Army Game* cast and crew. As co-writer Mayo Simon put it: 'It wasn't a major coup to get Paul Newman.' The live broadcast of the teleplay was attended by a young director named George Roy Hill, a friend and colleague of Schaffner. During the performance, Newman's trouser zipper got stuck between costume changes, obliging the actor to go on set with his flies wide open.

Newman reunited with Schaffner for *Rag Jungle*, another Kaiser Aluminum Hour presentation. Transmitted on 20 November 1956, this teleplay dealt with Mob infiltration of New York's garment industry. Newman starred as Charlie, a clothes manufacturer who takes a courageous stand against the gangsters, despite the loss of his business. Obviously inspired by *On the Waterfront*, *Rag Jungle* proved disappointing, hampered by a weak script and uninvolving characters. Having missed out on the Elia Kazan movie, Newman found himself in a poor television imitation. With his film career still in the balance, Newman could not afford this kind of misjudgement.

When the Academy Award nominations were announced in January 1957, Newman's performance in *Somebody Up There Likes Me* was not included. A surprised and disappointed Robert Wise offered Newman his commiserations. Joseph Ruttenberg's photography won an Oscar, as did the art direction, credited to MGM department head Cedric Gibbons and Malcolm F. Brown. The night of the Academy Awards ceremony, Wise and Charles Schnee threw a consolation party for Newman, held at the director's Santa Monica home. Newman was presented with a 'Noscar', a neat parody of the traditional Oscar statuette. Instead of standing upright, the familiar bald figure leaned on his sword, resigned to defeat. By way of compensation, Hollywood's Foreign Press Association handed Newman a Golden Globe award as Most Promising Newcomer. With three films to his name, Newman barely qualified as a Hollywood novice, although neither *The Silver Chalice* nor *The Rack* had made much impression. He shared the Golden Globe with Anthony Perkins and John Kerr, suggesting the FPA was hedging its bets. Newman and Perkins later acted together in *WUSA* (1970) and *The Life and Times of Judge Roy Bean* (1972). At the time, the Golden Globes were not taken seriously by the film-making community, and being named joint winner in an also-ran contest gave Newman little comfort.

Three years after *The Silver Chalice*, Newman finally made his second film for Warner Brothers. It was another biopic, *The Helen Morgan Story* (1957), the tragic 'true-life' tale of a 1930s singer. Originally entitled *The Jazz Age*, the production was inspired by two hit MGM biopics about troubled female entertainers: *Love Me or Leave Me* (1955), starring Doris Day as singer Ruth Etting, and *I'll Cry Tomorrow* (1955), with Susan Hayward as Broadway and Hollywood star Lillian Roth. Like Etting and Roth, Helen Morgan had a brief film career, appearing in James Whale's *Showboat* (1936), among others. Steadily dragged down by alcoholism, Morgan died in 1941, barely into her forties.

The Helen Morgan Story had been knocking around at Warners for over a dozen years, variously suggested as a vehicle for Judy Garland or Jane Wyman. The project was assigned to prolific Hungarian director Michael Curtiz, an accomplished craftsman with few pretensions to grandeur. A long-time Warner employee, Curtiz is best known for his films with Errol Flynn and for having directed *Casablanca* (1942). *The Helen Morgan Story* starred Ann Blyth, a trained opera singer active in films from the age of sixteen. Blyth had previously worked with Curtiz on *Mildred Pierce* (1945), cast as Joan Crawford's selfish daughter. Blyth's vocals were dubbed by Gogi Grant, as the actress's classically trained voice was unsuited to Helen Morgan's style of 'torch' singing.

The Helen Morgan Story – Larry Maddux charms Benny Weaver (Alan King) and Dolly (Cara Williams)

Hot from *Somebody Up There Likes Me*, Newman could only have regarded *The Helen Morgan Story* as a slap in the face from Jack Warner. The critic Ethan Mordden describes the film as 'outrageously disingenuous even for a Hollywood bio'. The multi-authored script dwells too much on Morgan's troubled private life, especially her failed relationships and chronic alcoholism. Curtiz directs with mechanical efficiency, going for easy sentiment rather than genuine pathos. Blyth, a competent actress, never captures the qualities that made Morgan a star, while Newman looks ill at ease as Larry Maddux, Morgan's selfish husband–manager. A con artist and arms dealer, Maddux is clearly bad news from the start. Newman felt the character was poorly defined, not to mention dislikeable. Certainly, his half-hearted performance made little impression on contemporary viewers. Having sat on its *Helen Morgan* project for years, Warner was beaten to the punch by Hollywood's deadly rival, television. On 16 May 1957, 'Playhouse 90' broadcast its own version of the tawdry tale, also entitled *The Helen Morgan Story*. The director, George Roy Hill, would go on to play an important part in Newman's career. The big-screen *Helen Morgan Story* didn't reach cinemas until 5 October 1957, nearly five months later. Promoted with taglines such as 'No Star Ever Climbed Higher – No Woman Ever Fell Lower!', the film failed to interest audiences. In Britain, where Morgan's name meant little, the film was retitled *Both Ends of the Candle*. *The Helen Morgan Story* proved to be Ann Blyth's last film. Years later, Newman's only comment on the movie was 'Ugggghhh'.

Feeling that Warner Brothers had mishandled him from the start, Newman openly rebelled against the studio. Jack Warner wanted him to co-star in *Marjorie Morningstar* (1958), the tale of an ambitious young Jewish woman from New York City who finds her dreams come to naught. Based on the bestselling 1955 novel by Herman Wouk, the film was a vehicle for Natalie Wood, who appeared in *The Silver Chalice* before finding fame in *Rebel Without a Cause*. Unimpressed with his role as Wood's older lover, Newman turned the film down, risking suspension. In the event, the part went to Gene Kelly, whose career had begun to slide as musicals went out of fashion. As an alternative, Newman suggested a film version of *The Death of Billy the Kid*, one of his favourite television roles. Studio politics aside, his instincts proved correct when *Marjorie Morningstar* failed at the box office.

Having more or less given up on Warner Brothers, Newman looked to Metro-Goldwyn-Mayer for better film roles. In the short term, he would be disappointed. MGM assigned him to *Until They Sail* (1957), which reunited him with director Robert Wise and producer Charles Schnee. This wartime romantic drama was based on a short story from James A. Michener's book *Return to Paradise*. For the screen-play, MGM signed respected playwright Robert Anderson. His script for *Until They Sail* did not impress Newman, who hoped to follow *Somebody Up There Likes Me* with an equally forceful starring role.

Instead, Wise and MGM were offering him a thinly written supporting part in an insipid 'woman's picture'. As Wise recalled: 'I had to sell Paul on the idea . . . he thought the part was a little mild, a little soft.' Aware of his debt to Wise, not to mention his contractual obligations to MGM, Newman signed on for the film.

Until They Sail starred British actress Jean Simmons, then at the peak of her Hollywood popularity following the success of *Guys and Dolls* (1955). Her older sister was played by fellow expatriate Joan Fontaine, the previous generation's premier 'English rose', most famously in *Rebecca* (1940). Newman took third billing, behind Simmons and Fontaine. The supporting cast included Piper Laurie and Sandra Dee, a fourteen-year-old model making her film début.

Until They Sail is a variation on the old 'overpaid, oversexed, over here' story, set in New Zealand rather than England. Four sisters living in a small village are faced with an influx of horny American soldiers, including Captain Jack Harding (Newman). Having waved her husband off to war, Barbara Leslie Forbes (Jean Simmons) embarks on an affair with Harding. The film has several points in its favour. The New Zealand backdrop is an unusual setting and Robert Wise directs with his customary polished professionalism. Newman and Simmons make for an agreeably unsentimental couple, well aware that their budding romance is more about convenience than true feeling. As the tagline put it: 'They Couldn't Have the Love They Wanted, So They Took the Love They Could Get!' For the most part, Robert Anderson's script is no more than soap opera de luxe, throwing in a murder plot and subsequent courtroom drama. Wise was pleased with Newman's work on the film: 'The part in *Until They Sail* was not his favourite, but he did a very good job.' Newman regarded his character as insubstantial: 'not much to play there'. Despite their differences over the film, Newman and Wise remained on good terms. Interviewed for a 2003 A&E *Biography* on Newman, Wise praised his old friend: 'I think he's just one of the very finest citizens of this country.'

Until They Sail premièred in New York City on 8 October 1957, only three days after *The Helen Morgan Story* opened nationwide. This near-simultaneous release of two Newman films could be attributed to his growing star status. On the other hand, neither Warner Brothers nor MGM seemed worried that their box-office receipts would be damaged by the competition. In truth, Newman was not the major selling point for either movie.

Joanne Woodward had been loaned to United Artists for *A Kiss Before Dying* (1956), suffering her own *Silver Chalice*-style trauma.

Based on a novel by Ira Levin, this thriller cast Woodward as a young woman seduced and then victimized by charming psychopath Robert Wagner. Woodward loathed the finished film, though some critics were impressed with director Gerd Oswald's visual flair.

Back at Twentieth Century Fox, Joanne Woodward's film career took off with *The Three Faces of Eve* (1957). This tale of multiple personalities was produced, scripted and directed by Nunnally Johnson, who'd been working in film since 1927. *Three Faces of Eve* was based on a real case, recorded in a bestselling book by Drs Corbett H. Thigpen and Hervey M. Cleckley, two neuropsychiatrists from Johnson's home town of Augusta, Georgia. Fox's first choice for the lead was Judy Garland, who hadn't appeared in a film since *A Star Is Born* (1954). When the notoriously unstable Garland wouldn't commit to the project, Johnson suggested the relatively unknown Woodward. Fox wanted a big name for the role, but with Johnson's support, Woodward eventually won the part of Eve White, a repressed Georgia housewife. If nothing else, Woodward came from the same southern state as her character. Orson Welles, who later worked with Newman and Woodward on *The Long Hot Summer*, felt the role was a surefire Academy Award winner.

As a study of schizophrenia, *The Three Faces of Eve* hasn't aged well, but the film benefits from Stanley Cortez's black-and-white Cinemascope photography and the experienced playing of co-stars Lee J. Cobb and David Wayne. Woodward's performance is still regarded as a *tour de force*. At the time, *Films in Review* critic Diana Willing suggested that:

> This none too important picture . . . will be long remembered for the performance of Joanne Woodward, who simulates three totally different kinds of women with a facility and effectiveness that could enable her to become one of the great actresses of this generation.

Woodward's forceful portrayal balances the script's implausible 'explanation' for Eve's split personality: as a child, she was made to kiss the cold, clammy cheek of her dead grandmother. When *The Three Faces of Eve* went on release, Woodward was acclaimed by many as *the* star discovery of 1957.

In August 1957, Newman and Woodward attended a preview of *The Three Faces of Eve* at Grauman's Chinese Theatre in Los Angeles. Newman agreed with the assembled press – and Orson Welles – that Woodward's performance could win her an Academy Award, 'If it's done strictly on merit.' This could be taken as a reference to the lack of industry recognition for his own performance in *Somebody Up There Likes Me.*

The Three Faces of Eve – Joanne Woodward as Eve Black

4 Tortured Minds

The Left-Handed Gun – William H. Bonney, aka Billy the Kid

This is the story
This is the song
Of a left-handed boy
Who never meant wrong.
   Title ballad, *The Left-Handed Gun*

The box-office failures of *The Helen Morgan Story* and *Until They Sail*
increased Newman's antipathy towards the Hollywood establishment.
His hard-won success with *Somebody Up There Likes Me* had been
undermined by studio incompetence. In early 1957, there had been a
glimmer of hope. Following persistent lobbying from Newman,
Warner Brothers finally agreed to make *The Left-Handed Gun* (1958),
based on Gore Vidal's teleplay *The Death of Billy the Kid*. Previous
screen incarnations of the celebrated outlaw had been highly
romanticized, leaving the way clear for an authentic film version of
the story.

   Getting *The Left-Handed Gun* off the ground had not been easy. At
one point, Newman claimed, Warners insisted on a happy ending, no
easy thing with the story of William Bonney. It's rumoured that Warners
hoped to cast James Dean in the role. According to Donald Spoto,
Dean became interested in making a film about Billy the Kid after
seeing Vidal's play. Whatever the case, discussions cannot have progressed very far: Dean died barely two months after *The Death of
Billy the Kid* was first broadcast.

   With Dean out of the picture, Jack Warner remained moderately
interested in the project. The final decision was delayed while he
attended Grace Kelly's wedding to Prince Rainier of Monaco. At this
point, Vidal was still an equal partner on the film. He'd expanded his
original teleplay to feature length, not the easiest task, since *The
Death of Billy the Kid* ran little more than forty-five minutes without
commercial breaks. A film version required double this material, at the
very minimum. That said, Vidal had already accomplished this with
The Catered Affair (1956), which was based on Paddy Chayefsky's
television play.

   Newman and Vidal intended *The Left-Handed Gun* to involve all
the major talents from the television version. Producer Fred Coe and
director Robert Mulligan were both recruited for the film. Mulligan
had recently made his feature-film début with *Fear Strikes Out* (1957),
a biopic of Boston Red Sox baseball player Jim Piersall, who succumbed
to schizophrenia. As a pre-production gift, Newman and Woodward
presented Vidal with two cocker spaniels, Billy and Blanche, named

after William Bonney and *A Streetcar Named Desire*'s Blanche DuBois.

For all the initial camaraderie, Vidal soon found himself sidelined from the production by Coe. In February 1957, Vidal arrived in Los Angeles for pre-production work on the film only to discover, to his dismay, that Coe had taken over the project. At this point, in Vidal's view, Coe was 'a television producer in need of a job'. Faced with the end of the live television drama era, Coe wanted to establish a film career. With this in mind, he was determined to make *The Left-Handed Gun* his film, not Vidal's. According to Vidal, he dropped Robert Mulligan in favour of Arthur Penn, who'd directed Newman in *The Battler*, also produced by Coe. Regarded as one of the television industry's top directors, Penn was looking for his big-screen break. Coe and Penn had a good working relationship, which presumably is one reason why Mulligan was ousted. Interviewed in the late 1960s, Penn claimed that he and Coe were the senior partners on *The Left-Handed Gun*. Coe had made the deal with Warner Brothers, sounding out director Delbert Mann before approaching Penn. Coe and Penn had Vidal's 'lousy' script revised by Leslie Stevens, a playwright making his film début.

In his autobiography, Vidal appears philosophical about Newman's failure to control his errant producer: 'Paul, no tower of strength in these matters, allowed the hijacking to take place.' Woodward later remarked that Newman simply disliked confrontation: 'When Paul sees trouble, he makes a run for it. Or ignores it.' Newman later expressed regret about the way things turned out: 'I wish Gore had written the screenplay. Maybe I should have pushed a little more for that to happen. But I didn't know much about the politics of Hollywood.' It's possible that Newman didn't want to clash with Coe and risk Warners scrapping the project, in which the studio had no great interest. It seems unlikely that Coe could have 'hijacked' the production without support from Jack Warner. Swallowing his pride, Vidal offered to rework the new script, with input from Coe, Penn and Stevens. Having won the battle, Coe turned him down flat.

Budgeted at around $700,000, *The Left-Handed Gun* had a twenty-three-day schedule. Much of the film, nicknamed 'The Left-Handed Jockstrap' by Newman, was shot on location in Santa Fe, New Mexico. Warners' front office adopted a largely hands-off attitude to the production. Preoccupied with big-budget projects such as Billy Wilder's *The Spirit of St Louis* (1957), starring James Stewart, the studio had little time for a low-budget western. Back in Hollywood, the town scenes were shot on the famous frontier standing set, seen in *High*

Noon (1952). Penn had carefully pre-planned *The Left-Handed Gun*, virtually shot for shot, but for all this preparation, he clashed with cameraman J. Peverell Marley. A Hollywood veteran, Marley had worked with director Cecil B. DeMille since the silent era. Meticulous and old-fashioned, he didn't care for Penn's use of two cameras and, having only lit for one, disowned the 'rogue' camera B takes. This aside, the working atmosphere remained relaxed. Once production wrapped on *The Left-Handed Gun*, the studio machinery took over. Having assembled a rough cut, Penn saw the footage disappear into Warners' editorial department, which had no interest in his suggestions. He would look back on *The Left-Handed Gun* as a bad experience.

The fracas over *The Left-Handed Gun* did not affect Vidal's friendship with Newman and Woodward. In late July 1957, while the film was still in production, Newman and Woodward rented Shirley MacLaine's house on Malibu Beach, which they shared with Vidal and Howard Austen. This unusual arrangement suited the couple for a number of reasons. During the mid-1950s, the idea of an unmarried couple cohabiting would have been frowned upon; a married man living with another woman was even worse. As Vidal put it, 'we were acting as beards for Paul and Joanne'. Newman and Woodward also needed a little economic support from their housemates. Under contract to Twentieth Century Fox, Woodward took home $500 a week. While Newman earned more, much of it went on child support. Though well-off by most people's standards, alone they could not afford the rent on a house in the exclusive Malibu district. Theresa and Arthur Newman Jr dropped by, Newman playing courteous host to his mother and older brother. Vidal noted that both Newman and Woodward seemed to have difficult relationships with their mothers. Now publicly separated from Jacqueline, Newman made regular trips back east to visit his children in New York. Despite this attempt to maintain contact, it soon became clear that his son Scott was not coping well with his parents' break-up, and Jacqueline subsequently moved herself and the three children to the San Fernando Valley in Los Angeles.

Newman expressed dissatisfaction with *The Left-Handed Gun*, dismissing the finished film as 'artificial'. The rewritten script hadn't worked, altering the original concept beyond recognition. While Vidal probably felt that this realization came too late, Newman at least owned up to his mistake. That said, *Time Out* critic Tom Milne rates *The Left-Handed Gun* as 'a key stage in the development of the western'. In his *Guide for the Film Fanatic*, Danny Peary cites the film as a clear influence on Sam Peckinpah; for example, in one scene, a small girl laughs at Deputy Ollinger's stray boot, blown off his foot by a shotgun blast. Writing in the late 1960s, critic Robin Wood argued that *The Left-Handed Gun* 'offers a remarkably complete thematic exposition of [Arthur] Penn's work to date'. Certainly, Penn had a very specific visual style in mind for *The Left-Handed Gun*: 'flat, black-and-white, hard edge'. While cynics might claim that he was simply employing his usual television style, it made the film stand out from the wide-screen, Technicolor westerns in vogue at the time. The harsh black-and-white photography is also in keeping with the film's bleak dramatic landscape. On the downside, *The Left-Handed Gun* seems disjointed in places, presumably due to studio tampering. Penn later claimed that some sequences were cut to pieces, while others run too long. To his credit, the deaths of Deputies Bell and Ollinger are well staged, employing vision blur and slow motion.

Drifting through Lincoln County, New Mexico, William Bonney is clearly in need of guidance. Introverted and inarticulate, Billy exhibits both intelligence and a keen moral sense. Adopted by cattle drover Tunstall (Colin Keith-Johnston), he becomes well-read, with a penchant for biblical allusion. Regrettably, Billy's relationship with father-figure Tunstall is underdeveloped, suggesting that key scenes were left on the cutting-room floor. When Tunstall is murdered, Billy hits the vengeance trail, impulsive and reckless in his quest for retribution. The film attempts to explore the nature of 'justice', depicting the law as ineffectual and corrupt. As the forces of law and order close in, Penn frames Billy though a shattered pane of glass, underlining his broken mind.

Newman's performance as Billy the mixed-up Kid suffers again from his reliance on the Method. Inevitably, this gesture-heavy acting now seems overly mannered. He also looks – and was – ten years too old for the part. Under fire, Billy curls into a ball on the floor, an action more suited to James Dean. Overall, Newman gives the impression of an actor trying too hard to reveal his character's psychological depths. Interviewed in 1998, Newman admitted that some of his 1950s screen performances were strained: 'If you watch my early films, you can see the actor working. You can catch glimpses of my machinery.' The end result, he felt, was a 'disconnection' between him and the character.

The most intriguing aspect of *The Left-Handed Gun* is the depiction of Billy the Kid as a celebrity. The journalist Moultrie (Hurd Hatfield) believes he has found a genuine star outlaw, an anti-hero for the masses. Uncertain of Moultrie's intentions, Billy cannot resist the trappings of fame. In one scene, a victim pleads for his life while Billy poses for a photograph. Imprisoned, Billy looks at a dime novel about himself. Moultrie abandons Billy when the outlaw falls short of his 'star' status: 'You're not like the books . . . You're not him.'

The Left-Handed Gun – Intended as a psychological character study, the film was sold as a conventional all-action Western

Having been through the post-production shredder, *The Left-Handed Gun* was left high and dry by Warner Brothers. The studio had doubts over the title, fearing that audiences wouldn't know what the film was about. The opening credits read 'Paul Newman as Billy the Kid . . . in The Left-Handed Gun'. After months sitting on the shelf, *The Left-Handed Gun* was given a throwaway release by Warners, opening in New York City on 7 May 1958 to mixed reviews and poor box office. Penn saw the film for the first time at Loews Theatre, on New York's 86th Street, as the bottom half of a double bill.

The Left-Handed Gun later became a 'sleeper' hit in Europe. Interviewed in 1982, Newman seemed more taken with the film – 'a little bit ahead of its time' – and pointing out its success overseas: 'I still get $800 at the end of the year. Go to Paris right now, and I bet you it is playing in some tiny theatre.' Gore Vidal remained unimpressed, dismissing *The Left-Handed Gun* as 'a film that only someone French could like'.[1]

Despite his disappointment with *The Left-Handed Gun*, Newman remained generous in his assessment of Arthur Penn, later commenting, 'It was evident that he'd really make it'. Disillusioned with Hollywood, Penn turned his attention to Broadway theatre; he didn't make another feature film until *The Miracle Worker* (1962), based on his 1959 Broadway hit, which reunited him with producer Fred Coe. The same year, original director Robert Mulligan scored a hit with *To Kill a Mockingbird*, starring Gregory Peck. During the early 1970s, John Calley, Warners' new head of production, asked Penn to restore *The Left-Handed Gun* to his original version. When Penn agreed, Calley approached Rudy Fehr, Warners' head of editing, only to be told that all the footage had been junked.

Newman and Joanne Woodward made their co-starring début in *The Long Hot Summer* (1958), which was also Newman's first film for Twentieth Century Fox. This Deep South melodrama was based on the writings of William Faulkner and was supervised by producer Jerry Wald, a former journalist and screenwriter. Wald had produced Fox's hit melodrama *Peyton Place* (1957), based on the bestselling novel by Grace Metalious. While *The Long Hot Summer* had a higher literary pedigree, it's a safe bet that Fox wanted the same commercial blend of sex, scandal and violence in small-town America. Rival studio Universal-International jumped on the William Faulkner bandwagon with *The Tarnished Angels* (1958), based on Faulkner's novel *Pylon*.

Looking for a director, Wald hired Martin Ritt, whose career – interrupted by his blacklisting – had recently got back on track. Signed on a long-term contract with Twentieth Century Fox, his first film under the deal was *No Down Payment* (1957), produced by Wald. This tale of seething passions in downtown Los Angeles starred Woodward and Tony Randall. Clichéd and overwrought, the film proved another Wald hit.

The task of adapting Faulkner's prose fell to Irving Ravetch and Harriet Frank Jr, a husband and wife writing team active in movies since the late 1940s. Ravetch and Frank assembled *The Long Hot Summer* screenplay from the Faulkner stories 'Barn Burning' and 'The Spotted Horses', and the novel *The Hamlet* (1940).

It's rumoured that Newman wasn't Fox's first choice to star in *The Long Hot Summer*. The studio considered both Robert Mitchum and Marlon Brando for the role of Ben Quick, the alleged barn-burner. Wald admitted that Newman had yet to escape Brando's shadow: 'Everyone says Newman is a road company Brando. It's like the Mark of Zorro on him.' Newman claimed he was regularly mistaken for Brando, adding, 'It bugs me'. Biographer Peter Manso argues that Newman – along with Ralph Meeker, James Dean and Steve McQueen – openly copied Brando's mannerisms and style of dress. Ritt, who knew both men from the Actors Studio, believed that Newman respected Brando and felt intimidated by him. Brando may have been given undue credit for establishing the classic Actors Studio style; he was simply the first of the group to become a major star, and everyone who followed in his wake risked being labelled a Brando-imitator, Newman included.

The Long Hot Summer was not intended as the first Paul Newman–Joanne Woodward movie. Fox wanted Eva Marie Saint, Newman's co-star from *Our Town*, for the female lead, Clara Varner. However, when Saint became pregnant, Woodward inherited the part. Newman and Woodward had been looking for a joint film vehicle and *The Long Hot Summer* seemed a solid prospect. At the time, Ritt rated Woodward as a more accomplished actor than Newman, an opinion shared by Gore Vidal. Despite her high-profile success with *The Three Faces of Eve*, Vidal felt she remained very much an actress, 'not a star like Paul, who only later will turn into an actor'.

The role of bullying patriarch Will Varner required a heavyweight character actor with star quality. Fox approached both Edward G. Robinson and James Cagney before settling on Orson Welles, back in Hollywood after a decade's self-imposed exile. Seriously broke, Welles was open to all offers of work. Unlike Robinson and Cagney, Welles had to be aged twenty years for his part in *The Long Hot Summer*, which necessitated a heavy make-up job. He received $150,000 for the film, money he badly needed to pay off his back taxes.

The Long Hot Summer – Newman and Woodward as Ben Quick and Clara
Varner

The Louisiana locations included the towns of Baton Rouge and Clinton. Prior to filming, Newman spent some time in Clinton for research,
taking in the local character and atmosphere. Not yet a world famous
face, he could hang out incognito in pool halls and bars. Budgeted at a
modest $1.5 million, *The Long Hot Summer* began shooting in Baton
Rouge on 23 September 1957. For the most part, the cast and crew got
on well. Newman liked the Ravetch–Frank script, sympathizing with
the character of Quick: 'He had a lifetime of having a bad reputation.

And for no cause.' Woodward felt she had a lot in common with her character, Clara. As a rule, she preferred roles that didn't overlap with her offscreen self. In this instance, she found that cutting her hair for the film brought Clara into focus. Angela Lansbury, who played Minnie Littlejohn, was struck by the chemistry between Newman and Woodward: 'They seemed to have such a total understanding of each other.' She also felt that Newman seemed 'very comfortable within himself, within his own beauty. He was like a young god.'

According to Irving Ravetch, Newman and Woodward did not socialize much: 'They were very reserved.' Probably Hollywood's best known unmarried couple, they spent most of their weekends off in New Orleans. Browsing in an antiques shop, they found a large brass bed, supposedly salvaged from a local whorehouse. Impressed, they bought the bed, which still resides in their Newport, Connecticut, home.

Newman and Woodward were totally professional on set. Orson Welles took a very different attitude, behaving, in Lansbury's words, like a 'sonofabitch'. He hated making the film, later telling Peter Bogdanovich, 'I've seldom been as unhappy in a picture.' From the start, Welles criticized the script as imitation Tennessee Williams, bearing no relation to Faulkner's work. Once filming began, he immediately clashed with Ritt, arguing over costumes, dialogue, line readings, body movement and camera angles. As Ritt later conceded, 'Two weeks after we started, you could bet we wouldn't finish the film.' Seriously overweight, Welles had problems with the intense Baton Rouge heat. The heavy make-up didn't help, causing Welles to sweat underneath his false nose. A classically trained performer, he also felt nervous about working with a cast of Method actors. Interviewed for a *Back Story* television documentary on the film, Woodward recalled:

> Orson had a hard time. It must have been a terrible, terrible feeling for him to have to be confronted by all these young hot shots who thought they were so great because they came from New York and the Actors Studio. It was a problem.

Nevertheless, Welles enjoyed working with Woodward and Lansbury. Apparently, he had less time for Newman.

Welles aside, Ritt had to contend with equally ferocious forces of nature. Bad weather, including several hurricanes, put the production nearly a week behind schedule. The climactic barn-burning took five days to shoot, as Ritt wanted all the elements to look just right. If the flames, sky, winds and sunlight didn't measure up during a take, the director rejected it. *The Long Hot Summer* finally wrapped on 21

November 1957. By the end of filming, Ritt had no doubts about Newman's star quality. Interviewed years later, he commented that Newman had a 'cool sexuality' and, rather more crudely, 'a great fuck-ability quotient'.

As the first Newman–Woodward movie, *The Long Hot Summer* has curiosity value but little else. Opening with a trite title song, delivered by Jimmie Rogers, the film is filled to bursting with overwrought dia-logue and performances. What Woodward described as 'juicy language' now seems as over-ripe as the symbolic watermelons, all glistening red flesh.

Things hot up at Frenchman's Bend when Ben Quick, drifter and alleged pyromaniac, hitches a ride into town. Pouting underneath his hat, Quick is cocky, self-assured and seemingly amoral. The film shamelessly exploits Newman's sexuality, putting the star in jeans and a dirty white vest, then stripping him down to white boxer shorts. Obsessed with perpetuating the family line, Will Varner soon has his eye on Quick, a 'prize blue-ribbon bull' and a 'big stud horse'. Bull or horse, Quick is prime breeding stock. An uptight spinster schoolteacher, Clara Varner wears her hair in a very tight bun, just waiting to spring loose. Quick immediately makes advances: 'Never walk when I can ride.' Clara acts cool: 'We're givin' you a ride and that's all we're givin' you.' As the horses go on the rampage, their flanks dripping with sweat, Clara finds her pent-up passions hard to control. Quick mocks Clara's interest in 'sissy' Alan Stewart (Richard Anderson): 'If you're saving it all for *him*, honey, you got your account in the wrong bank.' Wary of Quick's 'cold blue eyes', Clara gives him a slap before allowing herself to be seduced. In this scene, there is a noticeable spark between Newman and Woodward.

While *The Long Hot Summer* awaited release, television audiences got their first glimpse of Newman and Woodward together in the 'Play-house 90' production *The 80 Yard Run* (1958). Based on a story by Irwin Shaw, the drama centres on a troubled former sporting hero and his ambitious wife. Richard Anderson, who appeared in *The Long Hot Summer*, played Newman's love rival. *The 80 Yard Run* follows the familiar path of youthful idealism soured by adult experience. Col-lege football star Chris (Newman) finds marriage to Louise (Wood-ward) a disappointment after their teenage romance. His new career as a businessman, organized by Louise's father, is similarly frustrating. Inevitably, their marriage starts to fall apart, perhaps irreparably. Directed by Franklin Schaffner, the teleplay utilized several filmed inserts, including sequences shot at the UCLA football stadium.

Typically outspoken, Woodward criticized the script as contrived and dramatically thin. Nevertheless, Schaffner biographer Erwin Kim credits Newman with a strong performance, despite the limitations of the material. By arrangement with Twentieth Century Fox, the broadcast featured a plug for *The Long Hot Summer* during a commercial break. Transmitted on 16 January 1958, *The 80 Yard Run* would be Newman's last live television play.

The Long Hot Summer received its world première in Baton Rouge, with Jerry Wald and Woodward in attendance. Newman, who didn't show up, was described in the theatrical trailer as 'America's most popular new star'. The film opened in the US on 5 March 1958, to mostly favourable reviews. It also did well at the box office, proving Fox's sixth biggest hit of the year, and Newman won the Best Actor award at the 1958 Cannes Film Festival, his first major prize.

Pleased with their success, Twentieth Century Fox commissioned a return trip to William Faulkner territory. *The Sound and the Fury* (1959), based on Faulkner's 1929 novel, reunited *Long Hot Summer* producer Jerry Wald, director Martin Ritt, screenwriters Irving Ravetch and Harriet Frank, and Joanne Woodward. Newman made way for Yul Brynner, a major star following the success of Fox's *The King and I* (1956). Newman remained happy with *The Long Hot Summer*, remarking years later: 'Everything worked. Everything pulled together.'

Having played out a happy ending onscreen, Newman and Woodward were determined to achieve the same thing in real life. In Gore Vidal's opinion, Woodward had waited, not always patiently, for Newman to 'free himself' from Jacqueline and marry her. When *The Long Hot Summer* finished shooting, Newman supposedly headed further south for Mexico. While the exact details of this trip have never been disclosed, Newman was divorced from Jacqueline shortly afterwards. Having steadfastly refused to grant Newman a divorce, Jacqueline either relented or had her hand forced. It's been suggested that she finally accepted her husband's unhappiness, granting his wish to end the marriage. The former Mrs Newman made no public comment on the financial settlement involved and, to date, has never discussed the divorce.

Newman and Woodward were married in Las Vegas on 29 January 1958 at the El Rancho Hotel-Casino. This seemed a surprisingly glitzy setting for a couple uninterested in Hollywood glamour. So began the most famously enduring marriage in show-business history. From the start, the couple laughed off the idea that they had the 'perfect' relationship. Newman has alluded to 'body-bending confrontations' with Woodward during their marriage, and there have been rumours of affairs and temporary separations. Kirk Douglas, who should know, claims that no long-running marriage is entirely monogamous. For the most part, Newman and Woodward have shrugged off the gossip, innuendo and speculation, and over forty-five years later, the relationship appears as strong as ever. Newman has suggested that the marriage works as an attraction of opposites, especially in terms of temperament. That said, there are common factors in their backgrounds. Both had favoured older brothers, named after fathers they found cold and distant. Whatever the case, the bond between Newman and Woodward has remained tight, displaying a chemistry that eluded most of their joint screen appearances. Newman once described Woodward as a 'functioning voluptuary', presumably a compliment. When travelling alone, he still phones Woodward every day.

After the Vegas ceremony, the couple headed for London, where they honeymooned at the Connaught Hotel in Mayfair. Gore Vidal and Howard Austen were in town, playing host to the newly-weds. Visiting Europe for the first time, Newman liked what he saw, especially Hampton Court. Appreciating a prime opportunity for favourable publicity, the happy couple allowed the international press into their hotel suite for interviews and pictures. Vidal felt that Newman and Woodward's public image was carefully cultivated, playing down their relatively privileged backgrounds: 'They made a calculated choice to present themselves as a folksy lower-middle-class all-American couple.' Surprisingly, Newman publicly attacked Warner Brothers for ignoring his marriage, the studio failing to arrange the customary flowers and theatre tickets. While this could be dismissed as a rare display of prima-donna behaviour, Newman harboured a deep-seated resentment towards Jack Warner. Career problems apart, Newman regarded Warner as a vulgar philistine, who repeatedly referred to Woodward as 'Joan'. This aside, the pair's media-friendly strategy paid off in spades. While the press could have portrayed Newman as a heartless cad who'd deserted his wife and three small children for a younger woman, there was very little public criticism of his separation, divorce and rapid remarriage. Things would have been very different if the press had discovered that Woodward was already four months pregnant. However, during the London honeymoon, in February 1958, she suffered a miscarriage. Naturally, the incident was hushed up. Vidal believes that the revelation could have ended Woodward's film career. Newman was due back in Los Angeles to begin work on *Cat on a Hot Tin Roof* (1958). Unable to postpone his start date,

Newman had to fly out from London before Woodward left hospital.

Following *The Long Hot Summer*, Newman travelled to the Deep South once more for Metro-Goldwyn-Mayer's *Cat on a Hot Tin Roof*, based on the hit play by Tennessee Williams. Back in 1943, Williams had signed a six-month contract with MGM, working on an unproduced film script that eventually became *The Glass Menagerie* (1945), his first major stage play. He consolidated his reputation with *A Streetcar Named Desire* (1948), a Broadway smash that won the playwright his first Pulitzer Prize. Seven years later, *Cat on a Hot Tin Roof* (1955), directed by Elia Kazan, brought him a second Pulitzer. While this helped sell the script to MGM, the studio was more interested in the success of Warner Brothers' film of *A Streetcar Named Desire* (1951), also directed by Kazan.

Cat on a Hot Tin Roof was primarily a vehicle for Elizabeth Taylor, one of MGM's most prized contract players. Taylor's husband, entrepreneur Mike Todd, had recently turned film producer, scoring a hit with *Around the World in 80 Days* (1956). Distributed by United Artists, this epic travelogue grossed $35 million and won four Academy Awards, including Best Picture. Todd intended to play a hands-on role in his wife's film career. It's been suggested that he pushed Taylor into making *Cat on a Hot Tin Roof*, arguing 'It's a great script and it will be a great picture.' Taylor owed MGM two films under her existing contract, including the *Cat on a Hot Tin Roof* project. In February 1958, she signed on for the film, which paid her a $125,000 flat fee. MGM had good reason to rush the deal through. Taylor's contract with the studio expired on 1 June 1958, after which Todd could demand a lot more money for her services.

As usual, Newman was not the first choice for the male lead, Brick Pollitt. MGM intended to partner Taylor with Montgomery Clift, her co-star from Paramount's *A Place in the Sun* (1951) and MGM's own *Raintree County* (1957), a big hit for the studio. Wary of his character's implied homosexuality, Clift turned the part down. While Clift was widely known within the Hollywood community to be gay, he had no wish to 'out' himself in a major film role. In the event, he need not have worried. By the time MGM finished with Williams's play, only the most perceptive audiences would question Brick's macho credentials. With Clift out of the picture, Newman was loaned out for a bargain $25,000. Co-starring with Taylor represented a step up in his career. Moreover, his role required the Actors Studio training largely wasted in his Warner films.

Cat on a Hot Tin Roof – Brick and Maggie Pollitt (Elizabeth Taylor)

MGM had offered *Cat on a Hot Tin Roof* to esteemed director George Cukor. A fan of the Tennessee Williams play, Cukor hoped to make a faithful screen version starring Vivien Leigh, who'd won an Oscar for her performance in *A Streetcar Named Desire*. When the lead went to Elizabeth Taylor, Cukor lost much of his enthusiasm. The director also expressed concerns over censorship, realizing that MGM had no interest in fighting the Production Code restrictions. Unwilling to be a party to this Hollywood 'emasculation', Cukor resigned from the project.

Following Cukor's departure, MGM reassigned the film to writer–director Richard Brooks. In Hollywood from the early 1940s, Brooks served his time as a lowly screenwriter, working on films such as *The Killers* (1946) and *Brute Force* (1947). Turning director in 1950, he scored a hit with *The Blackboard Jungle* (1955), produced by MGM. Taylor approved the choice of Brooks, who had directed her in MGM's *The Last Time I Saw Paris* (1954).

Having paid Williams $450,000 for the rights to *Cat on a Hot Tin Roof*, MGM budgeted the film version at a modest $2 million. Teetering on the edge of financial ruin, the studio had staked its future on a costly remake of *Ben Hur* (1959). In early 1958, studio boss Sam Zimbalist proposed casting Newman in the title role. Gore Vidal, who worked on the *Ben Hur* script, had to explain Newman's aversion to 'cocktail skirt' movies. According to Vidal, Newman felt he was lacking in at least one crucial department: 'I don't have the legs for it.'

Uncertain of *Cat*'s commercial potential, MGM intended to make the film in black and white. In addition to reducing the production costs, this underlined the movie's status as serious dramatic fare. Both *A Streetcar Named Desire* and *Baby Doll* (1956), scripted by Williams, had eschewed Technicolor. Brooks begged to differ, feeling that black and white would waste the combination of Elizabeth Taylor's deep violet eyes and Newman's famous blues. Meeting with some resistance, he appealed to Todd, who persuaded the MGM executives to change their minds. Having upgraded the production to Technicolor, the studio hired veteran director of photography William Daniels, who was famous for being Greta Garbo's favourite cameraman. The supporting cast for *Cat on a Hot Tin Roof* was led by Burl Ives, who starred as Big Daddy in the original Broadway production.

Scheduled as a brisk thirty-four-day shoot, *Cat on a Hot Tin Roof* commenced production on 5 March 1958. While Brooks and his co-screenwriter James Poe had attempted to tone down Williams's play without emasculating the material, there were still major script problems. The Motion Picture Association of America (MPAA)-enforced Production Code forbade any mention of the word 'homosexual'. Williams's original third act was completely rewritten for the movie. During rehearsals for one scene, Newman played one of his on-set jokes, donning Taylor's nightgown mid-speech. This reference to Brick's homosexuality reduced the cast and crew to stunned silence, probably not the intended reaction. Newman liked Taylor, praising his leading lady as 'a real pro . . . she's got a lot of guts'.

Shooting slowed down when Taylor fell ill, stricken with a high temperature, but the production soon faced a far more serious problem. On 22 March 1958, Mike Todd was killed in a plane crash. Overcome by grief, Taylor became hysterical for several days, refusing to eat, and there were fears that she would attempt suicide. Todd's funeral was held on 25 March and, inevitably, production on *Cat on a Hot Tin Roof* had to be shut down. While Brooks could shoot around Taylor for a few days, he quickly ran out of scenes that didn't feature her character. Newman filmed the opening sequence – Brick attempting some drunken hurdling – during this period. Todd thought Taylor looked beautiful in the rushes, which is one reason she eventually returned to the film. However, Taylor needed to resume work, if only for financial reasons: once Todd's back taxes and debts had been cleared, his estate left her with only $13,000.

Todd's death came just four days before the 1958 Academy Awards ceremony. One of the major contenders was *The Three Faces of Eve*. Twentieth Century Fox's publicity department had pushed Woodward for the Best Actress nomination, not always with her co-operation. In interviews, she appeared supremely indifferent to the Academy seal of approval: 'If I had an infinite amount of respect for the people who think I gave the greatest performance, then it would matter.' When the nominations were announced, Woodward found herself up against Anna Magnani (*Wild is the Wind*), Lana Turner (*Peyton Place*), Deborah Kerr (*Heaven Knows, Mr Allison*) and the newly widowed Elizabeth Taylor (*Raintree County*). Woodward seemed an outside chance, the big money being on Taylor and Kerr. Taylor had the advantage of being in a big-budget historical drama, heavily hyped by MGM. Co-star Montgomery Clift had been involved in a near-fatal car crash during production, giving *Raintree County* a morbid curiosity value. Against this, both Taylor's performance and the overall film were mediocre. For good or bad, Todd's fatal accident came too late in the day to generate a sympathy vote for Taylor. To Fox's consternation, Woodward refused to play the Academy game, declaring, 'I don't feel the performance was my best.' She suggested that Kerr deserved the award. At least *Heaven Knows, Mr Allison* was another Fox release, undermining accusations of disloyalty. Interviewed by Wanda Hale, Woodward declared: 'I don't care one way or the other.'

During the ceremony, held at the Pantages Theatre, Newman and Woodward jointly presented the Academy Award for Best Editing. When Woodward's name was announced as the Best Actress winner, she appeared stunned. She received her Oscar from John Wayne, the embodiment of traditional, conservative Hollywood values. Aged only twenty-seven, the surprise Best Actress winner was suddenly in the major league. British journalist Alistair Cooke – who appeared at the start of *The Three Faces of Eve* – credited Woodward with shedding genuine tears of joy when her name was read out. Twenty years later, British punk band Siouxsie and the Banshees paid their own tribute with the song 'Eve White, Eve Black'. For Woodward, the elation of winning soon wore off: 'It was exciting for five or ten minutes. Sitting in bed afterward and drinking my Ovaltine, I said to Paul, "Is that it?"'

Elizabeth Taylor made her official return to *Cat on a Hot Tin Roof* on 14 April 1958. Her dressing room was filled with flowers, red roses from the cast and violets from the crew. Taylor, who'd lost twelve pounds in weight since Todd's death, remained very fragile for the rest of the shoot. There were further delays, as her medication made her drowsy in the mornings. Brooks rescheduled her scenes to accommodate this problem. Deeply traumatized, Taylor used the film to keep herself together: 'When I was Maggie, I could function. The rest of the time I was a robot.' She would eventually suffer a nervous breakdown.

Cat on a Hot Tin Roof is probably the best known of Newman's 1950s movies. It was also the first since *Somebody Up There Likes Me* to suggest that he could cut it as an A-list star. He rated *Cat* as 'pretty good', despite feeling that his performance still showed the Method mechanics. Knowing the value of stillness, Newman gives a low-key performance as Brick Pollitt. First seen engaged in some drunken hurdling, Brick is haunted by his past sporting glories as a star football player. Following a symbolic fall to earth, he appears even more symbolically leaning on a crutch. Now a virtual recluse, knocking back the booze, Brick shows no interest in his wife, Maggie 'The Cat' Pollitt (Elizabeth Taylor).

The scenes between Newman and Burl Ives have some force. Big Daddy is a cold, remote figure, unable to show his son any affection. Newman drew on his ambivalent feelings for his own father, not to mention his real-life drinking problem. Invited to talk, Brick is not interested: 'It gets nowhere and it's painful.' Did Newman feel the same way? Brick finally confronts Big Daddy, expressing his feelings on the nature of love, ambition and success. One line is particularly telling: 'All I wanted was a father, not a boss!' Newman brings real conviction to this moment, perhaps a reflection of his long days at the family sporting goods store. The sense of reconciliation between father and son is something Newman never achieved in real life. At least Brick and Big Daddy agree that there's too much 'mendacity' in the world, particularly their own household.

It comes as no surprise when Brick finally leans on Maggie rather than his crutch. From the start, MGM argued that audiences would riot if Newman and Taylor didn't get together in the last scene. Taking a pragmatic view, Richard Brooks went along with this happy ending. Following a passionate clinch, shown in the theatrical trailer, Brick tosses a second pillow onto the double bed.

Opening in the US on 20 September 1958, *Cat on a Hot Tin Roof* proved a hit, despite the new controversy surrounding Taylor. Putting Todd's death behind her, she had become involved with singer Eddie Fisher. At the time, Fisher was married to wholesome MGM star Debbie Reynolds. While the nation's moral guardians fumed over this high-profile affair, paying audiences didn't seem too bothered. Taking $10 million in North America alone, *Cat on a Hot Tin Roof* was one of the year's top box-office attractions. However, Tennessee Williams loathed the film, which he regarded as a vulgar, gutless travesty of his original play.

Cat on a Hot Tin Roof received Academy Award nominations in all the major categories: Best Picture, Best Adapted Screenplay, Best Director, Best Actor and Best Actress. William Daniels's slick photography was also recognized. Newman found himself up against Spencer Tracy (*The Old Man and the Sea*), Sidney Poitier (*The Defiant Ones*), Tony Curtis (*The Defiant Ones*) and David Niven (*Separate Tables*). On the night, Niven took the Oscar for his brave performance as a bogus war hero and child molester. At least Newman lost in good company, *Cat* failing to win a single Oscar. Interviewed in 1986, the year he won an honorary Academy Award, Newman claimed that his first Best Actor defeat didn't bother him: 'Nah. That was too early.'

Now an official Hollywood couple, Newman and Woodward moved to a rented house in Laurel Canyon, which conspicuously lacked the obligatory movie star swimming pool. In interviews, the couple discussed their personal lives with unusual frankness, Newman openly referring to his time in psychotherapy. They made a joint appearance on a 1958 edition of *Person to Person*, a television chat show. While Woodward knitted, Newman joked about the football team incident at Kenyon College, praising his *alma mater* as 'a wonderful school'. Woodward predicted that her husband would eventually turn to directing. Newman concurred, claiming to see himself as an administrator rather than a creative talent: 'I think I'm better equipped to be a producer or director. I don't get much fun out of acting.'

Following the success of *The Long Hot Summer*, Twentieth Century Fox wanted to reunite the celebrity couple in another heavyweight drama, but Newman was more interested in trying his hand at comedy. Both he and Woodward were keen on the topical satire *Rally 'Round the Flag, Boys!* (1958), which seemed a good joint vehicle. Woodward had already turned down the MGM melodrama *Some Came Running* (1958), largely because she didn't want to co-star opposite Frank Sinatra. Though a gifted screen actor, Sinatra had a reputation for impatience, refusing to rehearse scenes and walking off the set after one take. Woodward had no time for this casual approach to the craft of acting.

Rally 'Round the Flag, Boys! was produced and directed by Leo McCarey.[2] The film was based on a 1957 novel by Max Shulman, and McCarey wrote the script with Claude Binyon. Unhappy with the screenplay, Twentieth Century Fox hired George Axelrod to undertake a few rewrites. A successful playwright, Axelrod had worked for the studio on *The Seven Year Itch* (1955), which was based on his 1953 stage comedy.

Having secured Newman and Woodward's services, Twentieth Century Fox intended to pair them with Jayne Mansfield, a more experienced comedy performer. Noted for her peroxide blonde hair and enormous chest, Mansfield had co-starred in the Fox productions *The Girl Can't Help It* (1956) and *Will Success Spoil Rock Hunter?* (1957). Unimpressed, Newman and Woodward lobbied for British actress Joan Collins, another Fox contract player and a good friend of the couple; at one time, Woodward and Collins intended to share an apartment. Collins's career at Fox was going nowhere in particular, and the Fox executives were not convinced by Newman and Woodward's choice of co-star. According to Collins, the received wisdom was that blondes were funny, not brunettes. However, Newman and Woodward eventually won out.

Rally 'Round the Flag, Boys! – Harry Bannerman cuts loose with Angela Hoffa (Joan Collins)

By no means dictatorial, McCarey encouraged his actors to make suggestions and improvise. That said, he supposedly didn't get on with either Newman or Woodward. A film-maker of the old school, McCarey felt uncomfortable with the new generation of New York Method actors. In her autobiography, *Second Act*, Collins pours cold water on 'all that Method nonsense'. Curiously, she claims that

Newman felt the same way. For the record, Collins doesn't recall any tension on set:

> I was so in awe of Leo McCarey myself that I simply didn't notice, but Paul and Joanne are so down to earth and 'un-luvvie' at that time, that I don't really think people were in awe of them.

Cast as married couple Harry and Grace Bannerman, Newman and Woodward look uncomfortable. Even allowing for the poor script and clumsy direction, they show little aptitude for the material. The Actors Studio training, with its emphasis on character psychology and motivation, gave them little grounding in either light comedy or broad farce. Newman had few illusions about his awkward acting in the film – 'I was probably weak' – while Woodward felt embarrassed by her performance: 'When I wasn't playing small, I was busy making faces. I loathed myself in it.' *Rally 'Round the Flag, Boys!* opened in New York City on 23 December 1958, going on general release the following February.

Newman returned to Warner Brothers for *The Young Philadelphians* (1959), based on a bestselling novel, *The Philadelphian*, by Richard Powell. The film version, which initially retained the book's title, was scripted by James Gunn and directed by Vincent Sherman. Newman's leading lady was old friend Barbara Rush. On the lookout for hot new talent, Warner hired Robert Vaughn, who'd made an unlikely film début in the title role of *Teenage Caveman* (1958). *The Young Philadelphians* began production in late 1958.

Efficiently made, *The Young Philadelphians* marked no great improvement on Newman's earlier Warner films. Sherman's smooth, anonymous direction fails to gloss over the clunky script, which throws in death and blackmail to little effect. While the film plays with some potent themes, notably social status and class snobbery, it's nothing more than a run-of-the-mill East Coast soap opera.

During production, Warners developed cold feet about using Powell's original title. Feeling that *The Philadelphian* lacked excitement and youth appeal, the studio changed it to *The Young Philadelphians*. Opening in New York City on 21 May 1959, it went on general release nine days later, proving popular with audiences. Of the four films Newman made for Warners as a contract player, only *The Young Philadelphians* showed a profit. In Britain, the film was retitled *The City Jungle*, an obvious nod to *The Blackboard Jungle* (1955). Newman later dismissed *The Young Philadelphians* as 'just kind of a cosmopolitan story that didn't demand very much'.

By the late 1950s, Newman was determined to break his Warner Brothers contract, feeling the studio had held back his career with uninteresting projects. *The Young Philadelphians* merely underlined Warners' blinkered view of Newman: a good-looking romantic lead who could handle big dramatic moments when required. Newman could see where this was heading: 'Once you got typed, then that's pretty much where you stayed.' While the studio had indulged Newman over *The Left-Handed Gun*, the film's box-office failure only confirmed their prejudices, and the loan-outs to Metro-Goldwyn-Mayer and Twentieth Century Fox were a clear sign that Warners had no confidence in him. Newman even claimed that studio boss Jack Warner had personally cheated him out of $5,000. While this seems a negligible sum by movie-star standards, Newman earned only $17,500 per film. Warner Brothers, on the other hand, charged other studios $75,000 for his services. Newman's representatives began negotiating with Warners to buy out the rest of his contract.

Disenchanted with Hollywood, Newman returned to the theatre, accepting the lead in the Broadway production of Tennessee Williams's new play, *Sweet Bird of Youth* (1959), directed by Elia Kazan. Returning to his Actors Studio roots, and the scene of his first professional triumph, Newman could revitalize his creativity. He was cast as Chance Wayne, an aging gigolo and failed actor who makes the big mistake of returning to his home town, down south. His co-star was Geraldine Page, one of the American theatre's most respected actresses. Page would play Alexandra Del Lago, a faded movie star who numbs her misery with alcohol and young men while dreaming of a comeback.

Newman and Woodward rented a Greenwich Village apartment. Their social circle included figures from the showbiz, literary and political worlds, notably Gore Vidal, Christopher Isherwood and Tennessee Williams himself. Furnishing this new home, Newman installed the antique brass bed purchased in New Orleans during the *Long Hot Summer* shoot. Now pregnant again, Woodward put her career on hold. Given the traumas of her previous pregnancy, still a big secret, Newman now discouraged media coverage of their home life. Off the record, he explained his position with extreme bluntness: 'What we do together in the evening and during weekends is nobody's fucking business.' The couple were rarely seen at the hot celebrity nightspots. Refusing to wear a tie, Newman shunned any establishment with a dress code. While his intellectual image and liberal views were fine in New York's theatre circles, they stirred some criticism back in Hollywood.

The first cast read-through for *Sweet Bird of Youth* proved a disaster. Unimpressed by Page's hesitant delivery, Williams left the session early. Page subsequently fled to her dressing room, convinced she was hopelessly miscast. Kazan managed to talk Page around, reassuring her that they would bring the character of Alexandra Del Lago to life. Kazan felt that Williams's text had major structural problems, Del Lago disappearing for the entire second act. To smooth over the cracks, the director employed a number of visual tricks, such as a giant television screen that emphasized the power of the monstrous Boss Finlay. To capture Chance Wayne's seediness, Newman tinted his hair red and shaved his hairline. During rehearsals, Kazan worked at demolishing Newman's new 'movie star confidence' to make the fact that his character was a loser more plausible. Newman went along with this approach and felt satisfied with the end result: 'By opening night, it was marvellous. I didn't have any security in the part at all . . . precisely what he wanted.'

While working on the Williams play, Newman attended classes at the Actors Studio. He later claimed to have learned more from his fellow 'students', notably Kim Stanley, Karl Malden, Anne Jackson, Eli Wallach and Geraldine Page, than any director. Actors Studio associate Jack Garfein begged to differ, feeling that Newman matured as a performer during his time with Kazan, emerging with a sharper, more direct approach.

Newman also produced and directed his first film, a short entitled *On the Harmfulness of Tobacco* (1959). This Anton Chekhov monologue, performed by actor Michael Strong, was shot over five days at New York's Orpheum Theatre. While Newman would not make his 'official' directing début until *Rachel, Rachel*, nearly ten years later, he was already testing his potential as a film-maker: 'I did that as an exercise for myself . . . I did it to see whether I could handle a camera and direct actors.' The end result disappointed him, despite a favourable review in the *New York Times*.

During tryouts for *Sweet Bird of Youth*, in Philadelphia, Newman did a press interview he later regretted. Talking between matinee and evening performances, the 'jumpy' star was not at his most effusive, focusing his energies on the play. Newman was angered when the reporter 'wrote that acting might be exciting, but actors are certainly dull people. Meaning me.'

Sweet Bird of Youth premièred in New York on 10 March 1959. While reviews for the overall show were mixed, most critics praised the performances. In any event, Newman's movie star appeal ensured a box-office hit. On 8 April 1959, Woodward gave birth to a daughter,

Elinor Theresa, named after her grandmothers. Newman and Woodward asked Gore Vidal to be their first child's godfather.

In the summer of 1959, Newman finally reached an agreement with
Warner Brothers, buying out the remainder of his contract for around
$500,000. While this was a serious amount of money, Newman's
agents assured him that he would make it back with his next two
films. After the success of *Cat on a Hot Tin Roof*, and the Academy
Award nomination, Newman could expect to earn at least $250,000
for his services. In public, he explained the split from Warners in
broad, non-accusatory terms: 'I had to find out just how far I could go
as an actor without commitments to any one particular company.'
Despite the hefty price tag, Newman never regretted the deal: '[It] kept
me poor for several years. But I was free to make my own decisions . . .
it was the best financial transaction I ever made.' While filming *Exodus* (1960), Newman complained that he still couldn't afford to trade
in his Volkswagen for a Mercedes 320. It would not be his only com-
plaint during this long, arduous production.

While Newman and Woodward were wary of being perceived as a
husband-and-wife team, they wanted to continue working together.
Following the conspicuous failure of *Rally 'Round the Flag, Boys!*, a
return to heavyweight drama seemed in order. Twentieth Century Fox
offered them *From the Terrace* (1960), produced and directed by
Mark Robson. Newman and Woodward would play an affluent married couple, who grow to hate each other. Freed from his Warner
Brothers contract, Newman received $200,000 to star in the film.
   During the late 1950s, Robson specialized in lush, widescreen melo-
dramas, scoring hits with *Peyton Place* (1958) and *Inn of the Sixth
Happiness* (1958), both distributed by Fox. *From the Terrace* was
based on a bestseller by John O'Hara, best known for *Pal Joey* (1940),
which became a hit musical. O'Hara's book was adapted by Ernest
Lehman, who'd scripted *Somebody Up There Likes Me*.
   Since *The Long Hot Summer*, Woodward's film work had been
generally unsuccessful. Neither *Rally 'Round the Flag, Boys!* nor *The
Sound and the Fury* were well received. She'd recently co-starred with
Marlon Brando and Anna Magnani in *The Fugitive Kind* (1960),
based on the Tennessee Williams play *Orpheus Descending*. Directed
by Newman's old friend Sidney Lumet, the film proved a gruelling
experience. Whatever Woodward's past relationship with Brando, she
now found him impossible to handle: 'He was not there . . . there was
nothing to reach out to.' Unlike the rest of the cast and crew, Woodward

got on well with the temperamental Magnani, who shared her disenchanted view of the Hollywood scene. Woodward's friendship with
Magnani seemed to antagonize Brando, who behaved disdainfully
towards the Italian actress. Released in April 1960, *The Fugitive Kind*
was Brando's first box-office flop, signalling the start of his steady
career decline.

The locations for *From the Terrace* included New York City and
Phoenixville, Pennsylvania. During the New York shoot, Newman
was still acting on Broadway in *Sweet Bird of Youth*. Having completed a day's filming, Newman would go on stage in the evening, a pun-
ishing schedule. In January 1960, he resigned from *Sweet Bird of*
Youth to concentrate on the movie.

At best, the film version of *From the Terrace* is high-gloss soap
opera, with none of the book's ironic edge. Anxious to establish their
movie as a quality product, Fox and Robson play the titles over a
bronze of Rodin's *The Kiss*, accompanied by the lush Elmer Bernstein
score. What follows is two and half hours in the company of the
amoral, promiscuous, self-loathing rich. Like *The Young Philadelphi-*
ans, the film is set on the East Coast, kicking off in 1946 Philadelphia.
David Alfred Eaton (Newman) returns from war service in the navy to
face the snobbish class system, where social standing is everything.
The product of a broken home, he falls for Mary St John (Woodward),
a spoiled rich girl. Can he avoid the mistakes that ruined his parents'
lives?

As a vehicle for Newman and Woodward, *From the Terrace* seems
misjudged, their characters' stormy relationship generating little heat.
The vaguely autobiographical elements count for nothing, with Newman seeming to walk through the movie. David Eaton has to deal with
a cold father, industrialist Samuel Eaton (Leon Ames), who favoured
his deceased eldest son. Though Newman could identify with this situation, the script gives him little opportunity to invest Eaton with real
emotion. Woodward plays Mary's transformation into a cold bitch
with some relish. Her many outfits include a bright red number, with
matching hat and gloves, and a bizarre 'wicked queen' ensemble,
topped by a tiara. Both Newman and Woodward are out-acted by
Myrna Loy, who pulls out all the stops as Eaton's alcoholic mother.

Newman and Woodward skipped the première for *From the Ter-*
race. Released in the US on 15 July 1960, the film did reasonably well
at the box office. While Newman later described it as 'pretty good
soap opera', no one could pretend that the film was a major achievement. The same year, Woodward became the first actress to receive a
star on the Hollywood Walk of Fame. Under the circumstances, this

high-profile accolade must have rung a little hollow. The next New-man–Woodward outing had to be more than a poorly conceived star vehicle that wasted both their talents.

Now a successful freelance, Newman was hired to star in *Exodus* (1960), for producer–director Otto Preminger. A major project with an important theme – the birth of modern Israel – the film was bound to draw attention. It was based on a 1958 novel by Leon Uris, which became the biggest bestseller since *Gone with the Wind*, shifting 50 million copies worldwide. According to Willi Frischauer, Preminger's friend and biographer, Uris was encouraged to write the book by MGM boss Dore Schary, who paid for the research in Israel and bought the film rights. When Uris delivered the completed manuscript, MGM got cold feet about the project, especially the anti-British slant, and sold the rights to Preminger. The director made a deal with United Artists, who had backed *The Man with the Golden Arm* (1955), his controversial film about drug addiction.

Uris adapted his book into a screenplay, which Preminger promptly discarded, claiming that Uris had no ear for dialogue. Preminger replaced Uris with blacklisted writer Dalton Trumbo, whose left-wing politics had incurred the wrath of the right-wing establishment. As one of the 'Hollywood Ten', Trumbo suffered prosecution and ten months' imprisonment in 1947. Officially unemployable, he continued to write screen stories and scripts, using a series of pseudonyms. As 'Robert Rich', Trumbo earned an Academy Award for his work on *The Brave One* (1956). Having hired Trumbo to script *Spartacus* (1960) in 1958, producer–star Kirk Douglas decided to credit the writer under his own name, boldly breaking the blacklist. Sympathetic to Trumbo, or at least aware of a good PR opportunity, Preminger followed Douglas's lead. While Trumbo had never visited Israel, he could deliver quality work fast. His agent happened to be Ingo Preminger, the director's brother.

According to some sources, Douglas wanted the lead role in *Exodus*. While Douglas makes no mention of this in his autobiography, he could have seen it as a chance to explore his Jewish identity in a major movie. Frank Sinatra also expressed an interest in the film, even proposing that Spencer Tracy play his father. Sinatra had given one of his best film performances in Preminger's *The Man with the Golden Arm*, yet he was never a serious contender. While Newman had Jewish ancestry on his father's side, he was not Jewish himself. Nevertheless, he seems to have been Preminger's first choice for the lead role of Ari Ben Canaan, exiled freedom fighter. Interestingly, while Newman had no time for organized religion, he occasionally referred to himself as a Jew, 'because it's more of a challenge'. The *Exodus* deal paid him $200,000.

After six months of pre-production work, *Exodus* began filming in Israel on 27 March 1960. Working on a relatively modest $4-million budget, Preminger had fourteen weeks to shoot his modern epic. Arriving on location, the director established a base at the Hotel Zion in Haifa. He secured official co-operation for the production through his friendship with Meyer Weisgal, one of the nation's founding fathers. With Weisgal's assistance, the director obtained permission to film in the historic locations in Acre and Jerusalem. The production later relocated to Cyprus for the film's opening scenes.

When Newman flew out to Israel for the start of production, Woodward and daughter Elinor came along. Newman had committed himself to three and a half months of filming, far too long to spend away from his family. Preoccupied with childcare, Woodward had put her own acting career on hold. When Newman was not required on set, he took his family on sightseeing trips, braving the inevitable crowds of fans.

While Preminger claimed to respect and like Newman, both as an actor and a man, he wouldn't treat him as an equal partner on *Exodus*. The day after his arrival, Newman approached the director with six pages of suggestions for script revisions. Preminger refused to look at Newman's ideas, even as a courtesy to his star. The director had little interest in actors who wanted to discuss character development and motivation. He certainly didn't appreciate being told how to improve his film. Preminger argued that, if he liked Newman's script revisions and decided to use them, Newman would inevitably suggest more changes. This would steadily undermine Preminger's authority as the film's guiding hand. Rather than risk a stand-up argument, Newman conceded that Preminger had a point. According to Frischauer, Preminger listened to Newman's ideas, only to dismiss them instantly: 'Very interesting suggestions. If you were directing the picture, you would use them. But I do not like them. As I am directing the picture, I shan't use them!'

Interviewed a decade later, during production on *The Life and Times of Judge Roy Bean*, Newman claimed that his approach to Preminger was nothing out of the ordinary:

I make a lot of suggestions to the directors. They can turn around and say, 'Well, that suggestion's really sort of awful. Exactly the opposite of that would be marvellous.' I'm indifferent, you know, to the fact that it's turned down. It's just that often something interesting comes of a suggestion.

In Preminger's defence, he was happy for Newman to work with the other cast members, as long as they stuck to the given dialogue. However, the director fell out with Lee J. Cobb, claiming the actor didn't know his lines. Eva Marie Saint, who'd worked with Newman on *Our Town*, still found him charming: 'He's serious but he's not solemn . . . there's a lightness to him . . . The ego does not get in the way.'

While Newman maintained an uneasy truce with Preminger, he regarded the *Exodus* production as one of the worst of his career. Preminger aside, Newman had other problems during the Israel shoot. On one occasion, local Arabs expressed their hostility towards the film by throwing stones at the star, who escaped serious injury.

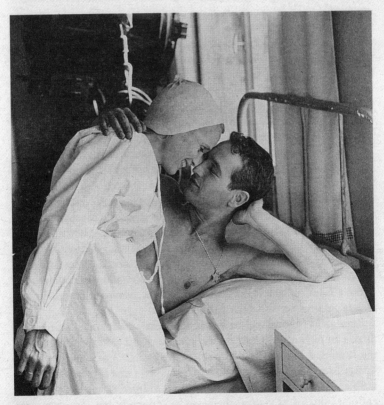

Exodus – Newman and Eva Marie Saint relax between takes. Newman's relationship with director Otto Preminger was not so good-natured

Interviewed on British television years later, Woodward made Newman's attitude clear: '*Exodus*! Paul can't bear to talk about it or even think about it!' Four decades on, Newman stills prefers not to discuss the experience. Preminger did at least pay tribute to Newman's personal life, informing a visiting reporter that 'He's an oddity in this business. He really loves his wife.' John Huston, a friend of both men, described Preminger as 'the kindest and most considerate of men in everyday life'. Sadly, Newman never saw this side of the director. Preminger finished *Exodus* ahead of schedule, completing post-production in London.

On the whole, *Exodus* is not highly regarded, with the honourable exception of Ernest Gold's outstanding main theme. Author Leon Uris supposedly disliked the film, hardly a surprise given his brief, ill-fated involvement. Many dismiss *Exodus* as a compromised piece of work, Preminger avoiding any serious examination of the moral issues involved. On the technical side, he displays a sure sense of composition and movement. Working in widescreen Super Panavision 70, he favours long takes, often with a fixed camera position. Trumbo's script is a mixed blessing, the humour sometimes as heavy-handed as the polemic. There's surprisingly little action for an epic. There are some nice touches, as when Ari's uncle, Akiva Ben Canaan (David Opatoshu), dies to a swinging arrangement of 'Greensleeves' playing on a car radio. While *Exodus* is never dull over its 220 minutes, the film lacks real passion and excitement.

Newman is first seen emerging from the sea at night, clad in khaki shorts. Favouring rolled shirtsleeves, he gives a muted performance, perhaps a reflection of his discontent during production. His character, Ari, is plain-speaking to the point of brusqueness, as determined as he is stoical. Chided for his hostility towards a gentile associate, Ari is unrepentant: 'We have no friends, except ourselves.' Newman occasionally stumbles; in one scene, Ari fools British soldiers with an assumed upper-class English accent. It doesn't sound too convincing. While Newman's work onscreen is never less than professional, he doesn't seem to believe in his performance. Newman described the *Exodus* experience as 'chilly', and it shows.

Exodus has been labelled blatant Zionist propaganda. Title aside, there's an obvious Moses parallel, with Ari leading his people back to the Promised Land. The film depicts the casual anti-Semitism of the British Army, the occupying force in Israel. Ari's first love was tortured, mutilated and killed by Arabs. David Mamet, a fan of the film, endorses one of its central themes – '. . . nobody but the Jews cares about the Jews' – though the film eventually softens this angle. *Exodus* moves towards its climax with the night-time evacuation of Jewish children from Gan Dafna, under threat from the Arabs. Ari and Kitty (Eva Marie Saint) place tape over the mouths of the smaller children, afraid that their cries will alert the enemy. The film seems to be building to a major Israeli–Arab battle, before opting for a low-key ending. For all his unhappiness in the role, Newman gives Ari's closing speech emotional force.

   Exodus opened in the US in late 1960, followed by a British release in the spring of 1961. Heavily promoted by United Artists, the film picked up some strong critical endorsement. The *Chicago Tribune* praised it as 'poignant, suspenseful, harrowing and timely', while the *New York Times* rated it 'a dazzling, nerve-tingling display that rips the heart'. Trumbo's involvement with the film prompted a series of pickets by the ultra-patriotic American Legion. To the latter's consternation, the paying public refused to be deterred. Despite mixed reviews, *Exodus* proved a major hit, grossing $8.7 million in North America. Worldwide, it took $21.75 million, becoming Newman's biggest box-office success to date. Gold's score won a deserved Academy Award, while cameraman Sam Leavitt and supporting actor Sal Mineo both received nominations. Ignored by the Academy, Newman had achieved the victory that really mattered. Having freed himself from Warner Brothers and survived the *Exodus* ordeal, he emerged as a *bona fide* Hollywood star.

5 Down and Dirty

The Hustler – 'Fast' Eddie Felson

Even if you beat me, I'm still the best.
  Eddie Felson, *The Hustler*

With the *Exodus* shoot behind them, Newman and Joanne Woodward headed for France, where they were scheduled to start work on *Paris Blues* (1961). Set in and around Paris's famous Left Bank, this drama featured Newman as a hedonistic jazz trombonist. The film reunited Newman with director Martin Ritt for the first time since *The Long Hot Summer*.

Distributed through United Artists, *Paris Blues* was co-produced by Pennebaker Incorporated, a company owned by Marlon Brando, in partnership with producer–director George Englund. Burdened by problems with the IRS, and Brando's long-delayed, vastly over-budget *One Eyed Jacks* (1961), Pennebaker needed to develop projects that didn't involve the star. For tax reasons, the films were made outside the US. Presumably, neither Newman nor Woodward had a problem with Brando as a sleeping co-producer. Brando considered starring in *Paris Blues* himself, opposite Marilyn Monroe, before losing interest in the project.

The movie was based on a novel by Harold Flender, which focused on a black couple. For commercial reasons, the film version added two white characters, played by Newman and Woodward. Jazz legend Duke Ellington agreed to provide the score, following his recent success with Otto Preminger's *Anatomy of a Murder* (1959).

Newman and Woodward were joined by Sidney Poitier, the first black American actor to achieve Hollywood stardom. Poitier and Ritt had previously collaborated on *Edge of the City* (1957). Whatever his co-stars' feelings, Poitier showed little enthusiasm for *Paris Blues*, dismissing the screenplay as 'a one-dimensional concoction'. His romantic interest was black actress Diahann Carroll, who'd appeared opposite Poitier in Preminger's *Porgy and Bess* (1959). Unlike Poitier, Carroll liked the *Paris Blues* script, feeling that it offered non-stereotypical, well-rounded black characters. Poitier believed the film would be better – and bolder – if the romantic pairings were switched around, giving him Woodward, and Newman, Carroll. It's rumoured that this was the original intention, until United Artists got cold feet over the double helping of interracial romance.

To prepare for his role, Newman received coaching from professional

trombonist Murray McEachern, a former member of the Benny Goodman Orchestra. Apparently, Newman became proficient enough with
the instrument for some of his own playing to be featured on the
soundtrack. In the interests of realism, and with an eye to the jazz
fans, the production employed a number of genuine musicians in acting roles. Prominent among these was Louis Armstrong, in an extended
cameo appearance.

Location filming for *Paris Blues* took place in the middle of winter.
Woodward had rented an apartment in Montmartre, thinking it
would be romantic. In reality, the building proved dark and cold.
Despite the chilly weather, both Newman and Woodward enjoyed the
experience. In the evenings, Newman liked to barbecue steaks in the
back yard of the apartment, watched by curious neighbours.

Newman and Woodward's co-stars were less comfortable, though
for reasons unconnected with the weather. Poitier and Carroll were in
the middle of a tortuous, if passionate, affair. Both were married and
suffered agonies of guilt and indecision. Under the circumstances, it
was not a good idea for them to be working together on a distant location. Staying at the Georges Cinq Hotel, Poitier was visited by his
wife, Juanita, and their three daughters. Well aware of Poitier's relationship with Carroll, Juanita made it clear that he would not get an
'easy' divorce.

More relaxed on set, Carroll got on well with Woodward, praising
her co-star as a great actor. Both Newman and Poitier were taken with
Paris. According to Poitier, Newman toyed with the idea of buying an
apartment and relocating to the French capital. Unlike Newman's
later interest in racing, this particular pipe dream soon vanished.
When production finished, Newman and Woodward hurried back to
the US, where they lent their celebrity support to Democrat John F.
Kennedy's presidential campaign. They also backed Gore Vidal's bid
for political office, the writer running as a Democrat candidate for
Congress. Aware that his 'confirmed bachelor' status could become an
issue, Vidal used his brief engagement to Woodward to counter any
gay rumours.

In terms of background detail, *Paris Blues* is mildly daring for its
time, featuring a mixed-race couple and, by implication, a gay couple.
While Newman and Woodward seem a comfortable screen pairing
this time out, they get little help from the script. Stranded with an
unconvincing character, Woodward wastes her heavyweight talent on
woefully thin material. Wiser than his wife in the ways of Hollywood
scripts, Newman seems more relaxed. Also, for all their in-depth
research, Newman and Poitier don't look convincing jamming along-

side real musicians. Only one member of the cast seems truly comfort-able: as jazz legend 'Wild Man Moore', Louis Armstrong more or less plays himself. *Paris Blues* ends on a downbeat note, as Newman's character, Ram, throws away a chance of true love, arguing that his music is more important. An aspiring composer, Ram seems fated to a life of heroic failure. His magnum opus, entitled 'Paris Blues', comes to nothing.

The theatrical trailer for *Paris Blues* promised something racy: 'It's all about two Americans who come to Paris, and throw all caution aside!' It opened in the US on 27 September 1961, just two days after *The Hustler*. In the wake of the latter's commercial success, *Paris Blues*' poor box office made little difference to Newman's career. The *Los Angeles Examiner* liked what it saw, advising readers that the film 'flows with life and humor'. Poitier, who had a miserable time making the movie, later dismissed it as 'all wrong from beginning to end'. Newman was more lenient: 'I had some fun . . . Not that it is a great film.'

After seven long years in the movies, Newman finally made his mark with *The Hustler* (1961), the film that brought him true stardom. If *Exodus* provided Newman with box-office kudos, *The Hustler* gave him the ideal role. For the first time onscreen, his talent truly shone. As Newman later put it, 'I had a good feeling about this one right from the start.' Ironically, he would have missed out on the role of 'Fast' Eddie Felson had it not been for Elizabeth Taylor's poor health. New-man intended to follow *Paris Blues* with *Two for the Seesaw* (1962), a bittersweet romantic comedy based on William Gibson's hit 1958 play. Produced by the Mirisch Company for United Artists, the film would reunite Newman with Taylor. Newman would play a discon-tented Omaha lawyer, adrift in New York City, who becomes involved with Taylor's eccentric dance teacher. However, Taylor soon dropped out, citing illness. Newman's contract for the film specified four acceptable replacements. When none of them proved available, he was released from the production.

Produced for Twentieth Century Fox, *The Hustler* was based on a little-known novel by Walter Tevis, published in 1959. As a college student, Tevis worked in a pool hall, where he met a player–hustler called Eddie Parker. To cover his tracks, Parker used several pseudonyms, including 'Eddie Felsen'. Parker later claimed that at least a third of *The Hustler* was based on his life. He'd come up against a player called 'New York Fats' and had his right forefinger broken after hustling the wrong pool hall. Tevis's book had already been turned into a 'Playhouse 90' television drama, starring Cliff Robertson.

A number of film-makers were interested in adapting *The Hustler* for the big screen. Frank Sinatra optioned the rights, only to lose interest. The project was eventually taken on by Robert Rossen, a producer–director–writer whose career had been blighted by the blacklist.[1] After a series of flops, *The Hustler* offered him a chance to re-establish his reputation as a serious film-maker. He knew the world it depicted, having hustled pool as an impoverished teenager. Years earlier, Rossen started writing a play about the game, *Corner Pocket*, only to discard it; second time around, he could not afford to leave the work unfinished. Sidney Carroll turned Tevis's novel into a screenplay, which Rossen subsequently revised. According to one account, Rossen had already cast the lead role when he heard that Newman might be available. Rossen sent the finished script to Newman, who was still busy shooting *Paris Blues* on location in France. Newman had a space in his schedule, thanks to his release from *Two for the Seesaw*. He read only half the *Hustler* script before contacting Rossen to say yes.

The key role of pool champion Minnesota Fats went to comedian Jackie Gleason, who'd achieved television superstardom with *The Honeymooners* (1949–54). Rossen also recruited respected stage actor George C. Scott, who had only two prior film credits, including Otto Preminger's *Anatomy of a Murder* (1959). Rossen's daughter, television actress Carol Rossen, hoped to play the female lead, Sarah Packard, a case study in emotional and physical disability. The part went to Piper Laurie, who had worked with Newman on the unremarkable *Until They Sail*. Disenchanted with Hollywood, Laurie hadn't made a film since then.

The film's technical advisor was Willie Mosconi, world billiards champion fourteen times over between 1941 and 1957. He had two weeks to coach Newman, supposedly a pool novice, though childhood friend James Stotter remembers differently. Newman installed a pool table in his dining room, where he practised with Mosconi. He rated Mosconi as 'a wonderful teacher', always very patient. Under Mosconi's tuition, Newman became a solid pool player. More importantly, he learned how to look like a hustler. On location in New York, Newman would practise in a local girl's high school, travelling there in disguise. Famed for his immaculate wardrobe, Mosconi also provided the inspiration for Gleason's Minnesota Fats costume. Gleason, already a gifted pool player, was close to professional level. During filming, Newman and Gleason would execute all but one of their characters' pool shots. Mosconi performed a tricky 'massé' shot, hitting two object balls into the same pocket. Impressed, Rossen used the shot in both Felson–Fats games, photographed from different angles. A major influence on *The Hustler*, Mosconi is seen on a poster in the pool hall and also plays a small role, without credit. Cast as 'Willie', he holds the bet money during the first Felson–Fats contest.

The Hustler – Eddie Felson takes on Minnesota Fats (Jackie Gleason)

Twentieth Century Fox agreed to two weeks full rehearsal for *The Hustler*. This proved something of a reunion for Newman and Laurie, who hadn't seen each other since the end of shooting on *Until They Sail*. Laurie had the idea of putting pebbles in her shoes to suggest Sarah's limp. Perhaps wisely, she abandoned this idea for the actual filming. Feeling that audiences would be distracted by Sarah's disability, Rossen didn't want it to be too obvious.

Rossen planned to shoot *The Hustler* on location in New York City, a decision resisted by the Fox front office. Faced with the spiralling costs of *Cleopatra* (1963), the studio had become wary of long-distance productions. Fox eventually gave in, accepting that any problems on *The Hustler* would be minor by comparison. The New York filming suited Newman, who rented a large apartment on the city's East Side. Most of the pool sequences were shot at Ames pool hall, on

47th Street, just off Broadway and Times Square, and Rossen spent over five weeks on these scenes, a reflection of their importance. The first Felson–Fats match was shot early on in the schedule, giving film editor Dede Allen much-needed time to fine-cut the intricate footage. Only a few studio sets were used, including Sarah Packard's apartment, built on New York's Movietone sound stage.

Piper Laurie found Newman easy to work with, if a little intense: 'He was always very serious, slightly apart from the so-called movie actors.' Convinced that *The Hustler* would be a major film, Newman gave the role of Eddie Felson his full attention. He got on well with Gleason. Despite their disparate backgrounds, the two men formed a strong working relationship. Overconfident of his cue skills, Newman once bet Gleason $50 on a game of pool. Having been soundly thrashed, Newman paid his co-star in pennies. Laurie never got to meet Gleason, as their characters had no scenes together, while George C. Scott tended to focus on the work, seldom engaging in small talk.

Throughout production, Rossen went through serious mood swings. At times, he seemed very confident about the movie, anticipating a major critical and commercial success. Unfortunately, the director was in poor health, suffering from diabetes and chronic stress. Still depressed by his career problems, he felt *The Hustler* could be his last chance as a film-maker. Ulu Grosbard, the second assistant director, recalled the working atmosphere as tense. Already under pressure to execute some complicated set-ups, the crew were given short shrift by Rossen. According to Grosbard, Rossen had a smoother relationship with the cast, the director aware that any strife could affect their performances. Newman rated him as a gifted director, able to guide an actor out of trouble.

Newman once described *The Hustler* as a 'gut' film and Eddie Felson as 'a great character, surrounded by great characters'. The movie begins with a pre-credits sequence, rare for the time, set in a dingy New York bar on a summer afternoon. During this opening hustle, Felson acts ingratiating and restless, puffing on a cigarette and unable to hold his liquor. Playing a finely honed routine with Charlie Burns (Myron McCormick), his manager, Felson walks away a few bucks richer. This is merely a warm-up for Ames billiards hall, where Minnesota Fats will surely appear. Charlie pronounces it 'Quiet'. 'Yeah, like a church,' Felson responds, showing reverence towards this sweaty, seedy, shabby establishment. Pool is his religion. He aims to become its God. Employing snappy exchanges and a cheesy grin, Felson comes across as confident and cocky, caressing the green baize with an expert hand: 'Nice clean pocket drop.' Unbeaten for fifteen years, Minnesota Fats is the one player Felson regards with awe. The big Felson–Fats game, which comes early in the film, is a *tour de force*. Rossen didn't want *The Hustler* to be endless shots of ball drops, arguing that the film was about character, not pool. It's this sense of 'character' which gives Fats the edge over Felson. Fats has all the class, immaculately turned out in a suit, tie, waistcoat and buttonhole. Drinking his scotch from a glass rather than the bottle, Fats knows the value of holding back. While Eddie gets drunk, Fats freshens up, placing talcum powder on his hands. Eddie doesn't know when to quit, which costs him the game. Unable to handle this defeat, he literally collapses onto the floor. The pool hall, of course, is a metaphor for America, sharply divided into winners and losers. For all the mutual respect between Felson and Fats, the young pretender is a long way from the throne. Put simply, Minnesota Fats has the 'character' of a champion that Felson lacks.

The Hustler is a superb piece of film-making. Rossen's fluid direction, which makes full use of the Cinemascope format, is complemented by vivid location work and Dede Allen's precision editing. Shot in high-contrast black and white, the film perfectly captures a twilight world of pool halls, bars and bus stations, inhabited by sad, lonely people on the margins of society. The script has a sexual frankness unusual for the time, with Felson and Sarah wrapped up in mutual carnal attraction.

For all his easy charm, Eddie Felson is revealed as an obsessive, selfish jerk who treats people badly. Newman's big achievement is to render this two-bit hustler as an intriguing, even likeable, figure. Felson's desperate desire to win, to be more than a small-time player, is palpable. No great shakes as a jazzman in *Paris Blues*, Newman is convincing as a hot pool player. Interestingly, he felt he'd misjudged some of his performance. Watching the film years later, he was 'very conscious of working too hard, which comes partly from lack of faith in your own talent and lack of faith that just doing it in itself is all the audience requires'.

Piper Laurie wins a measure of sympathy for her character. The script depicts Sarah as a compulsive liar, which makes her hard to assess. Unfortunately, Sarah's subsequent suicide doesn't have the intended impact, perhaps because the film never gets inside her head.

The second Felson–Fats game is deliberately anti-climactic. Sarah's death has given Felson the 'character' to beat Fats, who knows he can't win this time. Felson regains his dignity, self-respect and soul, but the price is too high. If Felson truly loved Sarah, as he now claims, his cry of 'How can I lose?' is bitterly ironic. Winning has become meaningless. The hustling, in and out of the pool hall, is over.

The Hustler was edited in New York rather than Los Angeles. Still wary of this 'runaway' East Coast production, Fox sent representatives to report back on progress in the cutting room. Faced with an impending release date, Rossen and Allen had to rush the post-production. Fox urgently needed box-office revenue to support the Cleopatra shoot in Italy, still months away from completion. Believing The Hustler ran too long, the studio wanted to drop the pre-credits sequence, arguing that it was unnecessary. Fox also worried that the extended pool-room scenes would alienate female audiences. Interestingly, Allen partly agreed with the studio, feeling The Hustler could have been tightened with more post-production time.

Under pressure from Fox to make cuts, Rossen hired PR expert Arthur P. Jacobs to campaign for his version of the film. Jacobs arranged a midnight preview of The Hustler in New York, assembling an impressive list of celebrity guests. When the screening proved a hit, Fox agreed to release Rossen's cut. According to critic Richard Schickel, the midnight show was arranged by Richard Burton, a friend of Rossen since Alexander the Great (1956).

Having given in to Rossen, Twentieth Century Fox remained uncertain about the commercial appeal of pool. The advertising for The Hustler emphasized the romantic element, depicting Newman and Laurie in a passionate clinch: 'It delves without compromise into the hungers that lie deep within us all!'

The Hustler premièred in Washington D.C. in September 1961, with Robert Rossen, Piper Laurie, George C. Scott and Willie Mosconi as guests of honour. Released on 25 September 1961, it did respectable rather than spectacular business. Fox had opted to give the film an immediate wide release, rather than let it build on critical acclaim and audience word-of-mouth. Teetering on the verge of bankruptcy, the studio could not afford to soft-sell its movies.

In early 1962, The Hustler was nominated for a slew of Academy Awards: Best Picture, Best Director, Best Adapted Screenplay, Best Actor, Best Supporting Actor, Best Supporting Actress and Best Cinematography. In the Best Actor category, Newman faced competition from Spencer Tracy (Judgement at Nuremberg), Maximilian Schell (Judgement at Nuremberg), Charles Boyer (Fanny) and Stuart Whitman (The Mark). Joanne Woodward was visibly upset when Schell took the Oscar, protesting that Newman had been cheated. Interviewed by Playboy magazine, Newman admitted to taking the defeat badly: 'I was really hurt by that one.' Eugene Schufftan's photography deservedly won an Academy Award. By way of compensation, the

British Academy of Film and Television Awards named *The Hustler* Best Picture and Newman Best Actor.

While *The Hustler* established Newman's star status beyond all doubt, his box-office standing remained uncertain and he failed to make Hollywood's 'Top Ten' list for 1961, which was headed by Elizabeth Taylor, Rock Hudson and Doris Day. While Newman and George C. Scott both gained kudos from *The Hustler*, the film did little for their co-stars and director. Jackie Gleason never found another decent film role. Piper Laurie retired from acting following her marriage to film critic Joseph Morgenstern, although, fifteen years later, she made a successful comeback in *Carrie* (1976). Robert Rossen directed only one more film, the offbeat character study *Lilith* (1964), before his premature death in 1966, aged fifty-seven.

The limits of Newman's star power were demonstrated when he became involved with one of Jack Garfein's film projects. Well established in New York's theatre scene, Garfein got his first Hollywood break through Elia Kazan, who employed him as an assistant director on *Baby Doll* (1956). The Actors Studio connection brought Garfein to the attention of producer Sam Spiegel, who hired him to direct *The Strange One* (1957), which dealt with unsavoury happenings at a Deep South military academy. Spiegel and distributor Columbia had scored an Academy Award-winning hit with Elia Kazan's *On the Waterfront* (1953), starring Actors Studio graduate Marlon Brando. Spiegel sold *The Strange One* as 'the first picture filmed entirely by a cast and technicians from The Actors Studio, New York'. In truth, Garfein lacked Kazan's grasp of the film medium and the performances by leads Ben Gazzara and George Peppard now seem mannered. Four years later, Garfein directed his second feature film, *Something Wild* (1961), starring Carroll Baker as a rape victim. For all the heavy Method acting and vivid New York locations, *Something Wild* scored only as intense soap opera. Looking for a more substantial project, Garfein wanted to adapt John Richard Hersey's novel *The Wall*, a harrowing account of the Warsaw Ghetto uprising. The controversial subject matter held particular resonance for the Jewish Garfein, who'd survived childhood internment at Auschwitz, before arriving in the US, aged fifteen. In need of funds for script development, he asked Newman to be part of the deal, hoping to trade on his friend's star status. Even with Newman attached, not one Hollywood studio showed interest in backing the project.

Newman was also approached by Italian film-maker Gillo Pontecorvo, a former journalist, resistance fighter and documentarian. A committed Marxist, Pontecorvo had a mixed track record in the cinema. The controversial *Kapo* (1960), set in a Nazi concentration camp, was an overplotted melodrama peopled by stereotypes. Pontecorvo wanted Newman to star in his new project, an indictment of colonial oppression in Indo-China. For various reasons, the film came to nothing. Pontecorvo later reworked his ideas into *The Battle of Algiers* (1966), a classic of political cinema.

Newman returned to Metro-Goldwyn-Mayer for *Sweet Bird of Youth* (1962), based on his 1959 Broadway success. The film version was adapted and directed by Richard Brooks, who'd given MGM a hit with *Cat on a Hot Tin Roof*. Brooks was currently riding high on the success of *Elmer Gantry* (1960), which earned him an Academy Award for Best Screenplay. Despite Tennessee Williams's antipathy towards the screen version of *Cat*, MGM secured the rights to *Sweet Bird of Youth*. Newman would be paid $350,000 to reprise his stage role.

The film reunited Newman with Geraldine Page, his co-star from the original Broadway production. While Page's theatre career dated back to the early 1940s, her Hollywood standing was negligible. Prior to *Sweet Bird*, she had only three movies to her name, including the 3D western *Hondo* (1954), opposite John Wayne. She subsequently appeared in *Summer and Smoke* (1961), based on Tennessee Williams's 1948 play, reprising the role she'd played in a 1952 stage production. While both films earned Page Academy Award nominations, the actress had no interest in movie stardom. According to rumour, MGM considered dropping Page from the film version of *Sweet Bird*; the studio was keen to pair Newman with a hotter aging leading lady, such as Ava Gardner, Lana Turner or Rita Hayworth.

The role of Boss Finlay went to Ed Begley. The film also employed original cast members Madeleine Sherwood and Rip Torn, who had successfully taken over Newman's role during the play's initial Broadway run. He and Page married in 1961, staying together until her death in 1987.

Newman's love interest, Heavenly (Boss Finlay's daughter), was played by Shirley Knight. A relative newcomer, Knight's film credits included *The Dark at the Top of the Stairs* (1960). It earned her an Academy Award nomination for Best Supporting Actress, thus boosting her market value. For all this acclaim, she disliked Hollywood, later telling critic and columnist Rex Reed: 'I find movies a big bore and very unfulfilling . . . Any actor who tells me he is fulfilled artistically by working in movies is full of it.'

From the start, the film version of *Sweet Bird of Youth* was undermined by Production Code restrictions and studio tampering. While MGM eventually cast Page, the actress underwent a radical makeover for the big-screen incarnation of Alexandra Del Lago. The studio insisted that she be given a conventional movie star look rather than the shrivelled painted harpy envisaged by Tennessee Williams and Elia Kazan. Newman was also glamorized, making Chance Wayne look like the movie star he longed to be rather than the aging loser he actually was.

Sweet Bird of Youth – Chance Wayne and Alexandra Del Lago (Geraldine Page)

Newman described the *Sweet Bird of Youth* film as 'pretty good'. Williams and Brooks were obviously inspired by Billy Wilder's superior *Sunset Boulevard* (1950), but, by and large, *Sweet Bird of Youth* is overheated and overplayed, with only glimpses of Page's original power on stage. Having toned down his stage role to Hollywood dictates, Newman delivers a bland performance that lacks both passion and conviction. Like Martin Ritt in *The Long Hot Summer*, Brooks exploits Newman's sexuality to the maximum degree. Chance is seen in an open shirt, then without his shirt, his torso apparently oiled. He also performs a slow-motion dive in white swimming trunks.

Sporting a grin a mile wide, Chance doesn't twig the danger he's in from Boss Finlay. As Ethan Mordden puts it, 'Everyone in Williams is a dreamer or a realist, and the realists murder the dreamers.' Thanks to MGM and the Production Code, this dreamer escapes with a few minor abrasions. Chance may get his pretty face bashed up, but it's preferable to the castration he suffers in the stage version. Interestingly, Brooks never intended to follow Williams's original finale. His preferred ending had Chance's body being dumped at sea from a garbage scow. Blatant symbolism aside, MGM did not want a downbeat conclusion and vetoed Brooks's idea. In the event, Chance rediscovers his pride and integrity, gets roughed up, and drives off into the night with Heavenly. As cop-out finales go, this takes some beating. On the upside, Boss Finlay offers a sound piece of advice: 'Only idiots laugh at nothing.'

Marketed with the tagline 'He Used Love Like Most Men Use Money!', *Sweet Bird of Youth* opened in the US on 21 March 1962. Neither critics nor audiences were impressed, and the film did little business. Surprisingly, it received serious Academy Award attention. Begley picked up the trophy for Best Supporting Actor, and both Page and Knight were nominated, for Best Actress and Best Supporting Actress, respectively.

Whatever the disappointments of Newman's film career, his home life seemed reasonably harmonious, under the circumstances. Scott, Susan and Stephanie, the children from his first marriage, were now aged eleven, nine and seven, respectively. When Newman was in Los Angeles, they spent most of their weekends with him, alongside Woodward and their stepsister Elinor. Susan and Stephanie seemed to have accepted their parents' divorce, and even Scott got on with Elinor. Already dealing with the tensions of a fractured family, Newman took care to shield his children from the media. On 17 September 1961, Woodward gave birth to a second daughter, Melissa Steward, in Hollywood, California. Melissa was named after Woodward's character in *Count Three and Pray* (1955), still one of her favourite roles. Already on a high from the successful previews of *The Hustler*, just a few days earlier, Newman had cause for a double celebration.

While Newman and Woodward's work commitments meant spending time in Los Angeles, they wanted a base on the East Coast, thousands of miles from Hollywood. The celebrity couple eventually settled on a property in Westport, Connecticut, where Newman had lived during the late 1940s. An affluent, cultured neighbourhood, Westport had no connections to the show-business world. Newman and Woodward purchased a house by the Aspetuck River. On winter mornings, Newman liked to break the ice and jump in the water after his daily sauna. Their neighbours included writer A. E. Hotchner and his wife Ursula, both good friends. Newman and Hotchner jointly owned the fishing boat *Caca del Toro* ('bullshit'), which became their base for heavy-duty beer drinking. While Hotchner had been friendly with Newman since *The Battler* (1955), he regarded the star as a loner: 'He is the most private man I've ever known. He has a moat and a drawbridge which he lets down only occasionally.'

Hemingway's Adventures of a Young Man – Newman reprises his characterization of the Battler, with Richard Beymer

Newman's friendship with A. E. Hotchner led to a 'guest appearance' in *Hemingway's Adventures of a Young Man* (1962). Directed by Martin Ritt, this Twentieth Century Fox release proved an ill-conceived flop the studio could ill-afford. Having served as Ernest Hemingway's official biographer, Hotchner turned several of the author's short stories into a feature film. He was intrigued by the figure of Nick Adams, an autobiographical character who appeared in *The Battler*, and *Adventures of a Young Man* was a large-scale reworking of Hotchner's television play *The World of Nick Adams* (1957). Following years of depression, Hemingway had committed suicide in 1961.

Presumably, Hotchner intended the film as a tribute to his friend and mentor, whereas Fox probably saw the project as a chance to exploit public interest in the late author.

Hemingway's Adventures of a Young Man was produced by Jerry Wald, who'd worked with Newman and Ritt on *The Long Hot Summer*. Newman's agents protested when he accepted a cameo role, arguing that stars didn't play bit parts. Newman had agreed to reprise his television role of Ad Francis, The Battler. Aside from his loyalty to Ritt and Hotchner, Newman wanted a second stab at the character. Curious to see how he'd grown and matured as an actor, he watched his old television performance prior to filming. As the star later explained, 'It was a good part.'

Hemingway's Adventures of a Young Man did badly at the box office. For all Hotchner's hard work, Nick Adams's journey of self-discovery seemed contrived and uninvolving. Newman felt he'd misjudged his own performance: 'I tried to do what I did in the TV show, and that wasn't the way to go at it.'

In early 1962, Newman, Woodward and Gore Vidal were celebrity guests on the cruise ship *Leonardo Da Vinci*, sailing from New York to Italy. In return for free passage and VIP treatment, they would promote the service with their presence. Paying guests were treated to screenings of *The Three Faces of Eve* and *Cat on a Hot Tin Roof*. A few years later, Newman, Woodward and Vidal embarked on a less successful cruise around the Adriatic. According to Vidal, an unauthorised landing on Greek territory angered local authorities. Only Newman's movie-star status got them off the hook. Whatever the downsides, Hollywood fame still had its privileges.

6 A Barbed-Wire Soul

Hud – Hud and Alma (Patricia Neal)

My daddy thinks that oil is something you stick in your
salad dressing.
  Hud Bannon, *Hud*

Newman got his career back on track with *Hud* (1963), possibly his best movie in terms of dramatic force. Texas cattleman Hud Bannon is Newman's nastiest role, a mean-spirited hedonist with no redeeming qualities. While *The Hustler*'s Eddie Felson at least searched for redemption, the concept has no meaning for Hud.

Hud was Newman's fourth collaboration with director Martin Ritt. Having lost their way on *Paris Blues* and, to a lesser extent, *Adventures of a Young Man*, director and star now found an ideal character. Ritt saw Hud Bannon as a Clark Gable-style cad who stays that way, never undergoing the expected reformation, 'the kind of American heel that had not yet existed in American films'. Newman compared the character with the Tennessee Williams tradition of exploring 'that premium which Americans place on external beauty'. Ritt and Newman had recently formed a business partnership, offering their joint services to Paramount. Ritt would direct two films, starring Newman, with a third open to further negotiation. As the first project under the deal, *Hud* got the new partnership off to a strong start.

The pair were joined by *Long Hot Summer* writers Irving Ravetch and Harriet Frank Jr. The *Hud* script was based on Larry McMurtry's 1961 novel *Horseman, Pass By*, in which Hud is a relatively minor character. Ritt also recruited top cameraman James Wong Howe, whose forty-year career encompassed *The Thin Man* (1934) and *The Sweet Smell of Success* (1957).

Newman's co-stars included Patricia Neal, a fine actress seen in *A Face in the Crowd* (1957) and *Breakfast at Tiffany's* (1961). Neal knew both Newman and Ritt from the Actors Studio in New York. She first met Newman there during the mid-1950s, when her film career was on hold. Pregnant with her daughter Olivia, Neal couldn't accept job offers but wanted to keep acting, 'to get back to the roots of my profession'. A former Actors Studio graduate, Neal asked Lee Strasberg if she could return. Introduced to Newman, she was struck by 'an earnest young actor with the most penetrating blue eyes I had ever seen'. Newman stayed in touch with Neal, introducing her to Joanne Woodward in Paramount's make-up department during production on *Breakfast at Tiffanys*.

Ritt had worried that Neal would think her role in *Hud* too small. As it happened, Neal was anxious to work, for both financial and emotional reasons. Tragically, Olivia had died from German measles in November 1962 and, since her daughter's death, Neal had only taken one acting job. Her husband, British writer Roald Dahl, gave the *Hud* script his seal of approval. However, Neal was unhappy with her work schedule for the film, which meant being apart from her family for two months. Sympathetic to Neal's predicament, Ritt offered her a break between the location shoot in Texas and the studio work back in Hollywood.

The cast also featured stage actor Melvyn Douglas, whose film career began in the 1930s. The role of Hud's hero-worshipping nephew went to former child actor Brandon De Wilde, best known for *Shane* (1953). As an adult, De Wilde gave a creditable performance opposite Warren Beatty in *All Fall Down* (1962), where he played an impressionable young man who idolizes his charismatic, amoral older brother, a useful dry run for *Hud*.

Hud – Hud Bannon comes between nephew Lonnie (Brandon De Wilde) and father Homer (Melvyn Douglas)

To prepare for his role, Newman worked as a cowhand on a Texas ranch for several weeks. He acquired authentic calluses on his hands and even developed a cowboy's lope. Newman also studied the real ranch hands, picking up on their character traits. Prior to the start of production, Ritt rehearsed his cast at the Paramount studios, and Patricia Neal's faith in the project was soon confirmed: 'I could tell from the first reading that this was going to be special.'

Initially titled 'Hud Bannon', *Hud* was filmed on location in the small town of Claude, Texas. Newman and De Wilde drove around the town at night, much like their characters in the film. Neal got on well with both Ritt and Newman. On one occasion, however, Newman's behaviour left her deeply upset. Early on in the Claude shoot, Neal talked with Newman about the recent death of her daughter Olivia. Still traumatized by the tragedy, Neal explained how she'd allowed her sisters-in-law to supervise the funeral. She particularly regretted not seeing Olivia in her coffin. Newman responded to this heartbreaking story with a single word: 'Tough'. Initially shocked by her co-star's 'brutal indifference', Neal later realized that Newman had replied in character, as Hud Bannon. Perhaps he saw this 'full-immersion' approach as the only way to sustain such a dark portrayal, far removed from his own personality. This incident aside, Neal regarded him as both kind and considerate. On set, they had what Neal described as an 'ace' working relationship. During filming on the big 'kitchen sink' scene between Hud and Neal's character Alma, the symbolic horsefly swatted by the latter appeared by chance.

Throughout the location shoot, Newman found himself pursued by women, some of whom tried to break into his hotel. Aware of Woodward's unhappiness with the situation, he treated these incidents as trivial, if tiresome: 'At first, it's flattering to the ego. At first.' Back in Los Angeles for the Christmas holiday, Newman and Woodward decided to bypass some of the traditional festivities. Rather than buy each other presents, they would donate money to the humanitarian organization CARE.

Filmed in monochrome Panavision, *Hud* turns a tale of cattle ranchers into something approaching high tragedy. The downbeat tone is set by Elmer Bernstein's melancholy, plaintive main theme, played on an acoustic guitar. The film benefits immeasurably from the overall attention to detail, rendering the dusty small-town setting utterly believable. The smart, sexually frank script is also outstanding.

Hud Bannon's character is carefully sketched in prior to his entrance: a drinker, brawler and womaniser. Stretching his 'aw-shucks' grin a mile wide, Newman gives a raw, mean performance, topped by a convincing Texan accent. Writing in 1982, *Time* journalist John Skow described Hud as 'a brawler with the looks of a fallen angel'.

Newman's sculpted features take on a menacing, satanic aspect, typified by what Skow called his 'cruelly curled' lips. Cynical and downright rude, Hud cuts an elegant, insolent figure, his thumbs hooked in his jeans pockets.

Hud is the diametrical opposite of his father, Homer Bannon (Melvyn Douglas), who loathes Hud's cold indifference to others. Law-abiding and decent, Homer is a proud, if mangy, old lion, defending his territory to the last. This generational struggle is observed by Alma Brown (Patricia Neal), the Bannons' live-in housekeeper. Shrewd and worldly, Alma has an earthy quality that appeals to Hud. While the attraction appears mutual, she resists his advances. For all Hud's charm, Alma sees the 'cold-blooded bastard' underneath. When she claims that her ex-husband turned her off men, Hud acts indignant: 'Honey, don't go shootin' all the dogs 'cos one of them's got fleas.'

Any hope for the Bannon clan's future rests with Lonnie (Brandon De Wilde), Hud's nephew. Lon sees Hud as a link to his dead father, killed in a road accident caused by Hud. Inevitably, he becomes torn between Hud and Homer, unable to reconcile the former's reckless excitement with the latter's staid integrity. In a scene cut from the film, Lon questions Alma about the meaning of life, getting a curt, world-weary response: 'Honey, you'll just have to ask someone else.'

While *Hud* never sympathizes with its title character, the film does attempt to explain his attitude. Hud has spent twenty-four years in service to his father, working on the Bannon ranch from the age of ten. Now he wants something in return, with no hogwash about love or duty. The whole world is corrupt and each man must grab his share, by any means necessary. Matters come to a head with an outbreak of foot-and-mouth disease, which leaves Homer Bannon facing financial ruin. When the state vet suggests prospecting the Bannon land for oil, Homer won't hear of it, much to Hud's disgust. Of course, Hud is partly right. Homer can't move with the times, and his fierce commitment to the old ways will kill the family business.

Eventually, Hud loses his cool exterior, assaulting Alma after a night on the booze. Drunk or sober, Hud can't accept that a woman doesn't find him irresistible. Disgusted by Hud's behaviour, Lon sees his uncle's true character: amoral, dishonest and selfish. With Homer in his grave, Alma and Lon depart the Bannon ranch. Hud ends up alone, maybe oil rich, maybe just the friendless loser he's always been.

Hud premièred in New York City on 28 May 1963, going on general release a day later. Critically acclaimed, the film was a box-office hit, supported by some shrewd marketing. The print advertising campaign, which won an award, proved particularly effective: 'Paul Newman IS Hud . . . The Man with the Barbed-Wire Soul.' Newman received some of the best reviews of his career, though *The New Yorker*'s praise seemed as barbed as Hud Bannon: 'How he rejoices in the mastery of his craft! Luckily, it's a joy without a trace of self-satisfaction, and therefore harmless.'

The film also drew some major Academy Award nominations: Best Director, Best Adapted Screenplay, Best Cinematography, Best Actress (Patricia Neal) and Best Supporting Actor (Melvyn Douglas). Newman received his third Best Actor nomination. This time, he was up against Albert Finney (*Tom Jones*), Richard Harris (*This Sporting Life*), Rex Harrison (*Cleopatra*) and Sidney Poitier (*Lilies of the Field*), his co-star from *Paris Blues*. Most observers expected Poitier to take the award. Directed by Ralph Nelson, *Lilies of the Field* was a sentimental fable, with Poitier cast as a handyman who helps German nuns build a church. Aside from the uplifting feelgood factor, giving Poitier the Oscar would show that the Academy had moved with the times. While Hattie McDaniel had won the Best Supporting Actress Academy Award for her performance in *Gone with the Wind* (1939), no black actor had ever taken the major trophy. Aware that *Hud* did not offer a positive role model, Newman played down his chances of winning. In public, at least, he lent his support to Poitier: 'I'd like to see Sidney Poitier get it . . . I'd be proud to win for a role I really had to reach for.' Significantly, Newman declined to launch his own campaign for the Oscar.

The ceremony was held on 13 April 1964 in Santa Monica. To no one's surprise, Poitier took the Best Actor trophy, for an admittedly appealing performance. As Newman predicted, Hud Bannon was just too amoral and unsympathetic for the conservative Academy voters. However, James Wong Howe, Patricia Neal and Melvyn Douglas all won Academy Awards for their work on *Hud*. Heavily pregnant, Neal could not attend in person. She later sent Martin Ritt a telegram: 'It was not too small.' While Neal had played a supporting role in *Hud*, she took the Oscar in the Best Actress category. Without detracting from Neal's performance, it's arguable that this 'promotion' reflected the chronic shortage of strong leading roles for women.

Newman later expressed some misgivings about the impact of *Hud*. He felt that some audiences had only seen the 'cool', superficial Hud Bannon, failing to pick up on the dark, amoral character underneath: 'I think it was misunderstood, especially by the kids.' Ritt disagreed, arguing that Hud's lack of values put him in tune with the cynical younger generation. For his part, Ritt had no time for Hud: 'Any man committed to his appetite finally is a prick.'

Hud was reissued on a double bill with Howard Hawks's *Hatari!* (1962), in which John Wayne leads a motley crew of safari trappers across the African plains. While both films centre on rugged 'men's men' doing their thing, Wayne's morally upright leader-of-the-pack is poles apart from Newman's complex, unsympathetic character study. In all likelihood, Paramount's distribution division saw a shrewd marketing opportunity: both films had one-word titles beginning with the letter 'H'.

Newman remained with Paramount for *A New Kind of Love* (1963), his second excursion into big-screen comedy. The film reunited Newman and Joanne Woodward for another Paris romance, this time with a happy ending. However, of all Newman's failed, compromised or generally misfiring movies, *A New Kind of Love* is the hardest to sit through. It was produced, scripted and directed by Melville Shavelson, who'd made a string of glossy, middlebrow comedies at Paramount.[1] Though commercially successful, few of his movies displayed much in the way of sustained wit or comic invention.

The driving force behind *A New Kind of Love* was Woodward, who dragged Newman on board. By the early 1960s, her Hollywood career had lost momentum. Her most recent film was *The Stripper* (1963), a Twentieth Century Fox release produced by Jerry Wald. This minor effort marked the feature début of director Franklin J. Schaffner, who'd worked with Woodward and Newman on the television drama *The 80 Yard Run*. Based on William Inge's 1959 play *A Loss of Roses*, *The Stripper* cast Woodward as a faded beauty queen, who becomes involved with teenage garage hand Richard Beymer. Woodward had a commitment to Fox under her old contract, accepting the film out of expedience rather than enthusiasm. Made up to resemble Marilyn Monroe, she looked ill at ease. Her stripping routines, demure in the extreme, were all approved by Newman.

Production on *The Stripper* proved troubled. The atmosphere at Fox was gloomy, the studio in deep financial trouble with the *Cleopatra* production, which was now absurdly over-budget and behind schedule. To make matters worse, Wald died suddenly mid-shoot, on 13 July 1962, aged only fifty. Without his support, *The Stripper* fell victim to studio tampering, undergoing substantial re-editing. Despite the best efforts of Woodward and Schaffner, the released version proved a dreary small-town melodrama. Whatever the quality of

Inge's original play, Woodward had landed back in Hollywood soap opera with a dull thud.

A New Kind of Love – Samantha Blake draws Steve Sherman's interest with her new look

In search of lighter material, Woodward read the script for *A New Kind of Love*, liked what she saw and asked her husband to co-star. While she regarded Shavelson's screenplay as 'cute', Newman had major reservations: 'Geez, this is yechh.' According to Newman, Woodward used emotional blackmail to change his mind. He recalled her exact words as 'You son of a bitch, I've been carting your children around, taking care of them at the expense of my career, taking care of you and your house.' This was undeniably true. Back in 1958, Woodward had informed her agent that she would only accept films shooting close to Newman's locations. Taking his wife's point, Newman agreed to make the film. As he later admitted, 'This is what is known as a reciprocal trade agreement.'

During production at Paramount Studios, Newman was interviewed for the film's merchandising manual and press book. Aware that *A New Kind of Love* was likely to be a failure, Newman used the opportunity to discuss his outside interests:

> I don't want people to get the idea I'm academic. It seems to me though that an actor, just because his life happens to be in public domain, doesn't have to always answer innocuous questions about his domestic life, what he eats, how he sleeps and what famous relatives are on his family tree. I am keenly interested in world events, the work of such dedicated people as Dr Albert Schweitzer and generally all phases of modern existence. I don't suppose the average reader cares much what an actor thinks about current trends such as the Common Market and atomic test control; nevertheless, I find myself thinking on these things and I like to discuss them with anybody and everybody.

Paramount had little to complain about here. Newman was just a regular guy, with a keen but not obsessive interest in current affairs. In later years, his concerns over weapons control would lead to more aggressive lobbying. Woodward offered a more concise take on her ambitions: 'I just want to keep acting better and better. And I want to be a good wife and mother. I also want to do some real good in the world.'

Newman also talked, in general terms, about his approach to acting:

> I like to think my roles out before I begin them. I'm a firm believer in rehearsals. And the farther the characterizations are from my own personality, the greater the challenge.

Woodward concurred: 'Paul begins with an intellectual approach to a role. It starts in his head and he thinks it through.' While Newman described Woodward as an instinctive actress, in contrast to his own approach, she commented, 'I believe I develop a character from the outside in.' Newman claimed that working on a film with his wife was always an enjoyable, non-stressful experience: 'We actually have a ball. We fully discuss our parts both on the set and at home. And we both have a profound respect for each other as artist and person.' Their latest joint appearance was something of a departure:

As for my role in *A New Kind of Love*, this is quite different. It's such a fast-moving comedy that you don't get much chance to think about it. Even Joanne confesses that she doesn't know what I'm going to do next in the sequence of comic situations. This is good for her too. It's sort of a new challenge.

Shavelson praised the star couple as true professionals, bringing their own spontaneity and invention to the film. He had particular respect for Woodward: 'The emotional sensitivity is all there. But you don't detect it in the actress's normal life because she has complete control of her emotional system.' Whatever his reservations about Shavelson's script, Newman remained tactful in print. For the record, at least, *A New Kind of Love* had been a good experience for Woodward and himself:

... both of us, along with ... Shavelson and the entire cast and crew, have had plenty of laughs as we went along. [I] hope the audience gets as many chuckles out of the film as we have had making it.

Filmed 'In Blushing Technicolor', *A New Kind of Love* boasted 'The most elaborate and spectacular costuming for a Paramount motion picture since *The Ten Commandments*.' According to studio publicity, the production employed one million dollars' worth of outfits by Pierre Cardin, Christian Dior, Lanvin and Yves Saint-Laurent. Newman worked on his own wardrobe with veteran costume designer Edith Head. Unfortunately, *A New Kind of Love*'s plot and characters were as flimsy as damp tissue. As Newman pointed out from the start, Shavelson's script is 'just a bunch of one-liners'. In bolder hands, *A New Kind of Love* could have been a sharp comedy of gender politics. As things stand, the film is merely heavy-handed and misogynistic. Woodward's decision to involve herself and Newman in the film suggests questionable judgement, to say the least.

A New Kind of Love opened in New York City on 30 October 1963. Newman's doubts about the project proved well-founded. Despite a massive advertising campaign, the film was a deserved critical and commercial failure. *Photoplay* reviewer Janet Graves proved kinder than most: '. . . an engaging romp, with more style in the gorgeous clothes than there is in the leisurely story-telling'. By 1963, Newman and Woodward had been displaced as Hollywood's première showbiz couple by Elizabeth Taylor and Richard Burton, thanks to *Cleopatra*'s notoriety. Newman and Woodward would not co-star in another film until *Winning* (1969).

Newman returned to Metro-Goldwyn-Mayer for *The Prize* (1963), in which an American writer uncovers a sinister conspiracy at the Nobel Prize ceremony. This Hitchcockian thriller was loosely based on a 1962 novel by Irving Wallace, which sold 100,000 hardback copies in the US alone. Wallace's book provoked controversy by suggesting that the Nobel Prize could be fixed and was banned in Sweden, home of the Nobel Foundation. Warner Brothers had enjoyed some success with *The Chapman Report* (1962), based on an earlier Wallace book, inspired by Dr Alfred Kinsey's famous report on America's sexual mores.

The Prize reunited Newman with producer Pandro S. Berman, from *Sweet Bird of Youth*, and Mark Robson, who had directed *From the Terrace*. The screenplay was assigned to *From the Terrace* writer Ernest Lehman, presumably on the strength of *North by Northwest* (1959), a big hit for MGM. Lehman's finished script for *The Prize* bore little resemblance to the original book, retaining only the Nobel backdrop and a subplot involving the kidnap of a German scientist. Newman, who hadn't read the book, felt Lehman's script offered a solid combination of comedy, romance and drama.

The Prize – Andrew Craig and Inger Lisa (Elke Sommer)

Newman's leading lady was newcomer Elke Sommer. Her character, who didn't appear in Wallace's novel, served as the token love interest. The cast also featured Edward G. Robinson, one of Hollywood's greatest character actors. By the early 1960s, the star of *Little Caesar* (1930) and *Double Indemnity* (1944) had been through some rough times. During location filming in Kenya for *Sammy Going South* (1963), he had suffered a near-fatal heart attack. In March 1963, Berman, an old friend of Robinson, offered him $75,000 to appear in *The Prize*.

Newman grew a beard for his role, feeling his smooth-chinned visage looked too fresh and youthful for a dissolute author with writer's block. Having paid good money for the classic Paul Newman, Berman and MGM rejected the idea out of hand, requesting an immediate shave. Newman, who often grew a beard between films, took this executive dictate in his stride and, despite press rumours of a prolonged argument between Newman and Berman, on this occasion the star backed down. Robinson, on the other hand, was required to wear a false beard.

Berman intended to shoot *The Prize* on location in Sweden, where the action was set. Locations had been secured and cars rented. Then an article appeared in a Stockholm newspaper, claiming that the film denigrated the Nobel Foundation and, therefore, all Sweden. The deals signed by MGM were abruptly cancelled. Berman relocated the production to Hollywood, recreating the required interiors on sound stages. The camera crew, led by William Daniels, was dispatched to Stockholm, filming location backdrops and establishing shots.

Prior to shooting, Mark Robson rehearsed his cast for a week on Stage 30 of the MGM studios in Culver City. A sequence set in a nudist colony, shot on a closed set over two days, drew the expected publicity. Six female extras supposedly stormed off the set, claiming they hadn't been told about the disrobing. According to actress Maria Schroeder, who played a small speaking role, Newman seemed relaxed, telling the remaining fifty-four extras: 'Okay, girls, you don't laugh at me, I won't laugh at you.' Needless to say, no one in the scene was actually naked, the production team handing out flesh-coloured briefs. Working under the strict Production Code, the actresses even had to cover their nipples with 'pasties'. In the finished film, careful framing and editing obscures all the forbidden body parts.

While Newman rated *The Prize* as 'a lark', most of the distinguished cast perform without enthusiasm. Lehman's laboured screenplay is no better than *From the Terrace*. In terms of plot mechanics, *The Prize* plays like a 'B' remake of his script for *North by Northwest* (1959). An innocent man, who happens to be a smooth charmer, is caught up in international intrigue and marked for death. No one believes his story except a cool blonde woman, who falls for him. He's pursued by a gaunt assassin, who gets shot by the cops, falling to his death on a national monument.

Decked out in heavy-rimmed glasses, Newman looks ill at ease as burned-out novelist Andrew Craig. His awkward performance displays little sense of comic delivery or timing. Battling a feeble script, Newman and Sommer generate negligible screen chemistry.

The Prize opened in the US on 25 December 1963, scoring a hit at the Yuletide box office. The film drew mixed reviews, with only Edward G. Robinson receiving unanimous praise. That year, Newman made the top ten box-office attractions list, finishing at number nine.

Newman made his second 'guest' appearance in *What a Way to Go!* (1964). This swinging black comedy was the brainchild of Arthur P. Jacobs, a movie publicist turned independent producer. As a PR man, Jacobs had assisted Robert Rossen during the director's battle with Twentieth Century Fox over *The Hustler*. *What a Way to Go!* would be produced by Jacobs's APJAC company, with distribution through Fox. The screenplay was by the writer-lyricists Betty Comden and Adolph Green, best known for the MGM musicals *On the Town* (1949) and *Singin' in the Rain* (1952). Looking for a director, Jacobs settled on British expatriate J.(ohn) Lee Thompson, whose success with *The Guns of Navarone* (1961) had launched his Hollywood career.

Jacobs wanted Elizabeth Taylor for the starring role – an unlucky, if wealthy 'serial' widow. When Taylor proved unavailable, Fox and Jacobs settled on Shirley MacLaine, Newman's former landlady. Fresh from Billy Wilder's *Irma La Douce* (1963), MacLaine looked set to be one of the big stars of the 1960s. Newman's fellow husbands were played by Dick Van Dyke, Robert Mitchum, Gene Kelly and Dean Martin.

What a Way to Go! is agreeable, if patchy, entertainment. MacLaine's character, a good-natured small-town girl, weds and buries a succession of millionaire husbands, all of whom meet with strange accidents. Cast as painter Larry Flint, Newman claimed to have taken the role 'out of whimsy'. If nothing else, he was permitted to play his character with a beard, something he'd been denied for *The Prize*.

Following a lavish Manhattan première, *What a Way to Go!* opened in the US on 12 May 1964. Shortly afterwards, Newman attended the Democrats National Convention in Atlantic City, lending his support to President Lyndon Johnson.

Newman attempted one of his most ambitious roles in *The Outrage* (1964), an MGM release directed by Martin Ritt. Originally entitled *The Rape*, this western drama was a remake of Akira Kurosawa's celebrated *Rashomon* (1951), starring Toshiro Mifune. Based on two short stories, 'Rashomon' and 'Inside a Bush', *Rashomon* explores the subjective nature of truth, depicting four widely differing accounts of the same events.

In 1959, *Rashomon* became a Broadway play, starring Rod Steiger and Claire Bloom, who married the same year. Kurosawa's screenplay was adapted by Michael and Fay Kanin, another husband-and-wife team, who retained the story's original setting. For *The Outrage*, Michael Kanin performed a major rewrite of his play, relocating the action to the Old West.[2]

The producer, Ronald Lubin, sent the finished script to Newman, who promptly turned it down. According to Lubin, Newman 'felt it wasn't right for him', the actor suggesting Marlon Brando as better casting. Twelve years earlier, Brando had played Mexican revolutionary Emiliano Zapata in Elia Kazan's *Viva Zapata!* (1952), scripted by John Steinbeck. Taking Newman's advice, Lubin approached Brando, whose film career was in trouble after the box-office failures of *Mutiny on the Bounty* (1962) and *The Ugly American* (1963). Brando claimed to 'love' the script but, typically, wouldn't commit to the project. Fortunately for Lubin and Kanin, his interest in the film spurred Newman to reconsider his initial refusal. Years later, Lubin recalled, 'When Paul heard how much Brando liked the script, his whole attitude changed, and he accepted the role.' While Newman had surpassed Brando as a box-office name, the old competitive spirit remained, it seemed. At the time, Newman claimed, without much conviction, that he trusted Brando's judgement more than his own.

According to Ritt, he and Newman had a more pragmatic reason for taking the project. Both men owed MGM a film and *The Rape* seemed the best script available. The studio soon got cold feet over the title, settling on *The Outrage* as less contentious. Ritt and Newman also served as co-executive producers, the latter through his own company, Kayos. Hot from the success of *Hud*, director and star had faith in their creative partnership. They recruited *Hud* cameraman James Wong Howe, again working in monochrome Panavision.

The pair assembled an impressively eclectic cast for *The Outrage*. Claire Bloom, a good friend to Newman and Joanne Woodward, agreed to reprise her Broadway role, albeit in western costume. Her husband was played by fellow British actor Laurence Harvey. Though not an obvious crowd-pleaser, *The Outrage* at least offered a touch of class.

Thorough as always, Newman spent two weeks in Mexico to research his role, picking up the local accent and atmosphere. Back in Los Angeles, he had brown contact lenses made for extra authenticity. While *The Outrage* would be photographed in black and white, Newman felt his blue eyes could still undermine his performance.

The Outrage – Juan Carrasco under arrest

The Outrage was filmed in early 1964. Newman, Bloom and Harvey spent six weeks on location in Arizona, filming in the desert near Tucson. While Bloom rated Newman as 'a very fine actor', many were unconvinced by his casting. When a visiting journalist joked about Newman's heavy make-up, the star seemed unfazed: 'Sure I look like a Mexican, but I think people will still recognize little Pauly Neuman from Shaker Heights . . .'

During the production, Newman realized how much he'd adjusted to film-making, completing one take against a backdrop of crew movement and noise: 'It really amazed me when I realized that I could block out stuff like that.' On the other hand, he'd had ten years of Hollywood experience to get used to film sets.

Bloom described *The Outrage* as 'nearly a good film'. If so, the line between success and failure is fine indeed. Set during the post-Civil War era, *The Outrage* is loaded with significance, even dispensing with 'distracting' opening credits. It's a dark and stormy night in the town of Silver Gulch, rain bouncing off the rail tracks. A preacher (William Shatner) takes shelter in a wooden shack. Encountering a Con Man (Edward G. Robinson) and a Prospector (Howard Da Silva), he has a strange story to tell: notorious bandit Juan Carrasco (Newman) met a gentrified Husband (Laurence Harvey) and Wife (Claire Bloom). What happened next, nobody seems sure . . .

At the time, Newman felt he'd given one of his best performances: 'I probably came closest to crawling out of my skin.' Outfitted with the contact lenses, black wig and moustache, and heavy stubble, Newman certainly looks distinctive. In truth, he is badly miscast as Juan Carrasco, the only character with a proper name. For all the in-depth research, his growling bandit is a parodic Mexican, complete with sombrero and poncho. While Newman's desire to push himself as an actor is laudable, he should have trusted his instincts. At least Marlon Brando seemed comfortable, and relatively convincing, in *Viva Zapata!*. At times, Newman looks like Brando playing Emiliano Zapata and Don Corleone simultaneously. Brando aside, Newman had let himself be seduced by the challenge of bringing Carrasco to life:

> He was an absolute primitive, which I had never played, with an entirely different sense of movement and an accent I was not familiar with . . . I did it because I didn't think I could do it.

If taken seriously, *The Outrage* is a deeply questionable piece of work. Driven by animal lust, Juan Carrasco sees what he wants and pursues it, unconcerned with white man's bogus morality. The frivolous attitude to rape is offensive, the Wife obviously welcoming Carrasco's attentions. Carrasco puts his spurred boot on the Wife's backside, claiming her as his property. An amoral slut, the Wife goads the Husband and Carrasco into a duel, played as farce.

MGM sold *The Outrage* as 'One of the most provocative motion picture projects ever undertaken by a major motion picture company.' A poster depicting Claire Bloom in Newman's clutches bore the legend: '. . . was it an act of violence or an act of love?' According to the press campaign, Newman regarded Juan Carrasco as his '. . . most difficult role'. *The Outrage* premièred in New York City on 7 October 1964, going on limited release the following day. The reviews were mixed, at best, and the film did badly at the box office. While Newman stood by *The Outrage*, he clearly had reservations about the finale: 'With the exception of the ending, I thought it was a good script.' Quality aside, the paying public would not accept Newman as a Mexican rapist.

In *Adventures in the Screen Trade*, writer William Goldman quoted Newman's thoughts on typecasting in Hollywood:

> One of the difficult things is that American filmgoers seems less able and willing to accept actors or actresses in a wide variety of roles – they get something they hook on to and they like, and *that's* what they want to see.

In the case of *The Outrage*, Newman hadn't offered audiences a viable alternative. The same year, Italian director Sergio Leone released *A Fistful of Dollars* (1964), an unauthorized remake of Kurosawa's *Yojimbo* (1960). Despite legal problems, it proved an international hit, relaunching Clint Eastwood's film career. By contrast, *The Outrage* was quickly forgotten.

Away from the film set, Newman became increasingly involved with the Civil Rights movement. In early 1963, Martin Luther King appealed for celebrity support in Gadsden, Alabama, a hotbed of racial tension where the Ku Klux Klan held sway. Newman, Marlon Brando and Anthony Franciosa responded to King's plea, though Newman felt their gesture of solidarity had little impact: 'We were wasting our time.' The local mayor, Lesley Gilliland, refused to meet with them, threatening to imprison the actors if they damaged public property or incited rioting. Newman and Brando also joined a sit-in in Sacramento, California, to protest at a whites-only housing development. In August 1963, they were among the select group of film stars to take part in King's March on Washington, DC, which culminated with a rally at the Lincoln Memorial. This Hollywood contingent had a natural leader in the form of Charlton Heston. At the time, Heston was President of the Screen Actors Guild, though he couldn't use this position to promote the Civil Rights cause. According to Heston, 'We didn't get as many film people as I'd expected.' Only twenty to thirty Hollywood figures turned up, including Sidney Poitier, Tony Curtis, Lena Horne, Burt Lancaster, Harry Belafonte, James Garner, Sammy Davis Jr and Dorothy Dandridge. Some high-profile liberal actors and directors dropped out, fearing trouble on the day and long-term harm to their careers.

The 200,000 strong March was financed by a benefit performance at the Apollo Theater, Harlem, in which Newman and Brando also participated. Unlike the trip to Gadsden, Newman had no reservations about this mass protest: 'I think there's too much fear of *not* speaking out . . . I'm proud I was there.' Newman, Brando and Lancaster also backed King's Southern Christian Leadership Conference, and Newman

held Civil Rights fundraisers at his Los Angeles home, attended by
Marlon Brando, among others.

Interviewed in late 1963 by *Photoplay* reporter Aljean Meltsir,
Newman made his position clear:

> Some people say that there is some personal gain involved in my
> stand on civil rights, that I'm doing it to get publicity. Other peo-
> ple warn me to stop because it will 'hurt' my career. Am I any less
> a citizen for being an actor? Any kind of immorality condoned by
> the community must be actively attacked by everyone . . . How
> can we question the immorality of other nations when we have
> this blight of Negro inequality hanging over ourselves?

Following Martin Luther King's assassination in 1968, Newman,
Brando and Barbra Streisand all pledged 1 per cent of their earnings to
King's Southern Christian Leadership Conference. Newman also
joined the advisory board for the American Civil Liberties Union of
Southern California, alongside Tony Curtis, Robert Wise and Sidney
Poitier. In 1970, he appeared as a commentator for the epic documen-
tary *King: A Filmed Record . . . Montgomery to Memphis*.

Newman renewed his long-standing relationship with the Actors Studio. The latter had recently ventured into commercial stage productions with the Actors Studio Theatre. When the first three shows
flopped, the management looked to its ranks of celebrity alumni for a
little star support. Back in the late 1950s, Newman had been asked to
star in an Actors Studio production of *Giovanni's Room*, based on
James Baldwin's controversial 1957 novel. Marlon Brando and Montgomery Clift were also approached to play the lead, a character with
a hidden gay life. The Studio hoped that a star name would ensure a
successful Broadway run. Of the three, only Brando showed any interest in the project, which stalled when he wouldn't commit himself.
Interviewed in 1963, during production on *The Prize*, Newman
seemed scathing about the state of contemporary American theatre:
'The theatre is being used badly. It has become a road company Freud,
surrounded by musicals. But when the theatre is truly imaginative it is
something else. It is art.'

Newman and Joanne Woodward agreed to co-star in the fourth
Actors Studio Theatre production, *Baby Want a Kiss?*. Written by
James Costigan, a friend of the couple, this comedy centred on two
aging movie stars, whose careers – and marriage – have seen better
days. Costigan also acted in the play, cast as a writer friend of the main
characters. Both Newman and Woodward were paid the Equity mini-

mum, taking home $117.50 a week. Other Actors Studio Theatre stars had demanded a lot more for their services, often in excess of $1,000 a week. *Baby Want a Kiss?* soon ran into problems, however. During rehearsals, director Frank Corsaro frequently clashed with Costigan, who fiercely resisted any changes to his text. Another old friend of Newman and Woodward, Corsaro disliked the play from the start: 'It really was not a good choice'.

A flimsy, weakly written piece, *Baby Want a Kiss?* had little to recommend it. While Newman and Woodward seemed to find their roles amusing, many felt they were doing the play as a favour to Costigan. Newman may also have been intrigued by his character, a closet homosexual who makes a pass at his male friend. The play premièred at New York's Little Theatre on 19 April 1964 and, as Corsaro predicted, the response proved largely negative. Geraldine Page, Newman's co-star from the stage and screen versions of *Sweet Bird of Youth*, made no attempt at diplomacy: 'I hated it.' Woodward loyally defended her husband's work in the play, claiming, 'The critics were just not bright enough to understand his performance.' In her view, Newman belonged back on the stage; the film medium inhibited his larger than life quality. *Baby Want a Kiss?* was the first – and only – Actors Studio Theatre production to make money. Hot from the success of *Hud* and *The Prize*, Newman was a surefire box-office draw and, despite bad reviews, the play was sold out for its entire four-month run. In the long term, *Baby Want a Kiss?* served as a poor advertisement for the Actors Studio. Four years later, in 1968, Newman served as a presenter for the 22nd Annual Tony Awards, broadcast on television. This was as close as he'd get to the New York stage for a long time. After *Baby Want a Kiss?*, Newman did not appear in another Broadway production for thirty-eight years.

Having taken a pay cut for *Baby Want a Kiss?*, Newman was not averse to a little easy money. Since the beginning of his stardom, Newman had refused to endorse commercial products in the US. Like most well-known actors, he didn't want his credibility tainted by cold hustling. That said, he agreed to star in an overseas advert for the German car company Volkswagen. If Laurence Olivier could flog cameras in Japan, who was he to turn down this lucrative offer? In fairness, Newman did drive a Volkswagen Beetle, albeit one fitted with a Porsche engine. Unperturbed by Volkswagen's Nazi connections, Newman lent his name to the product: 'I do like that little bug.' To balance this shameless endorsement, he appeared in several public-service adverts back home, promoting safety belts and the Library Association.

Newman's career hit a low point with *Lady L* (1965), co-produced by Metro-Goldwyn-Mayer and Italian movie mogul Carlo Ponti. Based on a novel by Romain Gary, this romantic comedy had started pre-production back in 1959. Tony Curtis, Gina Lollobrigida and Ralph Richardson were set to star in the film, under the direction of George Cukor. Following various disagreements between Cukor and producer Julian Blaustein – largely over the script and casting – the project was shelved, with $1 million already spent on sets and costumes.

Ponti felt *Lady L* could be a good vehicle for his wife, Sophia Loren. Despite creditable appearances in *Houseboat* (1958) and *El Cid* (1961), Loren's Hollywood career hadn't taken off in a big way. Her most acclaimed performance was in Vittorio de Sica's *Two Women* (1961), for which she won an Academy Award. She had recently finished work on *The Fall of the Roman Empire* (1964) and, if this ambitious big-budget epic failed, Loren would need a major hit. Incidentally, Loren had been Cukor's first choice for *Lady L*. In this instance, at least, Cukor's casting instincts would be proved wrong.

Ponti had wanted Loren to star in the epic romance *Doctor Zhivago* (1965), which he produced for MGM, in partnership with director David Lean. Lean and scriptwriter Robert Bolt were not interested in Loren, casting British actress Julie Christie instead. Newman was MGM's first choice for the title role, presumably due to his success in *The Prize*. Having sat through the Mark Robson film, Lean felt that Newman looked too practical and decisive for the poetic Zhivago: 'I can discover nothing of the dreamer about him.'

Still keen to pair Newman and Loren, MGM proposed reviving *Lady L* as an alternative vehicle.³ Newman had a commitment to the studio and accepted Tony Curtis's old role rather than wait around for another script. He would play Armand, a romantic French anarchist. The deal with Ponti gave Sophia Loren top billing.

The multi-talented Peter Ustinov signed on as writer, director and supporting actor, accepting the *Lady L* project on the condition that he adapted the Romain Gary novel from scratch, discarding the existing scripts. Newman and Loren were joined by David Niven, who'd beaten Newman to the Best Actor Academy Award back in 1959.

In August 1964, Newman took his family to Paris for the start of shooting. At one point, all five of his children were around, and Joanne Woodward was now pregnant with the sixth. Visitors included Gore Vidal. A truly European production, *Lady L* was filmed in France, the Swiss Riviera and Castle Howard, North Yorkshire, England.

While Newman and Woodward got on well with Ustinov, *Lady L* proved a troubled production. Conceived as a sweeping, epic romance, the film soon fell victim to executive nerves. When *The Fall of the Roman Empire* proved a box-office disaster, MGM ordered Ustinov to radically shorten his script. Preoccupied with shooting, Ustinov felt this last-minute rewrite damaged the film. Hoping to sell *Lady L* as family entertainment, MGM also became nervous about the brothel scenes. Thankfully, there was no realistic way of cutting these from the film.

Both Woodward and Vidal were intrigued by Sophia Loren. Newman seemed reluctant to discuss his leading lady, mentioning little more than her occasional lateness on set. A stickler for punctuality, Newman had a problem with tardy co-stars. According to Vidal, Woodward became worried that Newman and Loren were having an affair. The widow of a well-known film star claims that Newman had a series of casual girlfriends, who kept him company during those long location shoots. In this instance, Woodward had nothing to worry about. Loren did not like Newman at all, regarding her co-star as vulgar and uncouth.

Both Ustinov and Newman appreciated that he'd been miscast. Newman spent the production in a state of depression – 'I woke up every morning and knew I wasn't cutting the mustard' – while Ustinov despaired at the lack of chemistry between his mismatched leads. Significantly, their screen arguments carried far more conviction than the love scenes. Attempting to salvage the film, Ustinov asked Newman and Loren to work at their relationship, both on- and offscreen. Loren, who respected the director, readily agreed. For whatever reason, Newman seemed unable to comply. Arriving for work one morning, Loren made an attempt at conversation, asking Newman how his false moustache was attached. According to Ustinov, Newman replied, 'Sperm.' (Approached for this book, Loren declined to comment on *Lady L* and Paul Newman.)

Casting problems aside, Ustinov felt that Newman hadn't realized his potential on film: 'Paul is overly cerebral about his role. As a result, he's a superb actor who has not yet hit his zenith.' Like Woodward, he predicted that Newman would naturally gravitate to directing: 'I believe Paul's true destiny is *behind* the camera . . . There he will have the room he needs to buttress his intelligence with his instinct.' Interviewed years later, Newman admitted that he never became totally immersed in a role: 'Even in a really emotional scene there is 15 to 20 per cent of you standing back like a camera.'

As a piece of film-making, *Lady L* shows hints of ambition. Ustinov may have been influenced by German director Max Ophüls, for whom he acted in *Lola Montes* (1955). There are some elaborate tracking shots through the lavish sets, emphasizing the production values if nothing else. Otherwise, the direction is perfunctory and often misjudged.

Judging from *Lady L*, Newman was not cut out to be an international man of mystery. First seen disguised as a tramp, Armand also impersonates an elderly gentleman and a priest. Sporting the infamous stick-on moustache, Newman is utterly implausible as a bank-robbing socialist anarchist. MGM would have been better off with Tony Curtis, who'd shown a flair for light comedy in *Some Like It Hot* (1959) and *Operation Petticoat* (1959).

Lady L – Impersonating an elderly gentleman

Lady L opened in Britain on 17 December 1965, to largely negative reviews. Faced with disappointing box-office returns, MGM delayed the North American release. When Newman's next film, *Harper*, scored a hit, MGM saw a chance to cut their losses, and *Lady L* opened in New York City on 18 May 1966, five months after its European première. In the event, *Harper*'s success made no difference, *Lady L* flopping with US audiences. Newman took responsibility for the film's failure: 'Anything wrong with *Lady L* was the fault of Paul Newman. I have a very American skin, and when I try to go out of my skin . . . I go wrong.' Now forty, Newman had suffered two commercial failures in a row. Fortunately, he'd already found a film vehicle which ideally suited his 'American skin'.

7 Reluctant Heroes

Harper – Lew Harper, a good man in a bad world

Only cream and bastards rise.
　Lew Harper

Whether by chance or design, Newman and Warner Brothers had avoided each other since *The Young Philadelphians* (1959). Jack Warner didn't forgive 'disloyal' actors lightly, and it's possible that he placed Newman on a personal blacklist. Gainfully employed by the other major studios, Newman had little reason to seek reconciliation. However, six years after breaking his Warners contract, he returned to the studio to star in *Harper* (1966). In need of a hit after *The Outrage* and *Lady L*, Newman put his faith in this slick private-eye movie, ersatz Raymond Chandler for the swinging sixties.

The *Harper* deal was put together by independent producers Jerry Gershwin and Elliott Kastner. Kastner had optioned a number of books, including *Boys and Girls Together* by William Goldman. At the time, Goldman was just another young writer, looking for his big Hollywood break. During one meeting, Kastner told Goldman that he was looking to make 'a movie with balls'. A big Raymond Chandler fan, he had long wanted to film one of the Philip Marlowe books, but couldn't obtain the rights. At Goldman's suggestion, Gershwin and Kastner optioned Kenneth Millar's crime novel *The Moving Target* (1949). Written under Millar's *nom de plume*, 'Ross MacDonald', the book featured a Chandleresque private detective named Lew Archer. Goldman turned Millar's novel, the first of the Archer series, into a workable script, for which he received $80,000.

At the time, there hadn't been a major private-eye movie for years, the genre having been co-opted by television. If nothing else, the project had a sense of freshness. Kastner soon drew the interest of singer–actor Frank Sinatra, looking to follow up on the success of his World War II adventure *Von Ryan's Express* (1965). When the Sinatra deal fell through, Kastner sought a less temperamental leading man. He sent Goldman's script to Newman in Paris, where he was shooting *Lady L*. *The Moving Target* came along at exactly the right moment. Looking for a vehicle to boost his career, Newman showed strong interest in a traditional American genre piece.

Katsner travelled to Paris for a meeting, accompanied by a Newman-approved director. While Kastner and Newman got on well, the negotiations hit a major snag. According to Goldman, the director announced that the script was 'a piece of shit' requiring a total rewrite. With the deal looking shaky, Kastner reassured Newman and fired the director. As a replacement, he selected Jack Smight, first ensuring that he was acceptable to Newman. Smight was an experienced television director, with two feature films to his name.

Newman requested some changes to the *Moving Target* script. Goldman obliged, well aware that Kastner would replace him if he failed to deliver. Despite Newman's recent run of flops, he remained a big name. Kastner had Warner Brothers interested in the deal and the studio would wait for Newman to come on board. One of Newman's requirements was a change of surname for his character. Since *The Hustler* and *Hud*, Newman had decided that titles beginning with 'H' were lucky for him. Thus, Lew Archer became Lew Harper. Fortunately, Goldman got on well with Newman, who gave the revised script his seal of approval. Kastner congratulated Goldman on his new Hollywood career: 'You just jumped past all the shit.' Having sold the *Harper* package to Warners, Kastner paid Newman $750,000 for his services, along with 10 per cent of the box-office gross. Meeting with Newman at his Connecticut home, Goldman noticed during a stroll that the star had a habit of turning his back to oncoming traffic. Off duty, away from Hollywood, Newman wanted to avoid the attention of strangers.

The cameraman on *Harper* was Conrad L. Hall. The crew also included Newman's older brother, Arthur Newman Jr, employed as a unit manager. By this time, Arthur Jr had abandoned the retail business, relocating to California for a new career in motion pictures. Still on good terms with Arthur, Newman was happy to help his brother out, brushing aside charges of nepotism. The experience proved mutually agreeable and Newman retained Arthur's services on several more films, usually as a unit manager, production manager or assistant to the producer.[1]

To give *Harper* an extra touch of class, Kastner hired a number of distinguished actors for small roles. These 'guest stars' included Lauren Bacall, Janet Leigh, Shelley Winters and Julie Harris. While none of them carried any box-office clout, their names were familiar to audiences. Bacall had the additional kudos of starring opposite Humphrey Bogart in *The Big Sleep* (1946), regarded by many as the definitive private-eye movie. Bacall already knew Newman socially, rating him highly as both an actor and a person. Like Newman, she was a high-profile Democrat who'd never been afraid to speak her mind. A former Warner Brothers contract player, Bacall shared Newman's antipathy toward Jack Warner, who placed her on suspension when she turned down film roles. Well aware of the *Big Sleep* connection, she signed up for one month's work. Most of her scenes were with Newman and, in her autobiography, *By*

Myself, Bacall remembers being 'more than pleased to have an opportunity to work with him'. Unthreatened by other actors, Newman welcomed this strong supporting cast.

Harper was filmed over the summer of 1965. On the first day of production, at the Warner Brothers studios, Jack Warner paid a visit to the set. By the mid-1960s, Warner was little more than a figurehead at the studio, out of touch with the day-to-day operations. Now in his seventies, he merely stopped by to wish the *Harper* cast and crew good luck. William Goldman was also on set, watching as Warner talked with old acquaintances Jack Smight and Newman. Despite his long-standing dislike of Warner, Newman agreed to be photographed with his former employer. Having freed himself from the shackles of his Warner contract, he had made it as a star on his own terms. Other films in production at Warner at the time included *Inside Daisy Clover* (1966), co-starring a little-known actor named Robert Redford.

Goldman praised Newman as 'the least starlike superstar I've ever worked with'. Focusing on the script and characters, Newman didn't demand extra close-ups, unlike Steve McQueen. Goldman felt he had a 'terrier' attitude to his work, never drifting through a scene. Newman concurred: 'I worry things like a bone. I never stop working.' The location filming in and around Los Angeles proved difficult. While Newman could maintain his privacy at home in Connecticut, he was frequently recognized and approached during the *Harper* shoot. Inconvenience aside, Newman found the experience depressing: 'They don't see you as a person but as an icon or object.'

Co-star Pamela Tiffin got on well with Newman, who seemed reserved but friendly: 'Paul is a very "normal" man who happens to act.' By no means narcissistic, Newman projected a tough, masculine quality. Stuck in the thankless role of Harper's estranged wife, Janet Leigh claimed to be in awe of Newman's authority and charisma: 'He *makes* you respond to him. That's the basis of his sex appeal.' For Lew Harper, Newman borrowed some mannerisms from a political acquaintance, Senator Robert F. Kennedy. Kennedy had a habit of listening to people without actually facing them, a 'sideways' approach that intrigued Newman.

A courteous professional, Newman was loyal and conscientious towards his co-workers, never playing the big star. Not one cast or crew member had reason to complain about his behaviour. For close-ups on other actors, he read his lines off-camera, a task normally undertaken by a script girl. During one scene, Newman was so impressed by Robert Wagner's tearful performance that he missed his own cue.

Newman's changes to Goldman's script included Lew Harper's

choice of car. Goldman had given Harper a beat-up old Ford, reasoning that a down-at-heel private eye couldn't afford anything more upmarket. Newman swapped the Ford for a Porsche, arguing somewhat spuriously that it suited Harper better. It certainly suited Newman. As a concession to Harper's shaky finances, Newman suggested that the Porsche's left fender and door should only have primer paint. His passion for fast cars made an impression on Tiffin, who later remarked, 'I think his *true* interest is racing.' When Joanne Woodward visited the *Harper* set, Tiffin found her a 'strong, sober' character, adding, 'Joanne doesn't have a great sense of humour.'

Goldman's script described Lew Harper as 'a good man in a bad world'. Moving among the rich and nasty, Harper gets a forcible reminder that nice guys finish last. The opening scene features an unshaven Harper in vest and boxer shorts. Short of groceries, he reuses the previous day's coffee grinds, retrieved from the kitchen bin. Chewing rhythmically, in best Method style, Harper salutes a photograph of his estranged wife, then swats a fly. Incidentally, this credits sequence was added during production, not featuring in Goldman's original script. Now back in New York, Goldman had delivered the new scene by return of post. He later discovered that the coffee gag immediately warmed audiences to Harper. Private eye or not, Lew Harper is just another working stiff, struggling to make ends meet in a harsh world.

Harper is a good example of efficient Hollywood professionalism. Goldman felt that director Smight handled the film 'with terrific pace and skill'. He later admitted that the dialogue-heavy script reflected his inexperience as a screenwriter.

Newman is clearly having a good time as Lew Harper. Interestingly, he regarded the character as 'pretty close to me. I didn't have to do a lot of work for that.' Goldman praised the 'wonderful work' from Newman, 'who simply shouldered the script and rammed it home'. Interviewed in the early 1980s, Newman described Harper as 'loose and funky and whimsical'. While the character gets by on Newman's charisma and blue-eyed charm, he's a comic-book figure without depth or substance.

Marketed with the tagline 'Girls Go for Harper', *Harper* opened in the US on 23 February 1966, scoring a box-office hit. The film was released in Britain as *The Moving Target*, reverting to the book's title. Its commercial success revived the private-eye genre.[2]

Newman and Woodward's third daughter, Claire Olivia, or 'Clea', was born on 21 April 1965. To celebrate, Newman presented his wife with a Cartier diamond tiger pin. When it came to daily childcare, however, he did not subscribe to shared parenting. Woodward once remarked that Newman 'takes pride in being a father of six children and having never changed a diaper'. Now thirty-five, Woodward took up ballet to regain her figure.

With *Harper*'s release still months away, Newman was offered a co-starring role in *Torn Curtain* (1966), the new Alfred Hitchcock picture. An admirer of the British director, Newman showed immediate interest. Espionage movies were currently big at the box office and *Torn Curtain* seemed a surefire hit. Newman hadn't enjoyed a commercial success since *The Prize*, another Cold War thriller. Guided by the acknowledged master of suspense, he couldn't lose.

Having launched his Hollywood career with *Rebecca* (1940), Hitchcock remained at the top for the next two decades. By the mid-1960s, however, he seemed to have lost his way. *The Birds* (1963), an expensive production with no star names, turned only a small profit, and his most recent film, *Marnie* (1964), had flopped at the box office, despite the presence of James Bond star Sean Connery. Critics and audiences were bemused by Hitchcock's attempt at a psychological character study and the film was dismissed as a failure.

Universal Studios, which financed *The Birds* and *Marnie*, was relieved when Hitchcock opted to make a more conventional spy thriller. Back in 1951, Hitchcock had been intrigued by the high-profile defection of British double agents Guy Burgess and Donald Maclean. Fourteen years later, he decided to turn this premise into a movie. The original script was by Ulster novelist Brian Moore, who'd written several successful thrillers under the pseudonym 'Michael Bryan'. While Moore got on well with Hitchcock, he had reservations about the director's approach to film-making. Interviewed by biographer Donald Spoto, Moore argued that Hitchcock had no sense of characterization, dealing only in ciphers. He claims to have suggested the lengthy murder sequence, the one scene in *Torn Curtain* that people remember.

A fan of Hitchcock's films, Newman had long wanted to work with the director. Their first meeting, to discuss the basic story, went well. From the start, however, Hitchcock seemed uneasy about the script. The director wouldn't show Newman the existing screenplay, claiming it still needed work. Confident that Hitchcock would sort out any problems, Newman signed for the film. When he finally received a script, this optimism diminished. Concerned, he sent Hitchcock a letter explaining his problems with the material, suggesting various revisions. Covering fourteen main points, Newman's detailed critique included the overall tone, specific scenes and his own character. Many elements lacked credibility, undercutting the suspense. Newman also disliked the title – 'a trifle arch'. As with Otto Preminger five years earlier, Newman's ideas fell on stony ground.

Newman and Hitchcock also clashed early on over matters of etiquette. Invited to a formal dinner party by the director, Newman turned up in casual wear. He then hung his jacket on the back of a chair and requested beer instead of the expensive vintage wine on offer. Worse, he insisted on fetching the beer himself, which he drank straight from the can. According to Hitchcock biographer John Russell Taylor, Newman wanted to show the director that he couldn't be pushed around. Perhaps he was determined not to repeat the *Exodus* experience, where Preminger treated him like a hired hand.

Whatever Hitchcock's feelings about Newman, the director was even less keen on Universal's choice of leading lady. The studio wanted Julie Andrews, a major star after *Mary Poppins* (1964), which won her an Academy Award, and *The Sound of Music* (1965), directed by Robert Wise. In need of a hit, Hitchcock allowed himself to be 'persuaded' by the studio. Andrews was in the middle of filming *Hawaii* (1966) when she received the script for *Torn Curtain*. While she greatly admired Hitchcock, she disliked the screenplay, especially her underused character. Her representatives convinced her that starring opposite Newman in a Hitchcock film would be good for her career. Andrews would receive $750,000 plus 10 per cent of the gross, a larger fee than Newman. Box-office appeal aside, her busy schedule meant that Hitchcock had to start filming *Torn Curtain* sooner than he intended. Rushed into production, the project remained half-baked in all departments. To make matters worse, Hitchcock was without two of his regular collaborators, cameraman Robert Burks and editor George Tomasini. Burks was unavailable, while Tomasini had died in 1964.

Torn Curtain was in production from November 1965 to February 1966. Universal budgeted the film at $5 million, $1.8 million of which went to Newman and Andrews. Having paid out for big stars, against his better judgement, Hitchcock had to cut corners elsewhere. The director required back-projection footage from Berlin and Copenhagen. Unable to send a second-unit crew from Hollywood for reasons of cost, Hitchcock had to rely on local camera crews, with disappointing results. Much of the film was shot at Universal City, in Long Beach, with limited location work on the University of Southern California campus. For the famous sequence involving an isolated farmhouse, the production team travelled to nearby Camarillo. Neither Newman nor Andrews left sunny California for the duration of the shoot, something painfully obvious in the finished film.

Unhappy with Moore's screenplay, which lacked sharp dialogue and humour, Hitchcock hired Keith Waterhouse and Willis Hall to undertake a rewrite. This critically acclaimed British duo were best known for the downbeat comedy *Billy Liar* (1963). Waterhouse and Hall started work on *Torn Curtain* just days before the cameras rolled, rewriting scenes throughout the production. Waterhouse recalled delivering new dialogue mere hours before it was shot. While Hitchcock felt that Waterhouse and Hall deserved a screen credit for their work, the Writer's Guild of America begged to differ. Ironically, neither Waterhouse nor Hall wanted their name on the film. According to Moore, there were major script rewrites by Hitchcock himself. Moore regarded the final screenplay as poor in all departments, with no grasp of narrative or character.

Newman later revealed that working from the weak script hurt his relationship with Hitchcock. As he explained, 'It sounded like an exciting story . . . but somehow the script didn't turn out the way he'd told it, and all during the shooting we all wished we didn't have to make it.' Newman summed up the general feeling during filming: 'We all knew we had a loser on our hands in this picture.' The awkward on-set atmosphere also caused problems at home. Joanne Woodward remarked that Newman could be a 'pain in the neck' when a film was going badly: 'He'll work much harder on a script he hates, and . . . he'll drink too much beer.'

It's no secret that Hitchcock regarded actors as childlike and egocentric. He also claimed that stars no longer knew their place, demanding more and more say in a production. While Newman admitted to having problems with Hitchcock, he insisted that 'it was not a lack of communication or a lack of respect'. Famous for his meticulous pre-planning, with every shot storyboarded, Hitchcock claimed to find the actual shooting of a film boring. As with Otto Preminger on *Exodus*, Newman found the director had no interest in discussing character and motivation. Questioned by Newman during rehearsals for one scene, Hitchcock allegedly responded, 'Your motivation, Mr Newman, is your salary.' Tired of Newman's queries, the director asked Waterhouse and Hall to deal with the star's script worries. No fan of the Actors Studio, the director supposedly cut one of Newman's scenes on the grounds that his performance was too 'Method'. Hitchcock biographer Donald Spoto claims that the short, rotund director was never comfortable with handsome leading men, suffering acute insecurity, resentment and jealousy. Julie Andrews also found herself at odds with Hitchcock: '. . . he was obviously more interested in manipulating people, and in getting a reaction from the audience, than he was in directing us'. Their working relationship stayed courteous but cool.

During post-production, Hitchcock fell out with composer Bernard Herrmann, who'd worked on all the director's films from *The Trouble with Harry* (1956) onwards. While Universal disliked Herrmann's music for *Marnie*, the studio agreed to him scoring *Torn Curtain*. Unfortunately, the end result was deemed old-fashioned and overly downbeat. Under pressure to deliver a marketable soundtrack album, Hitchcock asked Herrmann to make changes. Famously temperamental, the composer wouldn't oblige and was either fired or resigned from the production. His music was dropped in favour of an entirely new score by British composer John Addison. Addison had won an Academy Award for *Tom Jones* (1963), which probably made him attractive to Universal. Hitchcock and Herrmann would never work together again.[3]

As Newman, Andrews and just about everyone else predicted, *Torn Curtain* is a dreary misfire. While Hitchcock's original idea had potential, the movie is rapidly derailed by the thin characters and weak dialogue. The depiction of Cold War espionage is on a par with the James Bond movies, only far less entertaining.

Michael Armstrong (Newman) is first seen in bed with fellow scientist Sarah Sherman (Julie Andrews), largely hidden under a pile of coats. While this love scene received some publicity at the time, the intimate close-ups of Newman and Andrews do not generate any notable screen chemistry. Hitchcock also toys with male nudity, showing Armstrong in the shower. While Newman is obscured by a plastic curtain, he's clearly wearing underpants. As bathroom scenes go, it's a long way from Janet Leigh's memorable shower in *Psycho*. Even the nudist-camp scene in *The Prize* is more risqué.

Newman seems uneasy throughout *Torn Curtain*. While Armstrong is supposed to be edgy, his cover at risk, the character just acts grumpy. Coming to the film with little preparation time, Andrews looks either hurt or reproachful.

Torn Curtain is best known for the prolonged, messy killing of Agent Gromek (Wolfgang Kieling), requiring a knife, shovel and gas oven. Hitchcock was enthusiastic about the sequence, which shows how hard it is for an 'amateur' to kill someone. Newman is out-acted by both Kieling and Carolyn Conwell, who plays Armstrong's fellow assassin, a US agent posing as a farmer's wife. Once Gromek is dead, the young woman takes control, washing the blood from Armstrong's hands as he goes into shock. Newman does better in a later scene, where Armstrong engages in duelling blackboard equations with Professor Lindt (Ludwig Donath), his opposite number in the Communist bloc.

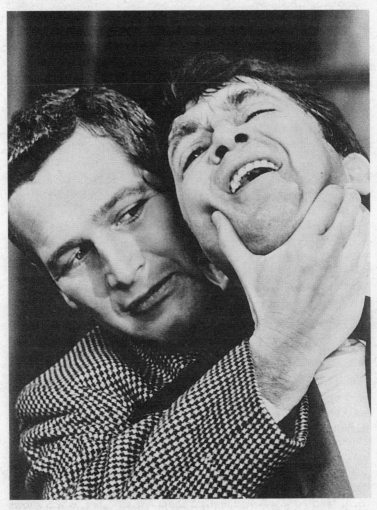

Torn Curtain – the prolonged, messy killing

A canny strategist, Armstrong goads and coaxes Lindt into revealing his secret formula. The subsequent escape by bicycle, bus, boat and wicker basket is less than thrilling. As Spoto suggests, the film can be read as an ironic reversal of the Orpheus and Eurydice myth, Sarah venturing into the underworld of Cold War espionage to 'rescue' her fiancé, Michael. As Spoto concedes, however, *Torn Curtain* lacks the narrative strength to sustain any subtext.

Promoted by Universal as Alfred Hitchcock's fiftieth feature film, *Torn Curtain* received its world première in Boston. Universal pulled all the stops out on launching the film, though early word of mouth was not good. While Hitchcock attended the Boston launch, both Newman and Andrews were conspicuous by their absence. The director took offence when he learned that Andrews had asked her friends not to see the movie. She explained that she disliked her own performance, not the overall film. Deeply disappointed by *Torn Curtain*, Hitchcock did not need to be reminded of his failure.

Torn Curtain went on general release in the US on 14 July 1966. The theatrical trailer promised big things: 'Alfred Hitchcock tears you apart with suspense!', accompanied by a romantic photograph, slashed with a knife, of Newman and Andrews. Hitchcock did the rounds of television talk shows in both America and his native Britain. Despite unfavourable reviews, the combined box-office appeal of Newman and Andrews turned *Torn Curtain* into a solid hit, grossing $6.5 million. For all Andrews' unhappiness during production, she at least saw a return on her percentage points. Hitchcock later blamed the film's problems on his miscast stars: 'Bad chemistry, that was.' In truth, the director knew full well that the project was fatally flawed from the start. He directed only three more films: *Topaz* (1969), *Frenzy* (1972) and *Family Plot* (1975), none of which featured a major star. Brian Moore placed the responsibility for *Torn Curtain* squarely on the director's shoulders: 'It's a bad film . . . Hitchcock simply ransacked his bag of tricks.' Interviewed in 1982, Newman concurred: 'Not so good.' In 1974, he attended Universal's seventy-fifth birthday party for Hitchcock, held at Chasen's restaurant in Los Angeles.

Adrift in the world of espionage, Newman retreated back to the Old West for *Hombre* (1967). Based on a novel by Elmore Leonard, this downbeat western reunited Newman with Martin Ritt. Since the failure of *The Outrage*, Ritt had revived his career and reputation with *The Spy Who Came in from the Cold* (1965). Recruiting *Hud* writers Irving Ravetch and Harriet Frank Jr, Newman and Ritt took the *Hombre* project to Twentieth Century Fox executive Richard Zanuck.

Newman's agents, Evarts Ziegler and Richard Shepherd, offered Zanuck a package deal – Newman, Ritt, Ravetch and Frank – for a total of $1.3 million. Newman would receive his standard $750,000 fee, plus 10 per cent of the box-office gross. The reunion of *Hud*'s key creative personnel included cameraman James Wong Howe.

Hombre

Newman's co-stars included Australian actress Diane Cilento and leading man turned character actor Fredric March, still going strong after nearly forty years in movies. Cilento had drawn Hollywood's attention with her supporting role in *Tom Jones*, picking up an Academy Award nomination. In need of a high-class heavy, Ritt cast Richard Boone, whose intimidating appearance made him ideal for malevolent characters.

Cast as a white man reared by Apaches, Newman researched his role by spending five days on an Indian reservation. Driving down the main street, he noticed a man standing outside the general store, with one foot up against the shop front and both arms crossed. Hours later, when Newman passed by again, the man was still there, in exactly the same position. Struck by this image, Newman used it as the keystone for his role: 'The whole character came out of that.'

Having cut down on his film work, Newman had a good time making *Hombre*: 'By then I was doing it less and enjoying it more.' Visitors to the Arizona locations included Cilento's husband, Sean Connery. At the time, Connery and Joanne Woodward were shooting *A Fine Madness* (1966) in New York City. Connery and Cilento's four-year marriage had parallels with the Newman–Woodward relationship. He was the big movie star, at least in the James Bond series, while she remained a highly respected actress with a negligible film career. Unlike Newman and Woodward, Connery and Cilento were encountering big problems in their relationship. According to biographer Michael Feeney Callan, Connery only accepted *A Fine Madness* to be near Cilento and save the marriage. In the event, their reconciliation proved shortlived, the couple divorcing in 1973.

Hombre is a revisionist update of John Ford's seminal *Stagecoach* (1939). John Russell (Newman), a.k.a. Hombre, is a white man who leaves his adoptive Apache community to live among 'civilized' people. He encounters the liberal, compassionate Jessie (Diane Cilento), a worldly landlady, and the less progressive Grimes (Richard Boone), an outlaw happy to steal from all races and creeds. Having put Jessie out of a job, Russell seems to care for no one. Joining a motley group of stagecoach passengers, they head out on a journey to nowhere. While *Stagecoach* had Apaches for bad guys, *Hombre* turns honorary Apache Russell into a reluctant hero, battling the white villains.

Hombre is extremely well crafted. Ritt maintains a deliberate pace, emphasizing that this is serious drama, not gung-ho western action. The Old West is coming to an end, the stagecoach making way for the railroad. The script is on a par with *Hud*, and the film shares *Hud*'s sexual frankness, dwelling on the place of women in the West. These are jaded, disillusioned people. Jessie is similar to *Hud*'s Alma, refusing to let her humanity be crushed by cynicism. Most of the characters are unusually articulate, always ready with a dry comeback.

Newman gives one of his most interesting, minimalist performances as the impassive, watchful Russell. Compared to his absurd Mexican *bandido* in *The Outrage*, he looks fine in long hair and full Native American garb. Even with short hair and civilized clothes, Russell remains an outsider. Caught between two cultures, he must deal with white racism, whether aggressive or genteel. No believer in peaceful protest, he smashes a whisky glass against a thug's face with his rifle butt. Russell is often framed in isolation from the other characters, unable and unwilling to make contact. He seems amused by white men's antics, all bluff and bluster. He and Jessie clash over their differing notions of responsibility. At first, Russell won't stick his neck out for any white person. Early on, Jessie observes: 'Takes a lot to light a fire under you, doesn't it?' As the film's liberal conscience, Jessie must push Russell into confronting his own prejudices. All people must be treated as equal, whatever their ethnic group or personal failings. In the event, Russell's ultimate course of action comes as no great surprise. Early on in the film, a symbolic black horse leads its herd to water.

Opening in the US on 21 March 1967, *Hombre* picked up favourable reviews and good box office. The *Los Angeles Times* rated the film as 'hard-hitting and exciting', while *Daily Variety* sung the star's praises: 'Paul Newman is excellent.' *Hombre* would be the last collaboration between Newman and Ritt. After nine years, and six movies, star and director called it a day.[4] Regarded as one of Newman's few close friends, Ritt remained generous in his assessment of the star. Interviewed in 1969, he defended Newman's avoidance of the Los Angeles party circuit:

> Paul is quite a homebody. He is a good father and husband and he prefers to live that way. He is a true professional who refuses to become part of the Hollywood game. He goes to work, does his work, then goes home and lives his own life.

8 Loveable Rogues

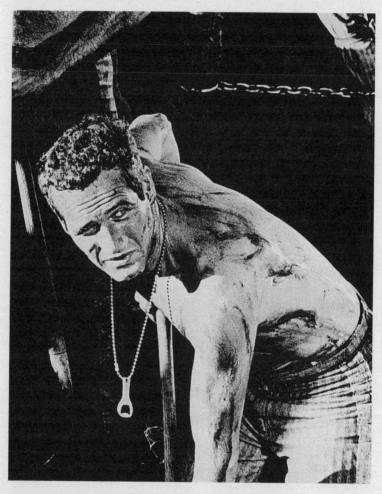

Cool Hand Luke – Lucas Jackson on the chain gang

Sometimes nothing can be a real cool hand.
    Lucas Jackson, *Cool Hand Luke*

With a run of box-office hits, Newman's career remained in good health. He was approached by Columbia, who wanted him to star in the film version of *In Cold Blood* (1967), a based-on-fact account of a brutal multiple killing in Kansas. The project originated with Richard Brooks, the writer–director of *Cat on a Hot Tin Roof* and *Sweet Bird of Youth*. He had bought the rights to Truman Capote's bestselling book, published in 1966. Columbia asked Newman and Steve McQueen to play the leads, though both men were much older than the real-life killers. Aware that Brooks did not want big names, Newman passed on the film, as did McQueen, the lead roles going to newcomers Scott Wilson and Robert Blake.

Four years on from *Hud*, Newman found another definitive role in *Cool Hand Luke* (1967), the existential tale of a free-spirited convict on a southern chain gang. This Warner release was produced by newcomer Gordon Carroll and was based on a novel by Donn Pearce, a former safecracker who served two years on a chain gang. Pearce agreed to adapt his book into a screenplay, subsequently rewritten by Frank R. Pierson, who co-scripted *Cat Ballou* (1965).

Surprisingly, Newman was not Carroll's first choice for the role of Lucas 'Cool Hand' Jackson. Carroll originally wanted character actor Telly Savalas for the lead. Savalas was in England filming *The Dirty Dozen* (1967). However, once the shoot was finished, Savalas insisted on taking a boat back to California, rather than fly as expected. Unable to accommodate this delay to his schedule, Carroll cast Newman instead.

Cool Hand Luke initiated Newman's four-film partnership with director Stuart Rosenberg.[1] Carroll also recruited Conrad Hall, whose camerawork distinguished *Harper*, and Argentinian composer Lalo Schifrin, who scored *The Cincinnati Kid* (1965). The supporting cast was led by George Kennedy, an imposing character actor. Hollywood veteran Bette Davis was approached for the brief role of Luke's mother, essentially an extended cameo. Still very much the star, at least in her own mind, Davis was not interested in bit parts. Undaunted, the producers cast Jo Van Fleet, who'd won an Academy Award for her début in *East of Eden* (1955). Having missed out on playing mother and son in *East of Eden*, Van Fleet and Newman finally got their chance. Van Fleet liked Newman, telling reporters, 'You'd better believe he treats me with respect.' The cast also featured Richard Davalos, who'd beaten Newman to the role of Aron Trask, only to be wiped off the screen by James Dean.

Cool Hand Luke boasted a role call of Hollywood's more offbeat character actors, led by Strother Martin, from *Harper*, Anthony Zerbe, Harry Dean Stanton and Dennis Hopper. A James Dean acolyte, Hopper had recently returned to mainstream films after several years in exile for his 'difficult' attitude. Still at odds with the square Hollywood mentality, he marked time in various small roles before scoring his own counterculture hit with *Easy Rider* (1969). In addition to his screenwriting duties, author Donn Pearce served as the film's technical advisor and played a small, uncredited role, as Sailor.

Newman had full confidence in the *Cool Hand Luke* script, describing his character as 'the ultimate non-conformist and rebel'. The most physically demanding scene for Newman was the famous egg-eating challenge. A Method man to the last, Newman supposedly ate all fifty hard-boiled eggs. According to most accounts, he suffered nothing worse than a bloated stomach as a consequence. Frankly, this seems unlikely. Warner Brothers were more concerned with Newman's eyes. Conrad Hall recalled shooting one scene five times after studio executives complained that Newman's famous blues were not prominent enough.

In contrast to Warners' earlier *I Am a Fugitive from a Chain Gang* (1932), *Cool Hand Luke* is more interested in allegory than social reform. Unlike Paul Muni's Robert E. Burns, a real-life figure, Newman's Lucas Jackson is guilty as charged. At the start of the film, he is seen wantonly decapitating parking meters. Sentenced to two years on a chain gang, Luke seems unperturbed.

Newman regarded Lucas Jackson as an ideal role: 'I had great fun with that part. I liked that man.' The blue prison uniform certainly matches Newman's eyes, complemented by a beer-bottle opener strung around his neck. Luke is first seen as a playful drunk, knocking back the beer as he trashes the parking meters. Critic Ethan Mordden describes this vandalism as 'murdering the rules for what can be allowed'. As Luke goes about his business, the red 'Violation' flag springs up on one meter, literally signalling his fate. Questioned about his behaviour, Luke offers no great insight: 'Small town. Not much to do in the evening.' A decorated war hero (Korea?) whose rebellious attitude got him demoted during his war service, despite an award for bravery, Luke is a dedicated non-conformist, scoring small points off the establishment. Offering no political or ideological agenda, he treats his battle with The Man as just another game.

Behind bars, Luke finds the ideal audience for his laid-back style of rebellion. In the sadomasochistic boxing scene, Luke takes a beating from Dragline (George Kennedy), the number-one convict, refusing to give in. The watching convicts' bloodlust soon turns to queasiness. Presumably, the audience is supposed to feel the same way. Inevitably, Luke wins the acceptance and respect of the other convicts. As Dragline puts it: 'You wild beautiful thing.'

The scene with Arletta Jackson (Jo Van Fleet), Luke's dying mother, is a mixed blessing. Though well acted by Newman and Van Fleet, the end result seems overly familiar. We learn that Luke never knew his father, yet another worthless drifter. Despite this lack of paternal guidance, Luke knows right from wrong, warning his young nephew not to stray. He reacts to news of his mother's death by singing 'Plastic Jesus', accompanying himself on the banjo. This is a memorable, even touching, moment, though Luke himself remains an enigma. Rosenberg saw Luke as 'the perfect existential hero', a symbol of defiance appealing to any number of oppressed minorities. Significantly, the only speaking black characters are two kids, who automatically side with Luke.

Cool Hand Luke is a blatant, if fuzzy, Christ allegory. Luke spends a lot of time in a white robe, actually the nightshirt worn in the punishment box. His prison number, 37, is a reference to Luke, Chapter 1, Verse 37 in the New Testament: 'For there is nothing that God cannot do.' Luke proves this by eating fifty hard-boiled eggs, a sequence scored like a 'swinging' caper movie. Triumphant, if exhausted, the now horizontal Luke adopts a 'crucified' position, clad in nothing but white shorts. If he is the Son of God, he has serious paternal issues with 'that big bearded boss'. In one mildly controversial scene, Luke challenges God to strike him down: 'Love me, hate me, kill me, anything. Just let me know it.' Failure to communicate is not limited to the earthly sphere.

Luke has become a symbol of freedom and rebellion for his fellow convicts. Eventually, this proves too heavy a burden, Luke yelling, 'Stop feedin' off me!' Sent back to the punishment box, he is short of ready quips: 'Callin' it your job don't make it right, Boss.' Whatever trick he pulls, the Captain Strother Martin always regains the upper hand. As Newman put it, 'Luke is detached and indifferent, but he can't beat the system he scoffs at.' When Luke breaks under the Captain's punishment regime, subjected to hours of symbolic grave digging, he loses the convicts' respect.

Luke's climactic escape, his third attempt, ends inside a church. Offering a prayer, he seems to find some kind of peace. Cornered by the Captain's gang of armed wardens, he is amused by this show of force: 'What we've got here is a failure to communicate.' God's own Son or holy fool, Luke faces martyrdom with a smile.

Cool Hand Luke – Luke finally breaks down under the punishment regime

Cool Hand Luke opened in the US on 1 November 1967, drawing favourable reviews and big audiences. Newman's character seemed in step with America's growing counterculture, quickly taking on icon status. Critic John Simon rated *Cool Hand Luke* as 'Maybe the best American film of 1967.'

Newman was subsequently offered the lead in *The Swimmer* (1968), another allegorical fable. Based on a story by John Cheever, this downbeat drama dwelt on the illusory nature of the American dream. Newman turned the film down, despite the chance to shoot in Connecticut, as did William Holden and Glenn Ford. The title role went to Burt Lancaster, who gave a strong performance as a middle-aged failure refusing to face reality. Distributed by Columbia, *The Swimmer* proved a box-office disaster.

From the start, *Cool Hand Luke* was tipped as a surefire Oscar contender. Newman's fourth nomination for Best Actor came as no surprise. The film was also nominated for Best Supporting Actor (George Kennedy), Best Adapted Screenplay and Best Original Score. Once again, Newman faced strong competition: Warren Beatty (*Bonnie and Clyde*), Dustin Hoffman (*The Graduate*), the late Spencer Tracy (*Guess Who's Coming to Dinner*) and Rod Steiger (*In the Heat of the Night*). The sentimental favourite was Tracy, who'd died shortly after completing work on *Guess Who's Coming to Dinner*. The film itself, a contrived fable of racial tolerance, compared badly with the competition. Putting aside past Oscar disappointments, Newman attended the ceremony with his daughter Susan. In the event, the award went to Steiger for his powerhouse performance as a bigoted, self-loathing Deep South cop, forced to confront his prejudices and failings during a murder investigation. According to Joanne Woodward, Newman didn't mind losing out to Steiger, a fellow Actors Studio graduate, commenting: 'It was like losing to a real pro.'

Of the *Cool Hand Luke* contenders, only George Kennedy emerged triumphant. Worried that *Luke* would be overshadowed by the year's 'big' movies, notably *Camelot* and *Bonnie and Clyde*, Kennedy spent $5,000 of his own money on trade adverts. His hard work, both on- and offscreen, was amply rewarded. As Kennedy put it, 'I didn't have to play only villains any more.'

Cool Hand Luke reaffirmed Newman's star status, with the accompanying public attention. While both he and Joanne Woodward could cope with this celebrity, they worried about its effect on the Newman children. Press photographers were dissuaded from taking pictures of the younger family members. Scott, Susan and Stephanie, Newman's children from his first marriage, found it hard to adjust to the contrast between his vast wealth and their mother's far more modest lifestyle. Well aware of this disparity, Jacqueline Witte was not happy when Newman and Woodward gave her children expensive gifts she could never afford. Presented with a fur coat by her father and stepmother, Susan correctly anticipated a major row with her mother.

The older Newman children made no public comment on the problems of having a famous divorced father. Nevertheless, Newman felt uncomfortable, unsure how to deal with the situation. Scott had grown into the archetypal troubled teenager, frequently clashing with his father. As far as Scott was concerned, Newman had deserted him and his sisters. While Susan and Stephanie dealt with the family break-up as best they could, Scott felt Newman owed him a lifetime of favours. Deeply resentful of Joanne Woodward, he often refused to speak to her. Susan and Stephanie got on well with Woodward, yet felt torn by their loyalty to Scott. Susan had her share of adolescent traumas, later describing herself as 'intolerable' between the ages of fourteen and seventeen. That said, Susan didn't feel that she and her siblings suffered any more than other children of divorced or separated parents, despite Newman's fame: 'Scott and Stephanie and I had a very normal, middle-class upbringing.' Despite the ongoing problems with Scott, Newman felt he had a solid relationship with his children, most of the time. Aware of his own failings, he admitted to a lack of patience. He claimed that his fiercest rows were with Woodward: 'I'm all in favour of a good screaming free-for-all every two or three months.' Newman and Woodward did their best to keep the family together. If Newman's film work took him on location for more than two weeks, Woodward and the children would travel with him.

Newman gave his comic talents another airing in *The Secret War of Harry Frigg* (1968). Made for Universal, this World War II farce was produced by former child actor Hal E. Chester. At Newman's suggestion, Chester hired *Harper* director Jack Smight. A modest talent, Smight earned the respect of 'serious' actors who didn't suffer fools gladly. Lee Remick, who starred in Smight's acclaimed *No Way to Treat a Lady* (1968), also got on well with the director.

The Secret War of Harry Frigg – Harry Frigg discusses tactics with Colonel Ferrucci (Vito Scotti)

Smight aside, *Harry Frigg* offered Newman a reunion with old friend James Gregory. Since *The Desperate Hours* (1955), Gregory had secured a niche in film history as the rabidly right-wing senator in *The Manchurian Candidate* (1962). Newman's love interest was Yugoslavian actress Sylva Koscina, who achieved minor fame opposite bodybuilder Steve Reeves in the Italian *peplum* epic *Hercules* (1957). The supporting cast included Tom Bosley, Newman's fellow Woodstock Player, and comedy writer–performer Buck Henry, who'd scored a big success co-scripting *The Graduate* (1967). Newman's older brother, Arthur Jr, served as the film's production manager. As with *Torn Curtain*, Universal was not interested in authentic locations and *Harry Frigg* was filmed in and around Los Angeles, the villa sequences being shot at a house in Sierra Madre. While the California backdrops are easy on the eye, they bear little resemblance to World War II Italy.

Private Harry Frigg (Newman) is a petty conman languishing in a US Army stockade. Frigg gets a shot at freedom when he's assigned to rescue five Allied generals captured by the enemy. He also hooks up with the glamorous Countess De Montefiore (Sylva Koscina). In terms of comic timing and delivery, Newman had learned little from *Rally 'Round the Flag, Boys!*, *A New Kind of Love* or *Lady L*. Co-star Gregory felt Newman misjudged his performance as the dim-witted Frigg: 'I didn't think he was playing it right.' Years later, Newman endorsed Gregory's verdict: 'A lurch at comedy. I didn't accomplish it very well.' Newman would do better as a confidence trickster in *The Sting*.

By the late 1960s, Newman admitted to feeling bored with acting. Far from developing as a performer with each new project, he felt he was simply repeating himself: 'It's all getting pretty familiar. The more I do, the more I duplicate. I'm not inexhaustible, like an Olivier. I don't have that kind of talent.' He revealed that he'd always enjoyed the research and preparation for a role rather than the actual performance, whether on stage or in front of a camera. As he once explained to Gore Vidal, 'That's the whole fun of acting, finding out all these things with other people.' While Newman loved to work on a character's development and motivation, he got no great thrill from sharing his discoveries with an audience: 'I guess I've never been that much of an exhibitionist.'

Newman's professed boredom with acting did not affect his long-standing commitment to the Actors Studio. During the late 1960s, Jack Garfein approached Newman with the idea of founding Actors Studio West, in Hollywood. Intrigued by Garfein's proposal, Newman donated $20,000 towards purchasing a building. Grateful for this support, Garfein noticed that Newman was downbeat about his own prospects as a 'serious' actor. According to Newman, his Hollywood status now precluded him from playing the classic roles, especially Shakespeare. Even if he took the chance, audiences would come to see Paul Newman the superstar and movie icon: 'I don't have the freedom anymore of an actor – just doing it . . .' While Garfein dismissed this attitude as a cop-out, Newman remained adamant. In truth, he seemed more interested in motor racing, eagerly discussing his plans to compete in amateur events, and by the mid-1970s, his film contracts would specify weekends off during the race season.

Already active as a producer, Newman decided to turn director with *Rachel, Rachel* (1968), a low-key character study of a spinster schoolteacher. Asked about his move behind the camera, Newman responded, 'Why merely be a first violinist, if you feel you can conduct?' While he'd been dissatisfied with *On the Harmfulness of Tobacco* (1959), a decade earlier, Newman had not lost interest in directing. A number of stars had attempted to direct their own vehicles, notably Robert Montgomery, Ray Milland, Ida Lupino, Burt Lancaster, John Wayne and even Marlon Brando. Newman had no interest in becoming an actor–director as such, exercizing maximum control over his movies. He wanted to develop as a film-maker, leaving Paul Newman, Superstar, on the sidelines: 'I'm curious about my taste, my dramatic selection, my technical ability with the camera.'

Rachel, Rachel was conceived as a vehicle for Joanne Woodward, whose film career was on the slide. Claire Bloom, a friend of Woodward, regarded her as 'an excellent actress who has never become a true star'. Ethan Mordden felt that she was 'the kind of star only critics care for'. There's a case for arguing that Woodward had little instinct for strong scripts. Certainly, the five Newman–Woodward films to date showed neither star at their best. Since *A New Kind of Love* (1963), Woodward had co-starred in *Signpost to Murder* (1964), *A Big Hand for the Little Lady* (1966) and *A Fine Madness* (1966). All of them did poorly at the box office.

Rachel, Rachel was based on the novel *A Jest of God* (1966) by Canadian writer Margaret Laurence. Having committed himself to the project as the producer and director, Newman looked for a suitable screenwriter to adapt Laurence's book. He approached Stewart Stern – still best known for *Rebel Without a Cause* (1955) – who had also written Newman's second film, *The Rack*. In Stern's view, Newman wanted to create a film role worthy of Woodward, whose talents had been largely wasted by Hollywood. Interviewed for *Time* magazine in 1982, Stern explained, 'Paul has a sense of real adoration for what

Joanne can do. He's constantly trying to provide a setting where the world can see what he sees in her.'

Rachel, Rachel – Rachel Cameron (Joanne Woodward)

Both Newman and Woodward worked with Stern on the *Rachel, Rachel* script, holding regular story conferences. The biggest disagreement concerned a brief scene where Woodward's character masturbates. While all three wanted the sequence in the film, Newman and Stern argued about Rachel's position while she masturbated. Unable to resolve the matter through discussion, Newman turned up on Stern's doorstep dressed as a Nazi SS officer, explaining, 'I just wanted you to know who's boss.' Dubious taste aside, he had made his point. Perhaps wisely, Woodward left Newman and Stern to sort out the rest of the script.

As an actor, Newman could now earn over $1 million a film. As an untried director, selling an intense, character-based script, he found the going much tougher. He hawked his pet project, which initially retained the book's title, around all the major studios, claiming he could make the film for a mere $350,000, both he and Woodward deferring their salaries. Faced with a series of rejections, Newman felt badly let down, commenting, 'There's not much loyalty in movie-making.' In truth, Newman seemed naive about the realities of the film business. Whatever its merits, *Rachel, Rachel* had minimal box-office potential and Woodward's fleeting brush with Hollywood stardom was ancient history.

Newman finally made a deal with Warner Brothers production head Kenneth Hyman. Recently installed at the studio, Hyman wanted to make important, even artistic, films at Warners, commissioning Sidney Lumet's *The Seagull* (1968), based on the Chekhov play, and Sam Peckinpah's *The Wild Bunch* (1969). As he explained to David Weddle, 'I wasn't a deal-maker . . . I was a picture maker.' Unlike the vast majority of studio heads, he believed in giving directors his full support. Impressed by Newman, Hyman agreed to meet *Rachel, Rachel*'s modest $700,000 budget, double Newman's original estimate. Aware that Newman was desperate to make the film, Warners could more or less name its terms. Newman committed himself to starring in two films for the studio, at 50 per cent of his usual fee. Woodward also agreed to make another film on a reduced salary. While neither was thrilled with this arrangement, their options were extremely limited. As Newman explained, 'They really had us over the barrel. We said okay.' If *Rachel, Rachel* ran over budget, he would have to meet the extra cost himself. On the bright side, Newman's agents secured an important clause in his *Rachel, Rachel* contract. If the creative management at Warners changed, the two-film commitment became null and void. While Newman trusted Hyman, 'I didn't want some idiot to be submitting scripts.' In the event, Hyman soon left Warners, freeing both Newman and Woodward from the agreement.

Newman made *Rachel, Rachel* through his own company, Kayos. Once Warner Brothers gave the green light, he assembled his cast and production team in just a few weeks. Aware of his novice status as a director, Newman hired high calibre back-up, notably *Hustler* editor Dede Allen, fresh from Arthur Penn's *Bonnie and Clyde* (1967). He also secured the services of composer Jerome Moross, who produced a memorable score for *The Big Country* (1958). Arthur Newman Jr came on board as a co-associate producer, a small step up from production manager.

The supporting cast was led by Estelle Parsons, whose performance as Blanche Barrow in *Bonnie and Clyde* would win her an Academy Award. The role of Rachel's lover went to James Olson, who had appeared in Jack Garfein's *The Strange One* (1957). Newman also gave a role to Frank Corsaro, the director of *Baby Want a Kiss?* (1964), possibly to make amends for Corsaro's bad experience on the play. The non-professionals in the cast included Newman's car mechanic and Elinor Newman, his oldest daughter with Woodward. Billed under her nickname, 'Nell Potts', Elinor played Woodward's character as a child.

Rachel, Rachel began production in the summer of 1967. Newman had opted to make the film in his adopted home state of Connecticut. Woodward admitted to feeling nervous about the project, essentially a vehicle for her: 'It just had to work.' Dede Allen recalled Newman's humorous plea to his crew on the first day of shooting: 'I'm a virgin, so be gentle.' In the event, *Rachel, Rachel* proved a largely harmonious production, with few arguments between director and star. If Woodward disagreed with Newman's approach to a scene, they tried it her way as well as his. Taking a relaxed attitude, Newman often directed in a T-shirt and shorts. According to Woodward, the entire cast and crew felt deeply involved with the film. Co-star Estelle Parsons had nothing but praise for Newman: '. . . he's wonderful. It's all been so relaxed and easy.' Interviewed in 1982, Stewart Stern echoed the sentiment:

> [Paul] is very sensitive to writing, and is the best director of actors I know. I think there's less impediment between his talent and its expression when he's directing. That's probably because 'Paul Newman' doesn't have to be there.

Protective of his cast, Newman only allowed key production personnel to view the daily rushes. People not directly involved with the film could easily form the wrong impression of the actors' work from the raw footage:

> I don't think it's fair to the actor. Actors experiment on the screen, and you may have a scene which goes very badly for three quarters of it, but you know you want to use the remaining one quarter.

Newman completed principal photography on *Rachel, Rachel* in six weeks. Post-production took eight months, Newman giving way to Dede Allen. Confident in Allen's abilities, he let her get on with the job, making occasional visits to view the cut sequences and discuss their options. Lacking Newman's faith, Stern became worried by Allen's early assemblage of *Rachel, Rachel*, feeling the film didn't work. In the event, both he and Newman were moved to tears by the final cut. Gore Vidal, who approved Newman and Woodward's joint screen appearances, felt they'd reached a new level as a director–actor partnership. During production on *Winning*, Newman's next film, he screened *Rachel, Rachel* for an audience of racing drivers, who were all crying by the end. Even this endorsement didn't reassure Newman, who worried that his and Woodward's presence had affected the reaction to the film. Back in Los Angeles, Stern organized a second unofficial preview, which produced the same response. Newman still seemed doubtful, perhaps unwilling to drop his guard until *Rachel, Rachel* was exposed to critics and paying audiences.

A melancholy small-town drama, lightened by a hint of optimism, *Rachel, Rachel* holds up well. Rachel Cameron (Woodward) is an unhappy schoolteacher, experiencing an early mid-life crisis. Aged thirty-five, she can no longer deal with her loneliness and sexual frustration, or the demands of a clinging, overbearing mother. When Rachel encounters the handsome Nick Kazlik (James Olson), a childhood friend making a trip home, she sees the possibility of a different life.

Newman's confident direction makes good use of tracking shots and the camera crane. The film's unorthodox structure incorporates flashbacks, fantasy sequences and interior monologue. Experimenting with distortion and slow motion, Newman underlines the script's themes with birdcage symbolism and dead child imagery.

Whatever the failings of their joint screen appearances, Newman and Woodward make Rachel Cameron a memorable, believable and sympathetic character. Rigid and uptight, she cuts a sad figure, her clothes as dowdy as her hairstyle. The self-loathing Rachel regards herself as a 'coward', afraid of life. An undertaker's daughter, she still lives above a funeral parlour. Her name is already on the family gravestone. Having grown up surrounded by the trappings of death, Rachel has never learned how to enjoy life. Any pleasure, especially of a sensual kind, is immediately smothered by guilt. Incidentally, the much contested masturbation scene is so discreet as to pass virtually unnoticed.

Rachel's only true friend is fellow teacher Calla Mackie (Estelle Parsons), a lonely lesbian who looks to the local evangelist church for solace. Their relationship suffers when Calla makes a pass at Rachel, neither one able to deal with this open expression of feeling. Nick Kazlik, on the other hand, has no problem articulating his desires.

Dispensing with small talk, Nick wants 'a little action'. Looking for love, Rachel embarks on an empty affair, refusing to see beyond the initial excitement and emotional rush. Bitter and selfish, Nick has little to offer Rachel other than a weekend's casual fornication.

If nothing else, Rachel's brief involvement with Nick initiates tentative steps towards a new life. Believing herself to be pregnant and abandoned, she discovers that her unborn 'child' is nothing more than a small cyst. Shaken out of her repressive, calcified routine, Rachel decides to leave the past behind, buying a one-way bus ticket to Oregon. While the sequence is muted, she has enjoyed her first small triumph. The closing credits roll over shots of Rachel on a beach with a child. Is this another fantasy or a glimpse of things to come?

Rachel, Rachel – Rachel begins her affair with Nick Kazlik (James Olson)

Lacking a big name, at least in front of the camera, *Rachel, Rachel* required careful selling. Newman and Woodward embarked on a major publicity campaign for the film, orchestrated by Warren Cowan, Newman's press agent. Usually shunning the media spotlight, their sudden availability became an event, and they did the rounds of television talk shows and appeared together on the cover of *Life* magazine. The accompanying article stressed that the couple had given up the Labor Day holiday to share their thoughts on life, each other and *Rachel, Rachel* with *Life* readers. Select audiences, usually no more than eight people, were invited to special previews at the Beverly Hills Hotel's Cinema Room. Newman usually put in an appearance after the screening, discussing the film over coffee.

During the publicity drive for *Rachel, Rachel*, Newman stressed his debt to Woodward, both personal and professional. As he explained, 'Joanne really gave up her career for me, to stick by me, to make the marriage work. That's one of the reasons I directed this film with her.' Interviewed by *Playboy* magazine, he related how Woodward had turned down film work to stay with him and their family: 'She's done this to the detriment of her career, I'm afraid, but it's helped keep us together.' Readers could be left in no doubt about Newman's feelings for his wife: 'Without her, I'd be nowhere, nothing.'

From a technical point of view, Newman felt his directorial début had gone well, proving much less exhausting than his usual acting work:

I didn't get anywhere near as tired directing as when I act . . .
When you're involved with every facet of the production . . .
you're constantly pumped up, and you don't have an opportunity
to slow down.

Finance aside, Newman's biggest fight over *Rachel, Rachel* was the position of his director credit. Concerned that audiences would be distracted by seeing his name at the start of the film, he didn't want it mentioned until the end credits. The Directors Guild rejected this strategy, arguing that the director's name had to be listed at the beginning. Undaunted, Newman asked director friends Elia Kazan and William Wyler to support his case. Both Kazan and Wyler carried a lot of weight with the Guild, and Newman won his appeal.[2]

As the film's star, Woodward did her share of media schmoozing, commenting, 'I wanted to do a film . . . that meant something to me.' Interviewed for the *New York Times*, she discussed Newman's struggle to get backing for the project: 'I'm afraid offering a package of the script and me was hardly like offering Elizabeth Taylor and Tennessee Williams.' Ironically, the new Taylor–Williams film, *Boom!* (1968), had recently died a quick death at the US box office. Asked about Newman's ability behind the camera, Woodward replied: 'Who could direct better than the person you live with?' While this sounds glib, she believed that no other director would have had Newman's fierce commitment to the film. Never one to undersell her husband's talents, Woodward compared Newman with acclaimed Swedish director Ingmar Bergman: 'Paul is an actor's director in that he is very specific, clear . . . I just wish Paul could direct every movie I'll ever do again.' Of the eleven feature films Woodward appeared in subsequently, Newman would direct three.

Rachel, Rachel received its official première at New York's Plaza Theatre, followed by a limited release in New York City and Los Angeles on 26 August 1968. Woodward talked about the film as if it were a new-born child: 'We hated to release it. It's like breaking the umbilical cord.' Critics praised Woodward's heartfelt performance and Newman's measured, sensitive direction. The film's sombre, intro- spective approach appeared to suit the mood of the times. Newman suggested that *Rachel, Rachel* appealed to audiences because it touched on universal themes: 'I think that this film went over because it dealt with the values we all deal with: loneliness, birth, death, change, despair.' It did solid box-office business.

The film's many admirers included Patricia Neal, who co-starred with Newman in *Hud*. Sadly, Neal had suffered a massive stroke in 1965, which badly affected her memory. Unable to recall Newman's name on the telephone, she still managed to praise his achievement: 'You did it beautifully.'

Without doubt, *Rachel, Rachel* re-established Joanne Woodward as a leading film actress. 'I guess *Rachel* has revived my career,' she admitted. The National Association of Theatre Owners named her as one of its 'Box Office Stars of the Year', alongside Steve McQueen, and both Newman and Woodward received Golden Globes, handed out by Hollywood's Foreign Press Association. The New York Film Critics Cricle also named the couple as Best Director and Best Actress. When the Academy Award nominations were announced, *Rachel, Rachel* received nods for Best Picture, Best Adapted Screenplay, Best Actress and Best Supporting Actress. Newman's direction, praised by most critics, was passed over. Furious at this omission, Woodward threatened to boycott the ceremony, despite her own nomination. However, the more diplomatic Newman persuaded her to change her mind. As the driving force behind *Rachel, Rachel*, he could claim the Best Picture nomination as his own. Woodward faced serious compe- tition from Katharine Hepburn (*The Lion in Winter*), Barbra Streisand (*Funny Girl*), Vanessa Redgrave (*Isadora*) and, ironically, Patricia Neal (*The Subject Was Roses*). For the only time in its history, the Academy declared a draw, with both Hepburn and Streisand taking the Best Actress prize. Stewart Stern lost the Best Adapted Screenplay award to James Goldman, William's brother, and *The Lion in Winter*. Under the circumstances, Newman and Woodward had few qualms about skipping the post-ceremony ball. Interviewed for *Time* magazine in 1982, Newman recalled *Rachel, Rachel* with 'great fondness. That is a really good film.'

Nineteen sixty-eight was also an election year. Newman backed Senator Eugene McCarthy's campaign to secure the nomination for the Democrat presidential candidate. As always, he played down his celebrity status: 'You can't consider yourself a disenfranchised citizen merely because you're in the acting profession.' He spoke out against the Vietnam War, a risky stance for a high-profile public figure, and attended the Democrat convention in Chicago, witnessing at first hand the brutal police suppression of anti-war protesters ordered by Mayor Richard Daley. In total, Newman spent twenty-five days campaigning for McCarthy. In the end, McCarthy was beaten to the nomination by Hubert Humphrey. Humphrey, in turn, proved no match for Republican candidate Richard 'Tricky Dicky' Nixon. Out on the campaign trail, Newman discovered that a Jaguar car he'd rented for the weekend was used during the week by Nixon, prompting him to leave a note inside the vehicle, advising Nixon of the 'tricky' clutch. Bad jokes and political differences aside, Nixon resented Newman for making the cover of *Life* magazine before he did, later putting him on his infamous 'enemies' list. Placed at no. 19, Newman seemed unfazed: 'Send G. Gordon Liddy to pick up my award.' For the record, Nixon once told Newman's friend and producer John Foreman, 'I think he's a first-rate actor even if he thinks I'm a lousy politician.'

Gore Vidal, a fellow Democrat, pushed Newman to take his political activism one stage further. Having failed to launch his own career in politics, Vidal felt Newman should run for the Senate in his adopted home state of Connecticut. As Vidal explained, 'He is one of the few people I know who has a good character.' Flattered by Vidal's endorsement, Newman graciously declined to follow this path: 'I don't have the arrogance, and I don't have the credentials.' He continued to act on his political beliefs from the outside, supporting the Centre for the Study of Democratic Institutions, based in Santa Barbara, California. In 1969, the American Jewish Committee recognized Newman and Woodward's activism with the William J. German Humanitarian Relations Award.

Newman's passion for fast cars found a tailor-made outlet in *Winning* (1969). This race drama is notable for initiating Newman's producing partnership with John Foreman; having guided both Newman and Woodward's early careers, the balding former agent had decided on a change of occupation. *Winning* would be a co-production between

Universal Studios and the newly formed Newman–Foreman company, and the film was executive-produced by Jennings Lang, another ex-MCA agent.

By the late 1960s, Universal was enjoying more success with its television product than its feature films. *Winning* began life at the studio as a humble TV movie, scripted by Howard Rodman, whose credits included *Coogan's Bluff* (1968), another Universal release. A racing fan for many years, Newman now arranged his work schedule to incorporate the Indianapolis 500 race, held on Memorial Day. The *Winning* project, though highly formulaic, seemed too good an opportunity to miss:

> . . . when the movie came up, even though I had some quarrels about their script, it was just sensational for me to be able to drive the big stuff . . . I get 'stoned' on automobiles . . . it's a natural high.

Newman's involvement with *Winning* prompted an immediate upgrade to 'A' feature status. He received $1.1 million for the film, his highest fee to date. Having paid big money for their star, Universal kept the production fairly modest in scope, budgeting *Winning* at around $4 million. Given the project's origins, the studio had no qualms about using a television director, James Goldstone.[3]

The film co-starred Woodward, acting opposite Newman for the first time since *A New Kind of Love*. Presumably, the couple felt like making another film together after their fruitful experience with *Rachel, Rachel*, because the *Winning* script lacked all the strengths Woodward normally favoured. Newman and Woodward were joined by Robert Wagner, who'd made the most of his supporting role in *Harper*.

Newman and Wagner trained for their roles as rival drivers at the Robert Bondurant Racing School in California. The film's schedule permitted only a small amount of pre-production preparation on the track, and both Newman and Wagner began filming with barely two weeks of training. Newman proved a fast learner, driving without an instructor within the first week. Starting off in a Lola T270, the standard car for new students, he soon demanded something faster, switching to a Ford GT 40. Confident behind the wheel, he insisted on doing all his own driving for *Winning*. Neither Universal nor Woodward were happy with this, though for different reasons: the studio worried about insurance problems and injury-related production delays; Woodward simply didn't want to become a widow.

Winning – Newman relaxes between takes with driving instructor Robert Bondurant

Most of the racing footage was shot at the Elkhart Lake track in Wisconsin, the cast and crew eating with the real drivers and their pit crews. For the interior scenes, Universal converted a garage into a makeshift film studio. Newman impressed stunt co-ordinator James Arnett with his driving expertise: 'Paul took to racing as though it were second nature to him.' The non-racing scenes included a bedroom encounter in which Wagner's character seduces Newman's wife, played by Woodward. Wagner was obviously nervous about the scene, looking to Newman for advice and, it seemed, approval. While Newman found the whole thing vastly amusing, he appreciated Wagner's discomfort, stifling his laughter. John Foreman also saw the funny side: 'Here's Paul giving Wagner several good points about how to behave in bed with his wife.'

Shot in ultra-wide Panavision, *Winning* never disguises its small-screen origins. James Goldstone's self-consciously modish direction utilizes fast cuts, zooms, tricksy focus shifts, slow dissolves, slow motion, distortion and multiple exposures. The relentless mood music is similarly distracting. With a nod to realism, the driving sequences feature no obvious back projection.

The film gives Newman and Woodward little chance to shine. In terms of solid characterization, the film is a non-starter. Frank Capua (Newman) is just another boozing, workaholic womaniser. Obsessed with victory on the racetrack, he can't see the strain this ambition has placed on his marriage. As Elora (Woodward) puts it, 'He just wants to win. He doesn't care what the stakes are.'

Competing at the Indianapolis 500, Capua scores the biggest win of his career, only to feel a strange emptiness. Without Elora at his side, professional triumph now means little. Having punched out Luther Erding (Wagner), several scenes too late, Capua turns up on Elora's doorstep. The open ending suggests their relationship may have a future.

Both Newman and Woodward are wasted on clichéd, underdeveloped characters who fail to generate interest or sympathy. If nothing else, *Winning* took Newman's passion for cars to a new level: 'It's the one thing that I can be genuinely adolescent about.' Woodward was markedly less enthusiastic about her husband's new hobby. Newman admitted: 'She thinks competitive driving is the silliest thing in the world. It is also very scary to her.'

Winning opened in the US on 22 May 1969, drawing largely negative reviews. Surprisingly, *New Yorker* critic Pauline Kael praised Newman's performance as one of his finest. Newman rated the film as a 'pretty good story about racing', though 'the people were not integrated well'. It did respectable business at the box office, comfortably turning a profit on its total cost of $5.2 million.

Promoting *Winning*'s British release, in the autumn of 1969, Newman did an interview for *Photoplay Film Monthly*. Reporter Robert Peer described the star as 'the most insecure actor I know', and Newman admitted to 'a recurring nightmare in which I always dream that the whole bottom is going to fall out of my career'. Despite his initial struggles and subsequent disappointments, Newman believed that he'd enjoyed a relatively smooth ride as a leading man and, because of this, he hadn't truly earned the benefits of stardom, financial and otherwise:

> Because acting comes to me very easily . . . it is very difficult
> for me to comprehend why the rewards for doing something
> that doesn't really seem to involve that much work should be
> so extraordinary.

Given Newman and Woodward's fraught screen relationship in *Winning*, questions about their real-life marriage were inevitable. Newman discussed his personal life in broad terms. In contrast to the impulsive, selfish couple in *Winning*, he and Woodward were still happily married off-screen. As he explained to Peer:

> We have things pretty well worked out between us. For instance, we've been married eleven years and we've been away from each other no more than ten or twelve weeks. And we're frank with each other about everything. This is important.

On the domestic front, Newman still faced major problems with his wayward son. Now eighteen, Scott had grown into a good-looking young man, compared by Joanne Woodward to 'a French film star'. Underneath, he remained bitter, angry and unhappy. An expensive private education came to naught, with Scott being expelled from school for his poor grades. Prone to bouts of heavy drinking, he got into several fights. Having been in the same situation, Newman felt both anger and guilt that history was repeating itself. For all his success, wealth and influence, he hadn't steered Scott away from trouble. While Scott deeply resented any show of parental authority, he clearly expected to share his father's affluent movie-star lifestyle.

Newman's five daughters seemed happier, and more resilient, than their troubled sibling. That said, Newman had not given them the most stable of childhoods. Leaving aside the divorce from Jacqueline, all the children had gone through a succession of schools, causing disruptions to their lives and the loss of friends. As a consequence, they were both shy and wary of new people, unwilling to form attachments that could soon be broken. Aware of this situation, Newman readily admitted to his failings as a parent: 'You simply don't know what the right choice is.'

Newman rounded off the 1960s, his most successful decade in films, with *Butch Cassidy and the Sundance Kid* (1969). While not on the level of *The Hustler* or *Hud*, this humorous, irreverent western pastiche is probably his best-loved movie. Produced for Twentieth Century Fox, it marked Newman's first collaboration with Robert Redford and director George Roy Hill.

Butch Cassidy and the Sundance Kid originated with screenwriter William Goldman, who delivered the goods for *Harper*. He was fascinated by these real-life outlaws, citing Cassidy, aka Robert Leroy Parker, as one of his favourite historical figures. Born in Utah in 1866, Cassidy evaded the law until 1909, when he and Sundance ran into the Bolivian army. In Goldman's view, the real Cassidy was much like the character in the film, a charming rogue who inspired genuine affection. By contrast, the lives of Sundance, born Harry

Longbaugh, and his lover Etta Place were not well documented. While Place may have been the schoolteacher depicted in the film, she was just as likely a prostitute.

Butch Cassidy and the Sundance Kid – Butch and Sundance, looking good

The story of Butch and Sundance had been filmed back in 1905, running to two reels (forty minutes). According to legend, the duo was fascinated by this fictionalized version of their lives, risking arrest to attend a screening. Goldman researched the characters for nearly eight years before embarking on a screenplay, initially titled *The Sundance Kid and Butch Cassidy*. In 1963, he met producer Lawrence Turman, who later made *The Graduate* (1967). With Turman's help, Goldman shaped his material into a rough storyline, writing the first draft of *Butch Cassidy* in 1966 in a mere four weeks. In *Adventures in the Screen Trade*, Goldman cites this screenplay as the most important of his career, certainly 'as a learning experience'.

Goldman's initial draft of *Butch Cassidy* stirred less Hollywood interest than he'd hoped. Already wary of westerns, a genre in decline, studio executives felt the screenplay lacked both action and humour, and Cassidy's tendency to run away was not typical hero behaviour. Curtis Kenyon, head of Warner Brothers' story department, nonetheless loved the script, urging studio boss Kenneth Hyman to buy it. However, Warners wouldn't meet Goldman's asking price of $400,000, plus a percentage of the box-office gross. Goldman's script also caught the attention of Peter Bart, a young executive at Paramount. Impressed by the 'brilliantly stylized writing', he offered Goldman $200,000 for the screenplay, despite the antipathy of Paramount's front office. Half expecting to be fired for reckless behaviour, Bart soon learned that he'd been outbid by Twentieth Century Fox. Studio boss Richard Zanuck and vice-president David Brown bought the *Butch Cassidy* script for $400,000, a record at the time. Goldman signed the deal with Fox on 27 October 1967.

The *Butch Cassidy* project was assigned to director George Roy Hill, a gifted craftsman still looking for his big break.4 Hill was immediately taken with Goldman's script. The director had a liking for nostalgic subjects, explaining, 'I read nothing but history for pleasure.' He worked on the screenplay with Goldman during June and July 1968. Throughout pre-production, Twentieth Century Fox pushed for changes to make Butch and Sundance more conventional western heroes. The studio also wanted an audience-friendly romance, which Sundance and Etta Place barely provided. Goldman and Hill fiercely resisted this executive tampering. Interviewed in 1970 for *Photoplay Film Monthly*, Hill explained Fox's problem with the characters: 'Butch is a likeable desperado and screen morality, until recently, didn't allow bad guys to be heroic, so to speak.'

Goldman's number-one choice for the part of Butch Cassidy was Jack Lemmon, inspired by the latter's performance in *Cowboy* (1958). He felt that Lemmon was both assured and amusing in the saddle, though his character, a former hotel clerk, rapidly tires of life on the range. Struck by Newman's impetuous, angst-ridden Billy the Kid in *The Left-Handed Gun*, Goldman thought he'd a make a perfect Sundance Kid.

Unlikely as it now seems, he saw Lemmon and Newman as an ideal combination: 'I thought they'd be great together.' In early 1967, months before the Fox deal was signed, Goldman met with Newman in Tucson, Arizona. At the time, the actor was busy shooting *Hombre*, a more downbeat western. Over several evenings, they discussed the *Butch Cassidy* script, Newman making his interest clear.

Though more than happy to cast Newman, Richard Zanuck and David Brown had no interest in Jack Lemmon, setting their sights instead on Marlon Brando. Nearly a decade earlier, Brando had directed and starred in the intriguing *One Eyed Jacks* (1961), a revisionist take on the Billy the Kid legend. Despite Brando's flagging career, and negligible comic touch, Zanuck and Brown viewed him as a serious contender. Brando proved impossible to contact, however, and Fox soon realized that the famously difficult star wouldn't play ball. The studio also considered Dustin Hoffman, a big name after *The Graduate* (1967), for the part of Butch. While Hoffman seems an unlikely contender for a Wild West hero, he later gave an outstanding performance in Arthur Penn's *Little Big Man* (1970).

Throughout the casting discussions, Zanuck lobbied for Steve McQueen to play Butch Cassidy. A born screen cowboy, McQueen had demonstrated his western credentials in *The Magnificent Seven* (1960) and the less impressive *Nevada Smith* (1966). Smelling a hit, McQueen accepted the film, on the condition that he played the more dynamic Sundance. Ever since *Somebody Up There Likes Me*, he had been fiercely competitive with Newman. Now a major star, the former $19-a-day extra rivalled Newman as a box-office draw. According to Newman, he and McQueen had already discussed co-starring in the film. McQueen invited Newman to his house, where they debated the script as a suitable joint vehicle. When Newman suggested buying the screenplay, splitting the $400,000 price tag fifty–fifty, McQueen got cold feet.

Unimpressed by McQueen, George Roy Hill wanted Newman for Butch Cassidy, only to find that the star had lost confidence. Following the abject failure of *The Secret War of Harry Frigg*, released in early 1968, Newman felt he couldn't handle comedy. Hill argued that the humour in Goldman's script stemmed from the situations, not the characters. Reassured, Newman came back on board for $750,000, with McQueen looking set to co-star. By this time, he no longer cared whether he played Butch or Sundance. Ultimately, his deal with Fox faltered over the question of billing. Neither he nor Newman could be seen to take second place. After some deliberation, the Fox executives proposed a workable solution. Both Newman and McQueen would be billed above the title, with the name on the left slightly lower than the name on the right. Feeling that both honour and equality had been satisfied, Newman agreed to take either position. The eternally wary and insecure McQueen was unconvinced and quit the project, much to Hill's relief. When Newman and McQueen did finally co-star in a movie, *The Towering Inferno* (1974), the same staggered billing strategy was used.

With McQueen out of the picture, Hill suggested Robert Redford, an experienced stage and television actor. At the time, Redford's Hollywood track record was not impressive. Having made his film début in *War Hunt* (1961), a low-budget drama, he disappeared from movies for the next few years. When he returned, it was in major flops such as *Inside Daisy Clover* (1965) and *The Chase* (1966). Redford's only hit to date was the marital comedy *Barefoot in the Park* (1967), in which he recreated his role in Neil Simon's 1963 Broadway success. While both Redford and co-star Jane Fonda gave accomplished performances, the film sold largely on the playwright's name. Cast in the Paramount western *Blue* (1968), Redford walked off the project, and the resulting legal wrangles put his film career on hold for nearly two years.

Hill had met Redford back in 1962 and had been struck by the actor's presence. Newman didn't share the director's enthusiasm, feeling that Redford looked more like 'a Wall Street lawyer type' than an outlaw. Weary of the endless casting discussions, he left the final decision to Hill, Zanuck and Brown. Initially, Zanuck fiercely resisted casting Redford, claiming that he'd rather cancel the production. Brown regarded the actor as 'an also-ran' for the role. Accepting that Steve McQueen was not an option, Zanuck now pursued Warren Beatty. However, hot from *Bonnie and Clyde* (1967), Beatty declined the part of Sundance, preferring to co-star opposite Elizabeth Taylor in *The Only Game in Town* (1970). Reassured by Hill, Redford cleared his work schedule and waited for the call, risking public humiliation if it didn't come. In need of support, Hill asked both William Goldman and Newman to back him. Goldman sent a telegram to Zanuck, while Newman phoned the studio boss, supposedly demanding Redford as his co-star. Interestingly, Newman later claimed that Joanne Woodward had suggested casting Redford. According to one version of events, Hill intended Newman to play Sundance, with Redford as Butch. At Redford's suggestion, the stars switched roles. Like the real-life Sundance Kid, Redford was left-handed. Once Newman had settled on Butch, the film officially became *Butch Cassidy and the Sundance Kid*, a reversal of Goldman's original title. As

Goldman famously pointed out, in the film business 'nobody knows anything'.

With the star roles finally cast, production on *Butch Cassidy and the Sundance Kid* began in earnest. Fox employee Paul Monash, who negotiated the deal with Goldman, had been made the film's producer. When Newman came on board, he brought John Foreman along. In the interests of diplomacy, Foreman took the producer credit, while Monash was made the executive producer. Newman also recruited cameraman Conrad Hall, recently employed on John Boorman's *Hell in the Pacific* (1969). Impressed by Hall's work on *Harper* and *Cool Hand Luke*, Newman specifically requested him for *Butch Cassidy*. According to director Sam Mendes, who worked with Newman and Hall on *Road to Perdition*, Hall both admired and respected actors, making him Newman's kind of cameraman. Twentieth Century Fox resisted hiring him, however, arguing that he was too expensive. When Newman insisted, the studio backed down. George Roy Hill had been struck by Hall's photography for Richard Brooks's *The Professionals* (1966), a cynical western adventure, and agreed he'd be the perfect choice for *Butch Cassidy*. Looking for a 'hip' score, Fox hired pop composer Burt Bacharach, who'd worked on the swinging comedies *What's New Pussycat?* (1965) and *Casino Royale* (1967).

The role of Etta Place went to Katharine Ross, whose performance in *The Graduate* (1967) earned her an Academy Award nomination. Hill regarded Ross as '. . . the sexiest girl I'd ever seen . . . just ravishingly beautiful'. Newman recruited Strother Martin, from *Harper* and *Cool Hand Luke*, for the part of an eccentric mine agent. Conrad Hall rated him as 'one of the best character actors of all time'.

As usual, Newman requested a full rehearsal prior to shooting. Twentieth Century Fox agreed to two weeks of cast read-throughs, beginning in early September 1968. Redford didn't favour this approach, feeling that 'rehearsal cuts into the spontaneity of what you're doing'. However, aware that he had little say in the matter, he played along: 'Newman was calling the shots, so I rehearsed.' According to Goldman, Redford used humour to cut any tensions, while Katharine Ross tended to keep quiet. During rehearsals, Newman and Hill argued for several days over one particular scene. Pursued by a 'super-posse', Butch and Sundance visit Sheriff Bledsoe, an old friend, who warns the outlaws that their days are numbered. Newman felt this exchange belonged at the end of the sequence, just before Butch, Sundance and Etta head for Bolivia, via New York, whereas Hill wanted the scene placed in the middle of the pursuit. In his view, Butch and Sundance already knew that they had to flee the US; they didn't need a climactic warning from the sheriff. Newman wouldn't let the matter drop, displaying his 'terrier' instinct. While Goldman joined in these lively discussions, Redford kept his distance, perhaps feeling that he lacked the clout of the others. When news of the row filtered back to Hollywood, rumours spread that Fox would have to shut down *Butch Cassidy*. The studio already had doubts about the film, feeling the $6.5-million budget was too high for an offbeat western. In the event, Hill got his way, Newman deferring to the director. For the record, many feel that Newman's idea was better.

Butch Cassidy and the Sundance Kid began filming on 16 September 1968. Twentieth Century Fox had the production scheduled for a twelve-week shoot, leaving little margin for error. Despite the front-office nerves, director George Roy Hill remained firmly in charge of the project, ordering non-essential personnel off the set if they bothered him.[5] Newman seemed insecure on the first day of shooting, over-playing the comedy. Hill persuaded him that the more droll approach agreed in rehearsal would work. It's possible that Newman still worried about his ability to handle humour, shaken by the failure of *Harry Frigg*. He was also nervous around horses, worried that he'd be kicked. Newman remained grateful for Hill's patient guidance, later remarking: 'He is truly a director in the best sense . . . when you're cooking, he leaves you alone.' Newman had further problems with a short scene featuring Butch and a friendly prostitute, Agnes (Cloris Leachman). Uneasy with the scripted dialogue, he suggested a little improvisation, not his usual approach. With Leachman's encouragement, he soon relaxed, though much of their ad-libbing would be cut from the finished film. Newman later described the *Butch Cassidy* shoot as 'a perfect example of film-making as a community experience . . . everybody was geared to invent and create'. He also expressed total confidence in the film's commercial potential, telling Redford: 'You're in your first twenty-million-dollar picture.'

Hill sensed an immediate rapport between Newman and Redford: 'It was a rare kind of relationship between those guys.' Newman's representatives worried that Redford was getting too many scenes and close-ups, but Newman himself didn't seem bothered. Only Redford's late arrivals on set caused friction with Newman, a stickler for punctuality. This aside, Hill observed that the stars were 'very fond of each other'. Redford had nothing but respect for Newman: 'He knew exactly what he wanted to do.' A fellow liberal activist, Redford also shared Newman's enthusiasm for fast cars and racing.

At dinner time on filming days, Newman would prepare a large dressed salad, to be shared between the cast and crew. He also filled a coffee pot with Scotch and ice, presumably available to anyone who wanted it. After dinner, the company would reassemble to watch the rushes of the previous day's filming. Newman usually turned up, despite claiming that viewing rushes made his hands sweat.

Interviewed by showbiz reporter Rona Jaffe, Newman outlined his daily routine during the *Butch Cassidy* shoot. Rising at 5.30 a.m., he would go for an hour-long session in the sauna and swimming pool. By 7.00 a.m. he was on the set, ready for work. Obviously taken with Newman, Jaffe praised the star as 'Just a super-nice, intelligent guy with charisma . . . A gentleman, but humorous with it.'

Having resolved the Bledsoe quarrel, Newman and Hill clashed off the set over the latter's supposed stinginess. Never one of life's reckless spenders, Hill declined to stand his co-workers a round of drinks. Newman 'settled' the dispute by sawing the director's office desk in half with a chainsaw. In his view, playing practical jokes on Hill helped both him and Redford get into character. For the record, Newman had nothing but praise for Hill, 'a sensational man, and a great director'.

Katharine Ross had her own problems with Hill, largely because of -2tically involved with cameraman Conrad Hall. Although Ross's character did not appear in the train robbery sequence, she turned up on location to be with Hall, and Hill became annoyed when Hall let Ross operate one of the cameras. This may have been for safety or union reasons. It's also possible that Hill resented Ross and Hall playing out their relationship on his set. Whatever the case, Hill barred Ross from the *Butch Cassidy* set when she wasn't required for filming. Camera shenanigans aside, Hill and Ross didn't communicate well, arguing over her character. Significantly, Hill remained on civil terms with Hall, despite some impatience with the cameraman's 'slow' working pace. Ross had a much easier time with Newman: 'He's a totally unpretentious person. He's not seemingly in it for himself and he is very generous. It's fun to work with him. He's a real human being.'

Most of *Butch Cassidy* was shot in Colorado, Utah and New Mexico. The Bolivian sequences were filmed in Mexico, a more convenient distance from Los Angeles. Most of the cast and crew, including Hill, had problems with the local water supply and were struck down by chronic diarrhoea. Newman, Redford and Ross stuck to soda pop and alcohol, remaining in good health.

The famous cliff-top jump was partly filmed at the Animus River Gorge, near Durango, Colorado. Newman and Redford did the initial leap, landing on a ledge cushioned with a mattress six feet below them. The river water was too shallow for the big plunge, which was to be executed by stunt doubles. The production team staged this shot back at the Fox Ranch in Malibu. British stunt co-ordinator Vic Armstrong singled out the cliff jump as one of the ten best stunts ever filmed: 'A fine example of a stunt being perfectly integrated into the story . . . it contributes something to our understanding of the characters and what they're willing to go through.' For the less spectacular bicycle sequence, Newman did most of the riding himself. When the stuntman on call proved short of ideas, Newman devised all the 'trick' shots of Butch showing off to Etta Place. At Fox's insistence, Newman was doubled for the shot where Butch crashes into a fence.

Butch Cassidy and the Sundance Kid had its share of production traumas. Prone to back trouble, Hill was incapacitated for ten days and directed from a stretcher. Worried that Twentieth Century Fox would replace him, he asked Newman and Redford to keep his condition a secret. The memorable fight scene between Butch and Harvey Logan (Ted Cassidy) also caused headaches. Thanks to weather and lighting problems, the various takes didn't match, and the required reshoots put the production two days behind schedule. Shooting the final sequence, Newman and Redford had to contend with explosive squibs and airgun pellets. While the stars emerged unscathed, Newman's stunt double, James Arnett, broke his hip executing a Bolivian cop's death fall.

Visitors to the set included Lulu Betanson, sister of the historical Butch Cassidy. The first scene Betanson watched involved Butch kicking Harvey Logan in the balls. She obviously liked what she saw, making frequent return visits. Between takes, she entertained the cast and crew with stories about her celebrity brother and his Hole-in-the-Wall gang. Betanson also gave her seal of approval to Goldman's script and Newman's portrayal, praising their accuracy. Apparently, Butch Cassidy really did have blue eyes and a winning grin.

Without exception, the creators of *Butch Cassidy and the Sundance Kid* regard the film as a highpoint in their careers. Goldman describes *Butch Cassidy* as 'a glorious piece of narrative, original and moving'. He saw the film as a tale of loneliness, the outlaws attempting to recapture their old way of life in a changing world. Newman characterized it as a buddy picture, in the best Clark Gable–Spencer Tracy tradition, with 'a lovely kind of hit-and-run sense of humour'. Certainly, *Butch Cassidy* works best as the ultimate lovable rogues movie. Opening with an ersatz silent film about the Hole-in-the-Wall gang, *Butch Cassidy* is extremely well made. Hall's photography evokes a sun-kissed landscape of forest, mountain and desert. Hill experiments

Butch Cassidy and the Sundance Kid – Perhaps the most famous bicycle ride in film history

with a number of visual tricks, notably the sepia prologue, photo montage and moment-of-death slow motion. This high level of craftsmanship rarely falters.

Burt Bacharach's jazz-influenced score includes the song 'Raindrops Keep Fallin' on My Head', which accompanies the bicycle scene. An *homage* to François Truffaut's *Jules et Jim* (1961), this sequence was devised by Hill to suggest romantic feelings between Butch and Etta. When Bob Dylan declined to sing 'Raindrops', the job went to B. J. Thomas.

In essence, *Butch Cassidy and the Sundance Kid* is a well-achieved star vehicle, thin on substance.[6] The film hangs on the camaraderie between the outlaws, expertly played by Newman and Redford. *Butch Cassidy*'s biggest failing is Etta Place. Soft-spoken and soulful, Etta doesn't have much to do. Newman rightly regarded the character as incidental to the film: 'I don't think people realize what that picture was all about. It's a love affair between two men.'

After the 'Raindrops' interlude, Cassidy rejects progress, in the form of the bicycle, continuing with his outlaw ways. The lengthy flight from the super-posse, nearly forty minutes of screentime, substitutes for narrative and character development. These pursuers are a faceless menace, seen only in long shot. Unable to shake the lawmen, Butch and Sundance keep the jokes coming: 'Who *are* those guys?' Mid-chase, Sheriff Bledsoe spells out the final act of the Butch and Sundance story: 'It's over . . . you're gonna die bloody and all you can do is choose where.' Etta has no appetite for this, making her exit before the outlaws run out of luck: 'I won't watch you die. I'll miss that scene if you don't mind.'[7]

While the *Butch Cassidy* shoot proved one of the best experiences of Newman's career, his personal life had come under increasing media scrutiny. There were persistent rumours that the Newman–Woodward marriage was in trouble, largely on account of his heavy drinking. Woodward's low blood pressure meant she had little tolerance for alcohol. Her social drinking was limited to the occasional glass of sherry, compared to Newman's coffee pots of Scotch and ice. Woodward conceded that she overreacted to Newman's drinking at times, though both of them appreciated that it set a bad example for Scott. Now mixing his booze with narcotics, he had become ever more volatile. He channelled some of his aggression into dangerous sports, notably skydiving. Scott also shared his father's enthusiasm for fast cars. Unlike Newman, Scott had no qualms about driving under the influence of alcohol. From this time onwards, Newman lived in fear of bad news. Turning his concerns to positive use, Newman supplied the narration for an anti-drugs film, shown in high schools.

Scott aside, the Newman–Woodward marriage could never be a tension-free zone. As Newman readily admitted, he and Woodward had very different personalities. He was bright and alert early in the morning, while she was grumpy. Woodward lost her temper easily, but quickly forgave and forgot. While Newman rarely became angry, he tended to hold grudges. Newman has compared Woodward to a light bulb and cannon, bright and explosive. On another occasion he explained, 'She's nitroglycerine and I'm diesel fuel.' In July 1969, Newman and Woodward paid $2,000 to place an advert in the *Los Angeles Times*. The message was simple: 'We Are Not Breaking Up.' The couple then took a short holiday in England, where they'd spent their honeymoon a decade earlier. Whether this destination was nostalgic or symbolic, Newman and Woodward had to deal with the painful memories of her miscarriage, something still hidden from the public. A few years later, all seemed to be well, Newman commenting: 'For two people with almost nothing in common, we have an uncommonly good marriage.'

Fox's distribution division wanted to open *Butch Cassidy and the Sundance Kid* in Texas on Memorial Day. Richard Zanuck liked the idea, though it meant cutting the post-production schedule. Already working fourteen-hour days on the film, George Roy Hill complained in the strongest terms. Newman also protested to the studio, unwilling to see his surefire hit screwed up by marketing executives. Wary of upsetting Newman, Zanuck soon dropped the plan. It probably helped that *Winning*, made by rival studio Universal, was already set for a Memorial Day release, and having two Paul Newman films opening on the same date would not be good for anyone. Newman and Zanuck remained on civil terms, subsequently working together on *The Sting*, *The Verdict* and *Road to Perdition*.

Hill delivered the first cut of *Butch Cassidy* on 20 April 1969. The deleted sequences included a short scene, towards the end of the film, where Butch and Sundance watch a silent movie about themselves, which ends with the outlaws' deaths. William Goldman recalls Newman disliking the scene, an obvious harbinger of doom, though Newman denies this. Fox pushed for the sequence to be cut, arguing that it slowed down the narrative. In the final edit, the silent film became part of the opening titles.

Twentieth Century Fox wanted Lulu Betanson, Butch Cassidy's sister, to endorse their film, in a series of cinema adverts. Betanson agreed, on the condition that she got to see the finished movie first. Fearing a negative response, the studio refused, claiming that such a

preview was out of the question. However, Robert Redford, a canny
operator, persuaded Betanson to plug the film unseen in return for a
fee.

Butch Cassidy previewed in San Francisco on 9 August 1969. The
screening was not an unqualified success. Feeling that the audience
laughed too much, Hill reduced the comedy elements for subsequent
screenings. B. J. Thomas's representatives thought he'd made a big
mistake getting involved with the film.

Butch Cassidy and the Sundance Kid premièred in Durango, Colorado,
on 2 September 1969, and New Haven, Connecticut, Newman's
adopted home town. The film opened in New York, in selected theatres
only, on 23 September 1969. This limited showcase screening was
followed by a nationwide release on 24 October. The reviews were
decidedly mixed. Writing in *The New Yorker*, Pauline Kael entitled
her review 'The Bottom of the Pit', one of Etta Place's lines in the film.
Kael seemed offended by *Butch Cassidy*, particularly the way it
glamorized outlaws and downgraded women: 'It's clear who is at the
bottom of the pit, and it isn't those frontier schoolteachers, whose
work was honest.'

Released at a time when the western genre was in decline, *Butch
Cassidy* didn't score an immediate box-office smash, but thanks to
positive word-of-mouth, the movie steadily built into a hit, becoming
the fifth-highest grossing film of its decade. By the time it received its
British première, in the spring of 1970, the film had become a motion-
picture phenomenon, taking $45.95 million at the North American
box office and another $50 million in foreign territories. The film was
the most commercially successful western in Hollywood history, until
Mel Brooks's *Blazing Saddles* (1974), a coarser form of
homage/parody. Newman claimed to have expected a hit all along: 'I
knew that [it] was going to be the biggest film I'd ever been in. There
was no way of missing with it.' Out on the publicity rounds, he also
commented:

> . . . I think we have a great picture here . . . I liked playing Butch,
> and I played him as he was, a man who ruled the wildest rustlers,
> bank and train robbers because he was smarter than they were:
> brains over brawn.

Playing down his own contribution, Newman later said, 'I'm not so
much proud of my performance, but I'm proud of the film.' Redford
found himself hailed as a major star, a position he still holds today. In
1981, he founded the Sundance Institute and the accompanying
Sundance Film Festival, named after his character in *Butch Cassidy*.

When Newman finished 1969 as Hollywood's number two box-office draw, behind John Wayne, Joanne Woodward brought her husband back down to earth: 'Look, he's forty-four, got six children, and snores in bed. How can he be a sex symbol?'

Butch Cassidy received several Academy Award nominations in major categories, including Best Picture, Best Director, Best Original Screenplay, Best Cinematography, Best Original Score and Best Song. On the night, William Goldman, Conrad Hall and Burt Bacharach all won Oscars, but *Butch Cassidy* and George Roy Hill lost out to *Midnight Cowboy* and John Schlesinger.

Despite an aversion to sequels, Newman admitted that Butch and Sundance were ideal characters for a long-running series: 'Too bad they got killed at the end, 'cause those two guys could have gone on in films for ever.'

9 American Nightmares

I think films can change the way people think in a very, very small way. They are more a reflection of our times.
  Paul Newman, 1970

The success of *Butch Cassidy and the Sundance Kid*, Newman's biggest hit since *Exodus*, took his career to new heights. Now in his mid-forties, he had never been a bigger star. Not inclined to play commercially safe, he followed *Butch Cassidy* with a more substantial drama that touched on contemporary issues. *WUSA* (1970) was a New Orleans tale of political corruption and conspiracy. Newman would play an impoverished drifter, hired as a disc jockey by a right-wing radio station.

WUSA was based on Robert Stone's novel *A Hall of Mirrors* (1966). Stone adapted the book – his first – into a screenplay for Paramount. Newman had a commitment to the studio and selected *WUSA* for its interesting, provocative ideas. While Stone's screenplay was far from perfect, it offered an uncompromising vision of a callous, unfeeling society that ruthlessly crushes its vulnerable and unwanted people. Well aware that *WUSA* would only get made with a major star attached, Newman adopted the movie as a personal project.

Reunited with John Foreman, Newman also recruited *Cool Hand Luke* director Stuart Rosenberg. His co-stars on *WUSA* included Joanne Woodward, cast as his emotionally fragile lover, who meets with a bad end. While *Winning* had dealt with cardboard characters, *WUSA* at least attempted a little depth. Newman also gave roles to Laurence Harvey, whose career had declined badly since *The Outrage* (1964), and Anthony Perkins, still trying to escape the shadow of *Psycho* (1960).

Newman had intended to retain Stone's original title, *A Hall of Mirrors*. At some point, it was decided that the radio station's call sign, 'W USA', had more resonance. *WUSA* began production in the spring of 1969, with location filming in Louisiana. Rosenberg found Woodward to be a very controlled actress, requiring little in the way of close direction or discussion. By contrast, Newman relentlessly probed and analyzed his character. Rosenberg tried to keep his star relaxed on set, damping down the thought processes. One scene required Anthony Perkins to cry. According to Perkins, when he failed to shed tears on cue, one of the production team gave him 'poppers' to moisten his eyes. Given Newman's antipathy towards the drug culture, this seems unlikely. Whatever the case, Perkins acquired a taste for poppers, which he attributed to the *WUSA* shoot.

WUSA – Rheinhardt and Geraldine (Joanne Woodward)

In June of the same year, Newman, Sidney Poitier and Barbra Streisand announced the formation of First Artists, their new production company. First Artists was the brainchild of agent Freddie Fields, co-founder of the Creative Management Agency. Significantly, all three stars were CMA clients. In theory, First Artists would give them almost full control over film projects, from conception through to release. Taking no salaries for their First Artists productions, the stars owned 10 per cent of the box-office gross. Inevitably, this venture was compared with United Artists, founded in 1919 by Douglas Fairbanks, Mary Pickford, Charles Chaplin and director D. W. Griffith. While UA still thrived fifty years on, it never brought its founders the creative and economic independence they sought. First Artists was launched at the Plaza Hotel, New York, where Newman, Poitier and Streisand signed the incorporation papers in front of the assembled press. The company offered enough star power to secure a distribution deal with Warners. The original star trio were later joined by Steve McQueen, who signed on in 1972, and Dustin Hoffman. It's been argued that Newman's work through First Artists came close to wrecking his career. Certainly, films such as *Pocket Money* (1972) and *The Life and Times of Judge Roy Bean* (1972) were not big hits. Most of the movies produced under the First Artists banner were commercial failures and the company eventually folded.

Not everyone at First Artists shared Newman's enthusiasm for *WUSA*. Creative executive Julia Phillips, who later co-produced *The Sting*, felt that Newman and John Foreman had misjudged the material's appeal. As Phillips put it, 'Wake up and smell the shit, John, *WUSA* is not where it's at right now.' She suggested Jim Thompson's crime novel *The Getaway* as a suitable First Artists project for Newman. Foreman disagreed, dismissing the book as vacuous, insignificant pulp. For the record, Phillips disliked Foreman, especially his supposed 'snotty tone' with her. In the event, Newman's First Artists partner Steve McQueen picked up *The Getaway*. Directed by Sam Peckinpah, the 1972 film proved a big hit for the star.

According to actor Robert Quarry, who played the small part of Noonan, the preview version of *WUSA* ran an epic 190 minutes. Realizing that Paramount wouldn't release a three-hour political drama, Newman and Foreman cut the film down to 117 minutes. Most of the supporting characters were reduced to walk-ons, losing much of their motivation and dramatic development.

Rooted in the social unrest of the late 1960s, *WUSA* is an attack on blind patriotism and intolerance. The film has been criticized as clichéd and pretentious. A novice screenwriter, Robert Stone doesn't develop the narrative or thematic elements, and the satirical possibilities of the material are left unexplored. By and large, *WUSA* takes itself too seriously, becoming oppressively doom-laden.

WUSA's big message concerns personal responsibility. When Rheinhardt (Newman) discovers that WUSA is a front for a neo-fascist organization, he must overcome his cynicism and political apathy. For much of the film, Rheinhardt is a selfish, if charismatic, figure. Even when stirred to action, his beliefs and motivation remain ambiguous.

On the plus side, *WUSA* is well-acted. Joanne Woodward gives a sympathetic reading of her character and Anthony Perkins contributes an outstanding performance as Rainey, a troubled social worker. Newman's scenes with Woodward have a chemistry that transcends the flawed script. Fans of *WUSA* find the film genuinely moving.

Given the troubled times, Newman expected *WUSA* to attract fierce criticism. Right-wing pundits would inevitably label it unpatriotic. While Newman and his associates remained committed to *WUSA*, Paramount had little faith in the project's commercial potential.

Angered by the studio's antipathy towards the film, Newman and Woodward went out on the publicity trail themselves. Newman put his reputation on the line, declaring *WUSA* 'The most significant film I've ever made and the best.' The publicity campaign was equally portentous. One poster design depicted the Stars and Stripes on the blade of a dagger, along with the legend 'Love it or leave it.'

WUSA premièred in New York City on 19 August 1970. As Newman predicted, many of the reviews were hostile, though critics attacked the film for its supposed pretentions rather than any political message. David Thomson compared Woodward's participation to 'a dutiful wife who goes along on the husband's fishing trips'. Stung, Woodward defended the movie: '*WUSA* is a fair statement about the country right now.' A major flop in the US, *WUSA* proved Newman's lowest grossing film to date. Ironically, he was now Hollywood's number one box-office star, thanks to *Butch Cassidy*.

While Newman was bitterly disappointed by *WUSA*'s poor reception, he seemed to concede that it suffered from a flawed, unrealized script. In one interview, Newman suggested that the cast and crew deserved points for 'making something almost good out of something that's mediocre'. *New York Times* critic Vincent Canby put the film on his Ten Worst list for 1970. Newman responded angrily, 'If he's right, I don't know my ass from a hole in the ground.'

Newman hoped that the film would find an appreciative audience in Europe, so offering a pointed rebuttal to his detractors back home. With Newman otherwise engaged, Woodward promoted the film's belated British release in the autumn of 1971. Some UK critics were impressed with *WUSA*'s ambitious agenda. Reviewing the film in *Time Out*, David Pirie praised Anthony Perkins' performance as 'less a character study than a kind of visible expression of the raw liberal conscience, a twitching, convulsive mass of uncertainty and pain'. He rated the overall film as 'one of the more important political statements to have come out of Hollywood in the early '70s'. Despite this endorsement, *WUSA* did not become a 'sleeper' hit overseas. According to some accounts, the *WUSA* experience left Newman with a permanent grudge against critics.

Interestingly, both Newman and Woodward later revised their opinions of the film. Performing a major turnaround, Woodward disowned *WUSA*: 'I don't think the film comes off, I never really liked it.' She now claimed that she'd only appeared in *WUSA* because Newman was involved and she liked the New Orleans location. On the plus side, Woodward still regarded her husband's work in the film as 'one of the best performances Paul ever gave'. Returning the compliment,

Newman praised Woodward's performance as 'very sexy, very vulnerable'. His biggest problem with the film was the overambitious script, which didn't realize the material's potential: 'It should never have been a political picture.' Newman also blamed himself for not addressing this problem during production: 'When you're an actor in a picture, you sometimes don't see where the whole thing is going . . . I should have.' In 1982, he described *WUSA* as 'a film of incredible potential, which the producer, the director and I loused up'. Interviewed in 2002, Newman had changed his mind once again: 'That film wasn't popular, but I have a great fondness for it. I love Joanne in that picture, she was so spectacular.'

Professional announcements aside, Newman remained wary of the media, citing inappropriate questions and misquotes. In fairness, he occasionally made rash statements he later regretted. Asked about his enduring marriage to Joanne Woodward, Newman famously replied, 'I have steak at home. Why should I go out for hamburger?' While no one doubted the sentiment, comparing the vegetarian Woodward with a piece of meat seemed crass. Newman later changed the comparison to a full-bodied burgundy and a cocktail. Conversely, it was easy for the press to depict Woodward's more unusual public spirited gestures as mere eccentricity. On trips to New York, she made a point of picking up trash in Central Park, assisted by whichever of the children were around. Onlookers rarely followed their lead, much to Woodward's disappointment. When the 1970s energy crisis bit, Newman and Woodward responded by ditching their 'unnecessary' electrical goods. Woodward also swapped her Mazda for a more fuel-efficient Honda. Concerned about their diets, both Woodward and Newman switched to organic foods.

The Newman–Foreman company continued to thrive, albeit in low-key fashion. Newman and John Foreman were the executive producers on *Puzzle of a Downfall Child* (1970), a Universal release. Directed by Jerry Schatzberg, a fashion photographer making his feature début, the film starred Faye Dunaway as a model recovering from a nervous breakdown. Filmed in the autumn of 1969, on New York locations, *Puzzle of a Downfall Child* was a labour of love for Schatzberg. Dunaway, a former lover, made the film for nothing. A pretentious psychodrama, the film fared poorly with critics and audiences. Nevertheless, Dunaway cites the film as a personal favourite.

They Might Be Giants (1971) reunited Newman–Foreman with Universal and *Winning* co-producer Jennings Lang. Unlike *Winning*, this unusual piece offered a substantial character part for Woodward. At the time, she commented: 'I only do films I believe in, and there aren't many of those.' As with *Puzzle of a Downfall Child*, Newman restricted his involvement to an executive role, while Foreman served as the producer.

They Might Be Giants was based on a 1964 play by James Goldman, first performed in London by Joan Littlewood's theatre company. The film version reunited Goldman with director Anthony Harvey and composer John Barry, who'd both worked with him on *The Lion in Winter* (1968).

The film co-starred George C. Scott, cast as a New York judge with a Sherlock Holmes complex. Scott's work with Newman on *The Hustler* played no part in his casting for *Giants*. While the two actors enjoyed a civil relationship, they were never close friends. No fan of the Actors Studio, Scott had little time for Method actors. According to Harvey, Newman considered playing Scott's role himself, intrigued by the part of 'Sherlock Holmes'. Aware that Goldman favoured Scott, Newman stepped aside. For the record, Harvey believes that Newman could have been 'absolutely marvellous' in the part.

Produced on a low budget, *They Might Be Giants* was largely filmed on locations in New York City. Newman turned up for the first day of shooting, to wish the cast and crew good luck. Harvey recalls Newman being 'wonderfully cheerful'. He didn't see Newman again until the first cut was assembled. Filmed during a very cold winter, *Giants* proved a physically demanding shoot. Manhattan had been hit by a garbagemen's strike, making conditions even less pleasant. While Woodward got on well with the cast and crew, she did not enjoy making *They Might Be Giants*. Weather and trash aside, her biggest problem was the film medium itself: 'You get no sense of joy.' According to Harvey, Woodward remained upbeat throughout filming, never letting her discontent show. George C. Scott, a heavy drinker with a bad reputation, was also the consummate professional.

They Might Be Giants is an offbeat romantic comedy–fantasy, the title lifted from Miguel Cervantes' *Don Quixote*. It is a hard film to categorize. The treatment is sometimes whimsical, combining slapstick and sentiment. While Goldman's script does not disguise its theatrical origins, the end result is engaging and well-acted. Woodward's portrayal of the spirited yet lonely Dr Mildred Watson is arguably her best film performance. Goldman seems to suggest that only those who defy society's conventions have the potential for true sanity and contentment. While several plot strands are left unresolved, the haunting finale is genuinely touching.

Predictably, Universal didn't know what to make of *They Might Be Giants*. The studio re-edited Harvey's cut of the film, removing several major scenes. For whatever reason, neither Newman nor Foreman championed Harvey's version. Presumably, their contract with Universal didn't entitle them to a 'producer's cut'. Sold as 'a delightfully different, slightly mad love story', *They Might Be Giants* opened in New York City on 9 June 1971. *New York Post* critic Archer Winsten described the film as 'delightful, sly, imaginative'. Despite this positive response, Universal had no faith in *Giants*, releasing it to a handful of cinemas with minimal publicity. Left to founder without studio support, *They Might Be Giants* did poorly at the box office. The film might have been more successful as a Newman–Woodward vehicle. Years later, Universal restored a three-minute sequence to *Giants* for television, video and DVD release. The other cut scenes may no longer exist.

Newman–Foreman subsequently announced plans to film Iris Murdoch's novel *A Fairly Honourable Defeat*. Retitled 'Mirror, Mirror', the screen version would star Joanne Woodward, James Mason, Louis Jourdan, Peter Ustinov and Deborah Kerr. While the actors were all enthusiastic, especially the semi-retired Kerr, the film didn't happen.

Newman's big project for Universal was *Sometimes a Great Notion* (1971), also made through Newman–Foreman. This rural saga of lumberjacks was based on a novel by cult author Ken Kesey, best known for the anti-establishment classic *One Flew Over the Cuckoo's Nest* (1963). Published in 1966, *Sometimes a Great Notion* flopped badly, prompting Kesey to abandon literature for many years. A big fan of the book, Newman quickly optioned the rights.

Sometimes a Great Notion reunited Newman with executive producer Jennings Lang, who'd worked on *Winning* and *They Might Be Giants*. From the start, Newman was torn between directing the film and starring in it. He felt that doing both was not an option, as this would require an impossible amount of preparation time. Opting to play a leading role, Newman put his faith in newcomer Richard A. Colla, a former television director. Colla had impressed Newman with his feature début, *Zigzag* (1970), an intriguing thriller starring George Kennedy, Anne Jackson and Eli Wallach. Arthur Newman Jr came on board as the unit production manager. Scott Newman would spend his summer vacation from college working with the second unit.

The distinguished cast for *Sometimes a Great Notion* included Henry Fonda, and Newman's screen wife was played by Lee Remick, his co-star from *The Long Hot Summer* (1958). Newman also cast

French-Canadian actor Michael Sarrazin, who trained at the New York Actors Studio. Under contract to Universal, Sarrazin hadn't yet achieved his career breakthrough. Both he and Remick had outstanding commitments to Universal, and *Sometimes a Great Notion* seemed the most attractive project on offer.

Sometimes a Great Notion – Hank Stamper educates half-brother Leland (Michael Sarrazin) in the ways of the lumberjack

Casting for the role of his brother, Newman settled on Richard Jaeckel, a burly character actor employed by director Robert Aldrich in *The Dirty Dozen* (1967). Jaeckel first met Newman back in the 1950s. At the time, he was acting in a West Coast production of *The Desperate Hours*, playing Newman's old role. Gracious as always, Newman complimented Jaeckel on his performance. According to Jaeckel, Newman offered him a role in *Sometimes a Great Notion* nearly two years before the film was made. Universal favoured George Kennedy, whose Oscar win for *Cool Hand Luke* had boosted his career. While Newman had no problem with Kennedy, he stuck to his original choice. Jaeckel felt that Newman cast him partly because he had the build of a lumberjack. At Newman's request, Universal agreed to two weeks of rehearsal. The cast also received basic training in logging techniques to lend their characters some authenticity.

Sometimes a Great Notion began production in the late spring of
1970 in Oregon. When the summer vacation broke, Joanne Woodward
and the girls visited Newman on the set. At the start, the working
atmosphere seemed relaxed. As Woodward discovered while shooting
A Big Hand for the Little Lady, Henry Fonda liked to do needlepoint
between takes.

Unfortunately, the on-set harmony didn't last long. Early on, there
were clashes between director Richard Colla and Fonda. Accustomed
to close, specific direction, Fonda didn't respond well to Colla's more
hands-off approach. Many in the cast felt the director was preoccupied with camera angles and set-ups, neglecting his actors. Aware of
the problem, Newman tried to help Colla, taking him aside to explain
what was required. When the director proved unresponsive, Newman
was faced with a difficult decision. Interviewed by *Films and Filming*
in 1971, Lee Remick offered her version of the events leading to
Colla's departure:

> . . . after about a month of shooting, he [Newman] and John
> Foreman, who were producing the film jointly, decided on a
> change of director. There had been what you might call a lack of
> meeting of minds between them and the original director. So Paul
> took over . . .

Newman explained that Colla 'didn't understand the subject in the
way I thought he should'. Fonda felt that Newman resisted firing
Colla, knowing he would have to take over the direction. Reluctant to
assume the dual role he'd dismissed as impractical, Newman asked
George Roy Hill to replace Colla. When Hill declined, Newman
approached Paul Bogart, another director friend. Bogart also turned
down the job, obliging Newman to bow to the inevitable. Calling a
crisis meeting for the cast and crew, Newman made the big announcement. Rather than abandon the film, he would reluctantly take on the
role of director. Nervous of the task ahead, he humbly requested his
colleagues' assistance and understanding: 'I'm gonna need all the help
you can give me.' Hill agreed to look at 15,000 feet of film shot by
Colla, which Newman hadn't even seen. Over three days, Hill ran the
footage and cut it together, telling Newman which shots he needed to
complete the sequences.

As Newman feared, directing himself in a film proved hard work.
Focused on the other actors, he missed his own cue during one lengthy
take. Away from the set, he crashed his motorbike, breaking an ankle.
This injury held up shooting, putting the film behind schedule and
over budget. Under considerable pressure, Newman hit the hard

liquor after hours, though this heavy drinking never affected his work on set. Impressed by Newman's dedication and tenacity, the cast and crew remained loyal, and principal photography was finished in mid-autumn 1970.

Sometimes a Great Notion is the story of a logging family, headed by aging patriarch Henry Stamper (Henry Fonda). Fiercely independent, the Stampers have little regard for popular opinion or union dictates. When they refuse to join a local strike, events turn tragic. The drowning scene that drew Newman to Kesey's novel is also the film's most powerful sequence: Joe Ben Stamper (Richard Jaeckel) is trapped underwater by logs, with Hank Stamper (Newman) unable to save him.

Promoting *Sometimes a Great Notion*, Newman explained the attraction of the subject matter: 'I wanted to do the picture because, like so many of my best pictures – I'm thinking of *Hud* and *Hombre* especially – it shows the life of simple Americans.' Even the right-wing critics who loathed *WUSA* would like his new movie, 'it's so much a picture of grassroots America'. Newman's commitment to *Sometimes a Great Notion* was not matched by Universal, who released the film with minimal advertising. It opened in New York to some positive reviews. *Time* critic Jay Cocks declared that 'Newman is better than he has been in years . . .' Writing in *New York* magazine, Judith Crist praised Newman's direction: '. . . he shows that he can go beyond the introspection and sensitivities of *Rachel, Rachel*, and deal with the harsh primitivism of man and nature'. Despite this acclaim, *Sometimes a Great Notion* did poorly at the box office. Faced with meagre returns, Universal pulled the film from distribution. Relaunched under the new title *Never Give an Inch*, the Stamper family motto, the lumberjack saga floundered once more. Co-star Richard Jaeckel later suggested that audiences wouldn't accept Newman as a loser. On top of the production problems and disappointing box office, Newman had to deal with his restless son. After finishing work on *Sometimes a Great Notion*, Scott dropped out of college and rented an apartment, where he lived alone.

Newman hoped that *Sometimes a Great Notion* would win favour with the Academy Awards committee. In the event, Jaeckel was nominated in the Best Supporting Actor category, which revived his career but did little for the film. It's been suggested that Newman expected a nomination for himself, whether as star or director, and resented the Academy's lack of recognition. On the bright side, Henry Fonda regarded his performance as the best of his career. Newman remained proud of *Sometimes a Great Notion*, 'a much better film than its popularity would signify'.

Having struck out with *WUSA* and *Sometimes a Great Notion*, Newman risked losing the box-office allure bestowed by *Butch Cassidy*. Committed to heavyweight dramas, he missed out on at least two major hits. Originally a vehicle for Frank Sinatra, *Dirty Harry* (1971) had been offered to Newman, Steve McQueen, John Wayne and Robert Mitchum. Newman quickly passed, ostensibly on the grounds that the character was too 'scruffy'. It seems more likely that Newman had a problem with the script's questionable politics. The role of Inspector Harry Callahan eventually went to Clint Eastwood, who, according to some sources, was suggested for the part by Newman. When *The French Connection* (1971) came along, Newman was considered for the role of rogue cop Jimmy 'Popeye' Doyle. Robert Mitchum, *Hustler* co-star Jackie Gleason and character actor Peter Boyle also made the shortlist. Director William Friedkin eventually settled on the relatively unknown Gene Hackman. Despite his recent box-office flops, Newman finished 1971 at number three in the 'Top Ten' list of film stars, behind John Wayne and Clint Eastwood. Steve McQueen came in at number four.

Newman attempted a curious change of image with *Pocket Money* (1972), a First Artists production distributed through Warner Brothers. Working with producer John Foreman and director Stuart Rosenberg, Newman cast himself as a small-time loser who keeps on losing. The film was based on a novel, *Jim Kane*, by J. P. S. Brown. The screenplay was assigned to John Gay, who'd adapted *Sometimes a Great Notion*. When Gay's script proved disappointing, Newman and Foreman hired a promising newcomer called Terrence Malick.[1]

The script for *Pocket Money* required a heavyweight co-star. First Artists approached Lee Marvin, who had appeared opposite Newman in *The Rack* (1956). Since the late 1950s, Marvin had steadily worked his way up from supporting actor to leading man. He finally broke through with the comic western *Cat Ballou* (1965), winning an Academy Award for his dual role, and the blockbuster success of *The Dirty Dozen* (1967) established him as one of Hollywood's hottest stars.

Newman personally asked Marvin to star with him in *Pocket Money*, a flattering invitation. Marvin liked the revised script, praising Malick as a 'brilliant guy'. He was also taken with the idea of playing a loser, especially alongside Newman, a major box-office star. Marvin even took a pay cut to make the film, accepting $500,000 up front, plus 20 per cent of the profits. Keen to have Marvin on board, Newman agreed to co-star in a second film of Marvin's choice. Marvin's contract for *Pocket Money* specified equal billing with Newman. First

Artists and Warner employed the compromise 'staggered billing' arrangement, originally proposed for Newman and Steve McQueen on *Butch Cassidy and the Sundance Kid*: Newman's name went on the left, with Marvin's on the right, slightly higher.

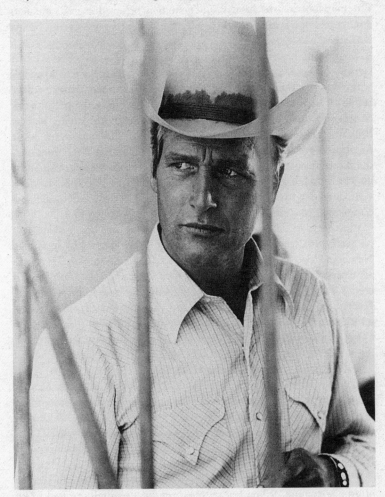

Pocket Money – Jim Kane

Initially retaining the source novel's title, *Jim Kane, Pocket Money* was filmed in the spring of 1971 in New Mexico and Arizona. Relations between Newman and Marvin seemed relaxed. Marvin remained enthusiastic about the project, telling his wife Pamela, 'Baby, you will never be on a better film in your whole life!' When Newman proved reluctant to wear a stetson, Marvin persuaded his co-star that it looked good on him. Pamela Marvin liked John Foreman, 'a humorous, gently-spoken "gentleman producer"'. A rarity in the business, Foreman looked after his cast and genuinely believed in art as much as commerce. She was also taken with the similarly soft-spoken Stuart Rosenberg.

Rosenberg described working with Marvin as 'a marvellous experience'. Director and star got on well, clashing only once. Marvin's stunt double, Bud Stout, was fired mid-shoot, presumably to save money. On location in Ajo, Arizona, Marvin turned up for work hopelessly drunk. Filming had to be delayed, Rosenberg sending Marvin back to his hotel. Pamela Marvin guessed that her husband hit the bottle to protest at Stout's dismissal. Whatever his intentions, Stout was quickly reinstated. Marvin also broke his toe on the leg of a hotel couch. Scheduled to film a dance scene, with Pupe Bocar, he stoically went ahead with the demanding routine. When the sequence was completed, Marvin's boot had to be cut off his swollen foot.

According to Pamela Marvin, both Newman and her husband got on well with the cast and crew, neither playing the big star. Like Newman, Marvin was a consummate professional, knowledgeable in all aspects of film-making. Discussing their late fathers, the stars discovered a lot of common ground, notably unresolved feelings and the never-ending search for approval. Marvin also shared much of Newman's political outlook, including his belief in the Civil Rights movement. In 1960, he supported John F. Kennedy's presidential campaign, attending the Democrat convention in Los Angeles. Unlike Newman, he had never become a high-profile liberal activist.

However, their attitudes to film-making certainly differed. Marvin biographer Donald Zec describes Newman as a slave to his star image. Newman's early morning fitness regime involved sit-ups, swimming and the sauna. Marvin, by contrast, was not a natural early riser. Once up and about, Marvin liked to stay on set, even if he wasn't needed. He felt this helped him get a handle on the continuity of the film.

While Marvin liked to hang out with the crew, Newman seemed unusually remote. When not required on set, he usually retired to his trailer, reading and listening to classical music, or relaxed in his portable sauna. Staying at La Fonda Hotel in Santa Fe, Newman blew the building's electricity supply when he plugged in the sauna. Significantly, he had recently sworn off hard liquor, one reason he preferred not to socialize with the hard-drinking Marvin. Questioned at the time, Newman didn't elaborate on his motives: 'I just decided to stop.' There'd never been any major press coverage of his drinking, despite his arrest back in 1956. It's possible that Newman's heavy drinking while filming *Sometimes a Great Notion* proved a turning point. Now that Scott had an alcohol problem, Newman didn't want to contribute to it by poor example. That said, he remained a dedicated beer drinker, lending his name to overseas campaigns for Coors and Budweiser.

Newman and Joanne Woodward made another major change to their lifestyle in 1971. Woodward had grown disenchanted with Los Angeles, sick of the pollution levels and ever-present earthquake threat. The major earth tremor of 9 February 1971, which registered 6.5 on the Richter scale and killed 65 people, proved the last straw. The couple sold their Los Angeles home, quitting the city for several years.

Pocket Money's final scene was also the last to be shot, at a railway station in Santa Fe, New Mexico. Unhappy with the scripted dialogue, Newman wanted to improvise the closing exchanges between himself and Marvin. This wasn't Marvin's style, especially with a script he liked. According to Zec, Woodward was due to pass through the station that day en route to New York. The company had arranged for the train to slow down, enabling Woodward to wave at Newman from her carriage. When the time grew near, filming ground to a halt, the cast and crew ready to greet Woodward. Unimpressed by this display, Marvin absented himself from the line-up.

After viewing the rough cut of *Pocket Money*, Newman supposedly offered Marvin a $1-million flat fee in exchange for his percentage points. By the time the film completed post-production, Marvin wished he'd accepted the deal. He felt that some of his best scenes had been heavily cut, losing much of the humour. Newman had deleted the entire dance scene, which Marvin had filmed under great duress. Interviewed by Jim Sirmans, Marvin made little attempt at diplomacy: 'It was Paul Newman's production company. By the time they cut the footage, Newman was the star. I dunno. I guess the old ego got the best of him.'

One-upmanship aside, Marvin felt disappointed with the finished film. Interviewed by *Rolling Stone* reporter Grover Lewis, he explained, 'We had it – we got it all down on film and it just didn't get on the screen.' For whatever reason, Newman had wasted a golden opportunity: 'He got the dough together, so if he wants to cut the finesse points out, he can do anything he wants.' Needless to say, plans for a second Newman–Marvin movie came to nothing. According to Pamela Marvin, Stuart Rosenberg was also unhappy with the final cut, even calling a meeting to protest at Newman's 'butchery'. The director assured Marvin that he'd had no say in the release print. Newman wouldn't work with Rosenberg again until *The Drowning Pool*.

There's not enough of anything in *Pocket Money*: character, story, humour or atmosphere. Newman seems ill-cast, giving an uncertain performance. The acting mechanics seen in some of his early movies are clearly visible here. Rosenberg shoots Newman from unflattering low angles, presumably an attempt to undercut the star's charisma. Newman is out-acted by Marvin, who looks far more assured as the twitchy, hard-drinking Leonard. Marvin's mannered acting style works well for the character, boisterous rather than aggressive. Unfortunately, Leonard is very much a supporting figure in the existing film, the character's potential unrealized. A number of Marvin's scenes end abruptly, lending credence to his claims of drastic cutting. While Newman seems an unlikely candidate for professional jealousy, he can't have been happy watching Marvin steal the movie. For whatever reason, the qualities Marvin saw in Malick's script didn't make it to the finished movie. *Pocket Money* doesn't so much end as fade away.

Pocket Money opened in the US on 1 February 1972. The reviews were mostly dismissive and the film flopped at the box office. Editing disputes aside, Rosenberg felt *Pocket Money* failed because of the very quality that attracted Marvin: the paying public wouldn't accept Newman and Marvin as losers. 'You could just feel the audience leaving,' he commented. A decade later, Newman attributed the film's failure to a flawed screenplay: 'Loved the character, the script never came together though.' The famously reclusive Terrence Malick declined to comment.

Forced to turn actor–director on *Sometimes a Great Notion*, Newman remained firmly behind the camera for *The Effect of Gamma Rays on Man-in-the-Moon Marigolds* (1972). This harrowing domestic drama is based on a Pulitzer Prize-winning play by Paul Zindel, written in 1965 but not performed on stage until 1970. Like *Rachel, Rachel*, *Gamma Rays* was primarily a vehicle for Joanne Woodward. However, second time around, Newman and Woodward misjudged the appeal of their central character.

The *Gamma Rays* project had an unusual genesis. Woodward found a book, Violet Weingarten's *Mrs Beneker* (1968), which she thought would make a good film. A deal for the rights was negotiated through agent Gil Parker, whose clients included author and playwright Paul Zindel. Parker suggested Zindel as a good choice to adapt *Mrs Beneker*. Having scored an off-Broadway hit with *Gamma Rays*, Zindel welcomed the chance to break into feature films.

Zindel got on well with Woodward and Newman, both professionally and socially. He admired the way Newman dealt with public
attention. He noted that the star refused to sign autographs under any
circumstances. According to old friend A. E. Hotchner, 'The majesty
of the act is offensive to him.' (For the record, Newman has signed
photographs, laserdiscs, DVDs and even ice-hockey pucks.) Trips to
the theatre were problematic, as Newman was always pestered by
fans. Unable to concentrate on the actual play, he sometimes gave up,
leaving during the interval. As he pointed out, 'Nobody can come to
respect and love their anonymity until they've lost it.'

With the *Mrs Beneker* project still at an early stage, Woodward and
Newman saw a performance of *Gamma Rays*. Both of them were
struck by the play's emotional impact. Zindel had drawn inspiration
from his traumatic childhood. His father, a policeman, abandoned the
family when Zindel was two. Zindel's mother, a qualified nurse, also
worked as a cloakroom attendant and hot-dog vendor. She supplemented this three-fold income by letting rooms to dying patients. The
central character in *Gamma Rays*, a middle-aged woman disappointed
by life, seemed tailor-made for Woodward. Sensing a great opportunity, Woodward and Newman asked Zindel for the film rights. A big
fan of *Rachel, Rachel*, Zindel thought Woodward and Newman would
be 'perfect' as the star and director of the film. With this in mind, he
sold the rights for $65,000, a modest sum given the play's Pulitzer Prize-
winning status. Perhaps tired of Universal's apathy, Newman–Foreman
made a production–distribution deal with Twentieth Century Fox.

Busy with the *Mrs Beneker* script, Zindel declined to handle the
screen adaptation of *Gamma Rays*, so Newman hired ex-television
writer Alvin Sargent. Ironically, Woodward rejected Zindel's first draft
of *Mrs Beneker*, arguing that she hadn't 'found' the character.

The role of Woodward's young daughter went to Elinor Newman, her
oldest child in real life. Having appeared briefly in *Rachel, Rachel*, Elinor showed no apparent interest in acting again. Nevertheless, she
agreed to co-star opposite her mother in *Gamma Rays*, still using her
'Nell Potts' pseudonym. Her big sister would be played by Roberta Wallach, daughter of Actors Studio veterans Eli Wallach and Anne Jackson.

Newman intended to shoot *Gamma Rays* on location in Staten
Island, the setting for Zindel's play. When union problems proved
insurmountable, he moved the production to Bridgeport, Connecticut,
closer to home. Working with a tight schedule and budget, Newman
rehearsed his cast for two weeks. The interiors were filmed inside an
abandoned parsonage rather than an actual studio. During location

shooting, crowds invariably gathered to look at Newman. Newman had a good working relationship with Elinor, despite her lack of acting experience: 'It's easy to direct her . . . Her quality not as a performer, but as a person carries her through.' Roberta Wallach praised Newman's open approach to directing: 'Paul lets you find your own way to do it.'

Having taken on a difficult, emotionally draining role, Joanne Woodward prepared herself for an arduous shoot. She dyed her hair a mousy shade of brown, feeling that the character of Beatrice had long lost her sense of self-worth. She also wore her mother's old clothes, dyed an 'icky' colour, to reflect Beatrice's lack of esteem. Unfortunately, her deep loathing for Beatrice affected her own state of mind: 'I was so depressed and suicidal during that film I couldn't stand it . . . I came close to sheer insanity.' During filming, Woodward argued with Newman over her interpretation of the character, worried she was missing the humour and pathos that balanced the monstrosity.

Woodward's inability to distance herself from Beatrice also caused problems off the set. Exhausted after each day's filming, she found it hard to deal with a house full of lively, demanding children. Shooting in Staten Island, far from home, would have suited her better. When filming finished, she drove to their New York apartment, leaving the family behind in Connecticut. Both physically and mentally worn out by her *Gamma Rays* role, Woodward intended to unwind with a few days on her own. The first night, she woke up at 4.00 a.m., screaming, later describing the feeling as 'like some terrible, demonic possession'. Panicking, she called Newman, who raced over to the apartment. Despite her commitment to *Gamma Rays*, she regretted making the film: 'That is the one picture I wish I hadn't done . . . it had a terrible effect on me . . . That picture left scars.'

The Effect of Gamma Rays on Man-in-the-Moon Marigolds is a claustrophobic character study, short on light and humour. Beatrice (Joanne Woodward), a reclusive single mother, lives with her two daughters, Ruth (Roberta Wallach) and Matilda (Elinor Newman). Resentful and unhappy, Beatrice loses herself in fantasies of a better life. She vents her frustrations on the children, acting in a cruel, abusive fashion. Compared to *Rachel, Rachel*, Newman's direction seems more refined yet less engaging. Woodward's powerhouse performance becomes hard to take, perhaps a reflection of her success at creating a repellent character. At its best, *Gamma Rays* is an unsentimental look at stunted, empty lives, lifted by small moments of happiness. Ruth's limited ambition, focused on cheerleading and sex, will lead her down Beatrice's path. The intelligent, introverted Matilda has more potential, symbolized by the school-science project of the title.

The Effect of Gamma Rays on Man-in-the-Moon Marigolds – Beatrice (Joanne Woodward) comforts Ruth (Roberta Wallach) while Matilda (Elinor Newman) looks on

In late 1972, Newman invited Paul Zindel to a screening of the rough cut. By this time, the *Mrs Beneker* project had been shelved, which inevitably cooled Zindel's relationship with Woodward. Hardly the most objective observer, the playwright came away from *Gamma Rays* sorely disappointed. Watching the film without sound effects or music, Zindel had reservations about the pace: 'It seemed slow to me. Very slow.' He publicly criticized the casting of Elinor Newman as a bad example of nepotism. The role required a real actress, not an inexperienced amateur. Nevertheless, *Time Out* critic Gilbert Adair felt that Elinor Newman stole the film.

Interestingly, Paramount asked Paul and Elinor Newman to co-star in *Paper Moon* (1973), playing father-and-daughter con artists in Depression-era Kansas. Scripted by *Gamma Rays* writer Alvin Sargent, the film was based on Joe David Brown's acclaimed novel *Addie Pray*. Assured that Elinor wasn't being cast for her gimmick value, Newman gave a provisional commitment to the project. Unfortunately, studio politics soon caused problems. The original director was dropped in favour of *wunderkind* Peter Bogdanovich, a major Hollywood player after *The Last Picture Show* (1971) and *What's Up Doc?* (1972). Wary of Bogdanovich's *auteur* status – and wildly inflated ego – Newman withdrew from the production, taking Elinor with him. Undaunted, Bogdanovich cast *What's Up Doc?* star Ryan O'Neal and his daughter Tatum, who went on to win an Academy Award for her performance.

The Effect of Gamma Rays on Man-in-the-Moon Marigolds opened in New York City on 20 December 1972, going on general release in early 1973. The film drew largely negative reviews, even for Joanne Woodward. While *Rachel, Rachel* had been lauded as a personal triumph for both Woodward and Newman, *Gamma Rays* quickly faded from view and, still sore from the critical mauling of *WUSA*, Newman took this failure badly. It fared better in Europe though, Woodward taking the Best Actress prize at the 1973 Cannes Film Festival.

A few years later, Paul Zindel watched *Gamma Rays* again on network television. Second time around, he liked it much more. He felt the film worked better on a small screen, broken up by commercials. Far from disrupting the carefully achieved mood, the adverts 'added considerably to the film'. While it's hard to read this as an outright compliment, Zindel appreciated elements of the film he'd previously dismissed. Woodward's performance seemed 'less strenuous, less transparent' and even Elinor Newman was adequate. Interviewed in the late 1980s, Zindel offered an unqualified endorsement of the film, praising Woodward and Newman for their impressive achievement: 'It was very sensitively done and very carefully thought out.' Ironically, Newman begged to differ, feeling he'd mishandled the material: 'Too much theater and not enough cinema. I screwed up there.'

Newman's children from his first marriage continued to cause him angst. While Scott remained an ongoing concern, Newman also clashed with Susan, his oldest daughter. More resilient than Scott, Susan Newman had her share of traumas. She became seriously ill after a crash diet, losing forty pounds in as many days through fasting. During her late teens, a love affair with an older man drew family disapproval. Far from being promiscuous, Susan was wary of losing her virginity, worried that potential lovers were attracted by her family celebrity. In one interview, she suggested that her famous father and his second family didn't live in the real world. While Newman never played the superstar, people invariably gave him special treatment; his celebrity got him off a speeding ticket at least once. Aggressive fans would push the Newman children aside to get a look at their idol. Interviewed for *Time* magazine in 1982, Susan still seemed fazed by the experience:

> It was pretty bewildering when we'd go out to dinner and 300 crazed women would approach our table . . . even in the fields of Italy, these kerchiefed people looking over the vines would be crying 'Paul-o Newman.' It wears you down. It's tiring.

One particular gripe was Newman's inconsistent attitude to money. After Susan graduated from high school, he happily paid for her to visit Europe. When it came to paying her air fare from Los Angeles to Connecticut, he complained about the cost. In Susan's view, life for the Newman children was frequently 'draining' and 'painful'.

Unhappy with this open criticism, Newman conceded that he'd made plenty of mistakes as a parent: 'I was all over the place, too loving one minute, too distant the next . . . It was very hard for them to get a balance.' Kept at arm's length emotionally by his own father, Newman was determined not to treat his children the same way. As a result, he sometimes overcompensated, before retreating into aloofness. He admitted that his personal hang-ups probably affected his parenting skills: 'Maybe I could have behaved consistently with the kids if I had felt consistently good about myself.' Prone to occasional bad moods, he realized he could be an intimidating figure to his children. Interviewed in 1982, Newman felt he'd been a good father 'in flashes' only.

10 Nostalgia Trips

For Texas and Miss Lillie!
  Judge Roy Bean

During the early 1970s, Newman was linked to numerous film projects which never saw the light of day, such as *Hillman* and *Where the Dark Streets Go*. Disappointed with the response to his recent work, both commercial and critical, Newman now looked for a strong script with obvious box-office appeal. He found what he wanted in a screenplay by John Milius, a newcomer with a handful of credits. Three years after *Butch Cassidy and the Sundance Kid*, Newman headed out West once more for *The Life and Times of Judge Roy Bean* (1972), his first film with veteran director John Huston.

The historical Roy Bean (1823–1903) was a legendary figure of the Old West. Born in Mason County, Kentucky, Bean drifted south to Vinegaroon, Texas, where he set up shop as a maverick lawman.[1]

John Milius had been active in Hollywood since the late 1960s, working for American International Pictures after a stint at the USC film school. He developed a script that became *Jeremiah Johnson* (1972), one of Robert Redford's better vehicles. Milius saw *Judge Roy Bean* as his big Hollywood break, the story of 'a man going off to a primitive culture and becoming a legend and a god'. Originally, he hoped to direct the film himself, and his first choice for Bean was character actor Warren Oates, best known for the Sam Peckinpah westerns.

Newman and John Foreman liked Milius's script, paying him an impressive $300,000. *Judge Roy Bean* became a First Artists production, with distribution through National General. However, Newman and Foreman had no interest in Milius as a director, even when he offered to take a 50 per cent pay cut. Newman wanted a more experienced hand, settling on Hollywood legend John Huston.[2] Huston respected Newman as a 'venturesome' actor: 'He likes playing dissimilar roles; this reflects his imagination and his willingness to take a flier.' The director also admired Newman's readiness to fail, rather than play it safe: 'He hits and misses.' Much like Huston himself. Huston also rated Newman, alongside Orson Welles and Charles Chaplin, as one of the few actors to successfully turn director. In his autobiography, he praised Milius's *Roy Bean* script for its 'splendid feeling for the old West'. He liked the offbeat humour, which had 'a weird and wonderful extravagance'. In Huston's opinion, *Judge Roy Bean* promised to be 'a lark of a picture'.[3]

Filmed in late 1971, *The Life and Times of Judge Roy Bean* had a $4-million budget and a ten-week schedule. Newman regarded the shoot as 'one of the best experiences I've had as an actor'. Initially, he felt overawed by John Huston: 'I always considered him such an artist. I felt very bourgeois around him. One always feels a certain sense of uneasiness around a man of genius.' In the event, director and star got on well together, enjoying what Newman termed an 'instant under-standing'. Newman regarded Huston as a total professional: 'Obvious-ly, John's a man with a functioning ego, but that ego never intrudes upon his work.' It helped that Huston was a gregarious maverick rather than an inflexible disciplinarian like Otto Preminger or Alfred Hitchcock. Or Arthur Newman Sr. Newman ranked Huston alongside Robert Rossen and George Roy Hill: 'He had that wonderful gift that is the mark of a good director: to speak when necessary and let his actors fly, if they were flying.' Huston's favourite piece of direction was 'Do what feels right.' When actress Victoria Principal uninten-tionally questioned Huston's authority on set, she received a stern lecture from Newman. In return, Huston praised Newman as 'one of the most gifted actors I've ever known'. Given Huston's previous work with Humphrey Bogart, Peter Lorre, Bette Davis, Edward G. Robinson, Katharine Hepburn, Deborah Kerr, Robert Mitchum, Burt Lancaster, Montgomery Clift, Richard Burton, Marlon Brando and his own father, Walter Huston, this was praise indeed. Years later, Huston cited Newman as a flawless talent:

> Acting on intuition, he'll come to instant decisions that stand all the tests of logic afterward. As a performer, he's capable of those quick transformations of personality that amount to the change of a mask.

Huston also liked Newman personally: 'His political and artistic opinions are invariably correct, and his insights are rare indeed.' Unlike Hitchcock and Preminger, Huston welcomed Newman's input and suggestions. During production on *Judge Roy Bean*, Newman told Huston that he'd rather be a racing driver than an actor. Huston was amused by this revelation, '. . . which I put down at the time as one of those idle dreams we all have'.

According to Milius, Huston drank straight vodka throughout the production, which might explain his playful mood. As usual, Newman was more easygoing with his co-workers. Victoria Principal praised her leading man as 'out of this world', babysitting for Newman and Woodward when the family dropped in. Other visitors to the set included Clint Eastwood and Marlon Brando, who'd worked with Huston on *Reflections in a Golden Eye* (1967).

Unlike Newman, screenwriter John Milius found working with Huston a traumatic experience. He felt Newman had chosen badly in hiring Huston: 'I don't think he was terribly interested in making the movie.' Despite his later comments, Huston showed scant respect for Milius's script, announcing that he would make 'a turd smell sweet'. Milius claimed that Huston 'blackmailed' him into making changes. If Milius refused, Huston's longtime assistant Gladys Hill would take over. Interviewed for *Film Comment* in 1976, Milius explained: 'We had a strange relationship. He tortured me constantly, changing things and doing scenes, I thought, deliberately wrong.' While Huston was happy to explain his choices to Milius, he never asked for advice. Significantly, the writing credit on *Judge Roy Bean* reads 'Original screenplay John Milius', suggesting subsequent revisions. Sidelined from the production, Milius was tempted to leave: 'I could have walked off, left them to ruin it, which they did anyway.' In the event, he stayed around for the entire shoot, bound by his sense of duty. He later cast Huston in his film, *The Wind and the Lion* (1975), which some interpreted as an act of revenge.

By the time 'guest star' Jacqueline Bisset turned up on location, the script tussles were largely resolved. Required only for the climactic scenes, Bisset spent just two weeks working on the film. Unfortunately, Huston had fallen ill. At Huston's suggestion, Newman directed all of Bisset's scenes. Out of respect for Huston, Newman's directorial contribution was not publicized. By late summer 1972, *Judge Roy Bean* was in post-production.

According to Milius, *The Life and Times of Judge Roy Bean* is a classic example of a fine script ruined by Hollywood incompetence. Milius intended *Judge Roy Bean* to have a much 'tougher, harder tone', in the cynical style of Sergio Leone's spaghetti westerns. He envisaged Bean as a harsh, authoritarian figure in the General Patton mould. Like the overall film, Newman's Judge was 'too soft and too cute'. During filming, Milius became convinced that Newman and Foreman wanted to make another *Butch Cassidy*. Significantly, Newman wore the same derby hat he'd used in the George Roy Hill hit. For his part, Newman claimed that Milius's original script would have made a 'pretty boring' film. In his view, 'Huston gave it class,' not to mention a new, outrageous quality. Huston wanted to bring a fragmented, illogical, arbitrary feel to the story. As the director explained, 'I loved the audacity of the film.' Huston biographer Axel Madsen claims that Newman felt nervous about playing Roy Bean, regarding Milius's character as too raunchy and immoral. Under the circumstances, it was inevitable that Bean would be toned down. In fairness, Milius didn't write with film stars' sensibilities in mind. His original script for *Jeremiah Johnson* had the title character eating his enemies' livers, something notably absent from the Robert Redford movie.

Many regard *The Life and Times of Judge Roy Bean* as an inferior copy of *Butch Cassidy*, Newman failing to capture the spirit and charm of the earlier film. It's true that *Judge Roy Bean* has a more frivolous feel, thanks to the episodic structure, broad humour and abrupt shifts in tone. That said, the film is both imaginative and enjoyable, and individual scenes have an undeniable power. While *Butch Cassidy* is more consistent and assured, *Judge Roy Bean* offers a potent vision of the Old West supplanted by creeping civilization.

Extremely well shot by Richard Moore, the film rivals *Butch Cassidy* for visual flair and stylistic quirks. Huston employs fast-motion, straight-to-camera addresses, multiple voice-overs, freeze-frames and sepia stills. Much of the narration is provided by bartender Tector Crites (Ned Beatty), though this isn't immediately obvious. The most obvious lift from *Butch Cassidy* is the musical break, Andy Williams singing 'Marmalade, Molasses and Honey' while Bean and his Mexican lover Maria Elena (Victoria Principal) enjoy their rural idyll. The agreeably cynical script becomes downright sentimental in its depiction of Maria Elena. Clearly, both Milius and Huston wanted to treat their one major Mexican character with appropriate respect. The more memorable cameo appearances include John Huston's Grizzly Adams. Looking for a good place to die, the fatalistic Adams dumps one of his bears on Roy Bean.

Newman's Judge Roy Bean cuts an imposing figure, distinguished by his scruffy beard, crooked neck and low growl. Bean is not so much a man as a shadow or ghost, crossing into the realm of myth after a close encounter with the noose. Equally at home in a bowler hat and sombrero, he promotes his own brand of justice and patriotism, literally draping himself in the Stars and Stripes. He's also a hopeless romantic, singing 'Yellow Rose of Texas' as he dreams of the unattainable Lillie Langtry. Lost outside his own territory, Bean quickly falls prey to city slickers. Some feel that Newman miscast himself as Bean. Biographer Susan Netter suggests western veteran John Wayne as a better choice for the role. However, it's unlikely that Wayne would have appreciated the film's offbeat style and satirical edge. Furthermore, Wayne had no wish to work with Huston again after their fraught relationship on *The Barbarian and the Geisha* (1958). Newman isn't obvious casting for Bean, a role tailor-made for Warren Oates or Sterling Hayden. That said, he does well with the part, turning Bean into a likeable anti-hero without glossing over his less attractive traits.

The Life and Times of Judge Roy Bean – Roy Bean and his Watch Bear (Bruno)

In terms of Bean's character, the much-debated rewrites probably help the film. In Milius's script, Bean is an amoral schemer, embracing the new civilization – embodied by the advancing railroad – and betraying his old friends. Newman's Bean is a more sympathetic figure, who values loyalty above all else. According to Huston and Jacqueline Bisset, Newman regarded Roy Bean as one of his best performances. It's certainly among his most memorable. Inevitably, Bean becomes an anachronism in the community he built, both embarrassing and dangerous. Lawyer Frank Gass (Roddy McDowall) represents the modern world, regarded by Milius as shrewd, crafty, Machiavellian and anonymous. Betrayed by his own men, Bean leaves Vinegaroon, a sad, if proud outcast. With Bean gone, Gass quickly takes control. Twenty years later, a mysterious stranger arrives in town.

John Huston saw *Judge Roy Bean* as an allegory on 'the vengeance of the past'. In Milius's script, Bean dies saving his daughter Rose (Jacqueline Bisset), who never discovers her saviour's true identity. Dispensing with this downbeat ending, Huston and Newman also pare down Bean's dialogue, underlining his status as a mythic figure from the Old West. Newman's make-up, courtesy of Monty Westmore, emphasizes his ghostly quality. Building up the tension, the film explodes into a well-staged gun battle. A brave but helpless bystander in Milius's script, Rose now gets a piece of the action, and Jacqueline Bisset gives a spirited performance. Judge Roy Bean goes out in a blaze of glory, destroying the community he built. The corrupt, oil-soaked town is burned to the ground, Bean vanishing into legend.

While Newman rated the first three quarters of *Judge Roy Bean* as 'classic', he had problems with the last act: 'We never came to grips with the ending.' In his opinion, 'the final fifteen minutes are the most important of any movie'. Whatever Newman had in mind, the existing finale seems an appropriate, satisfying pay-off. In this instance, at least, Newman and Huston improved on Milius's script.

National General did a hard sell on *The Life and Times of Judge Roy Bean*, inviting comparisons with *Butch Cassidy*. It opened in the US on 18 December 1972, receiving mixed reviews, including a thumbs-up from Judith Crist, writing in *New York Magazine*: 'As smooth and entertaining as "Butch Cassidy", what with Newman providing a dandy bravura performance.'

Judge Roy Bean did disappointing business, falling well short of *Butch Cassidy*'s success. The film grossed $5 million in the US and Canada, barely recovering its production costs. Newman attributed the poor box office to the weak ending: 'Maybe it had no ending. But if we had found one, then the picture might have been a serious classic.' John Huston had a more balanced perspective on the movie: 'I thought it was a quite well-done film . . . in the fine old American tradition of the Tall Tale . . . At the same time, it said something important about frontier life and the loss of America's innocence.'

Taking advantage of the positive reviews for Newman, National General pushed his performance for Oscar consideration. Newman hadn't received an Academy Award nomination since *Cool Hand Luke*. However, westerns rarely did well with the Academy and *Judge Roy Bean* proved no exception. Ironically, the song 'Marmalade, Molasses and Honey' was nominated, which must have delighted John Milius. Around the same time, Marlon Brando emerged from a decade in the wilderness with *The Godfather* (1972) and *Last Tango in Paris* (1972). The former netted Brando an Academy Award, which he rejected in protest at the treatment of Native Americans. At the time, Newman must have wondered if Brando would reclaim his position as the pre-eminent American film actor. Both *Godfather* and *Last Tango* were motion-picture events, celebrated and condemned the world over. By contrast, Newman's recent films had barely caused a ripple.

Having found a kindred spirit in John Huston, Newman recruited the director for his next starring vehicle, *The Mackintosh Man* (1973). This unremarkable spy drama is a classic example of a film being made for all the wrong reasons, with both Newman and scriptwriter Walter Hill having outstanding commitments to Warner Brothers. Though by no means terrible, the movie showed how variable Newman's decision making was.

Under contract to Warners, Hill's relationship with the studio soured after a row over money. He wrote the *Mackintosh Man* script, based on Desmond Bagley's novel *The Freedom Trap*, to get out of his contract. Offered a selection of Warner properties, a resentful Hill chose the one he considered least suitable as film material. Having knocked together a script in five days, he was amazed when Newman and John Foreman showed an interest. The relative failure of *Judge Roy Bean* left Newman in need of a hit, so when Warner suggested *The Mackintosh Man*, Newman decided to go with it. Spy movies often did well at the box office, though the downbeat school of espionage lacked the appeal of the James Bond franchise.

Looking for a sympathetic director, Newman first offered the job to Robert Wise, who'd set him on the road to stardom with *Somebody Up There Likes Me*. While Newman supposedly made a formal offer to Wise, the director has no recollection of the project, suggesting their discussions didn't get very far.

When Wise turned down *Mackintosh Man*, Newman tried a few more directors before approaching John Huston. After shooting wrapped on *Judge Roy Bean*, Newman announced: 'If John Huston ever wants to direct another one of my pictures, he's got it.' Ironically, Huston had no pressing desire to direct *The Mackintosh Man*. Like Wise, he thought little of the weak script, which lacked a proper ending. Realizing that Newman faced major problems, Huston finally agreed to help out. Grateful for this support, Newman was candid about the director's involvement: 'Huston agreed to do it as a friend. He turned it down at first, then his conscience got to him . . . I don't think he ever thought very much of it.' After thirty years as a director, Huston knew all about contractual hassles: 'It was only done because it relieved Paul of a commitment. None of us had any illusions as to its worth.' Friendship aside, Huston was open about the reason for both his and Foreman's involvement: 'Foreman, I gathered, needed the money, and I certainly did.' At the time, Huston was recovering from a recent bout of pneumonia. Faced with a flawed script and an ailing director, Walter Hill didn't rate the production's chances. As he explained to biographer Lawrence Grobel: 'I thought these guys were going crazy, because the story didn't make sense.'

The Mackintosh Man began filming in November 1972. The international locations included London and Malta. While Huston hoped to recapture the Judge Roy Bean camaraderie, the production proved troubled. According to Hill, Huston saw The Mackintosh Man as a serious Cold War drama, along the lines of his earlier film The Kremlin Letter (1970). Hill felt it could only work as a lighthearted Hitchcockian thriller. As with John Milius on Judge Roy Bean, Hill soon realized that Huston wasn't interested in his ideas. Unlike Milius, Hill didn't prolong his suffering, leaving the production after the first week of filming. According to Axel Madsen, the screenplay remained incomplete two weeks into shooting. Hill's script was revised by veteran screenwriter William Fairchild, though Hill believes that most of the final script was written by Huston and Gladys Hill. His own contribution to the finished film amounted to 'about 60 per cent of the first half'. Huston continued to rewrite throughout production, something he'd wanted to avoid. The director more or less admitted defeat, claiming, '[we] did the best we could with it'. Looking to enliven the shoot, Newman played one of his trademark practical jokes, throwing a dummy sixty feet from a window. Believing they'd witnessed Newman plummet to his death, the shaken cast and crew didn't see the funny side.

Still in fragile health, John Huston seemed detached from the film, only talking to Newman and co-stars James Mason and Dominique Sanda in person. The supporting cast took their instructions from the assistant director, Colin Brewer. This approach didn't go down well with Michael Hordern, who claimed that Huston was 'hopeless at any tactful direction'. According to cameraman Oswald Morris, several entire scenes were directed by Brewer, Huston unable – or unwilling – to make the effort. John Foreman had worried that Huston's poor health might affect the production. Interviewed by Lawrence Grobel, Morris had another explanation for the director's lack of interest: 'John only did The Mackintosh Man for the money. You could tell if he was bored by how late he arrived.' In this instance, Huston rarely appeared on set before ten o'clock. A stickler for punctuality, Newman didn't protest at the director's frequent tardiness, perhaps making allowances for Huston's ill health. Morris expected Newman to be more assertive, telling Grobel: 'John was always the top dog. Paul would never do anything to cross John. Paul was a bit of a boy scout.' In fairness, Newman knew that Huston had accepted the film as a personal favour.

Interviewed on Hammer Films' official website, actor Shane Briant recalled *The Mackintosh Man* as a good experience. He praised Newman as 'A genuinely good bloke. Worked with all the actors as equals. Never the star.' Happy to share his considerable film experience, Newman helped Briant get the best from his role: '[He] showed me how to work a camera – by that I mean look after myself and look good.' During one fight scene, Newman hit Briant too hard, splitting his lip. While Newman was genuinely shocked, former boxer John Huston appeared unconcerned. Sitting fifty feet away, puffing on his trademark cigar, Huston merely asked for another take: 'We'll go again.' However, Huston praised Briant's performance once he'd finished work on the film.

John Huston once described *The Mackintosh Man* experience as 'mutual misfortune' for all concerned. In truth, the film is perfectly watchable, the action unreeling to Maurice Jarre's jaunty score. Despite Huston's indifference, *The Mackintosh Man* is technically sound, though one shot features a member of the crew reflected in a car window. Patchwork script aside, the film suffers mainly from over-familiar ingredients. The violence is relatively vicious, Reardon (Newman) going up against the hard-kicking Gerda (Jenny Runacre). It is one of the few Newman movies in which he hits women. In terms of acting, the film largely wastes its stellar cast. During the last week of shooting, Huston and Gladys Hill finally came up with a decent ending, which the director described as the best thing in the film. Unfortunately, the movie didn't build to it properly, undermining the effectiveness. In the final analysis, Huston felt he'd upgraded the project from 'out-and-out disgrace' to mere mediocrity.

After a series of unsuccessful previews, *The Mackintosh Man* opened in the US on 25 July 1973. While critics didn't share Huston's view that the film was his worst ever, most dismissed it as a tired espionage caper. Audiences showed little interest and *The Mackintosh Man* did poorly at the box office. Writing in the late 1970s, Huston remarked: 'I know of hardly anyone who has even heard of it.' Walter Hill regarded the film as 'the bottom out' of Huston's career, and Newman conceded that he'd made a mistake: '[I] thought we could make an effective melodrama out of that, and I was wrong.'

Newman and Huston talked of reuniting for *The Man Who Would Be King* (1975), one of the director's most personal projects.4 Based on a story by Rudyard Kipling, this cynical adventure concerns two 'retired' British soldiers, seeking wealth and power in the mountainous country of Kafiristan. As Huston explained, 'In our mutual guilt following *The Mackintosh Man*, Paul and I were eager to do something we could hold our heads up about afterwards.' John Foreman, who also got on well with Huston, believed the project would be ideal for Newman. Usually wary of period pieces, Newman liked the existing scripts, which Huston had commissioned over the years. There was talk of Robert Redford playing the second starring role. A Newman–Redford reunion, just two years after *The Sting*, would draw immediate studio interest. Excited by this prospect, Huston and Gladys Hill wrote a new script. Newman loved the revised screenplay, but now felt that he and Redford would be miscast. As Newman demonstrated in *Exodus*, he was not too convincing as an English military man. The leads should be played by British actors. Newman even suggested the perfect casting: 'For Christ's sake, John, get Connery and Caine!'5

No longer based in Los Angeles, Newman maintained a medium–high profile among the movie community. During the early 1970s, Newman and Joanne Woodward regularly attended parties held by super-agent Sue Mengers at her home on Dawn Ridge Drive. Despite the informal setting, the Mengers gatherings were primarily business opportunities, a place to mingle for established and rising film people. It says something about the state of Newman's career that the normally party-shy star felt obliged to show up at these events. Woodward would sit in a chair, knitting. If anyone lit up a joint, the couple made their excuses and left. While Newman and Woodward were liberal in most respects, they had no wish to be associated with the drug culture, soft or otherwise. Newman didn't fit into the 'New Hollywood' scene, in more ways than one.

Newman finally arrested his slump into the box-office doldrums with *The Sting* (1973), a slick tale of loveable conmen in 1936 Chicago. Reunited with *Butch Cassidy* co-star Robert Redford and director George Roy Hill, Newman cranked up the superstar charm, reminding audiences that they enjoyed seeing him in feel-good movies. For the time being, in-depth characters and scripts with Something to Say were placed on the back burner.

The Sting – Newman and Redford reunited

A Universal release, *The Sting* was brought to the screen by the producing team of Tony Bill and married couple Michael and Julia Phillips.
Scripted by David S. Ward, *The Sting* centred on con artists Henry Gondorff and Johnny Hooker, supposedly named after blues guitarist John
Lee Hooker. In the initial drafts, Hooker was out to avenge the murder
of his brother, a boxer who refused to throw a fight. Ward developed his
script with Redford in mind for Hooker but, approached with the *Sting*
project, Redford initially declined the role. At some point, the part was
offered to Jack Nicholson, a rising star after *Carnal Knowledge* (1971).
Dismissing *The Sting* as 'creatively . . . not worth my time', Nicholson
opted instead to star in *The Last Detail* (1973). While Redford eventually agreed to star in the film, he wasn't expecting another *Butch Cassidy*-style blockbuster. He certainly didn't see *The Sting* as the obvious
vehicle for a reunion with Hill and Newman.

As it happened, Redford and Hill had already signed with Universal
to make *The Great Waldo Pepper* (1975). For various reasons, the
project had to be postponed, leaving star and director free to work on
other films. Even so, Hill only saw the *Sting* script by accident. Unlike
Redford, he was immediately taken with the project, offering his services as the director. *The Sting*'s twist-heavy plot and conspicuous lack
of depth didn't bother him: 'I've always wanted to do entertaining

films. I'm not a very deep thinker. I'm more for entertainment than something that has deep meaning to it.'

Since *Butch Cassidy*, Hill had regularly discussed his projects with Newman. The second conman, Henry Gondorff, was written as a supporting role for a character actor. Julia Phillips had already earmarked the part for Peter Boyle. Newman read Ward's script and expressed an interest in the role. According to Phillips, he contacted Hill to ask: 'Would I be ruining the movie if I wanted to play Gondorff?' Newman is said to have put it more bluntly: 'You're making another film with Redford and there's no part for me?' Hill felt that Gondorff could be built up into a starring role, played as 'a riverboat gambler'. In the director's opinion, Ward's script was not an untouchable 'classic' of screenwriting craft. Furthermore, Newman had a lot more audience appeal than Boyle.

William Goldman suggests that Newman was drawn by *The Sting*'s 'package' deal, with Redford and Hill, rather than by the script *per se*. While Newman later described Ward's screenplay as 'first-class material', this came with the benefit of hindsight. Since *Butch Cassidy*, he had starred in five consecutive flops, producing two more. Even the biggest Hollywood stars couldn't survive a long run of commercial failures. Some felt that his preoccupation with 'message' films, such as *WUSA*, had derailed his career. In need of a hit, Newman pushed his way into *The Sting* deal. While he and Redford received the same $500,000 pay cheque, a significant reduction on their standard fees, Newman also got top billing and a percentage of the box-office gross. Grateful to Newman for the *Butch Cassidy* break, Redford also respected his co-star's senior status. Newman's research for *The Sting* included watching old William Powell movies. Little known today, the debonair, wisecracking Powell was a major star of the 1930s, most notably in the *Thin Man* series (1934–47) and *My Man Godfrey* (1936). Although he lived until 1984, it's not known if he ever saw Newman's performance in *The Sting*.

The deal with Universal was brokered by executive producers Richard Zanuck and David Brown, who worked on *Butch Cassidy*. Now freelance operators, they needed a big movie to launch their new partnership. Balancing *The Sting*'s uncertain appeal against the Newman–Redford combo, Universal agreed to a $5.5-million budget, less than *Butch Cassidy*.

Instead of an original score, Hill used the music of Scott Joplin, famous for his 'ragtime' style. Written between 1900 and 1910, Joplin's tunes were reworked by composer–arranger Marvin Hamlisch.

The Sting featured a major villain, Irish gangster Doyle Lonnegan.

Hill felt the part was tailor-made for Richard Boone, a memorable badman in *Hombre* (1967). According to Julia Phillips, Boone's heavy drinking had damaged his film career. When Boone proved unresponsive to Hill's overtures, the director had David Ward rewrite the part, making Lonnegan a stronger character. Just a few weeks before the start of filming, Boone rejected the role. Suggestions for his replacement included Irish actor Stephen Boyd, whose career had declined badly since *Ben Hur* (1959). Universal also considered British star Oliver Reed, a forceful, charismatic lead in *The Devils* (1971). Approached by the studio, Reed turned down the chance to test for Lonnegan, one of several bad decisions in his patchy career. The Phillips–Bill team wanted a more 'classy' actor, favouring Laurence Olivier, Hugh Griffith, who appeared in *Exodus*, and Robert Shaw. While Olivier and Griffith proved unavailable, Shaw seemed a viable option. Despite strong performances in *From Russia with Love* (1963) and *A Man for All Seasons* (1966), Shaw's film career was going nowhere. John French, Shaw's former agent and biographer, claims that Newman suggested casting the actor. The *Sting* script had Gondorff adopting the name 'Mr Shaw', which made Newman think of Robert Shaw. At the time, late 1972, Newman was shooting *The Mackintosh Man* in Ireland, near Shaw's home. He hand-delivered a copy of the *Sting* script to Shaw, who showed immediate interest. (According to French, Newman simply made a phone call.) Frustrated with his career, Shaw regarded *The Sting* as a big deal, and he certainly appreciated the chance to work with Newman and Redford. A few days before the start of production, he injured his right knee ligaments on a handball court at the Beverly Hills Hotel Racquet Ball Club. Rather than disguise the resultant limp during filming, Shaw incorporated it into the character of Lonnegan. He later described his role in *The Sting* as 'the most intellectual performance I've ever done'.

The *Sting* began production in February 1973, following a week of cast rehearsal. George Roy Hill felt *The Sting* should look like a 1930s movie, eschewing the harsh Depression-era realism envisaged by David Ward. Hill intended to shoot the entire film on location, until art director Henry Bumstead argued that the period setting made this impractical. After reviewing the situation, Hill agreed with Bumstead, filming most of the exteriors on the Universal backlot. The production also filmed for two weeks in Chicago, Illinois, where hundreds of people turned up to glimpse Newman and Redford. While Newman's box-office appeal had dwindled since *Butch Cassidy*, he still drew major attention, and Robert Shaw claimed that the National Guard were needed to hold back the crowds. In the film, Newman's character,

Henry Gondorff, performs a series of elaborate card tricks. These were devised by technical advisor John Scarne, who also doubled Newman's hands for the close-ups. Though a quick learner, Newman didn't have time to train as a card sharp.

Off set, Robert Redford didn't socialize much. Based at the same Chicago hotel, Newman and Shaw occasionally went out for a drink. However, aside from a shared interest in cars, the actors had little in common. Newman's trademark dirty jokes didn't impress Shaw. While Newman claimed to dislike attention, Shaw noticed an inconsistency in his behaviour. Ushered into the private booths of two bars, Newman soon left, dragging Shaw into the main bar of a third. Inevitably, the fans soon gathered, pestering Newman for autographs. Newman merely shrugged at Shaw, 'It always happens, everywhere I go.' It's possible that Newman's recent box-office failures had made him insecure.

By and large, Newman, Redford and Hill recaptured the rapport they'd enjoyed on *Butch Cassidy and the Sundance Kid*. Hill regarded Redford as an instinctive actor, poles apart from Newman's intellectual approach. During production on *The Sting*, Hill rented Newman's house on Heather Drive. One of many practical jokes involved the compacted wreck of a Porsche, which Redford sent to Newman as a birthday gift. Newman in turn had Redford's face printed on sheets of toilet paper, not just one roll but 150 cartons. Uncertain of Redford's response, however, he never sent them. As he later explained, he and Redford were just 'close acquaintances'. Now a major star in his own right, Redford still turned up late for work. *The Sting* finished shooting in April 1973 and, after the wrap party, Hill discovered his new sports car cut in half with a blowtorch. Newman paid for a replacement. Julia Phillips regarded Newman as 'seriously weird', claiming he took offence at the smallest things.

Newman once described *The Sting* as 'very long on plot and very short on character'. Despite this shortcoming, he rated the end result as 'great fun'. Most viewers tend to agree, regarding Gondorff and Hooker as worthy successors to Butch and Sundance. Unlike the doomed outlaws, the conmen have right on their side, robbing a fellow crook rather than innocent members of the public. Newman and Redford aside, *The Sting* is a nostalgia trip, opening with the old Universal Pictures logo in glorious sepia. Henry Bumstead's art direction captures the 1930s atmosphere, though the resemblance to American films of the era is negligible. George Roy Hill's smooth, impersonal direction endorses his claim to be an 'administrator' rather than an *auteur*. He utilizes such classical Hollywood devices as iris shots, picture flips and a succession of horizontal, vertical and diagonal wipes. The film also features actors' introductions, illustrations and even chapter headings. From the first shot, *The Sting* announces itself as a Movie, leaving grim reality far behind. That said, the most memorable image is a group of off-duty hookers riding on a carousel. Ironically, the film's biggest anachronism is the jaunty Scott Joplin score: by the 1930s, ragtime music had gone out of fashion.

When Gondorff (Newman) finally appears, half an hour into the film, he's not at his best. He's discovered in a drunken stupor, face pressed against a wall. Snoring loud enough to wake the dead, Gondorff doesn't appreciate Hooker's (Redford) wake-up call: 'Glad to meet you, kid. You're a real horse's ass.' That said, he now has a reason to get off the floor. Unlike Butch and Sundance, these crooks are wary strangers, Hooker keeping vital information from Gondorff. Newman is probably better cast than Redford, who looks too old for Hooker. Tangling with gangsters and bent cops, the relaxed Gondorff stands out in his vest, braces and hat. The famous poker sequence features Newman's best ever drunk act, playing a character pretending to be half-cut. Hill loved Newman's performance in this scene, describing it as 'one of the best pieces of comedic acting I've ever seen. I defy any actor to play that scene better.'

While the Newman–Redford interplay works well enough, the male bonding that distinguished *Butch Cassidy* is absent. For all the rewrites and top billing, Newman's part isn't a *bona fide* starring role. Once the big con is underway, *The Sting* becomes an ensemble piece, Gondorff and Hooker making way for fellow 'artists' J. J. Singleton (Ray Walston) and Kid Twist (Harold Gould). As Newman pointed out, the film is entirely plot-led. The Lonnegan operation is everything, the initial revenge motive becoming secondary. Gondorff even remarks, 'Revenge is for suckers.' The climactic scam is extraordinarily elaborate, not to say expensive. While the con artists pick up a little cash, the big reward seems to be pride in a job well done. The final twist lacks dramatic punch, despite the $500,000 payoff.

The Sting didn't score an immediate hit with Universal. The studio's publicity department was unimpressed by the rough cut, which lacked the optical effects and all-important Joplin score. The pace seemed slow, the plot ridiculously contrived. Thankfully, preview audiences loved the film, reassuring Universal executives that they had a hit on their hands. Robert Shaw received a telegram from Richard Zanuck and David Brown: 'We had extraordinary preview and exhibition of *The Sting* and your performance was received with special delight and interest.' Presumably, Newman and Redford were sent similar messages.

Marketed with the tagline 'All It Takes Is a Little Confidence!', *The Sting* opened in the US on 23 December 1973. The poster art featured a grinning Newman, lighting his cigar with a dollar bill. Newman did his share of publicity, praising the film's period setting:

I love the '30s; I always have. It was a decade of crisis for the nation, and a lot of artists, particularly writers, were stirred to serious thought by the events that took place.

The reviews were generally favourable. *Sunday Times* critic Dilys Powell regarded the film as first-rate entertainment: '*The Sting* is directed and played with great verve; the 1936 underworld is re-created with delight; and the victims deserve what they get.'

The movie grossed over $78 million in North America alone, making nearly as much again in foreign rentals. Preoccupied with a new era of crisis, embodied by Watergate and Vietnam, the paying public were grateful for two hours of high-grade escapism. *Variety* placed *The Sting* at number six in its all-time 'Top Grossers' chart. After four years of critical and commercial flops, Newman had regained his position as a major Hollywood player. By the end of 1973, he was the seventh biggest box-office draw.

On 2 April 1974, *The Sting* scored a second triumph, this time at the Academy Awards. Going head to head with William Friedkin's *The Exorcist* (1973), *The Sting* won Best Picture, Best Director, Best Original Screenplay, Best Art Direction, Best Costume Design, Best Editing and Best Scoring. The Best Picture presentation, by Elizabeth Taylor, was preceded by an onstage streaker, sex-shop owner Robert Opal. Robert Redford and cameraman Robert Surtees both lost out, and to date, Redford has yet to receive a second Oscar nod. Newman, who hadn't been nominated, was probably grateful to be spared another Best Actor miss. *The Sting*'s Best Picture win supposedly added $30 million to its box-office gross. Looking to exploit the Newman–Redford combination, Twentieth Century Fox reissued *Butch Cassidy and the Sundance Kid* with the tagline 'Butch & The Kid Are Back! Just for the Fun of It!' Re-released on 27 June 1974, it took around $13 million. For the time being, audiences couldn't get enough of Paul Newman.

11 A Burning Sensation

One tiny spark becomes a night of blazing suspense!
 Tagline, *The Towering Inferno*

In January 1974, Joanne Woodward agreed to appear in August Strindberg's play *The Dance of Death*, produced by Joseph Papp at New York's Lincoln Center. She would co-star alongside Robert Shaw. The production was scheduled for a brief four-week run in April and May. Unfortunately, Woodward and Shaw fell out during the first week of rehearsal. Shaw later claimed that Woodward seemed nervous about returning to the stage after a long gap. It seems more likely that Woodward objected to Shaw's heavy drinking, especially during rehearsals. Never a big social drinker, she had little time for actors who mixed work with alcohol. She resigned from the play, to be replaced by Zoe Caldwell, who'd worked with Shaw on the Royal Court's 1961 production of *The Changeling*. Woodward and Shaw avoided public comment on her departure, which generated minimal press coverage. *The Dance of Death* proved a personal triumph for Shaw, scoring a critical and box-office hit. Sadly, his chronic alcohol abuse would lead to his early death, in 1978, at the age of fifty-one.

Producer Richard Zanuck hoped to cast Newman in *Lucky Lady* (1975), another caper movie set during the 1930s. Zanuck and David Brown had bought the script from Willard Huyck and Gloria Katz, whose credits included *American Graffiti* (1973), a sleeper hit for Universal. While *Lucky Lady* was lightweight material, Newman expressed interest in the project as a First Artists co-production. He'd recently seen the Zanuck–Brown film *Sugarland Express* (1974), a downbeat love-on-the-run story directed by newcomer Steven Spielberg. Newman felt that Spielberg would be ideal for *Lucky Lady*'s offbeat comedy, featuring a trio of loveable bootleggers involved in a *ménage à trois*. Unimpressed with this package deal, Spielberg turned the film down, arguing – correctly – that Newman was the wrong choice for the script's broad farce. Newman lost interest in *Lucky Lady* and Spielberg went on to direct *Jaws* (1975), another Zanuck–Brown production.

Newman's box-office renaissance continued with *The Towering Inferno* (1974), producer Irwin Allen's follow-up to *The Poseidon*

Adventure (1972).[1] *The Towering Inferno* made film history as the first joint production between two major studios. This came about through expedience rather than intention. Allen wanted Twentieth Century Fox to buy the film rights to *The Tower*, a novel by Richard Martin Stern. Looking to exploit the disaster-movie boom, Warner Brothers outbid Fox for the book, paying Stern $390,000. Two months later, Allen and Fox optioned *The Glass Inferno*, an as-yet unpublished novel by Thomas M. Scortia and Frank M. Robinson. Having read the book in proof form, Allen acquired the rights for $400,000. Faced with two burning skyscraper movies competing at the box office, Fox and Warners agreed to a co-production, splitting the film's $15-million budget fifty–fifty. The box-office gross was also divided evenly, Fox taking the North American receipts, while Warner got the overseas revenue.

The screenplay was assigned to Stirling Silliphant, co-writer of *The Poseidon Adventure*. Working from both *The Tower* and *The Glass Inferno*, Silliphant combined the books' titles, main characters and grand climaxes. The film would be directed by British expatriate John Guillermin. Irwin Allen opted to handle the second unit himself, taking a credit as 'director of action sequences'. He also supervised many of Guillermin's scenes, his authority never in question.

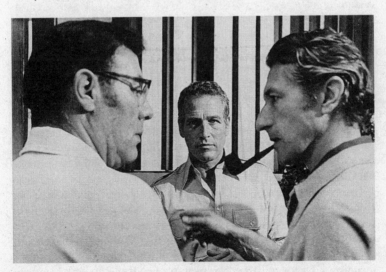

The Towering Inferno – Newman stands by while director John Guillermin (right) confers with producer Irwin Allen (left)

The Towering Inferno – Newman and Steve McQueen manage a smile for the camera

Fire aside, *The Towering Inferno*'s big selling point was Newman and Steve McQueen, together at last. Allen had succeeded where *Butch Cassidy* failed, luring both stars with a surefire hit and big money. Since early 1972, McQueen had been part of the First Artists partnership, alongside Newman, Sidney Poitier and Barbra Streisand. However, this business association did nothing to temper McQueen's hostility towards Newman. During the 1972 presidential election campaigns, McQueen made it clear that he didn't want First Artists funds used to support Democrat candidate George McGovern.

Irwin Allen wanted McQueen to play idealistic architect Doug Roberts, whose grand design for the Glass Tower is fatally compromised by sneaky cost-cutting and corporate corruption. McQueen declined, opting for the role of Fire Chief O'Halloran, a hard-nosed professional who saves lives and takes no shit. More secure with his machismo, Newman had no problem playing Roberts. Both Newman and McQueen were paid $1 million, plus 10 per cent of the box-office gross. McQueen's deal for the film, signed on 12 April 1974, would make him $12 million. Reading through the script, he discovered he

had twelve fewer lines than Newman. McQueen insisted that Silliphant make up the difference. Either he went into the film on equal
terms with Newman or he didn't turn up at all. When it came to
billing, both stars were happy with the staggered arrangement originally
proposed for *Butch Cassidy and the Sundance Kid*. For whatever
reason, McQueen no longer regarded this compromise with suspicion.
He told friends that getting 'superior' billing to Newman was the highpoint of his career.

If nothing else, *The Towering Inferno* boasted a better class of
supporting actor than *The Poseidon Adventure*. William Holden was
one. Years of alcohol abuse were etched on his face and few producers
now considered him for major roles. While Holden dismissed the
Towering Inferno script as 'lousy', giving all the action to Newman
and McQueen, he needed the work. He was paid $750,000 to appear
in the film, his biggest pay cheque in years. Newman's token love interest was played by Faye Dunaway. Dunaway had revived her flagging
career with *Chinatown* (1974). While *The Towering Inferno* hardly
offered the same acting challenge, she happened to be available and
she liked both Newman and McQueen, with whom she'd co-starred in
The Thomas Crown Affair (1968). More to the point, her agent argued
that a hit disaster movie would help her career. The older generation
of Hollywood stars was represented by Fred Astaire and Jennifer Jones.

The bit-part actors included Scott Newman. Now based in Los
Angeles, Scott had decided on a career in films, despite the inevitable
comparisons with his famous father. While many found Scott intense
and over-sensitive, he had a fine sense of humour to counter his stubborn,
arrogant streak. Frequently short of funds, he preferred to borrow
money from friends rather than his parents, wary of questions about
his spending habits. Having enrolled in acting classes, he proved a
poor student, frequently failing to show up. He seemed ambivalent
about his long-term prospects as an actor, claiming to prefer stunt
work. In this field, at least, Scott would not be measured against his
father and found wanting. Whatever his lingering resentments
towards Newman, he was not too proud to turn down a job on *The
Towering Inferno*. At Newman's suggestion, Irwin Allen cast Scott in
the small role of a fireman. Most of his scenes would be opposite Steve
McQueen, rather than Newman. His involvement with the film
attracted a disproportionate amount of publicity.[2] Even at his most
blinkered, Scott must have realized he was drawing attention as
Paul Newman's son, not as a promising young actor in his own right.

The Towering Inferno commenced filming on 13 May 1974, and
was scheduled for a seventy-two-day shoot. The production required

four camera crews and fifty-seven specially built sets, most of which
would be burned. The numerous stuntmen employed on the film
included John Landis, later a respected director. Both Newman and
McQueen offered to do their own stunts, where possible, presumably
out of professionalism rather than rivalry.

According to director John Guillermin, *The Towering Inferno*
proved a smooth shoot, with no ego clashes: 'We got along like one
big happy family.' In fact, Guillermin had to contend with at least two
sources of star temperament. Both Steve McQueen and Faye Dunaway
operated a strict 'no visitors' policy while working on set. McQueen
also refused to give interviews, wary of questions about his recent
marriage to actress Ali MacGraw, who co-starred with him in *The
Getaway*. The more easygoing Newman merely requested that he be
informed of any visitors. William Holden took a strong dislike to
Dunaway, who once kept him waiting on set for two hours. According
to Bob Thomas, Holden's biographer, the veteran star threatened
physical violence if Dunaway was ever late again.

Many expected Newman and McQueen to clash at some point.
Neile McQueen, the star's first wife, later shed some light on his attitude to Newman. During production on *Somebody Up There Likes
Me*, the unknown McQueen supposedly vowed to become a bigger
star than Newman. By taking top billing on *The Towering Inferno*, as
he saw it, McQueen had achieved his goal. There's little doubt that he
resented Newman and envied his 'privileged' background. He regularly dismissed his perceived rival as a 'fuckwit'. Aware that Newman got
on better with the cast and crew than he did, McQueen claimed not to
care. In truth, his hostility towards Newman contained as much bluster as substance. His inner circle of friends included actor Don Gordon,
cast in *Towering Inferno* as a fellow fireman. A few years earlier, Gordon had played a supporting role in *WUSA*, without incurring
McQueen's wrath. Whatever the case, Newman and McQueen didn't
fight on set. Judging from the humorous out-takes, they actually got
on at least some of the time. Newman pulled a number of his trademark gags, including wielding a giant prop telephone while McQueen
tried to make a call. Perhaps McQueen found Newman harder to dislike in person. Interviewed for a 2003 A&E *Biography* on Newman,
co-star Susan Blakely recalled enjoying the shoot: 'The most fun was
Paul Newman. He definitely liked to have a good time. He has a very
naughty sense of humour.' Dunaway described Newman as 'great to
work with – one of the single sexiest men in the movies'. McQueen put
his fireman training to good use, on 6 May 1974 helping to tackle a
blaze at the Samuel Goldwyn Studios on Santa Monica and Formosa.

The Towering Inferno completed principal photography on 11 September 1974. Newman offered a qualified endorsement of the movie: 'Of its kind, rather good. Get the actors off and the stunt men on as quick as you can.' While the film was clearly a demanding, physically arduous production, the end result unwinds to a very tired formula. Smoothly made, The Towering Inferno's special effects – supervised by L. B. Abbott, A. D. Flowers, Frank Van der Veer and Douglas Trumball – have dated surprisingly little. The script is less impressive, offering a collection of predictable situations and dull characters. The human drama is strictly by the numbers. Most of the big names perform in a vacuum, barely interacting with their co-stars. McQueen and Dunaway, who played a memorable game of chess in The Thomas Crown Affair, have no dialogue together. Only odd moments linger in the mind. The prolonged death of Bigelow (Robert Wagner) is both risible and disturbing. Covering his head in a blue towel, like an ersatz Virgin Mary, Bigelow stumbles through a blazing office before falling out of the window. The script's one surprise is letting Jim Duncan (William Holden) live, though his skyscraping career is probably over. While McQueen seems more comfortable than Newman, neither actor is at their best.

The publicity for The Towering Inferno promised a sensational viewing experience. Twentieth Century Fox and Warner Brothers even suggested that disaster movies were 'the new art form of the twentieth century'. The theatrical trailer mentioned Steve McQueen before Newman, presumably a contractual obligation. Preview audiences certainly liked what they saw, suggesting that Irwin Allen hadn't lost his magic touch.

The Towering Inferno premièred in New York City on 10 December 1974, going on general release in the US four days later. Some of the reviews were highly favourable, the New York Times praising the film as 'old-fashioned Hollywood make-believe at its painstaking best'. It grossed $48.8 million at the North American box office and proved equally popular overseas, taking more than $67 million. The film earned over $16 million in Japan alone, more than its production cost. Obviously, the Japanese appetite for urban apocalypse had not been sated by twenty years of Godzilla films. Irwin Allen offered Steve McQueen $3 million up front to make a sequel, but McQueen slammed the door in his face – literally, by all accounts.

Newman finished 1974 as the third biggest box-office draw. Approaching his half century, Newman had lost none of his sex appeal, receiving fan mail from teenagers.[3] He claimed to have no worries about growing older: 'I am lurching toward fifty with all the eager anticipation of a kid having a woman for the first time.'

12 Out in the Cold

My daddy died without ever seein' me as the star.
  William F. Cody, *Buffalo Bill and the Indians*

After the blockbuster success of *The Sting* and *The Towering Inferno*, Newman had the commercial muscle to make any film he wanted. His first post-*Inferno* vehicle seemed an odd choice, neither blockbuster nor heavyweight drama. He reprised the role of Lew Harper in Warner Brothers' *The Drowning Pool* (1975), based on a 1950 novel by Ross MacDonald. Returning to the character after nine years suggested a lack of ideas on Newman's part, rather than fond nostalgia.

Newman's original choice of director was Jack Garfein, his old friend from the Actors Studio. Garfein's film career had been on hold since *Something Wild* (1961), and he hoped to get another shot at the big screen. When he first approached Warner Brothers, independently of Newman, he was dismissed out of hand. The studio had no interest in a New York theatre director, whose two minor film credits were ancient history. Short of options, Garfein appealed to Newman's sense of loyalty. Newman rose to the occasion, insisting that Warner hire Garfein. This unlikely reunion proved short-lived. According to Garfein, Newman was approached by Stuart Rosenberg, who'd fallen out with the star over the editing of *Pocket Money*. Garfein claims that Rosenberg had suffered a major personal crisis, leaving his life and career in tatters. Rosenberg begged Newman for the *Drowning Pool* job, and the star felt unable to refuse. Appreciating Newman's position, Garfein gracefully withdrew from the production. While his version of events is hardly impartial, there seems little reason to doubt his story. Whatever the case, it's possible that Newman felt bad about the *Pocket Money* fiasco. On a more practical level, Rosenberg had far more film-making experience than Garfein. For *The Drowning Pool*, Rosenberg received valuable support from cameraman Gordon Willis, acclaimed for his work on *Klute* (1971) and the first two *Godfather* films (1972/74).

The Drowning Pool co-starred Joanne Woodward, her first screen appearance opposite Newman since the ill-fated *WUSA*. At the time, her film career was going nowhere in particular. Despite the failure of *A New Kind of Love*, she remained partial to lightweight material, especially comedies. She'd hoped to star in the film version of *Forty Carats*, a hit Broadway comedy about a New York divorcee's affair with a younger man. In the event, Columbia's 1973 screen version starred Liv Ullmann, Edward Albert and Gene Kelly. The end result proved disappointing, partly due to the miscasting of Ullmann.

The Drowning Pool – Reprising the role of Lew Harper

Since *The Effect of Gamma Rays on Man-in-the-Moon Marigolds*, Woodward had appeared in *Summer Wishes, Winter Dreams* (1973). Cast in yet another angst-ridden role, she found the experience depressing. She had problems with the director, Gilbert Cates, which led to arguments over his handling of the material. Treading a fine line between sensitive character study and melodrama, *Summer Wishes, Winter Dreams* didn't repeat *Rachel, Rachel*'s 'sleeper' success. The producer, Ray Stark, pushed the film for Academy Award consideration, obliging a reluctant Woodward to hit the interview trail. In the event, she received a Best Actress nomination for her committed performance, losing out to Glenda Jackson's comedy turn in *A Touch of Class* (1973). Woodward seemed unconcerned, claiming an Oscar win was only significant as 'a political or a business gesture'.

Now in her mid-forties, Woodward was well acquainted with mid-life crisis. She felt she'd been found wanting as both an actress and a mother, commenting, 'My career has suffered because of the children, and my children have suffered because of my career.' Interviewed for

Time magazine in 1982, Woodward described herself as 'a creative dilettante'. She also admitted that motherhood had seemed an obligation rather than a choice: 'I think what I really wanted was to have a life with no children, but I was raised in a generation that taught us otherwise.' She didn't regret putting her career on hold for Newman and their daughters. At the same time, she believed her life, and decisions, could have been easier: 'It was instilled in me to believe it couldn't be Paul *and* me, it had to be Paul *or* me.' She later blamed herself for 'choosing to be in Paul's shadow'. Taking a supporting role in *The Drowning Pool*, Woodward was philosophical about her involvement in Newman's latest film: 'He's the big movie star, and I'm a character actress.' She received special billing, more a reflection of her famous husband than an Oscar-winning film career.

Interviewed in 1982, Newman dismissed *The Drowning Pool* as a disappointment: '[The] only time I ever played the same character twice, and it didn't work.' At the time, he claimed to love playing Lew Harper: 'I simply adore that character, because it will accommodate any kind of actor's invention. He can do the most outrageous things.' Unfortunately, there is nothing inventive or outrageous about this private eye. Afflicted by car trouble and a smart mouth, Harper hasn't changed much since his first outing. The ritual roughing up from both cops and crooks doesn't seem to bother him. Still in good shape at fifty, Newman poses variously in swimming trunks, a bath towel and boxer shorts. Harper certainly draws the interest of Schuyler Devereaux (Melanie Griffith), the promiscuous teenage daughter of old flame Iris Devereaux (Woodward).

The Drowning Pool opened in the US in July 1975. The film had tested poorly with preview audiences, most of whom knew little of *Harper*. Nine years is a long time in popular culture and the original movie had faded from public consciousness. Despite this disappointing response, Newman and Warner Brothers hoped to score one of the big hits of the summer season. Instead, *The Drowning Pool* met with negative reviews and audience apathy.

The film marked the last collaboration between Newman and Stuart Rosenberg. Of their four films together, only *Cool Hand Luke* had been successful. While *Pocket Money* may have suffered from Newman's 'tampering', there were no ready excuses for *WUSA* and *The Drowning Pool*.

In the mid-1970s, Newman and Joanne Woodward re-established their base in Los Angeles, buying a house in Beverly Hills. The couple's busy schedules kept them apart for long periods; over the average year, they might be together for six months. Putting the *Drowning Pool* flop behind him, Newman served as a host for the documentary *McCarthy: Death of a Witch Hunter* (1975). He also made a guest appearance in a 1976 edition of *The Gong Show*, one of the tackiest television programmes of all time. Created and hosted by Chuck Barris, this legendarily awful 'talent' contest remains a cult favourite. Barris later claimed to have alternated his small-screen career with regular assignments as a CIA hitman.

Back on the big screen, Newman agreed to play a cameo role in Mel Brooks's *Silent Movie* (1976). Hot from the success of *Blazing Saddles* (1974) and the superior *Young Frankenstein* (1974), Brooks was Hollywood's reigning king of comedy. Newman's fellow guest stars included Burt Reynolds, James Caan, Liza Minnelli and mime artist Marcel Marceau, who speaks the film's only line of dialogue. *Silent Movie* is patchy, to say the least, alternating moments of manic inspiration with a slew of weak gags. Newman takes part in a wheelchair chase, dressed in racing gear. While he deserves points for sending up his famous hobby, the scene is less than hilarious.

Newman was linked to Richard Attenborough's all-star war epic *A Bridge Too Far* (1977), scripted by William Goldman, though he eventually passed on the film. He was also offered the lead in *Islands in the Stream* (1977), based on a novel by Ernest Hemingway. The film was directed by Franklin J. Schaffner, who'd worked with Newman back in the late 1950s on live television dramas. Newman turned it down, suggesting George C. Scott as a better choice for the main character. It's difficult to picture Newman as a hard-drinking expatriate artist, confronted with his estranged sons and the onset of World War II. Scott turned out to be the best thing in the completed film, which did poorly at the box office.

Newman claimed to have no special interest in working with particular actors or directors. While he praised Stanley Kubrick and John Cassavetes as original film-makers, it was a backhanded compliment: 'That doesn't necessarily mean that they're good, but they're original.' As always, he put his faith in strong material: 'I only have a very real desire to find a script that's genuinely distinguished.' In this respect, Newman seemed disenchanted with the Hollywood scene, claiming that most of the scripts he saw were 'uniformly bad'. The new generation of screenwriters lacked real craft: 'There's a visceral rather than an intellectual process.' This plaintive lament contained as much nostalgia as truth, for Newman had contended with plenty of bad scripts during the 1950s and 1960s. Hedging his bets, he didn't condemn the block-buster mentality outright: '"Entertainment" films are fine, as long as they're not all you do.' He supposedly turned down some films because of their violence. While this could be seen as a moral stance, he simply claimed to be 'bored' by screen brutality. Newman singled out Sam Peckinpah, the maestro of slow-motion bloodspurting, as a director he disliked.

He toyed with making a film version of Patricia Nell Warren's novel *The Front Runner* (1974), about an athletics coach who falls for one of his male students. Newman wanted to star as the coach, a daring departure from the red-blooded heterosexuals he usually played. Even his character in *Cat on a Hot Tin Roof* had merely been 'confused'. Fired with enthusiasm, he approached Robert Redford for the student role. Too old for the part, Redford had a bigger problem with the material. More conscious of his screen image than Newman, he didn't want to play a gay character. Surprisingly, Newman also offered the part to Steve McQueen, who wasted no time turning him down: 'I could never play a fag.' Brought down to earth by these blunt refusals, Newman realized that his fans wouldn't accept him as a homosexual. While audiences loved the Newman–Redford chemistry in *Butch Cassidy* and *The Sting*, any gay element in these buddy movies was kept safely clos-eted. While several film magazines announced *The Front Runner* as a forthcoming production, Newman soon shelved the project for good.

Frustrated, Newman looked for material that offered depth and sig-nificance. What he ended up with was *Buffalo Bill and the Indians, or Sitting Bull's History Lesson* (1976). Co-written and directed by Robert Altman, a self-styled Hollywood maverick, this clinical dissec-tion of western myth had potential. Unfortunately, the end product was a single idea in search of a movie.

Newman had a fascination with the historical character of William Frederick Cody (1846–1917), a.k.a. Buffalo Bill: 'He was a butcher, and we made him a hero . . . we create legends because that's the nature of our need.' A guide, scout and hunter, Cody played his part in wiping out the Native Americans, slaughtering the buffaloes they depended on for food. Dime novelist Ned Buntline turned Cody into a celebrity with *Buffalo Bill – The King of the Border Men* (1869). Turn-ing showmen in 1883, Cody and Buntline discovered a more lucrative line of work and, at its peak, their Wild West show grossed over $1 million a year. Newman described Cody as the 'first movie star'. While *The Left-Handed Gun* touched on similar territory, he regarded his Billy the Kid movie as a compromised failure.

Buffalo Bill and the Indians – William Cody, aka Buffalo Bill

Buffalo Bill and the Indians was based on Arthur Kopit's play *Indians* (1969), an acclaimed, controversial piece about the treatment of Native Americans in the Old West. Intrigued by the material, Newman and John Foreman bought the film rights soon after *Indians'* Broadway début in October 1969. Newman paid $500,000 – a steep price given the play's offbeat, near-surreal style. Just weeks after Kopit's play opened, *Variety* announced the *Indians* movie as a forthcoming production. Newman would play Cody, with George Roy Hill directing. In the event, the project didn't get off the ground, and Newman allowed his option to lapse.

The rights passed to Italian movie mogul Dino De Laurentiis, who arranged a production–distribution deal with United Artists. The film was produced by David Susskind. Looking for a suitable director, Susskind approached Robert Altman, whose erratic career seemed back on course with *Nashville* (1975). Well known for his love of overlapping dialogue, on-set improvisation, low-key lighting and slow, contemplative zooms, Altman was capable of near-brilliant work. Favouring offbeat characters, quirky humour and a dreamlike, surreal atmosphere, the director reworked familiar genres, playing on audience expectations. On the downside, he could be overly casual in his approach, throwing in ideas and jokes to little effect.

For all the acclaim surrounding *Nashville*, Altman needed a film deal. A string of recent projects had fallen through, notably *Breakfast of Champions*, *Eight Men Out* and *North Dallas Forty*. That said, he initially turned down *Buffalo Bill and the Indians*, showing little interest in Kopit's play. The director had his eye on the forthcoming *Ragtime*, based on the novel by E. L. Doctorow. Newman had also been linked to this ambitious period piece, set in 1906 America. The film rights to Doctorow's book were held by Dino De Laurentiis and, hoping to forge an alliance with De Laurentiis, Altman reconsidered the *Buffalo Bill* option. If the production proceeded smoothly, he had a good chance of securing the *Ragtime* deal. Questioned by journalists, Altman rationalized *Buffalo Bill and the Indians* as his ironic contribution to America's forthcoming bicentennial celebrations. Newman admired Altman's work and the director seemed an ideal choice for a star keen to subvert his established image. The pair may also have bonded through their shared dislike of Jack Warner. Altman claimed to have fought with Warner over the editing of *Countdown* (1968), his first studio assignment, though producer James Lydon disputed this version of events.

Buffalo Bill and the Indians began pre-production in May 1975. Altman co-wrote the script with Alan Rudolph, his assistant director on *Nashville*. The Altman–Rudolph screenplay shifted the emphasis from Sitting Bull to Buffalo Bill. Budgeted at $6 million, *Buffalo Bill and the Indians* began production on 11 August 1975. According to the credits, the film's sole location was the Stoney Indian Reserve, in Alberta, Canada. At Altman's request, the crew built Cody's winter camp two weeks before the start of filming, and Altman encouraged his cast to hang around the outdoor set, absorbing the atmosphere. Co-star Burt Lancaster spent less than a week on location, completing his scenes in around four days. Newman had known Lancaster for years, largely through their shared commitment to liberal causes. On set, the stars treated each other with respect rather than warmth. Lancaster subsequently asked Newman to co-star in *Twilight's Last Gleaming* (1977). Directed by Robert Aldrich, this political thriller blended nuclear blackmail and Cold War conspiracy. Newman would play the President of the United States, forced to come clean on Vietnam by Lancaster's renegade general. While the subject matter was close to Newman's heart, he turned the movie down.

Newman enjoyed working with Altman, describing the director as 'very interesting, a real explorer'. The two men shared a raucous, vulgar sense of humour. Still the practical joker, Newman placed three hundred live chicks inside Altman's trailer. Newman reconciled his belief in rehearsal and the written word with Altman's penchant for on-set improvisation. That said, Newman felt the director's ad-lib tendencies had been misunderstood. As he later explained, during production on *Quintet*:

> I think all this talk about Bob's ad-libbing is a lot of things that the actors bring in. This is what he wants. But these things are all incorporated and rehearsed before they're shot. You don't just get up on a set and start improvising and shooting.

Newman also praised the democratic atmosphere of an Altman production: 'The most marvellous thing is that there are no egos on the set.' He felt the director treated each member of the cast and crew as his equal. Uninterested in star pampering, Newman was in his element: 'You can experiment and explore comfortably, knowing that everybody else is allowed the same privilege.' *Buffalo Bill and the Indians* finished production in late October 1975, and Newman seemed happy with the end result, announcing to the press:

> *Buffalo Bill* has a clout people won't realize until they start thinking about the film three days later. What it does is shoot down all those legendary people. That includes Buffalo Bill and me and Redford and Muhammad Ali and Churchill and Stalin and Roosevelt.

Newman regarded William Cody as a gift of a role, the perfect antidote to mainstream blandness. Just as Cody reinvented himself as Buffalo Bill, so Newman could cut loose as the fabricated Wild West star: 'This picture is an adult fairy tale that accommodates almost any kind of actor's invention. But you have to be careful that the invention has the size of the character.' Hidden underneath a flowing wig and false beard, Newman seems to be having a good time. Sporting a cheesy grin, Cody is a vain, drunken, cowardly, vindictive braggart. Even his serial womanising is a sham, Bill muttering apologies for his impotence. Altman biographer Patrick McGilligan praises Newman's Cody as 'a consummate performance . . . alternately comical and eerie'.

Cody's philosophy of showmanship is simple: 'What we do is to make the best look better.' For Buffalo Bill, history is a truth-free zone, unfettered by tiresome facts. Sitting Bull (Frank Kaquitts), diminutive and frail, dismisses White Man's history as 'disrespect for the dead'. However, the contrast between Cody and Sitting Bull, supposedly the heart of the film, lacks the necessary force. Altman seems ill at ease with the Native American characters, reducing Sitting Bull and inter- preter William Halsey (Will Sampson) to peripheral figures. The historical Sitting Bull saw little hope for his people: 'The Indians must keep quiet or die.' If Cody truly believes his own myth, others are happy to exploit it. According to President Grover Cleveland (Pat McCormick): 'It's a man like that made this country what it is today.' Even Sitting Bull's ghost, silently reproachful, fails to shake Cody's faith. Having drunk his inner demons to the surface, he faces them down.

The film's best scene is Cody's one encounter with Burt Lancaster's Ned Buntline, his discarded creator. Unlike the lackeys, groupies and political opportunists, Buntline no longer indulges Cody's fantasy world. Unable to deal with reality, Cody can't tolerate dissenters in his camp. Buntline's parting shot to Cody, 'See you in hell, Bill,' was the original last line from Richard Brooks's *Elmer Gantry* (1960), which starred Lancaster as a conman preacher. The Catholic Legion of Decency threatened to give the film a 'C' (Condemned) rating if this dialogue wasn't cut. Like Sitting Bull, Buntline will quickly fade into the past. Back in the arena, Cody feeds off the adulation of the crowd. He has nothing else.

While *Buffalo Bill and the Indians* proved a smooth, relaxed shoot, Altman had to rush the film through post-production. De Laurentiis wanted to launch *Buffalo Bill and the Indians* at a high-profile New York press show, giving Altman an absurdly tight deadline. The two had already clashed over the editing, the producer feeling that Alt- man's cut ran too long. Both Altman and Newman attended the post- screening question-and-answer session. Newman joked with the assembled journalists, 'I hope you left your grenades at the door,' while Altman admitted to feeling nervous. While the director and star were not given a hard time, there was a sense of disappointment. Crit- ics expecting another *Nashville* felt Altman had come up short. That said, the film had its admirers, scoring a hit at the 1976 Berlin Film Festival and taking the Golden Bear award for Best Film. Ironically,

De Laurentiis entered the film in competition against Altman's wishes.

Buffalo Bill and the Indians opened in the US on 24 June 1976, eight days after *Silent Movie*. United Artists' marketing played down the intellectual debate in favour of carnival thrills: 'Presenting the Wildest Wild West Show of Them All!' Given a minimal release, the film failed to win much-needed support from the critics. Pauline Kael, a longtime Altman supporter, wrote a negative review. Writing in *Time* magazine, Richard Schickel praised *Buffalo Bill and the Indians* as 'a sly, wry, wise study of what fame does to people cursed with that most mixed of blessings'. Audience-wise, *Buffalo Bill and the Indians* was a major disappointment, proving Newman's lowest grossing film to date.

Unhappy with *Buffalo Bill and the Indian*'s poor performance, De Laurentiis re-edited the film, taking out twenty minutes. While Altman's contract ensured that his version was released in the US, the UK and France, De Laurentiis had the final say in other territories. It came as no surprise when De Laurentiis dropped Altman from *Ragtime*, handing the project to Milos Forman. Whatever Altman's initial doubts about *Buffalo Bill and the Indians*, he later seemed fiercely attached to the film. During the director's mid-1980s 'exile' in Paris, he hung a large *Buffalo Bill* poster in his office. In contrast, Newman dismissed the film as a missed opportunity: 'Don't know what happened to that one. Made a mistake somewhere, along the line.' By the end of 1976, Newman was no longer among the top ten box-office stars. The number-one spot went to Robert Redford.

Four years on from *The Sting*, Newman reunited with Universal and George Roy Hill for *Slap Shot* (1977), probably the definitive ice-hockey movie. A foul-mouthed black comedy, *Slap Shot* comes close to being an exceptional film.

It began life as a proposed documentary on the minor league ice-hockey scene. Scriptwriter Nancy Dowd's brother, Ned Dowd, played for the Johnstown Jets, and Nancy Dowd spent four weeks with the Jets for research purposes. Dowd's project drew the attention of Hill, who met with her and persuaded her that *Slap Shot* would work as a feature film. Hill showed the finished *Slap Shot* screenplay to Newman, who expressed immediate interest. Still on the lookout for strong, 'significant' material, Newman regarded Dowd's script as a highly original piece of work. The main character, Reggie Dunlop, was based on John Brophy, a player-coach who enjoyed a lengthy minor-league career. While Hill had worried about Newman's reaction to the strong language, it never became an issue. The *Slap Shot* project also drew the attention of Al Pacino, now a bigger star than Newman. Acclaimed for his recent performance in *Dog Day Afternoon* (1975), Pacino felt he would be perfect for the lead. Famously temperamental, Pacino took offence when Hill asked if he could ice skate. According to Pacino, this 'facetious' question showed that Hill didn't take him seriously. Given Hill's commitment to Newman, Pacino may well have been right. Whatever the case, Pacino later expressed regret that he'd missed out on the film.

Newman's co-stars included Canadian actor Michael Ontkean. A gifted sportsman, Ontkean attended the University of New Hampshire on a hockey scholarship, later receiving an offer from the New York Rangers. When it came to being cast in *Slap Shot*, his prowess on the ice rink probably counted for as much as his acting ability. Susan Newman, the star's oldest daughter, was given the small, uncredited role of a pharmacist. Skipping college, Susan had shown interest in an acting career. Taking a different route to Scott, she moved to New York rather than Los Angeles, enrolling in drama classes. Concerned that people only saw her as Paul Newman's daughter, she took to using the name Susan Kendall. Still haunted by his late father's disapproval, Newman didn't dissuade either Scott or Susan from acting. Both were learning the hard way that the profession was tough and unfair. As the children of a world famous film star, they were bound to fall short of expectations, especially their own. Susan made her off-Broadway début in *We Interrupt This Programme*. When the play flopped, Newman offered his commiserations and encouragement. He felt his daughter had done a good job under difficult circumstances. Significantly, he said little about the play itself. By the mid-1970s, Susan had become depressed with the state of her career. Like Scott, she found the big breaks elusive. Newman hadn't seen much of his daughter for a couple of years and hiring her for *Slap Shot* at least gave them the chance to spend time together. In addition to her acting role, Susan worked on the film as a 'Girl Friday', spending a total of fourteen weeks with the production. Newman kept his advice on film acting brief: 'Learn how to relax when you're not on.'

Ontkean aside, Hill had trouble finding actors who could ice skate. He auditioned several television stars, including Peter Strauss, a big name after *Rich Man, Poor Man* (1976). When Strauss broke a leg on the ice, Hill admitted defeat. Dowd's script featured the three Hanson Brothers, borderline psychopaths who become Reggie Dunlop's star players. Hill eventually cast Jack, Jeff and Steve Carlson, real-life hockey-star brothers who played alongside Ned Dowd for the Johnstown Jets. The Carlsons did two readings for Hill, who seemed satisfied with their acting abilities. Shortly before the start of production, Jack Carlson was recruited by the Edmonton Oilers, who required his services immediately. Fellow Jets player David Hanson took over his role.

Newman and his fellow actors trained hard to look convincing as seasoned skaters. Newman, who'd played hockey as a youth, practised for seven weeks prior to the start of filming. Pleased with their progress, he claimed that during shooting 'you couldn't tell the skaters from the actors'. The Johnstown Jets players in the cast helped the actors with their hockey moves, especially the all-important stick fighting; Jeff Carlson, Steve Carlson and David Hanson all paid tribute to Newman's skating skills.

Filmed over the spring and summer months of 1976, *Slap Shot* had a sixty-eight day schedule. Required on set every day of the shoot, Newman sometimes looked weary. Working with Newman for the third time, Hill felt the star had lost his passion for film-making: 'I think Paul is bored with acting. It's too bad. He has the capacity to become a great actor.' Hill also suggested that Newman remained ambivalent about his star status: '. . . being a celebrity is a process of dying, and that has been the hardest thing for Paul to cope with'. Now in his early fifties, Newman often faced reminders of his passing youth and vigour. While he rarely looked at his old films, the media never tired of printing pictures from the *Hustler* or *Cool Hand Luke* or *Butch Cassidy* eras.

The *Slap Shot* production had a good working atmosphere. Newman pulled a number of practical jokes, even faking a car crash to spook Hill. Discovering a local shortage of Coors beer, Newman brought in his own supply. Required to film a sex scene with Newman, actress Melinda Dillon found the star relaxed and good-natured; as a result, the bedroom encounter proved 'a breeze' to shoot. Equally comfortable on ice, Newman was only doubled for the more intricate stickwork, performed by Rod Bloomfield. As he explained: 'I do everything the script requires myself if I can . . . It's not a matter of machismo. It's a feeling of responsibility for the performance.' Michael Ontkean seemed thrilled by the ice antics: 'Newman was my hero as a kid, so it was a pretty amazing experience to work with him and play hockey . . .' Hill didn't give the hockey players much direction, letting their stickwork do the talking. For the hockey sequences, the camera was placed on a sledge, which could be easily manoeuvred around the ice rink. While the sledge left visible marks, most viewers would not distinguish them from skate tracks.

Newman later remarked that working on the film led to a coarsening in his vocabulary: 'Ever since *Slap Shot* I've been swearing more. I knew I had a problem one day when I turned to my daughter and said: "Please pass the fucking salt."' According to *Gamma Rays* writer Paul Zindel, back in the early 1970s Newman referred to his New York apartment as a 'fuck flat'. Newman also claims that spending time with Rocky Graziano for *Somebody Up There Likes Me* left him foulmouthed. Whatever the case, he cited *Slap Shot* as his most enjoyable film experience.

According to *Sports Illustrated*, *The Sporting News* and *ESPN.com*, *Slap Shot* is 'One of the Top Ten Sports Movies Ever!' Newman describes it as 'Just delicious . . . one of my favourite movies.' At its best, *Slap Shot* is genuinely funny, offering bad language, bad driving, bad fashions and bad hair, both real and synthetic. The aggressive, childlike Hanson brothers are a memorable trio, with their long lank hair and nerdy glasses. The broad comedy elements are supplemented by touches of satire. The credits play against the American flag, accompanied by the national anthem. The ice-hockey arena is a microcosm of the new America. The fans are a bloodthirsty mob, no different from the crowds who turned out for gladiators and crucifixions. As George Roy Hill explained, 'The hockey is really a metaphor for modern cultural trends.'

The film's celebration of locker-room culture is dubious. *Slap Shot* is one of Hill's few movies with a contemporary setting, yet the attitudes expressed are Neanderthal. Though written by a woman, *Slap Shot* seems to endorse its protagonists, in all their homophobic, misogynistic glory. The female characters are peripheral at best. Lily Braden (Lindsay Crouse), a hard-drinking player's wife, does little more than sulk and drive too fast. Suzanne (Melinda Dillon), Dunlop's bisexual lover, is more interesting. Confined to one scene, Dillon makes a strong impression. As Steven Spielberg remarked, 'She gives off a lovely light.'

Reggie Dunlop cuts a distinctive figure, favouring a blue turtleneck and black leather coat with fur trim. The character seems tailor-made for Newman, who couldn't play comedy until he learned to relax. Newman also looks good on ice, wielding his hockey stick like a pro. When Ned Braden (Michael Ontkean) protests at the Chiefs' illegal tactics, Dunlop claims that 'Most folk heroes started out as criminals,' an obvious reference to *Butch Cassidy and the Sundance Kid*. Newman later joked that he and Dunlop had much in common: 'That character is a lot closer to me than I would care to admit – vulgar, on the skids.'

Slap Shot – Reggie Dunlop attempts a little crowd control

Universal gave *Slap Shot* a lavish press launch at the Tavern-on-the-Green, a top Manhattan restaurant. Newman agreed to selective one-to-one interviews, orchestrated by publicists Rogers and Cowan. Only journalists with a pro-Newman track record were given access to the star. George Roy Hill defended the film's more provocative elements: 'There's a certain rawness to the script which I liked . . . The harsh language and obscenities in it may provoke criticism, but they are essential to the presentation of this culture. Anything else would be dishonest.' Newman backed his director, dismissing any controversy: '. . . that has to be their problem . . . it was a locker-room picture and it was true to its origins'.

Slap Shot tested well with preview audiences, calming executive nerves over the script's profanities. Universal hoped for a major box-office success, announcing, 'There's never been a film like *Slap Shot*. There may never be another.' Opening in the US on 25 February 1977, the film received mixed reviews. Influential critics Gene Siskel and Roger Ebert gave the movie a 'thumbs down', though both later recanted this harsh verdict. The strong language may have alienated some of Newman's more delicate fans, and Newman conceded that 'for many people it was too blasphemous'. Nevertheless, *Slap Shot* proved a solid hit with audiences, grossing $28 million. While the movie fell short of blockbuster status, it did better commercially than most Newman films of the era. With Newman still a box-office draw, Universal re-released *The Sting* in New York City on 28 April 1977. Newman later cited *Slap Shot* as 'probably my most original work, thanks to the screenplay'.

If nothing else, *Slap Shot* proved that Newman could still cut it as an action man, athletic and virile. Despite his advanced years, he was considered for the role of *Superman* (1978), along with Robert Redford, James Caan, Nick Nolte and Muhammad Ali. On balance, the *Superman* producers made a wise choice in Christopher Reeve.

Slap Shot would be Newman's last film with his older brother. Arthur Newman Jr continued to work as a production manager, based in Lake Arrowhead, California. Susan Newman won a co-starring role in another Universal production, *I Wanna Hold Your Hand* (1978). Scripted by Bob Gale and Robert Zemeckis, who also directed, this comedy about Beatlemania drew praise for its authentic period atmosphere. The film certainly appealed to Steven Spielberg, who served as an executive producer. Set in 1964, the story has four New Jersey teenagers hitting New York, determined to get tickets for The Beatles' appearance on *The Ed Sullivan Show*. Susan Newman's part was intended for *Star Wars* actress Carrie Fisher, who dropped out just a few days before the start of production. Auditioning for the role as 'Susan Kendall Newman', Susan was pleased when Zemeckis didn't immediately connect her to Paul Newman. When Newman asked Susan about her percentage deal for the film, she felt he'd lost touch with the realities of being an 'ordinary' actor. Newman visited Susan on set, posing with her for publicity photographs. He also arranged to appear with her on several magazine covers, aware that his celebrity would draw public interest. Unfortunately, *I Wanna Hold Your Hand* did poorly at the box office and Susan Newman's promising film career faded.

Having finished work on *Slap Shot*, Newman took an eighteen-month break from films to concentrate on his racing career. Since the early 1970s, he had taken his passion for fast cars to a new level. Out on the track, Newman could be one of the guys, his Hollywood status counting for nothing. Driver Brock Yates praised him as 'the most normal superstar of them all'. Interviewed by Lawrence Donegan in 2003, Newman explained:

> The first thing that attracted me was the speed. That, and the faint possibility that I might get good at it one day . . . Racing just

grabbed hold of me. I used to just slink off from doing pictures in order to try and get my licence.

By 1972, Newman had succeeded, starting off driving a four-cylinder Datsun. He was assisted by Bob Sharp, a Connecticut dealer and former racing champion. Interviewed for *Time* magazine in 1982, Sharp praised Newman's concentration, delicacy, wits and sheer guts. For the next four years, Newman competed as an amateur, using the *nom de track* P. L. Newman. In 1975, he established his own team, PLN Racing, with Bill Freeman, a friend and fellow enthusiast. Newman also appeared in and narrated *Graham* (1972), a television documentary about British racing champion Graham Hill. There's no evidence that Newman's film career suffered because of his commitment to racing. That said, he became unavailable for six months of every year: 'I turned my schedule round so I could take off from March until the beginning of October. I just wouldn't work at all, except in winter.' If he felt he'd lost out on some great film roles, he never let it show.

In 1976, Newman became the Sports Car Club of America national champion, Class D, driving a Triumph TR6. He would win the SCCA championship a total of four times, scoring his second victory in 1979. Le Mans winner Rob Dyson, who started in SCCA races around the same time, was highly impressed: '. . . he was a terrific driver, as committed to the craft as he was to acting. This is a guy who could have gone to the top levels of racing had he not come to the sport so late.' Newman secured sponsorship deals with Budweiser – 'I liked the beer' – and the Nissan Motor Company. He agreed to appear in a commercial for the latter, for Japanese audiences only. He also became an official driver for Datsun, earning a princely $5,000 a month. Newman's mother, Theresa, had reservations about his hobby, pointing out that her youngest son was 'no spring chicken'.

Nineteen seventy-nine proved one of Newman's biggest years in racing. In the spring, he entered a celebrity contest at the Riverside Raceway in California. His fellow racers included Clint Eastwood, Gene Hackman and James Brolin. Newman also took part in the heavy-duty Le Mans twenty-four-hour race, with co-drivers Dick Barbour and Rolf Stommelen. At fifty-four, he was the oldest competitor in the event. Barbour, the team boss, seemed unconcerned, rating Newman as a world-class driver: 'He's not just good, he's tremendous. Those machines cost 140,000 dollars each, and I wouldn't ask Paul to risk either his neck or my car if he couldn't handle one.' Never a fan of Newman's racing career, Joanne Woodward tried to dissuade her husband from the notoriously gruelling Le Mans event. As Newman admitted, 'She was really very frightened about me driving in this one, and she made it clear she didn't want me to race.' As always, Woodward's concerns over Newman's high-risk hobby counted for little. Worried about unwanted attention, Newman hired a leading public relations firm to keep the press and fans at a distance. A few days before the race, he arrived at the Le Mans circuit for the trial laps, surrounded by armed police. Despite these precautions, he later described Le Mans as 'the worst paparazzi experience of my life'. Competing in a Porsche 935, his team finished in second place, a personal triumph for the star. As Newman put it:

> Perhaps now people will stop taking me for a stupid actor who is simply playing at racing and accept me as a serious racer. That's what I want more than anything else. Racing is the best way I know to get away from all the rubbish in Hollywood. I'll always remember this race. It was much more interesting than making a film.

In one interview, Newman claimed that if he'd taken up motor racing at the age of thirty, rather than forty-five, he would have quit acting to try his luck as a professional driver. Reminded of this quote years later, Newman put it down to drunken exuberance:

> . . . I must have had four beers at the time. Looking back, to have done that would have been an insanity because I had too big an investment in my profession.

In 1980, Newman suffered the first serious accident of his racing career. Competing at the Golden State Raceway in Sonoma, California, his car overturned. He emerged from the wreck with only a gash to his forehead. Though shaken by this incident, Woodward didn't push her husband to quit racing and, by 1982, she claimed to enjoy watching him compete: 'Paul likes to test himself. That's what makes Paul run.' Newman sounded more pragmatic: 'We have a deal. I trade her a couple of ballets for a couple of races.' During the 1982 season, Newman drove a $70,000, 170 mph, turbo-charged Datsun 280ZX, one of the fastest cars on the circuit. Interviewed for *Time* magazine, he sounded as passionate as ever about his favourite sport:

> I enjoy the precision of racing, harnessing something as huge and powerful as a car and putting it as close to where you want it as you can. Besides, it's a kick in the ass.

Newman hoped to make another film about motor racing. In 1979, he announced plans to star in *Stand on It*, playing a reckless driver who takes increasingly dangerous risks. In the event, he never found the right script. Interviewed by Lawrence Donegan, Newman admitted:

> I don't think there's really ever been a great script about racing, where the characters propel the compulsion of the people to drive and where that compulsion propels the story.

Asked about his long break from films in 1979, Newman played down his racing achievements:

> I decided to take that year and a half off because it was time. I'd been working since I was thirteen, and I figured I was due to put a bunch of time together. It's really funny, though, because I found out that I didn't do anything of consequence. Either sweeping out the old head or the kind of travel that I would have liked to have done. Very peculiar.

According to A. E. Hotchner, Newman seemed happiest during their trips on the *Caca del Toro*, drifting around Long Island Sound.

The film offers continued to come in. Newman was approached by Steven Spielberg, who turned down the chance to work with him on *Lucky Lady*. Riding high after the success of *Jaws* (1975) and *Close Encounters of the Third Kind* (1977), Spielberg was now working on his first comedy, the World War II farce *1941* (1979). He wanted Newman to star in his remake of *A Guy Named Joe* (1943). Produced by Metro-Goldwyn-Mayer, this sentimental wartime fantasy starred Spencer Tracy as a flyer, killed in action. Returning to earth as a ghost, he watches over grieving girlfriend Irene Dunne, encouraging her tentative romance with young pilot Van Johnson. A fan of the film since childhood, Spielberg had acquired the rights and, with an eye to *The Sting*'s box-office success, offered the leading roles to Newman and Robert Redford. Both stars wanted to play the Tracy character, however, and the project stalled. Spielberg later claimed that, at the time, he lacked the emotional maturity to tackle the material. A decade later, the project reached the screen as *Always* (1989), starring Richard Dreyfuss, Holly Hunter and Brad Johnson.

Newman returned to the screen in *Quintet* (1979), distributed by Twentieth Century Fox. This strange science-fiction allegory reunited him with director Robert Altman. Newman and Altman had stayed on good terms since *Buffalo Bill and the Indians*, whatever their differing opinions of the movie. That said, Newman criticized Altman's taste for cheap white wine, which he likened to goat urine. He once presented the director with a baby goat, proclaiming, 'Here, now you have your own vineyard.' Like *Buffalo Bill and the Indians*, *Quintet* seemed a nebulous project, more concerned with ideas than story or character. The title referred to a 'game' involving ritual murder. Cast as Essex, a mysterious hunter–avenger, Newman placed his faith in Altman for a second time.

Since the failure of *Buffalo Bill and the Indians*, Altman had found a new patron, Fox executive Alan Ladd Jr. After the success of *Star Wars* (1977), Ladd could afford to indulge Altman, whose defiantly non-commercial approach alienated most of the big studios. It helped that the director worked non-union, keeping his budgets low. *Three Women* (1977) did well at international film festivals, though many American critics disliked it. Altman had less success with *A Wedding* (1978), a failed attempt at a *Nashville*-style epic. The director cast Susan Newman in a small role, giving her several scenes opposite Italian actor Vittorio Gassman.

Supposedly inspired by one of Altman's dreams, *Quintet* had a troubled script genesis. Altman commissioned a treatment from Lionel Chetwynd, a British-born, Canadian-raised author and playwright. Dissatisfied with the *Quintet* outline, Altman asked for rewrites, yet seemed unsure what he wanted. Chetwynd delivered a second draft, only to be fired from the project. Altman then hired Patricia Resnick, who worked on *Three Women* and *A Wedding*. Resnick felt that Chetwynd's outline borrowed too heavily from *The 10th Victim* (1965), an Italian–French science-fiction satire. She also realized that the central game of Quintet made no sense. According to Resnick, Altman remained vague about the script, leaving her with little direction. Having discarded most of the Chetwynd version, she quit the production. Altman brought in Frank Barhydt Jr, the son of his old boss at the Calvin Company, a Kansas-based outfit specializing in industrial films. Altman tried to remove both Chetwynd and Resnick from the credits, only to be overruled by the Writers Guild.

Still without a workable script, Altman rushed *Quintet* into production, fearful that Twentieth Century Fox would cancel the project. While *Star Wars* had made science fiction a hot genre, *Quintet* didn't have the makings of a blockbuster. When plans to shoot in Chicago fell through, Altman quickly found an alternative location. As with *Buffalo Bill and the Indians*, he opted to film in Canada. This reduced the production costs and put a convenient distance between the director and the Fox executives. *Quintet* was filmed in Montreal, Quebec and

Frobisher Bay during a harsh winter. In Montreal, Altman's team found an old exhibition centre, 'Expo '67: Man and His World', abandoned for ten years. The freezing temperatures fell as low as −40 degrees. To maintain the ice-age chill, Altman shot the interior scenes on outdoor sets built into an existing steel-grid structure on the Ile St Helen.

Quintet – Newman as Essex, the 'anesthesized detective'

Given the murkiness of *Quintet*'s origins, it's unlikely that Newman had a clear idea of Altman's intentions. In the *Quintet* pressbook, Altman explained: 'Games have always fascinated me as they are the reflections of our cultures . . . We've developed Quintet as a game representative of the human condition we present in the film.' Interviewed on location, Newman seemed bemused by Altman's lack of focus. According to Newman, the script had been heavily revised since he joined the production. While Altman had given him an idea of the plot, and one of the many script drafts, 'that plot and that script certainly do not resemble the plot or script we have today'. The cast were sometimes given their rewritten scenes just minutes before they shot them.

Freezing weather aside, *Quintet* was an atypical Altman shoot, with little of the 'party' atmosphere favoured by the director. Nor did the cast get to ad-lib around the scripted dialogue. As Newman explained:

It's pretty hard to get away with improvisation. This picture is too out of our time, it's out of our vernacular. It has to be mysterious without being bewildering. It has to have a lot of double meaning, which is very difficult to add to with any accuracy.

According to Tommy Thompson, Altman's assistant director, the cast and crew still believed that the Altman 'magic' would bring the film to life. Despite the script problems and difficult working conditions, the director seemed on form throughout the shoot. By the end of production, Thompson felt the actors had been let down. As he explained to Patrick McGilligan: 'They trust the director to have the long picture in mind, and I don't think we did.'

The pressbook for *Quintet* promised 'a totally unique motion picture experience'. While this is probably true, most people find the experience unimpressive. But for all its flaws and pretensions, the film has a certain fascination. Altman saw it as 'a grim Grimm's fairy tale', while others rate it as a potent Cold War allegory.

Both intriguing and tedious, *Quintet* is oddly memorable, beginning with distant figures in a frozen landscape. Altman's slow zooms and endless pans have a near-hypnotic quality. He also blurs the edges of the frame, drawing the viewer towards the centre. Despite the futuristic setting, the character names have a quasi-medieval quality. According to Altman, the names, originally Slavic, were changed to correspond with each player's Quintet pieces. According to production designer Leon Ericksen, the sets 'had a remarkable strangeness about them, a feeling of being out-of-time, symbolizing the leavings of a culture'. In this respect, Ericksen felt *Quintet* had achieved the desired fairy-tale quality. The film also benefits from Tom Pierson's score, highlighted by a haunting harp motif.

Slow and dreamlike, *Quintet* badly lacks humour to counter its depressing theme. Only Essex's wife Vivia (Brigitte Fossey) – both childlike and with child – represents hope for the future. Her violent death, early in the film, leaves an atmosphere of unrelenting gloom. The film's imagery is fairly graphic, featuring burned hands, slashed throats and skewered faces.

As a Paul Newman vehicle, *Quintet* seems calculated to alienate his fans. Newman described Essex as 'a detective – a deducer', lacking in emotion:

He's pretty well anesthetized except in this survival-detective kind of way. A lot of human functions, like making love, are simply vague memories in the back of his consciousness . . . Beyond that there really isn't much.

Remote and dispassionate, Essex displays little of the famous Newman charisma. Concerned only with survival, he dismisses hobbies like Quintet as 'just something to do, for no reason'. Earnest and impassive, Essex loosens up when drunk, yet gives little away. Only one scene suggests real feeling underneath: after Vivia's murder, Essex places his wife's body in a flowing river, rather than leave her for the dogs.

According to Twentieth Century Fox's publicity department, Altman asked his cast and crew not to discuss *Quintet* prior to its release. Officially, this was to maintain a sense of mystery around the project, especially the central board game. In all likelihood, both studio and director worried that the movie would be killed by negative publicity long before it hit the theatres. Altman seemed more interested in the commercial potential of the Quintet game, which he felt could catch on with the public. According to the director, the concept had been bought by Kenner and Company, though nothing came of this. The pressbook for the film included a set of rules, which seem complicated, if playable. Intentionally or not, the printed rules gave away the film's plot.

Marketed with the tagline 'One Man Against the World', *Quintet* opened in the US to hostile reviews. Pauline Kael, who once championed Altman's work, described his latest effort as 'a Monty Python show played at the wrong speed'. Many critics wondered why Newman had returned to the screen with such a poor choice of vehicle. The film did little better overseas, with a few exceptions. Discussing *Quintet* in *Punch* magazine, British critic Dilys Powell was enthusiastic: 'I find it mysterious, exciting, tenacious.'

According to Altman, *Quintet* also cost Alan Ladd Jr his post at Fox. The studio's board of directors included Princess Grace of Monaco, the former Grace Kelly. In 1980, the board's annual meeting was held in Kelly's adopted country. During the discussions, Kelly supposedly asked Ladd why he let Altman make such a bad film with such a great actor, Paul Newman. Ladd didn't take kindly to this criticism, making his feelings known in blunt terms. Shortly after, Ladd and Twentieth Century Fox parted company. In truth, Ladd probably fell out with the Fox management over *The Empire Strikes Back* (1980). George Lucas made the studio pay dearly for the *Star Wars* sequel and someone's head had to roll.

Newman loathes *Quintet*, making his feelings clear whenever it's mentioned. Interviewed in 1982, Newman gave the film short shrift: 'Made a mistake somewhere.'

Away from the movies, Newman's ongoing commitment to the Democrat Party brought an invitation from President Jimmy Carter. Impressed by the star's concern over the nuclear issue, Carter appointed Newman a public delegate to a 1978 United Nations special session on disarmament. Predictably, the right-wing press attacked Newman's selection, arguing that a film star had no place in the political arena. Flattered by Carter's invitation, Newman felt futile and out of his depth.

13 Family Tragedy

I don't think I'll ever escape the guilt.
Paul Newman on the death of his son

By the time *Quintet* appeared in cinemas, Newman had endured the worst crisis of his life. For the past few years, Scott Newman had been a major source of concern, unable to get his life together. Still resentful and suspicious, Scott believed that people only valued him for his father's celebrity. At the same time, he had no qualms about trading on the family name when it suited him. Since *The Towering Inferno*, his tentative film career had gone nowhere. He found occasional stunt work, but little in the way of acting jobs. George Roy Hill and Robert Redford hired him as a stuntman and bit-part actor on *The Great Waldo Pepper* (1975), an obvious favour to Newman. Both Newman and Joanne Woodward joined Redford at the film's première, held at New York's Rivoli Theatre. The celebrity line-up also included Dustin Hoffman, Redford's co-star in the forthcoming *All the President's Men* (1976). Despite their presence, Newman seemed to be the focus of attention. Scott also won a small role in *Breakheart Pass* (1975), a western murder-mystery starring Charles Bronson. This United Artists release was produced by Elliott Kastner and Jerry Gershwin, who'd revived Newman's career a decade earlier with *Harper*. Once again, the shadow of his father loomed large over Scott's film work. Cast as Trooper Rafferty, Scott had four lines of dialogue, his features hidden underneath a military cap. Caught up in a nefarious conspiracy, Rafferty is bashed with a wrench and presumably killed. Secret-service man Bronson seems unconcerned. While Scott was billed in eleventh place on the closing credits, his performance drew little attention.

Short of movie offers, Scott accepted a 'guest' role in Universal's hit television show *Marcus Welby, MD*, now in its sixth season. His solid performance in the episode 'Four-Plus-Hot', transmitted on 4 February 1975, proved he didn't have to depend on his father's reflected fame. A few weeks later, Scott could be seen in an episode of *Harry O*, 'Lester', first broadcast on 20 February 1975. His last television role was in the *S.W.A.T.* episode 'The Vendetta', which premièred on 11 October 1975. For all this gainful employment, Scott Newman had to face some harsh truths. A good-looking man and capable actor, he would never have his father's charisma, screen presence or talent.

Writer–producer Charles Gary Allison asked Scott to appear in

Fraternity Row (1977), a semi-professional film project. This perceptive look at 1950s campus life centred on 'hazing' initiation ceremonies, one of which ends in tragedy. Directed by Thomas J. Tobin, the film employed students from the University of Southern California as its cast and crew. Scott co-starred alongside the more experienced Peter Fox, who'd appeared in *Airport '77* (1977), and Gregory Harrison, seen in the hit TV movie *Trilogy of Terror* (1975). Cliff Robertson agreed to serve as the film's narrator, while Don McLean contributed to the original score. Distributed by Paramount, *Fraternity Row* earned some respectful reviews, especially for the performances. The film never found much of an audience, however, and did little for Scott's career.

Scott raised his public profile with a guest spot on Merv Griffin's television talk show. Whether by chance or design, Scott was on his best behaviour, emerging as a charming, articulate young man. After the show went out, Newman congratulated his son for making a good impression. By and large, their relationship remained fraught and unresolved. As Newman later revealed, 'We were like rubber bands, one minute close, the next separated by an enormous and unaccountable distance.' While Scott occasionally joined his father at motor racing events, they tended to talk around the big issues, focusing instead on the track action.

Whatever Scott's potential as an actor, his troubled personal life continued to drag him down. He had few close friends, alienating people with his volatile temperament and heavy drug use. His aggressive behaviour got him into trouble with the law, the charges ranging from disturbing the peace to assault and battery.[1] Faced with similar problems twenty years earlier, Newman had sought professional help. Aware that Scott wouldn't follow his example, Newman decided to take action, sparing no expense. A medical doctor and two psychologists were placed on twenty-four-hour call, in case Scott needed immediate assistance. Parental duties aside, Newman's past troubles gave him some sympathy for Scott's predicament. By contrast, Joanne Woodward supposedly ran out of patience with her stepson. Tired of Scott's errant behaviour, she deeply resented its effect on Newman.

At the time, Woodward had her own problems. By the mid-1970s, she felt she'd become an 'appendage' to her famous husband. Increasingly insecure, she wanted to be known as 'Miss Woodward', not 'Mrs Newman'. Newman and Woodward had a very public row in Sardi's, a New York restaurant popular with show-business figures. Attending a charity auction at the RCA Building in the Rockefeller Center, the couple quarrelled over a successful bid made by Woodward. As media speculation about the state of the marriage increased, Newman's PR people launched a damage limitation initiative. The normally press-shy couple were suddenly available for selected interviews, openly discussing the ups and inevitable downs of their long relationship. Newman admitted to some 'pretty bad hassles' along the way. For all the arguments, Woodward remained fiercely loyal to Newman: 'Paul is one of the few genuinely kind people I know.'

In the autumn of 1978, Newman returned to Kenyon College, where he'd studied drama thirty years earlier. Despite his mixed feelings about Kenyon, he retained a sense of loyalty to his *alma mater*. In 1973, when Kenyon announced the construction of a new $2-million theatre, Newman pledged to direct its first production. Five years later, with the theatre building completed, he honoured this promise. Taking no fee, he would direct Kenyon drama students in Michael Cristofer's *CC Pyle and the Bunyon Derby*. Cristofer happened to be a friend of Woodward. Reminiscent of *The Sting*, *CC Pyle* involved conmen during the 1920s. Playing down his movie-star status, Newman got on well with the students, who found their celebrity director friendly and approachable. Newman praised the talents of his young cast: 'They act with a built-in naturalism.'

By early 1978, Scott Newman's acting career had ground to a halt. Looking to escape his father's shadow, he relaunched himself as a nightclub singer, using the name 'William Scott'. He hoped to record an album, produced by Don McLean. By this time, there was no real communication between Newman and his son. It's been suggested that Scott felt too ashamed to approach Newman. Having measured his career against that of a superstar, Scott despised himself as a failure.

On Sunday 19 November 1978, Scott was staying at the Ramada Inn in west Los Angeles. A recent motorbike accident had left him with shoulder and rib injuries. In considerable discomfort, he countered the pain by increasing his already excessive intake of alcohol and drugs. When a friend supplied him with eight Valium tablets, Scott downed them all at once. Unable to cope, he contacted one of his psychologists, Dr Mark Weinstein, who prescribed Darvan. Weinstein also sent an associate, Scott Steinberg, to watch over Scott at his apartment. This had been a regular arrangement for some time, Weinstein increasingly concerned for Scott's well-being. Though used to dealing with Scott, Steinberg couldn't keep him under surveillance all the time. Retreating to the bathroom, Scott downed several Quaaludes, a barbiturate popular with the Hollywood crowd, and snorted cocaine. Some time after midnight, Steinberg noticed that Scott was having trouble breathing. He immediately summoned paramedics, who rushed Scott to hospital. All attempts at resuscitation failed and Scott Newman was declared dead at 1.07 a.m. on Monday 20 November 1978. While his death is sometimes described as suicide, there's no evidence he made a conscious decision to end his life.

Newman was busy with the student play at Kenyon when he heard the bad news. Grief-stricken, he decided to stay on at the college. If nothing else, the production gave him a much-needed focus, distracting him from the tragedy. Clair Bass, a student involved with the play, recalled Newman explaining, 'I need the show, I need all of you. I need the rowdiness.' Unsure what to do, a group of students presented Newman with some beer and a bottle of Jack Daniels. Graciously thanking his cast for the gifts, Newman took his first drink of hard liquor in eight years.

Newman received unexpected support from Steve McQueen, one of the first Hollywood figures to offer his sympathy. McQueen had worked with Scott on *The Towering Inferno*, playing the seasoned firefighter to Scott's nervous rookie. While McQueen rarely got close to anyone, he probably saw something of himself in the restless, insecure young man with a quick temper. With Newman no longer a threat, either in terms of star status or box-office appeal, McQueen took the occasion of Scott's death to make peace. This newfound respect, bordering on friendship, would last until McQueen's own death in 1980.

The obituaries for Scott Newman were non-sensational. Most stated that Paul Newman had been on good terms with his son, despite their limited contact. There was no media suggestion that Newman had failed in his duties as a parent. This press absolution meant little to Newman. Years later, he was still haunted by a sense of failure, commenting, 'I had lost the ability to help him.' Scott's death brought home a harsh truth. If someone is determined to self-destruct, there is little anyone else can do to stop them. Jacqueline Witte, Scott's mother, made no public comment about her son's tragic death. Scott Newman's funeral was conducted in private. His show-business friends, including the actors Allen Garfield and Mimi Leder, held a memorial service at Actors Studio West on 24 November 1978.

In the wake of Scott's death, Newman and Joanne Woodward served as the narrators for *Angel Death*, a documentary about the dangers of PCP, or Angel Dust. This television special was produced by disgraced Columbia executive David Begelman, who once worked for First Artists. Recently convicted of embezzlement, Begelman's sentence included community service. Newman and Woodward also became involved with the Scott Newman Foundation. This organization was founded by friends and associates of the couple. Woodward quickly came on board, as did Susan Newman, who became the SNF's spokesperson. Following their example, Newman financed an anti-drugs film produced by the foundation. Both Newman and Woodward did publicity to promote the SNF. More forthcoming than her husband, Woodward later discussed Elinor Newman's drug problem, which was mercifully shortlived. In 1981, the SNF funded *Say No*, a documentary dealing with substance abuse and peer pressure.

On 7 December 1978, Pearl Harbor Day, Newman was in Washington DC for a one-day conference on the nuclear weapons issue. He had contributed $25,000 of his own money to fund the event, which attracted over three hundred delegates. Partly because of Newman's involvement, the televised conference drew strong media coverage. The generally favourable public response was deeply gratifying to Newman.

The commercial failures of *The Drowning Pool*, *Buffalo Bill and the Indians* and *Quintet* left Newman's career in an uncertain state. Even *Slap Shot*, a modest hit, seemed a box-office disappointment compared with *The Sting* and *The Towering Inferno*. That said, *People* magazine had recently named Newman as the leading male film star. Robert Redford had to be content with second place. Newman had been offered $3 million to star in *Madonna Red*, only for the project to stall. he also remained in demand for more offbeat projects. Director–choreographer Bob Fosse wanted Newman to star as self-destructive genius Joe Gideon in *All That Jazz* (1979). Best known for *Cabaret* (1972) and *Lenny* (1974), Fosse was the kind of domineering *auteur* film-maker Newman preferred to avoid. It didn't help that the script, co-written by Fosse, was semi-autobiographical, featuring a workaholic, womanising, substance-abusing stage director. Newman had no wish to serve as Fosse's screen alter ego and turned the part down.

Newman's decision to star in *When Time Ran Out* (1980) – originally *The Day the World Ended* – suggested misjudgement tinged with desperation. Produced by Irwin Allen, this inept melodrama brought the 1970s disaster cycle to an end. Newman was paid $2 million to play Hank Anderson, a rough-hewn oil driller who runs into trouble when a volcano explodes on a Pacific island. Unfortunately, reuniting with Allen didn't guarantee a hit. Hoping for another *Towering Inferno*, Newman soon realized he'd made 'a terrible mistake'.

Faced with a bad script which seemed unfixable, Allen fell back on his standard all-star strategy: 'The way to make this picture is to plaster it with names.' He assembled a cast of disaster-movie veterans, including Newman and Jacqueline Bisset, who appeared in *The Life and Times of Judge Roy Bean*. Having paid out for two star names, Warner Brothers felt obliged to press on with the film, despite severe misgivings. The cast also featured William Holden (*The Towering Inferno*), and Ernest Borgnine and Red Buttons (*The Poseidon Adventure*).

Budgeted at $20 million, *The Day the World Ended* was filmed on location in Hawaii, with the interiors shot back in California at the Burbank Studios and MGM's Stage 30. Director James Goldstone had arranged for pre-filming rehearsals, held at the Kona Surf Hotel. While this could have been a concession to Newman, the main objective was to salvage the script. In vain, Goldstone and his cast attempted to inject some suspense and even characterization into the lifeless screenplay. Increasingly unhappy, the actors boosted their morale with a series of specially cooked dinners. Newman took Jacqueline Bisset to the local food market, explaining the importance of fresh ingredients. Bisset offered an Italian pasta dish, William Holden came up with a red hot chilli and Newman served up his speciality chargrilled hamburgers. When Joanne Woodward visited Newman during the Hawaii shoot, he presented her with a new evening gown. The couple flew out to a golf course on the coast, where they enjoyed a fine dinner, accompanied by a string quartet.

While Goldstone was in the director's chair, Irwin Allen remained the production's driving force, closely supervising each day's filming. As Bisset explained, 'He was the boss.' Working in humid conditions, everyone found the shoot physically demanding, and a series of torrential rainstorms caused delays, putting the production behind schedule. Between takes, Newman would look through prospective scripts, anxious to find a more promising project. Always professional on set, he knew that the film was doomed. As Bisset puts it, 'He must have said that to himself many times.'

Script and weather aside, the cast and crew had to contend with William Holden's chronic alcoholism. Normally a dedicated professional, Holden became edgy and uneasy, lashing out at people for no reason. Worried that he might injure himself or a fellow actor, Goldstone summoned professional help. Things didn't improve when the production moved back to Los Angeles. Scheduled for an early start on the MGM stage, Holden turned up hours late and then drank himself in a stupor. Deeply embarrassed by this behaviour, he agreed to be hospitalized, returning to the production six days later. Nevertheless, Bisset recalls Holden as charming. Interviewed by Bob Thomas, Holden's biographer, Newman explained: 'The curious thing is that nobody was pissed off at Bill . . . such was the reservoir of good will that Bill had established, everyone just felt concerned for him.' *The Day the World Ended* completed production $2 million over budget. Interviewed for the pressbook, Bisset was admirably diplomatic: 'It was as extraordinary an experience as I'd hoped.'

The Day the World Ended was in deep trouble long before it hit cinema screens. Advance word on the film was bad, Hollywood insiders predicting a major flop. A nervous Warner Brothers decided that a title change might save the movie. *The Day the World Ended* promised an all-out global apocalypse the film didn't deliver. *When Time Ran Out* seemed a reasonable alternative, ominous yet vague. Under either title, Newman's second disaster movie is an embarrassment for all concerned. Most of the film's budget went on the hefty star salaries, leaving little for the special effects set pieces. As Bisset points out, the grand finale proved a very damp squib. The film received an unexpected publicity boost when real-life volcano Mount St Helens blew its top. However, even this natural disaster couldn't stir audience interest. Released in the US on 28 March 1980, *When Time Ran Out* grossed a pitiful $1.7 million. Newman just wanted to put the experience behind him: 'I'm trying desperately to look the other way.'

As Newman foundered in a sea of fake lava, his former co-star Robert Redford found his career thriving, with starring roles in *Three Days of the Condor* (1975), *All the President's Men* (1976) and *The Electric Horseman* (1979). While Newman struggled to sustain his career as a leading man, Redford made an accomplished directing début with *Ordinary People* (1980), based on a novel by Judith Guest. This well-crafted tale of family trauma was scripted by Alvin Sargent, who'd worked on *The Effect of Gamma Rays on Man-in-the-Moon Marigolds*. Like Newman, Redford preferred not to direct and act in the same film. For *Ordinary People*, he cast Donald Sutherland as the grieving father forced to deal with the death of a son and the end of his marriage. Eliciting fine performances from his cast, Redford won the Academy Awards for Best Picture and Best Director, not a bad haul for a first attempt. Alvin Sargent and co-star Timothy Hutton also took home Oscars.

Newman was among the many Hollywood stars considered for *Once Upon a Time in America* (1983). Conceived, co-written and directed by Sergio Leone, this ambitious gangster epic looked set to relaunch the Italian film-maker's stagnant career. Best known for his cynical, visually audacious 'spaghetti' westerns, Leone hadn't directed an entire feature film for ten years. First mooted back in 1967, *Once Upon a Time in America* finally reached the pre-production stage in early 1980. Leone had Newman in mind for the lead role of gangster David 'Noodles' Aaronson. However, the brutality, misogyny and questionable morality of the script ruled that out. Furthermore, Leone was not an actor's director, treating his cast as just another part of the cinematic canvas. The part of Aaronson eventually went to Robert De Niro. Newman opted to star in a more low-key crime story, *Fort Apache, The Bronx* (1981), playing a character on the right side of the law.

14 Natural Justice

We've been paid to look the other way.
  Frank Galvin, *The Verdict*

Following a run of box-office failures, *Fort Apache, The Bronx* (1981), produced by Time Life, salvaged Newman's flagging career. The film was co-produced by David Susskind, who worked with Newman on *Buffalo Bill and the Indians*. Heywood Gould's script, written in the mid-1970s, was originally intended for Steve McQueen. Gould based his screenplay on the experiences of former policemen Thomas Mulhearn and Pete Tessitore. Both were based at New York's notorious 41st Precinct in the South Bronx, known as 'Fort Apache'. When the semi-retired McQueen turned the script down, the project was put on hold.

Newman's deal for *Fort Apache, The Bronx* paid him around $3 million, plus 15 per cent of the profits. Susskind considered most movie-star fees outrageous, inflated way beyond the actors' drawing power. In Newman's case, Susskind remained diplomatic: 'At least with Paul Newman you know there won't be production delays.' Money aside, Newman felt that *Fort Apache, The Bronx* had something to say, at a time when most films were pure escapism: 'As people get fed more and more movies that are baby food, I think it's important to hit them emotionally with a battle-ax.' Newman seemed disillusioned with the Hollywood scene, observing that the most popular characters of recent years were 'two robots and a shark'. Where did this leave the actors?

Fort Apache, The Bronx reunited Newman with Canadian director Daniel Petrie. Nearly twenty-five years earlier, Petrie had directed Newman in the live television play *Bang the Drum Slowly* (1956). His recent television work included the acclaimed drama *Sybil* (1976), scripted by Stewart Stern, which starred Sally Field as a disturbed woman with multiple personalities. Joanne Woodward, who'd played a similar character in *The Three Faces of Eve* (1957), gave a fine performance as Field's psychiatrist. Premièring on the NBC network in November 1976, *Sybil* proved a hit, Field winning an Emmy award. With her film career more or less on hold, Woodward now found herself in demand for high-quality television work.

The *Fort Apache* crew included Elinor Newman, who served as a production assistant. In the summer of 1981, Elinor had worked as an intern on a theatre programme at Kenyon College. During the late 1970s, Elinor admitted to using drugs, and even Scott's tragic death didn't deter her from substance abuse. Though never an addict, she badly scared her family.

Fort Apache, The Bronx. Newman poses with co-star Edward Asner (left) and director Daniel Petrie (centre)

Cast as a veteran beat cop, Newman wanted John Travolta to play his rookie sidekick. This seemed a shrewd move, as Travolta was one of Hollywood's hottest young stars after *Saturday Night Fever* (1977) and *Grease* (1978). In the event, Travolta passed on *Fort Apache*, perhaps wary of playing second fiddle to Newman. The role went to Ken Wahl, a relative unknown.

Preparing for the movie, Newman talked to ex-cops Thomas Mulhearn and Pete Tessitore, who served as advisors on the film. Tessitore expressed his admiration for the star:

> He's a true professional. We described a lot of our own experiences which he said had been helpful to him, but what really impressed us was his power of observation – the way he was able to pick up mannerisms and the jargon of the cops on the beat.

Researching the Bronx district, Newman admitted to being disturbed by the poverty and urban decay:

The Bronx is a revelation. To realize that you live on its doorstep and never realize what's going on inside your own city came as something of a shock to me.

Newman's enthusiasm for the *Fort Apache* script was not universally shared. Location filming in the South Bronx was picketed by Puerto Rican residents, who believed the film would stereotype their neighbourhood as a crime-ridden slum. Activists set up the 'Coalition Against Fort Apache', operating from a local store. When Daniel Petrie tried to shoot dialogue scenes, coalition members yelled out during takes, rendering the sound recordings unusable. Newman suffered verbal abuse from a group of youths, who also jumped on his car. Opposition to the shoot wasn't confined to the local population. Ed Koch, the mayor of New York City, lent his support to the campaign, condemning the 'racist' production. Presumably, Koch hoped his bold stand against Hollywood exploitation would be popular with voters. William Kunstler, a well-known radical lawyer, filed a libel action against the film on the coalition's behalf.

Wary of bad publicity – and going over schedule – the *Fort Apache* producers called a press conference to placate the locals and reassure the media. This hurriedly organized meeting partially backfired. Newman took exception to the *New York Post*'s coverage, which he considered sensational, biased and misleading: 'The *Post* made the conference sound like a racist thing.' From this point on, he became a dedicated enemy of both the *New York Post* and its right-wing owner, media magnate Rupert Murdoch. The feeling proved to be mutual. The *Village Voice*, another Murdoch publication, attacked Newman and the *Fort Apache* production. *Voice* journalist Richard Goldstein alleged that Newman had verbally abused him at the same press conference. Used to dealing with temperamental stars, Goldstein felt so intimidated by Newman that he left the conference early, unable to take any more. Newman and Petrie denied that their film had a racial slant, with Newman feeling that *Fort Apache* was being misunderstood: 'The film is tough, but it's toughest on the cops.' There was no intent to slander the South Bronx's law-abiding citizens: 'Most people there try to make a decent living for themselves, but it's not easy in those conditions.'

Fort Apache, The Bronx is a series of loosely related set pieces. Seasoned cop Murphy (Newman) attempts to uphold law and order on the streets, giving rookie partner Corelli (Ken Wahl) the benefit of his experience. While Murphy's unorthodox methods work, he regularly

clashes with Connolly (Edward Asner), his by-the-book superior. Heywood Gould's formulaic script is given straightforward treatment by
Petrie. Attempting a little visual excitement, he uses a steadicam, then
a relatively new device, operated by inventor Garrett Brown. Cameraman John Alcott had worked with Brown on *The Shining* (1980), and
it's likely he suggested the steadicam shots.

Fort Apache's star turn is undoubtedly Pam Grier, cast as Charlotte,
a drug-crazed, razor-wielding prostitute. At the start of the film, Charlotte shoots two cops, turning the already tense 41st Precinct into a
war zone. Regrettably, Grier and Newman don't have any scenes
together. While *Fort Apache* seems headed for a grim finale, the film
ends on an upbeat freeze-frame, Murphy finally catching an elusive
mugger.

Whatever the film-makers' intentions, the advertising for *Fort
Apache, The Bronx* played up the sense of urban terror: '15 minutes
from Manhattan there's a place where even the cops fear to tread.'
Released in the US on 6 February 1981, the film grossed a respectable
$29.2 million at the box office. For all the controversy over stereotyping
and outright racism, *Fort Apache* drew largely favourable reviews.
Out on the publicity trail, Newman seemed pleased with the finished
film: 'It's a tough movie in more senses than one. At one time the 41st
Precinct was considered the most dangerous in the country, with the
cops under almost constant siege.' Director Daniel Petrie reiterated his
view that *Fort Apache* was neither partisan nor sensationalist:

> What we are dealing with here is the constant battle between
> the policemen assigned to a violent precinct and the local minority
> citizens who feel the cops are their enemies . . . we haven't pulled
> any punches. We have, however, tried to treat both sides fairly.

Petrie praised Newman as a consummate professional, with one
reservation. In his view, Newman had drifted through his less substantial movies: 'I was lucky to get Paul in a more dedicated mood
than he was in, say, doing *The Towering Inferno*.' While *Fort Apache,
The Bronx* put Newman's career back on track, it did little for his co-
stars. Ken Wahl's movie career never took off and *Fort Apache*
remains his last film of note. Interviewed in 1982, Newman's enthusiasm for *Fort Apache, The Bronx* had waned: 'Some good moments, I
guess.'

Newman's second career as a film director had been on hold since *The
Effect of Gamma Rays on Man-in-the-Moon Marigolds*. He went
back behind the camera for *The Shadow Box* (1980), a made-for-

television drama. Scripted by Michael Cristofer, author of CC *Pyle and the Bunyon Derby*, *Shadow Box* began life as an acclaimed stage play, winning both a Pulitzer Prize and a Tony Award. The story centres on three terminally ill patients and their families. As with *Rachel, Rachel* and *Gamma Rays*, *Shadow Box* was primarily a vehicle for Joanne Woodward.

During the late 1970s, Woodward's small-screen career thrived. Following *Sybil*, she appeared in a British-made version of William Inge's *Come Back, Little Sheba* (1977), produced by Granada Television. Woodward starred opposite Laurence Olivier, an actor she'd admired since childhood. During production, Newman took a break from his racing season to visit Woodward in London. Back in the US, Woodward starred in *See How She Runs* (1978) as a restless housewife who competes in the Boston Marathon. She won an Emmy Award for her performance in this engaging drama, in which Melissa Newman made her acting début, playing one of Woodward's teenage daughters. *See How She Runs* was produced by George Englund, the husband of Cloris Leachman. Woodward had clashed with Englund during the filming of *Signpost to Murder* (1965), dismissing his direction as inadequate. Perhaps in the interests of diplomacy, Englund left the direction of *See How She Runs* to Richard T. Heffron. A television veteran, Heffron's major credits included the pilot for *The Rockford Files* (1974), which boosted James Garner's flagging career. Woodward also starred in *A Christmas to Remember* (1978), a sentimental tale set during the Depression. Scripted by *Rachel, Rachel* writer Stewart Stern, this polished drama benefited from the high-power playing of Woodward, Jason Robards and Eva Marie Saint. Woodward had her work cut out in *The Streets of LA* (1979), cast as a recklessly brave woman in pursuit of the teenage thugs who damaged her car.

Woodward's only recent feature film was *The End* (1978), a patchy black comedy starring Burt Reynolds, who also directed. Woodward played Reynolds's ex-wife, not the most likely piece of casting. While *The End* received fair reviews, Woodward made the film strictly for the money. A keen student of ballet, she had hoped to star in *The Turning Point* (1977), produced for Twentieth Century Fox. Scripted by Arthur Laurents, the film featured two former friends, one a star ballerina, the other a married dance teacher. Ballet aside, Woodward could identify with the script's major themes: friendship, disappointment, lingering resentments and the inevitable conflict between career and family. She supposedly approached Fox chief Alan Ladd Jr, only to be told she wasn't even an outside contender for the film. Worse, Ladd disliked Woodward personally and apparently made no attempt

to hide his feelings. Given Newman's collaboration with Ladd and
Twentieth Century Fox on *Quintet*, this seems unlikely. In the event,
the leading roles went to Shirley MacLaine and Anne Bancroft.

For all Woodward's career disappointments and self-doubt, she
never considered abandoning acting: 'I wouldn't know how *not* to act.
It's like being born with a deformity: you not only learn how to live
with it, you wouldn't know how to live without it.' By 1987, she had
become more guarded in discussing her craft: 'Acting is like sex. You
should do it, not talk about it.' Newman tended to agree:

> It's so hard to explain what it takes to be able to tap the emotion
> that you carry with you. Sometimes you have to dig for it. Other
> times it's at your fingertips and you don't even have to call on it.

The Shadow Box was another highpoint in Woodward's small-
screen career. A good friend of Michael Cristofer, Woodward wanted
to make a television version of his play. *The Shadow Box* would be
produced by Susan Newman, who'd now abandoned her acting career
to work for the Scott Newman Foundation. Realizing that the *Shadow
Box* project lacked commercial appeal, Susan asked her father to
direct the teleplay. Newman's involvement secured a deal with the
ABC network, which agreed to a $1.9-million budget, two weeks of
rehearsal and a twenty-one-day shoot. Once Newman came on board,
he showed total commitment to the project. Working for a token
salary, he agreed to cover any budget overruns personally. Having sold
out on *When Time Ran Out*, he wanted to prove that he could still
handle heavyweight material. *The Shadow Box* also offered a chance
to work closely with both his wife and oldest daughter. Interviewed at
the time, Newman praised Cristofer's original play:

> It's distinguished theatre, and as a director I like to deal with
> material that has some emotional link with the characters in it.
> The play says that we should use our time, not wait until
> tomorrow or until we are facing death, but use it *today*.

Woodward was persuaded by her director and producer to play a
different character from the one she'd intended. Both Paul and Susan
Newman felt she was better suited to the play's most flamboyant figure, who offered more of a challenge. As Newman later explained,
'Given the right parts, she is a great actress. She can find so many different facets of herself to play.' Despite some reservations, Woodward
agreed to this switch, growing in confidence during rehearsals. She
was joined on the film by Christopher Plummer, Valerie Harper and
Sylvia Sidney.

The Shadow Box was filmed during the summer of 1980. Newman disrupted his racing season to direct it, perhaps making a point to Susan about his sense of priority. The production's main location was a Salvation Army camp in the Santa Monica mountains, which doubled as a hospice. Set in California, the drama takes place over one day as the patients and their families visit a rural retreat. The interiors were shot back in Hollywood. It's been suggested that Susan Newman worried about charges of nepotism. Her acting career independent of Newman and Woodward had not worked out. In the event, she got on well with both her father and her stepmother during filming, their dual relationships causing no friction. She also devised a trade-paper advertising campaign for the film. Co-star Melinda Dillon praised Newman as a 'wonderful' director, who handled his cast with great skill. She felt that Newman was still developing as an artist, refusing to be constrained by his icon status: 'He's fought that star thing so hard that he's remaining alive and growing better and better.' According to Woodward, her husband had one special strength as a director: 'He keeps me from crying.' In her other films, the directors seemed unable to restrain this tendency: 'When I'm happy I cry, when I'm sad I cry; no matter what I am, I cry.' Newman declared himself satisfied with the end result: 'I take some pride in that one.'

Eager to promote *The Shadow Box*, Newman put aside his dislike of the media circus. For the first time in five years, he did the talk-show circuit. There was, however, one strict proviso: interviewers were to avoid any questions about Scott Newman's drug habit. Interviewed by Mike Douglas, Newman joked about his discomfort in front of the television cameras: 'Two things make me sweat: live TV and the government.' He sounded positive about *The Shadow Box*, describing it as 'very close to my best work'. Though only in his mid-fifties, Newman admitted that the play's theme held some resonance for him: 'You get to my age and can't avoid thinking about time . . . a year goes by in two and a half months.'

ABC premièred *The Shadow Box* on 28 December 1980. This post-Christmas scheduling was hardly the best slot for a downbeat tale about coming to terms with death. To Newman's disappointment, the network had not found a big-name sponsor for this first broadcast. Though hardly a ratings sensation, *The Shadow Box* drew favourable reviews, and Newman received an Emmy award nomination for his sensitive direction.

Whatever its limitations, *Fort Apache, The Bronx* marked a modest renaissance in Newman's career. He was offered the lead role in *That*

Championship Season (1982), based on a play by writer–actor Jason
Miller. The film version would be directed by William Friedkin, who
cast Miller in *The Exorcist* (1973) as the tormented, self-sacrificing
Father Karras. The main character in *That Championship Season* was
a retired college basketball coach, who enjoys a bittersweet twenty-
fourth anniversary reunion with his old star players. Newman passed
on the film, as did George C. Scott, William Holden, Lee Marvin and
Burt Lancaster. Friedkin eventually abandoned the project, leaving
Miller to direct his own script for infamous producers Menahem
Golan and Yoram Globus. Robert Mitchum played the coach, backed
by Stacy Keach, Bruce Dern, Martin Sheen and Paul Sorvino.

Newman's dislike of tabloid journalism found a tailor-made vehicle in
Absence of Malice (1981), a Columbia release produced and directed
by Sydney Pollack. As with *WUSA* and *Buffalo Bill and the Indians*,
Newman's enthusiasm for the subject matter seemed to blunt his
judgement of strong screen material.

   If nothing else, *Absence of Malice* boasted strong credentials. A television veteran, Pollack made a series of films in partnership with
Robert Redford, notably *Jeremiah Johnson* (1972), *The Way We Were*
(1973), *Three Days of the Condor* (1976) and *The Electric Horseman*
(1979). *Absence of Malice* was written by Kurt Luedtke, a Pulitzer
Prize-winning journalist and former reporter with the *Detroit Free
Press*. Luedtke had been disturbed by a recent Supreme Court ruling,
'*Times* versus Sullivan', which changed America's libel laws in favour
of the defendant. Pollack praised the 'tremendous authenticity' of
Luedtke's screenplay. Nevertheless, the director felt the script needed
revision, hiring David Rayfiel to undertake the rewrites.

   The lead role was intended for Al Pacino, who'd worked with Pollack on *Bobby Deerfield* (1977), a downbeat tale of doomed love and
motor racing. However, Pacino dropped out shortly before the start of
production, opting instead to star in the comedy *Author! Author!*
(1982). In need of a last-minute replacement, Pollack approached
Newman, who praised *Absence of Malice* as 'a marvellously con-
structed script'. The film's main theme struck a chord with Newman,
whose relationship with the press remained prickly: 'Journalists and
newspapers protect each other, like doctors do . . . it's unfortunate
when responsible newspapers won't take the irresponsible ones to
task.' Interviewed for the DVD release, Newman explained that the
film came along at the right time: 'The press was just starting to get a
little more reckless. And revenge has always been one of my favourite
personal motives.' Once Newman came on board, the main character's

ancestry was changed from Italian to Irish. Newman's main antagonist was played by Sally Field, also his tentative love interest.

Absence of Malice – a vehicle tailor-made for Newman's dislike of tabloid journalism

Budgeted at $12 million, *Absence of Malice* began production on 20 November 1980. Dispensing with sound stages, Pollack shot for three months on locations in Miami, Florida. He obtained permission to film in the *Miami Herald*'s newsroom and offices, despite the script's anti-press slant. The *Herald* remained operational throughout shooting, Pollack working between midnight and dawn. He felt that Newman's

acting exhibited 'a greater degree of maturity . . . you're seeing him
now at the top of his form'. In contrast, Sally Field worried she hadn't
captured her character's toughness and sexuality. Newman had problems with a scene where he physically assaults Field. The script called
for a high level of violence, which Pollack intended to reflect both
anger and sex. When Newman proved too gentle, Field deliberately
frustrated her co-star by breaking from his grip. After several abortive
takes, Newman had no problem finding his aggressive side. The following day, Field reported for work with a severe case of whiplash.
The climactic scene involved the Assistant US Attorney General,
played by Wilford Brimley. Newman was concerned about Brimley's
limited acting experience, but trusted Pollack's judgement. Years later,
Newman still seemed impressed: 'He was just spectacular. I can't think
of anybody who could have done it more effectively.'

Absence of Malice is a manipulative lecture on media ethics. Playing
ten years younger than his actual age, Newman admitted that the role
of Michael Gallagher was 'a relatively easy part for me'. Pollack
seemed awed by Newman's performance: 'You really can *feel* him
thinking in this movie. You can see in the silences the wheels turning.'
When Absence of Malice was previewed, audiences expressed disappointment that Newman and Field didn't get together. At Pollack's
request, Newman went into the studio, adding a shot where he hints
that they will meet again.

Selling Absence of Malice to the nation's media presented obvious
problems. The film's subject matter, the abuse of press freedom, was
bound to attract criticism. Hoping for the best, Columbia launched
Absence of Malice at Manhattan's Tavern-on-the-Green restaurant.
Sydney Pollack, Kurt Luedtke and Newman were in attendance, along
with co-stars Sally Field and Wilford Brimley. From the start, the
atmosphere seemed confrontational. According to Newman, '90 per
cent of what people read about me in the newspapers is untrue'.
Television was no better: 'TV broadcasts in a sensational vein. Their
news is for the lowest common denominator.'

Following the Fort Apache incident, the Rupert Murdoch-owned
Village Voice and New York Post were out for Newman's blood.
Newman had also criticized the Washington Post, for an unfavourable
piece on Jimmy Carter, and the New York Times, which he accused of
under-reporting the UN conference on the nuclear threat. His most
vocal opponent was Village Voice reporter Arthur Bell. Newman
rejected Bell's assertion that he despised all the press: 'Only some
aspects. The New York Post being an example.' Bell wrote a scathing
piece on the launch, singling out Newman for attack: 'Just like the

Absence of Malice screenplay, his slanted rhetoric went under the guise of contemporary social truths.' Bell also claimed that Newman had snubbed *New York Post* journalist Diana Maychick, telling her, 'I hate your paper.' Faced with such celebrity aggression, honest journalists had to fight their corner:

> Are we supposed to write attractive copy about one of the most bankable movie stars in the world when he obviously doesn't like us and is using the press to make him more bankable for his next project?

Bell concluded with a personal dig: 'Poor put-upon Newman. If only he were broke and a nobody.'

Absence of Malice went on limited release in the US on 19 November 1981, with a general release on 18 December. ABC-TV critic Joel Siegel praised the film as 'One of the best pictures of the year,' but the print media proved less enthusiastic. According to Pollack, sections of the press claimed that Field's naive reporter wasn't a credible figure. Despite some hostile media coverage, *Absence of Malice* grossed $19.68 million in North America, taking another $21 million in foreign territories. Two decades later, Newman clearly relished Michael Gallagher's stylish, dignified victory over the *Miami Standard*: 'He meticulously nailed them and that's a worthy ambition.' That said, Newman felt the situation with the press hadn't improved, commenting that 'the libel laws in this country are pretty hard to overcome'.

The same month *Absence of Malice* went on wide release, Newman lobbied in Washington to protest at the proposed deregulation of natural gas. Asked why he was there, Newman took the long view: 'I don't want to put on my tombstone that I wasn't part of my time.'

Newman's performance in *Absence of Malice* netted his fifth Academy Award nomination for Best Actor. He went up against Warren Beatty (*Reds*), Dudley Moore (*Arthur*), Burt Lancaster (*Atlantic City*) and Henry Fonda (*On Golden Pond*). While Lancaster had given the finest performance, playing an aging loser who regains his self-respect, the smart money was on Fonda. Now in poor health, the frail star had never won an Oscar, and the Academy of Motion Picture Arts and Sciences knew there wouldn't be another chance to honour him. Having guided Fonda to a strong performance in *Sometimes a Great Notion*, Newman didn't begrudge his old co-star the trophy. At the ceremony, held on 29 March 1982, *On Golden Pond* took the awards for Best Adapted Screenplay (Ernest Thompson), Best Actor and Best Actress (Katharine Hepburn). While most critics had reservations about the film, a treacly, sentimental concoction, few were surprised when Fonda won.

Having enjoyed his revenge fantasy against the press, Newman concentrated on the real world. In the summer of 1981, Newman and Joanne Woodward purchased a second residence in Westport, Connecticut. Situated on the other side of the Aspetuck River, this eighteenth-century farmhouse offered eleven acres of fields and woodland. The old house was retained as a residence for visiting Newman children.

Newman found another definitive role in *The Verdict* (1982), a potent combination of courtroom drama and character study. Cast as Frank Galvin, a burned-out lawyer who redeems himself, Newman gave his strongest performance since *Judge Roy Bean*. Released through Twentieth Century Fox, *The Verdict* reunited him with producers Richard Zanuck and David Brown, who worked on *Butch Cassidy and the Sundance Kid* and *The Sting*.

The Verdict – Frank Galvin, in need of a miracle

The Verdict was based on a 1980 novel by Barry Reed, a practising lawyer. While Reed's book made little impression, the *Verdict* project attracted a lot of interest in Hollywood, and Zanuck and Brown were approached by Roy Scheider, William Holden, Dustin Hoffman and even the long-retired Cary Grant. Frank Sinatra campaigned hard for the leading role, seeking to re-establish himself as a serious actor.

Looking for a suitable director, Zanuck and Brown hired Arthur Hiller; the adaptation was done by playwright David Mamet. Hiller approved the choice of Mamet, who promptly delivered a first draft screenplay. Unfortunately, the end result didn't please Zanuck, Brown and Hiller, who felt Mamet had deviated too much from the book. Worse, the screenplay ended before the jury returned the crucial verdict, leaving Frank Galvin's fate uncertain. Hiller then quit the project.

Dismissing Mamet, Zanuck and Brown hired a new writer, Jay Presson Allen, who had worked with director Sidney Lumet on *Prince of the City* (1981). Allen's rewrite of *The Verdict* met with Zanuck and Brown's requirements. At this point, the producers offered the lead to Robert Redford. Taken with the film's theme, Redford didn't like Allen's screenplay, regarding Frank Galvin as too seedy and unappealing. When Redford suggested giving the project to writer–director James Bridges, Allen was fired. This new partnership didn't work out, Redford rejecting Bridges' script and a subsequent rewrite. When Redford turned down Bridges' third draft, the director quit, with little to show for nine months of work. Redford then approached Sydney Pollack, an old friend and regular collaborator, without consulting Zanuck and Brown. Furious, Zanuck dropped Redford from the project. As no contract had been signed, Redford could hardly cry foul, given the circumstances. According to William Goldman, Zanuck publicly criticized Redford's behaviour, a highly unusual move. Rumours spread that Roy Scheider had been signed for the lead.

Running out of time and patience, Zanuck and Brown offered *The Verdict* to Sidney Lumet. Lumet had seen David Mamet's *Verdict* script long before Zanuck and Brown came calling. Having signed for the film, he read through the various rewrites, which got progressively worse. Whatever its faults, Mamet's draft was the strongest by far. Aware of Zanuck and Brown's reservations, Lumet felt the script could easily be fixed. His biggest problem with Mamet's screenplay was the open ending, which left the crucial verdict hanging in the air. Audiences would not accept this after two hours of heavy drama, so Lumet persuaded Mamet to provide a clear, positive resolution. Having been fired from the project once, Mamet remained philosophical about the experience: 'It's my job, when I take a job, to do it the best

I can.' At this point, Redford supposedly got back in touch, only to find himself out of the running.

Lumet sent the script to Newman, who was finishing off *Absence of Malice* at the time. The pair had been friends since their days in live television, back in the 1950s. Newman felt the revised Mamet script was a powerful piece of drama, with a demanding lead role. Less bothered than Redford about Galvin's character flaws, he agreed to star in the film. As he later explained:

> It's a very interesting character for me, because he's so unlike Cool Hand Luke, Butch Cassidy or any of the other cool, collected types I've played. Galvin's frightened. He's living on the edge and he's panicking . . . he's a believable, fallible human being and I think that's why people will be able to identify with him.

Newman empathized with at least one of Galvin's foibles: 'I could certainly understand his attraction to booze.' Co-producer David Brown felt they'd made the right decision: 'Paul Newman sets the standard by which all superstars should be measured.' Never prone to temper tantrums or bad moods on set, Newman made no outrageous demands and didn't travel with a vast entourage. According to Brown, 'His only demands are that he be supplied with popcorn – and some beer.'

Newman's co-stars included James Mason, who had appeared with him in *The Mackintosh Man*. Like Newman, Mason had worked with Lumet on several live television plays, as well as films such as *The Deadly Affair* (1966). Interviewed at the time of *The Deadly Affair*, Mason praised Lumet: 'Sidney is a marvellous director . . . I work better if a director will needle me, discipline me, help sharpen up my ideas.' For his part, Lumet rated Mason as one of the three finest movie actors, alongside Spencer Tracy and Henry Fonda. Lumet first offered Mason the sympathetic role of Mickey Morrissey, Galvin's long-suffering colleague and best friend, but Mason was more interested in the part of Edward Concannon, the elegantly ruthless defence lawyer. Despite his past collaborations with Lumet, Mason had trouble persuading the director to recast him. Determined to change Lumet's mind, he even read scenes over the phone to show he could play the 'bad' lawyer. The role of Morrissey eventually went to character actor Jack Warden, one of the jurors in Lumet's *Twelve Angry Men* (1957).

Very much an actors' director, Lumet shared Newman's belief in pre-production rehearsals: 'Good acting is really self-revelation . . . it takes time to get people free enough to do that.' Zanuck and Brown agreed to three weeks of rehearsal, winning Lumet's praise as supportive, non-interfering executives. *The Verdict* began production in early

1982. Newman's schedule included several night shoots in damp, bitterly cold winter weather. The all-important courtroom was a studio set, as the genuine article would have limited Lumet's options for camera set-ups and lighting. During filming in an apartment, a wooden batten holding eight lights crashed to the ground, missing Newman by inches. The chief grip, responsible for equipment safety, broke down in tears.

Newman welcomed the chance to play a character close to his actual age: 'It was such a relief to let it all hang out in the movie – blemishes and all.' He drew on his old Method techniques for a scene where Galvin arrives at a meeting out of breath, running around a sound stage until he was exhausted. Describing Galvin as a 'very compelling and difficult character', Newman didn't find him completely until filming began. He gave most of the credit to his fellow actors: 'They're like litmus paper. You throw something at them and they flash back an extraordinary colour that you respond to.' For him, *The Verdict* was a prime example of cinema as 'a community medium'. Interviewed for a 'making-of' featurette, Newman declared, 'I'm having a wonderful time.' Lumet praised Newman as 'a complete actor', unconcerned with his screen image. Newman's co-stars were impressed by his dedication to the film and lack of vanity. Charlotte Rampling seemed taken with her leading man: 'Paul is so attractive because he's *so* human.' She liked Newman a lot, finding him refreshingly different from many of her male co-stars. Milo O'Shea felt Newman had matured into a fine actor, leaving behind the 'pretty boy' image that limited his opportunities: 'Paul was "sold" on his looks. Now there are some lines and wrinkles in his face, giving him the character that perhaps he has been seeking.' O'Shea also suggested that the tragic death of Newman's son 'had a great effect on his work and his life. He really is feeling his way into a deeper part of himself, to a layer that has never been exposed before.'

The extras employed for the climactic courtroom sequence included an aspiring young actor named Bruce Willis. A decade later, Willis reunited with Newman for *Nobody's Fool* (1994). Now a major star, Willis agreed to play a supporting role.

Prior to the jury's verdict, Frank Galvin delivers an impassioned speech on the nature of justice. Newman did a great first take, only for Lumet to discover that the film had been scratched by dirt in the camera. Fortunately, Newman's second take was even better. *The Verdict* finished production on schedule. Confident in the film, Lumet had enjoyed the experience, and Newman credited him with keeping the shoot moving: 'He's the only guy who could double park in front of a whorehouse. He's that fast.'

Newman felt satisfied with his work on *The Verdict*, an opinion endorsed by others. Old friend A. E. Hotchner saw a new boldness and maturity in Newman's performance: 'I feel that he's finally opened himself up as he used to on the stage . . . now he's not playing it as safe in his films.' Lumet described *The Verdict* as a 'very good movie', thanks largely to Newman.

An effective legal drama, *The Verdict* works best as a study of frail humanity. Frank Galvin is first seen in a dingy bar, knocking back the beer as he plays pinball. The camera slowly tracks in on Galvin's shadowy figure, revealing a worn, troubled face. Galvin has progressed from ambulance chasing to corpse stalking, staking out funeral homes for vulnerable clients. Drawing on his own experience, Newman is utterly convincing as an alcoholic, with flushed complexion, stumbling speech and unsteady walk. For all Galvin's hearty bar camaraderie, his glazed eyes and open mouth tell the real story. Unable to lift his whisky glass, thanks to a bad case of the shakes, Galvin lowers his head and takes a sip. Newman gives a powerful performance.

Many of Galvin's mannerisms and character traits were not in Mamet's script. The pinball, one of Lumet's touches, conveys both inner turmoil and the desperate urge to win. Newman suggested that Galvin use eye drops, as he did, and breath freshener, to cover the smell of booze. He also improvised the business of Galvin wiping his mouth with a bar cloth. A non-smoker, Newman puffs on a cigarette with nervous conviction.

Newman embarked on a major publicity drive for the film. He appeared on several magazine covers, including *Rolling Stone* and *Time*, a publication he'd criticized in the past. He also agreed to be interviewed for *Playboy*, unperturbed by its soft-porn image. Playing safe, Newman stressed that *The Verdict* wasn't an attack on the legal system, the Catholic Church or hospitals: 'These institutions are merely a springboard for the development of the Galvin character. They're metaphors for what seem to be insurmountable obstacles all around him.' Written by John Skow, the reverential *Time* profile described Newman as 'possibly the most commanding male presence in films during the past three decades'. His very appearance made 'men's eyes mist over, and women's knees go wobbly'. Characters such as Eddie Felson and Hud Bannon were 'scapegrace heroes', ingrained into America's collective psyche. At the age of fifty-seven, Newman could pass for a man in his mid-forties. Rising above the herd of mere stars, he was 'Reddi Wip topping with jimmies – a superstar!' Susan Newman offered a more down-to-earth perspective on her celebrity father:

'Who knows? None of us in the family has a handle on how Old Skinny Legs made it.'

Opening in the US on 8 December 1982, *The Verdict* earned Newman some of the best reviews of his career. *US Magazine* was ecstatic: 'Paul Newman blesses us all with one of his most galvanising [*sic*] performances.' *Time* journalist John Skow rated Newman's acting as 'brilliant . . . his voice has the breathy rasp of a drinker, his walk the uncertainty of a strong man going down'. *The Verdict* took $26.65 million at the North American box office. Worldwide, the film made $54 million, an impressive total for a grim courtroom drama.

August 1982 saw the launch of Newman's Own food products. Newman devised this charitable concern with his Connecticut friends and neighbours, A. E. and Ursula Hotchner and photographer Steve Colhoun. The first Newman's Own product, an oil-and-vinegar salad dressing, was based on Newman and A. E. Hotchner's original recipe, a favourite with family and friends for many years. As Jacqueline Bisset discovered while filming *When Time Ran Out*, Newman took his food very seriously. Some time in the 1970s, Newman and Joanne Woodward were dining at Chasen's, a chic Los Angeles restaurant popular with the show-business set. Presented with a ready-dressed salad, Newman took it to the men's room, washed it, and returned to his table, where he redressed the salad himself. As *Time* journalist John Skow pointed out, this seemed 'a fairly gaudy stunt for a man who does not like to attract attention'. Newman talked of opening his own restaurant in Westport, Connecticut. As Hotchner recalls, Newman found most of the local establishments unimpressive.

In 1978, Newman and Hotchner offered their home-made salad dressing to local shops. Half-intended as a joke, this initial product-testing proved an unexpected success. During the Christmas season of 1981, Newman and Woodward filled old wine bottles with the salad dressing, handing it out to friends and neighbours on their carol-singing jaunts. When people came back for more, Newman and Hotchner started thinking seriously about marketing their product. While this sounds like the stuff of myth, Newman swears otherwise: 'That was actually, truly, how it got started.' Interviewed by Brian Baxter in 1987, he explained:

> I wanted it to be just a cottage industry at first, a small personal thing, but there were all sorts of regulations, controls on bottling – we couldn't just use up our old wine bottles – and shelf life.

Interviewed by Ron Hogan, Hotchner credited Newman as the driving force behind the project: 'At first I didn't think he was serious about trying to bottle his dressing.' An astute businessman, Newman commissioned a market survey before taking the plunge. Though the results proved encouraging, Newman and Hotchner had no illusions about the risk involved: 'We just expected to throw $40,000 into the wind and that would be it.' According to Hotchner, he and Newman were driven more by curiosity than a sound business plan: 'It became a game for us, a hell of a challenge . . . it was intriguing to learn about the food business.'

From the start, the Newman's Own enterprise was intended as a charity fundraiser. Newman and Hotchner pledged to produce an annual report, published in the national press, detailing how the profits had been spent. Newman's Own salad dressing was manufactured in a Boston factory, in accordance with federal regulations. Initially sold only in New England, the dressing proved an instant hit. The market soon expanded to New York, New Jersey and Connecticut, with limited distribution in Boston, Washington, Baltimore, Minneapolis and Chicago. By Christmas 1982, Newman's Own Olive Oil and Vinegar Dressing was available nationwide. Over the next few months, it became an established bestseller. A television advertising campaign featured the slogan 'It's time to rev up your summer salads . . . Go ahead, pour it on!' John Skow was struck by Newman's confidence in his product: 'Newman is the sort of man who questions his acting ability, but is sure he makes the world's best salad dressing.' Interviewed in September 1982 by New York Times reporter Mimi Sheraton, Newman declared: 'I guess I've had more fun doing this than anything else I've done in a long time.' Perhaps his time with the Newman-Stern sporting goods store was paying off at last: 'I came from a family of retail people.' He also went for a light-hearted political jibe: 'But remember, it's really my way of telling Ronald Reagan that his salad days are over.'

The launch of Newman's Own was tinged with sadness. The same month, Theresa Newman died of cancer. Having outlived Arthur Newman by more than three decades, Theresa spent her last years in Riverside County, California. After losing his son and mother in the space of four years, Newman became ever more determined to use his time wisely.

In May 1983, Newman's Own launched a spaghetti sauce, Fra Diavolo ('Devil's Brother'), based on one of Ursula Hotchner's recipes. A. E. Hotchner felt they were doing a public service, as 'everything else was just so awful. People have forgotten how bad spaghetti sauce was back then.' Made with natural ingredients, a Newman's Own trademark, Fra Diavolo met with Hotchner's approval: 'Putting that on spaghetti is my idea of heaven.' Like the salad dressing, it was a hit. The Newman's Own range later included Old-Style Picture Show Popcorn. A longtime popcorn fan, Newman wanted to share his passion with the world. Naturally, the Newman's Own popcorn would be organic. Lest Joanne Woodward feel excluded, Newman praised his wife's hollandaise sauce as the best in the world: 'She has never been topped by any restaurant.' In the summer of 1987, Newman's Own launched its Old-Fashioned Roadside Virgin Lemonade, with Newman claiming that 'Joan Collins was restored to virginity after drinking four quarts of it.' A. E. Hotchner suggested that Newman could enjoy another hit with his own brand of hamburger, 'which he says has never been duplicated by man'. Newman and Hotchner also considered a Newman's Own beer, negotiating with a brewer in Norwalk, until Woodward vetoed the idea. Newman eventually supplemented the original salad dressing with Newman's Own Caesar Dressing. The label featured a mock-up bust of Newman as a Roman emperor. Having shunned toga roles since *The Silver Chalice*, he made an exception for charity. Five years after its launch, Newman's Own had an annual turnover of $24 million.

To date, the profits from Newman's Own have gone to the AIDS Medical Foundation, Cystic Fibrosis, the Alzheimer's Disease Association, Inc., the Actors Studio, the American Ballet Theatre, Kenyon College and Yale University. In 1985, Newman's Own donated $250,000 to drought relief in Africa. A. E. Hotchner spoke about Newman's Own at Yale's business school. Interviewed in 2000, Newman still seemed bemused by the huge success of his food products venture:

> I can only say that, if someone told me twenty years ago that I'd have my face on a bottle of salad dressing, I'd have got them committed. But it's turned out in a way that we've never, ever expected.

According to its founder, the Newman's Own motto is 'From salad dressing all blessings flow.' Twenty years on, Newman is still a reluctant food magnate. As Hotchner explains, 'He really doesn't like the hustling.' The pair chronicled the Newman's Own saga in a book, *Shameless Exploitation in Pursuit of the Common Good: The Madcap Business Adventure by the Truly Oddest Couple* (2003). This project came about after a friend pointed out to Hotchner that 'maybe half the people who buy our products don't know our money goes to charity'.

In the autumn of 1982, Newman gave an hour-long interview to Ted Turner's Cable News Network (CNN). The topic under discussion

PAUL NEWMAN

was Proposition 12, a nuclear freeze initiative. Newman, of course, supported the move. He also spoke at a rally in Los Angeles, which carried the slogan: 'With Enough Shovels . . . The President's Men Could Dig Our Country's Grave.' Joanne Woodward gave her full backing: 'He's got a lot of courage, a highly underrated element in people's lives these days.' After twenty years of high-profile political activism, Newman still felt awkward as a public campaigner. He appeared on the ABC show *The Last Word* to debate the nuclear weapons issue, his opponent being fellow film star Charlton Heston, a one-time liberal turned reactionary. Newman found the experience frustrating, feeling he hadn't argued his case well. On reflection, he rated his performance as adequate: 'I've done better and I've done worse, but in the final analysis, it was better than not doing anything at all.' In the long term, he doubted that the success of Proposition 12 would have much effect on the Reagan administration. As a political 'traitor', Heston ranked low in Newman's estimation. A few years later, the Scott Newman Foundation held a ceremony in Los Angeles, honouring television and film people involved in anti-drug campaigning. When Newman learned that Heston would introduce him at the awards dinner, he objected strongly. Heston was replaced by the acceptably liberal Donald Sutherland.

On the domestic front, Newman's life seemed reasonably harmonious. His youngest daughter, Clea, now seventeen, had become an enthusiastic horsewoman, showing some promise. In the autumn of 1982, she took part in the National Horse Show, held at Madison Square Garden. When her performance proved disappointing, Joanne Woodward was on hand to offer condolences. 29 January 1983 marked Newman and Woodward's twenty-fifth wedding anniversary, and the couple celebrated with a small party at their Connecticut home. According to Gore Vidal, Newman had a simple explanation for the success of the marriage: 'It's because we have absolutely nothing in common. I race cars. She goes to the ballet.' Jokes aside, Newman made his feelings for Woodward clear:

> Joanne has always given me unconditional support in all my choices and especially with my racing, even though she has never stopped disapproving. To me that's love.

As his salad dressing flew off the shelves, Newman seemed on the verge of Academy Award success. *The Verdict* was nominated in most of the major categories: Best Picture, Best Director, Best Actor, along with Best Adapted Screenplay and Best Supporting Actor (James

Mason). Sixth time around, Newman faced his toughest competition yet: Dustin Hoffman (*Tootsie*), Ben Kingsley (*Gandhi*), Peter O'Toole (*My Favourite Year*) and Jack Lemmon (*Missing*). Ironically, Lemmon was nominated for a role Newman had turned down. Interviewed on the Florida location for *Harry and Son*, Newman offered a measured appraisal of the Oscar race:

> To say that I'm not interested would be hypocritical . . . I'm enough of a pragmatist to realize that the Academy Awards are good for the industry, they're good for a film . . . it's very comforting to be recognized by your peers.

Newsweek magazine suggested that Newman was covertly lobbying for the award, via the Rogers and Cowan agency. While this tactic is hardly rare practice in Hollywood, Warren Cowan responded with a fierce letter of denial. Both Newman and Woodward flew from Florida to attend the ceremony in Los Angeles. Richard Zanuck recalls begging Newman to show up, promising the star that his time had come. On the night, Ben Kingsley took the award for his extraordinary performance as Mahatma Gandhi. As usual, Newman proved gracious in defeat: 'I flew to the coast only to prove I'm a good loser.' Sidney Lumet made his feelings clear: 'Paul was robbed.' To date, Newman had lost the Best Actor trophy to David Niven, Maximilian Schell, Sidney Poitier, Rod Steiger, Henry Fonda and Ben Kingsley. Of the six, only Poitier and Fonda had obviously won for reasons unrelated to their performances.

Discussing the 1983 awards, Clint Eastwood offered his own theory:

> The Academy Award group . . . is political and so often gives Oscars to actors who don't have popular appeal and therefore aren't threatening – people like Ben Kingsley. I'm not putting these people down. I'm just saying that a popular movie star like Paul Newman, who competes for jobs with Academy members, doesn't have a chance against them.

If nothing else, Newman's situation offered a certain irony. After a dry patch in the late 1970s, he had bounced back with a run of box-office hits and two consecutive Oscar nominations. Now in his late fifties, he was too successful for his own good.

15 Creative Angst

I want to work and can't. You can and don't.
  Harry Keach, *Harry and Son*

With or without the Oscar, Newman's triumph in *The Verdict* confirmed his career renaissance after several lean years. While he would never have another hit on the scale of *The Sting* or *The Towering Inferno*, the box-office grosses of his last three movies were more than respectable. Significantly, Newman proved selective in his choice of projects, unwilling to work as a star-for-hire. He turned down a co-starring role opposite Jane Fonda in *Rollover* (1981) and also passed on Costa-Gavras's *Missing* (1982) and Robert Zemeckis's *Romancing the Stone* (1984). While the latter could be dismissed as just another frivolous blockbuster, *Missing* seemed the ideal Newman vehicle. Set in 1973 Chile during the US-backed coup, the based-on-fact script used its thriller format to explore the themes of political corruption and troubled family relationships. Newman would play a conservative American businessman searching for his political activist son against a backdrop of chaos, paranoia and brutality. Costa-Gavras eventually cast Jack Lemmon. Around the same time, Marlon Brando announced plans to make a film about the notorious 1864 Sand Creek Massacre, a subject previously covered in Ralph Nelson's *Soldier Blue* (1970). Taking no fee, Brando tried to recruit both Newman and Robert Redford as his co-stars, presumably at bargain rates. Like most of Brando's personal projects, the Sand Creek movie quickly fell by the wayside.

One of Newman's pet projects was *King of the Hill*, based on an autobiographical novel by A. E. Hotchner. Set in 1930s St Louis, this coming-of-age story centred on an imaginative twelve-year-old boy growing up during the Great Depression. Newman and Joanne Woodward acquired the film rights but couldn't get the production off the ground. Hotchner's book was finally brought to the screen in 1993 by writer–director Steven Soderbergh. Co-produced by Robert Redford's company, Wildwood, the film drew praise for its strong ensemble playing and evocative atmosphere. Newman and Woodward also talked with writer friend Stewart Stern about a sequel to *Rachel, Rachel*. This came to nothing, possibly because Rachel Cameron's story had reached its natural end in the original movie.

Newman followed *The Verdict* with the generation-gap drama *Harry and Son* (1984), his first feature film as a director in over a decade. It was loosely based on a novel, *A Lost King*, by Raymond DeCapite. Published in 1961, *A Lost King* centred on a young man living with his widower father and his problems adjusting to modern life. Dispensing with a professional screenwriter, Newman adapted the book himself, in collaboration with old friend Ronald L. Buck, a Los Angeles-based lawyer, restaurateur and builder. Newman and Buck worked on the script for over two and a half years and more than twenty-five drafts. In the process, Newman cut out a lot of humorous lines, dismissing this approach as a cheap trick. He also felt that the early drafts overdid the intense emotion. Audiences would be drained long before the denoument. Buck agreed that this extensive rewriting 'vastly improved' the screenplay and praised Newman's skill as a writer, especially his ear for dialogue. Newman stressed that the screenplay wasn't a veiled account of his relationship with Scott. While he planned to make a film about his son's death, the time hadn't yet come. If anything, the script reflected Newman's relationship with his own father. Buck took a different view, recognizing Newman and Scott in the characters of Harry and Howard Keach.

Newman touted the finished script, entitled *Harry's Boy*, around the major studios. Throughout the project's long gestation, he had never intended to play the blue-collar Harry Keach himself, feeling that Gene Hackman would be ideal for the role. It soon became clear, however, that the film would not get made without Newman in the lead. While *The Verdict* had reaffirmed Newman's stardom, his career as a director remained both intermittent and precarious. No studio was interested in a Paul Newman film which didn't have Paul Newman in it.

After his experiences on *Sometimes a Great Notion*, Newman had no further desire to direct and star in the same film. While Clint Eastwood seemed happy with the arrangement, Newman saw it as doomed to failure: 'Something's got to suffer. You can't pay enough attention to the other actors when you're acting, and you can't do your role justice when you're directing.' Already on board as the producer, director and co-writer, Newman felt cornered: 'I didn't want to bring in someone else to direct, and I couldn't get the movie made with anyone else in the role.' Bowing to harsh economic reality, he made a deal with Orion Pictures, a company founded in 1978 by former United Artists executives. At the time, Orion had a reputation as a director-friendly studio, backing John Boorman's *Excalibur* (1981) and Woody Allen's *A Midsummer Night's Sex Comedy* (1982). In Newman's case, the relationship had got off to a shaky start.

Committed to making *Harry and Son* on Orion's terms, Newman chose Robby Benson as Harry's son Howard. Benson's love interest was played by Ellen Barkin, who'd given an accomplished performance in *Diner* (1982). The role of Harry's brother went to Wilford Brimley, who so impressed Newman on *Absence of Malice*. Newman gave a small role to struggling actor Morgan Freeman, whose movie career at the time consisted of bit parts in *Brubaker* (1980) and *Eyewitness* (1981). Freeman had been on the verge of quitting the business before he was hired by Newman.

Harry and Son also marked a modest film 'comeback' for Joanne Woodward, whose recent television work included *Crisis at Central High* (1981). Set in Little Rock, Arkansas, in 1957, this powerful based-on-fact drama explored the furore over racial integration in education. Woodward played the real-life figure of Elizabeth Huckaby, a high-school teacher caught up in the events. The following year, Woodward made her directing début with *Come Along with Me* (1982), made for PBS's American Playhouse series. This offbeat drama was based on Shirley Jackson's last, unfinished novel, published in 1968, three years after her death. Estelle Parsons, from *Rachel, Rachel*, played a widow with psychic powers who moves into a boarding house inhabited by odd characters. Newman contributed a voice-only cameo.

By early 1983, Woodward felt she'd gone into 'artistic hibernation'. Keen to support her husband, she took a small role in *Harry and Son*: 'I just wanted to go, to do something.' Despite the difficult circumstances, Newman welcomed the chance to act opposite his wife, explaining, 'When we work together, we both know we can't get away with any old tricks.'

Harry and Son was filmed in Florida over the spring of 1983. Throughout the production, Newman seemed unhappy. In truth, he'd made too many compromises to get the film off the ground. He later admitted, 'I threw caution to the wind, and as far as the workload, I really regretted it . . . you can't do your best work when you're beat.' Now pushing sixty, he worked fifteen-hour days, six days a week. When Newman returned from the Academy Awards ceremony, having lost out on the Best Actor prize for the sixth time, he received a round of applause from the cast and crew. Visiting *Life* journalist Peter W. Kaplan noted the star's bashful reaction: 'Newman's skin got redder than usual, and his white teeth got wider, and his blues pointed straight to the ground.' While Newman appreciated this show of support, the sour Oscar experience didn't help his mood on set.

Woodward's part, originally just a few lines, was expanded to a major supporting role. At Newman's request, she also directed Harry Keach's death scene. Still unhappy with his dual responsibilities, Newman wanted to concentrate on his acting for this crucial sequence. Both Woodward and a visiting Newman daughter were moved to tears by his performance. With typical modesty, Woodward played down her behind-the-camera contribution: 'Did I direct him? I *couldn't* direct Paul.' During post-production, Newman and editor Dede Allen noticed an unusual problem with the footage. In some scenes featuring Newman's character, he was obviously watching the other actors as a director, rather than playing his own role. While Allen carefully excised these shots, their presence was a pointed reminder of the production problems. There could be little doubt that Newman had overstretched himself. Exhausted by the *Harry and Son* shoot, he vowed that his first outing as a producer–director–writer–star would also be his last: 'never again' was his verdict.

It's unfortunate that Newman's most personal project is also one of his weakest. Studio politics aside, his passion for the subject matter seems to have clouded his judgement. Significantly, Newman never felt satisfied with the script, which he rewrote throughout filming. As a piece of film-making, *Harry and Son* has none of the flair shown in *Rachel, Rachel*. Newman's direction is no more than competent, which could have worked with a stronger script. The most impressive visual touch comes right at the start. As the credits roll, Harry's crane demolishes an old building, the wrecking ball swinging in hypnotic slow motion. Through a trick of perspective, the ball takes an age to connect with the brickwork, building unexpected suspense.

Harry and Son's biggest failing is the central relationship. It's arguable that Newman miscast Robby Benson, a specialist in shy, sensitive teenagers. In this instance, Benson's acting ability is overshadowed by his big eyes and gleaming white teeth. Newman doesn't convince as the elderly, worn-out Harry Keach. In fairness, he never felt comfortable in the role, which he'd only taken under duress. Woodward plays an old friend of Harry's late wife, who offers the chance of late blossoming romance. The understated attraction between the characters is quite well played. Having learned to live again, Harry promptly dies. If Newman was aiming for tragic irony, the movie falls short.

Harry and Son opened in the US on 2 March 1984. Orion Pictures had little faith in the film, releasing it with minimal publicity. When the initial box-office returns proved disappointing, Newman tried to save his film with a round of newspaper, magazine and television interviews. Despite the many production problems, he still believed in *Harry and Son*, feeling it gave audiences 'an emotional experience they can identify with'. Questioned about his son Scott, he again denied that the film was an exorcism of their relationship: 'You can't fictionalize grief.' For all the press speculation about the film mirroring Newman's relationship with Scott, *Harry and Son* never drew audience interest.

Putting the disappointment of *Harry and Son* behind him, Newman devoted much of 1984 to motor racing. By the mid-1980s, his commitment to his favourite sport had reached a new level. In 1983, he became co-owner of Newman–Haas Racing, competing in the Championship Auto Racing Teams (CART) series. For several years, Newman had enjoyed a fierce rivalry with fellow driver Carl Haas. Mario Andretti, a Formula One world champion, talked Newman and Haas into joining forces. Realizing that Newman might be sceptical, Andretti promised to drive for the Newman–Haas team. As Newman later explained to Lawrence Donegan, this was a deal he couldn't refuse: 'Who is going to turn down the chance to own a race car team when Mario Andretti offers to be your driver?' Asked about his regrets in 1982, Newman expressed a wish to be either Laurence Olivier or Mario Andretti, 'but I guess I don't wish it hard enough or fiercely enough'. Having failed, in his own eyes, to become a great actor, Newman also fell short of being a champion driver.

At the time, Newman had been contemplating his future in racing: 'I thought I was going to retire . . . and I might need a little protection. It was just an alternative to driving.' His name secured the sponsorship deals his team needed to get off the ground. According to Andretti, Newman–Haas was not a union made in heaven. The racetrack antagonism had developed into a strong mutual dislike, the two men barely speaking at the start of their partnership. It didn't help matters when Newman–Haas Racing got off to a bad start, making little impression in its first year. Disappointed with this result, Andretti nearly quit the team, until Newman persuaded him to stay for another season. The following year proved the breakthrough year, Andretti winning the 1984 CART championship for Newman–Haas. Over the next twenty years, the Newman–Haas team would win a total of sixty-eight CART races. In 1993, they recruited British driver Nigel Mansell, who'd retired from Formula One the previous year. Newman heaped praise on his new star: 'Watching people like Nigel drive is just . . . awesome. Believe me. I feel the same way about them as other actors feel about Olivier.' Mansell went on to win the championship.

While Mansell raced to CART victory, Newman remained a top-class driver in his own right. In 1985, he won the Sports Car Club of America Championship – GTI Class, Road Atlanta – for the third time. Turning sixty did nothing to diminish his competitive nature. As Mario Andretti explained to Lawrence Donegan, 'Paul's passion is real. This isn't some Hollywood rich boy, posing around – the guy just loves cars and racing.' A notorious perfectionist, Andretti rated Newman eight out of ten as a driver:

> The thing about this guy is that he's so competitive. He hates getting beat – hates it. The other thing he has going for him is that he is so methodical. He's a serious driver . . . If he's not quicker than the next guy he likes to understand why.

Newman was more modest, telling Donegan:

> I suppose the best you could say is I'm pretty smooth. I was always better at the high speed stuff on tracks, rather than the road stuff. I didn't muscle the car enough for the roads.

Away from the racetrack, Newman pursued his political interests, campaigning for Democrat presidential hopeful Walter Mondale. However, hardline Republican Ronald Reagan won his second term in office with a landslide victory.

In early 1985, the Scott Newman Foundation became affiliated with the Health Behavior Research Institute, based at the University of Southern California. The SNF would now be known as the Scott Newman Center for Drug Abuse Prevention and Health Communications Research. In her capacity as spokesperson, Susan Newman criticized Hollywood's notorious drug culture. To her disappointment, if not surprise, a proposed anti-drugs campaign gained little support from the Motion Picture Association of America and the big studios. Many people in the film-making community had good reason to stay silent on the issue. By this time, Newman's first wife – now Jacqueline McDonald – worked for the Scott Newman Center alongside her daughter. No mention was made of her relationship with Paul and Scott Newman, presumably at her own request. The SNCDAPHCR board included producer Michael Phillips, who worked with Newman on *The Sting*. Ironically, Julia Phillips, his co-producer and ex-wife, had become notorious for her cocaine abuse.

Apart from Susan, the Newman children had chosen to live outside the media spotlight. At their request, Newman and Woodward didn't discuss them in interviews, saying nothing about where they lived or

what jobs they did. Both Newman and Woodward were vocal sup-
porters of Save the Children, 'adopting' seven children through the
STC programme and appearing in print advertisements for the charity.

16 Seems Like Old Times

For some players, luck itself is an art.
  Opening narration, *The Color of Money*

During the mid-1980s, Newman's personal income was estimated at around $2.5 million a year. While this was a modest sum by movie-star standards, Newman could well afford to turn down film work that didn't interest him. After two years' absence, he returned to the screen in *The Color of Money* (1986) – a belated follow-up to *The Hustler* – directed by Martin Scorsese.

The Color of Money was based on author Walter Tevis's own sequel to *The Hustler*, published in 1984. Sensing a golden opportunity, Newman grabbed the film rights straightaway. He commissioned a script from Tevis, who delivered a first draft before his death later the same year. Undaunted, Newman hired another writer to revise Tevis's screenplay, which stayed close to the original film, even incorporating scenes from *The Hustler*. At the British press conference for *The Color of Money*, Newman gave his opinion of Tevis's version:

> The sequel Walter Tevis wrote is a sweet book. Fast Eddie is
> trying to sell a six-table pool hall with a view to cleaning up
> when it becomes a shopping mall. Then he meets an aristocratic
> lady and wins a pool tournament in Las Vegas. I didn't believe in
> this character. I knew Eddie would still be a hustler . . .

Jake LaMotta, the subject of Scorsese's *Raging Bull* (1980), had made his acting début in *The Hustler*, cast as a bartender. Newman had been impressed by *Raging Bull*, the dark flipside to his more upbeat boxing biopic, *Somebody Up There Likes Me*. He sent his *Color of Money* script to Scorsese. Intrigued by the idea of revisiting Eddie Felson, the director regarded the existing screenplay as a wasted opportunity. As Newman recalled, Scorsese didn't believe in the 'weak' central character. Meeting with Newman to discuss rewrites, he suggested 'a whole new idea'. Newman agreed to drop several elements, notably flashbacks to Felson's childhood, the pool-hall subplot and a lengthy reunion with Minnesota Fats.

With Newman's consent, Scorsese brought in a new writer, novelist Richard Price. Like Scorsese, Price argued that Felson wouldn't still be playing pool: 'It's a young man's game.' It made more sense, and better drama, if Felson had 'become the guy he loathes: George C. Scott'.

Price also felt that the existing script drafts required in-depth knowledge of *The Hustler*. Given the twenty-five-year gap, Newman couldn't count on audience familiarity with the first film. A Malibu meeting between Newman, Scorsese and Price threw up more ideas. Price eventually delivered an all-new eighty-page script, which Newman disliked. Playing the mediator, Scorsese persuaded Price that the revised screenplay had to fit Newman's conception of Felson. Scorsese and Price wanted to emphasize Felson's meanness, giving more weight to his redemption. In Price's script, Felson had become a typical Scorsese protagonist, shot through with the director's Catholic sensibility. While Newman saw Felson as an anti-hero, he felt the character had become too unlikeable. After nine months, Price delivered a workable screenplay, acceptable to all parties. Scorsese and Price travelled to Newman's home in Westport, Connecticut, to hammer out the deal. Newman asked the director if he was 'good at holding an actor's hand'. Scorsese assured the star that he was. Both Newman and Scorsese were now committed to the project. The script development had proved an expensive process, with extra fees paid to the Walter Tevis estate.

Newman hoped that *The Color of Money* would reunite him with Jackie Gleason, his co-star from *The Hustler*. Newman approached Gleason with the project, though Minnesota Fat's role had radically diminished in the revised script. Gleason declined to reprise his most famous film character, feeling Fats had become a mere cameo, playing no part in the story.

Price's script introduced a new character, Vincent, a younger version of Eddie Felson. Both Newman and Scorsese wanted to cast Tom Cruise, who'd shown star quality in the teen comedies *All the Right Moves* (1983) and the darker *Risky Business* (1984). A fan of *All the Right Moves*, Scorsese felt Cruise would be ideal as the gifted, arrogant young player who hasn't a clue how to realize his potential. At the time, Cruise was working on *Top Gun* (1986). Scorsese and Newman had a successful meeting with Cruise, who liked and admired both of them. He was also taken with Price's screenplay and signed on for the film. Along the way, Cruise's character was toned down a little, losing his cocaine habit.

Offering *The Color of Money* as a package deal, Newman and Scorsese had problems raising the finance. According to Scorsese, the recent box-office failure of *Harry and Son* didn't help matters. Twentieth Century Fox, which produced *The Hustler*, showed some interest in the sequel. However, unhappy with the script and proposed casting, the studio eventually rejected the project. When Columbia also passed on *The Color of Money*, Newman and Scorsese took their film to Touchstone Pictures, Disney's 'adult' division, where executives Jeffrey Katzenberg and Michael Eisner agreed to a deal. Scorsese originally planned to shoot *The Color of Money* in black and white, *à la Raging Bull*, matching the visual style of *The Hustler*. Unsurprisingly, Touchstone dismissed the idea as a box-office kiss of death, though Scorsese claims to have dropped the plan himself, feeling that direct comparisons with *The Hustler* were unwise. Uncertain of the film's commercial potential, Touchstone budgeted the production at a modest $14.5 million. As a show of faith, Newman agreed to a pay cut, and both he and Scorsese put up one third of their salaries as collateral against budget overruns.

The Color of Money – Eddie Felson and Vincent (Tom Cruise)

The producers on *The Color of Money* were Barbara De Fina, Scorsese's fiancée, and Irving Axelrad, Newman's lawyer and trusted friend. Scorsese recruited German cameraman Michael Ballhaus, who had worked with the director on 1985's *After Hours*. Editor Thelma Schoonmaker had collaborated with Scorsese since the 1960s, winning an Academy Award for *Raging Bull*. The crew also included *Hustler* editor Dede Allen's son, Tom Fleischman, employed as a sound mixer.

The score was entrusted to Robbie Robertson, formerly of The Band, the subject of Scorsese's concert movie *The Last Waltz* (1978). The supporting cast included Mary Elizabeth Mastrantonio, best known as Al Pacino's doomed, coke-snorting sister in *Scarface* (1983).

The Color of Money – Eddie with girlfriend Janelle (Helen Shaver)

Tom Cruise trained with pool professional Mike Sigel, impressing Newman with his aptitude for the game: 'He learned to play pool better in six weeks than I did in five months twenty-five years ago.' Newman brushed up on his own cue skills. During the early 1980s, Eddie Parker, the real-life inspiration for Felson, produced a video and workbook on pool, entitled *What You've Always Wanted to Know About Pocket Billiards, But Were Afraid to Ask*. Newman watched it while preparing for *The Color of Money*, the fictional Eddie still learning from the real thing. At Newman's request, or insistence, Scorsese arranged for two weeks of rehearsal, with writer Richard Price sitting in. Newman claimed that both Scorsese and Cruise, who'd never rehearsed a film before, found the experience a revelation.

The Color of Money commenced production in January 1986, with location filming in Chicago, Illinois. Working on a slim budget, Scorsese had to complete the movie in fifty days, including additional location shooting in Atlantic City and New Jersey. Tom Cruise did all his own pool shots, except for a two-ball jump pot, which was executed by Mike Sigel. Scorsese and Price both made cameo appearances, as did singer Iggy Pop and Scorsese's dog. Scorsese also served as the film's uncredited narrator. Despite the tight schedule, the *Color of Money* shoot went smoothly, helped by the good working atmosphere. Most of the cast and crew participated in a daily 'Worst Joke' competition. Newman, who knew a thing or two about bad jokes, usually did well. On the telephone to Joanne Woodward, he expressed surprise at how well the production was going. This conversation found its way into the film, Eddie confiding to his girlfriend that Vincent's on-the-road education is progressing *too* smoothly. The respectful Cruise addressed his senior co-star as 'Mr Newman', until asked to use 'Paul' instead. Newman approved of Cruise: 'We worked well together.'

Martin Scorsese claims to have been awed by Newman's iconic presence. Newman enjoyed working with Scorsese, who gave his actors freedom to create, guiding them out of trouble when necessary. Interestingly, Newman paid the same compliment to *Hustler* director Robert Rossen. According to Newman, Scorsese's most useful piece of direction was to underplay the humour: 'Try *not* to be funny.' Richard Price had a more fractious relationship with Newman, who regularly suggested rewrites during production. While Price conceded that Newman's instincts were usually sound, he learned to dread the phrase 'Guys, I think we're missing an opportunity here.' For the record, Newman praised Price's dialogue as 'sharp and original'. He later described the *Color of Money* shoot as 'a wonderful, collaborative experience'. The film came in one day ahead of schedule and $1.5 million under budget.

Scorsese declared himself satisfied with the finished movie: 'I think I've done something that's personal.' In his view, *The Color of Money* was a follow-up to *The Hustler*, not a sequel. Newman stayed in contact with Cruise after *The Color of Money* wrapped, inviting him to stay at his Connecticut home. Cruise also attended many of Newman's races during the 1986 season. Inevitably, it was alleged that Newman regarded Cruise as a surrogate son. He enjoyed a close relationship with the young actor, something he'd never had with Scott.

By the mid-1980s, Newman had been making films for three decades. Now sixty, he showed no sign of retiring, despite his many off-screen interests. Nevertheless, Hollywood insiders felt that he deserved a few trophies before fading into the night. While his performances had been recognized overseas, he'd never won a major prize in his native country. In 1985, both Newman and Joanne Woodward were handed the Screen Actors Guild Annual Achievement Award. The Academy of

Motion Picture Arts and Sciences also came calling, looking to make up for Newman's six unsuccessful Best Actor nominations. During production on *The Color of Money*, Newman learned that he'd won an Honorary Academy Award. This was the Academy's standard deal for veteran stars who'd reached the twilight of their careers without winning an Oscar. Previous recipients included Charles Chaplin, Cary Grant and Barbara Stanwyck. Well aware of the trophy's consolation-prize status, Newman didn't feel overcome by gratitude: 'This award is usually given to someone whose career is ending, and I don't feel that way at all.' According to Irving Axelrad, Newman harboured a grudge against the Academy: 'He said they'd always treated him as second best, and now they were acting as though he were old and through.'

Tempted to refuse the award, Newman decided this wasn't a viable option. Whatever his feelings towards the Academy, he could ill-afford to alienate the wider Hollywood community. After consultation, he decided to be gracious, arguing, 'You don't kick people in the butt who are trying to be nice to you.' As a compromise, he declined to attend the actual ceremony, pointedly staying away. Still based in Chicago for location work on *The Color of Money*, he had the perfect excuse. On the night, the award was presented by Sally Field, Newman's co-star from *Absence of Malice*. The citation was the usual hyperbole: '. . . in recognition of his many memorable and compelling screen performances and for his personal integrity and dedication to his craft'. Newman accepted the award via satellite link-up, seated on the *Color of Money* set in Chicago. Audiences – and studio executives – were reminded that Paul Newman was still very much in the business. His acceptance speech included the expected jokes: 'I'm grateful this award didn't come wrapped as a gift certificate to Forest Lawn.' At the same time, Newman made it clear he had no intention of retiring: 'My best work is down the pike in front of me.' He later remarked that honourary Academy Awards were for 'people who are already up to their knees in weeds'. An Oscar only had real value if it was in recognition of a specific role.

The Color of Money is distinguished by Martin Scorsese's 'high style' direction, employing time-lapse shots, jump cuts and gliding pans. The most memorable images are the close-ups of pool balls falling down pockets and slamming into each other, and the chalk dust flying off the cue tips. Scorsese treats the climactic pool tournament as a near-religious experience. Furious that Vincent threw their competition match, Felson forfeits on the semi-final. Scorsese admitted to problems with the ending, which seems deliberately anti-climactic. Felson gets down and dirty with Vincent, demanding his 'best game'. Breaking off, Felson seems well satisfied: 'I'm back!' The climactic freeze-frame is open to interpretation, Felson's future in the game still uncertain. As Scorsese put it, 'Eddie's just back where he's supposed to be. It doesn't mean he's winning.' Newman's solid performance can't disguise the fact that *The Hustler* didn't require a sequel, and Scorsese felt he'd compromised his hard-edged style for bigger box-office receipts. Newman later commented that *The Color of Money* 'was just more of the same, I guess'.

Whatever the initial reservations, Touchstone Pictures now had high hopes for *The Color of Money*. While Newman's recent Academy Award played a part in this newfound optimism, there was another, more crucial factor. The blockbuster success of *Top Gun* had turned Tom Cruise into a major star and sex symbol. The Don Simpson–Jerry Bruckheimer film became the biggest box-office hit of 1986. Despite Cruise's new status, Newman retained top billing on *The Color of Money*. In August 1986, Touchstone held a sneak preview in Paramus, New Jersey, with Scorsese, Newman, Woodward and Cruise in attendance. The response proved so favourable that Touchstone brought the release date forward from December 1986 to mid-October. Having skimped on the budget, the company now pushed *The Color of Money* with a major media campaign. Newman and Cruise appeared on the cover of *Life* magazine, lying on top of a pool table.

The film received a charity première at New York's Ziegfeld Theatre. Tickets cost $250 a head, with proceeds going to the Actors Studio. Newman, Woodward, Cruise and Mary Elizabeth Mastrantonio turned up to face the media barrage. Distributed through Disney's Buena Vista subsidiary, *The Color of Money* opened in the US on 17 October 1986. The tagline kept it simple: 'The Hustler Isn't What He Used to Be, But He Has the Next Best Thing: A Kid Who Is.' The reviews were mixed, though *People* magazine enthused: 'Paul Newman makes everything he's learned in three decades of screen acting pay off in this forceful follow-up to his 1961 role.' *Newsweek* critic David Ansen went even further: 'Newman is mesmerising, moving and as sharp as a double-edged razor – this is as trenchant a performance as he's ever given.'

Newman travelled to London to promote *The Color of Money*'s British release. Writing in *Films and Filming*, Brian Baxter rated his performance as 'probably the best he has ever given'. When interviewed, Newman stated:

It's a very personal film for me. A film about the rekindling of passion, about the competition between youth and old age. Of course, it's not really a sequel to *The Hustler* . . . It's an extension of the character of Eddie examined from a different angle.

Curiously, Newman praised *The Color of Money* at the expense of his earlier movies: 'I have to say that I haven't liked much of the work I've done in the past twenty-five years. I'm just learning what this business is all about and I've a long way to go.' Having dismissed most of his films since *The Hustler*, he also claimed that he'd been bored with acting throughout the 1970s: 'I realized that I was beginning to duplicate myself, rely on mannerisms and the easy way out.' Only motor racing gave him a real sense of excitement: '. . . I guess my passion for automobiles has bled into my other passions – acting, directing, business and politics.'

The Color of Money proved a solid commercial success, taking $24.43 million at the North American box office. Worldwide, it made $52.29 million, making it Martin Scorsese's biggest hit to date. On the back of this success, Newman signed a three-year contract with the Walt Disney company. Under the terms of this deal, he would develop scripts at Touchstone, as both an actor and director. At the time, Newman explained: 'I've an agreement for four projects. Three of them in which I will act and one which I will direct.'

In the autumn of 1986, Newman and A. E. Hotchner announced the formation of the Hole-in-the-Wall Camp for children with leukaemia and other life-threatening diseases. Named after the outlaw gang in *Butch Cassidy and the Sundance Kid*, this $8-million project would occupy a 300-acre site in Ashford, north-east Connecticut. Affiliated to the Yale-New Haven Medical Centre, the Hole-in-the-Wall Camp was the first such outfit specially designed for child cancer sufferers, with doctors and nurses on twenty-four-hour call. Newman donated the first $4 million himself. The rest of the money came from an unexpected source, the King of Saudi Arabia contributing $5 million. Aware of Saudi Arabia's despotic regime, Newman felt able to turn a blind eye, given the circumstances. As Roman Polanski once pointed out, money has no smell. Discussing the success of Hole-in-the-Wall, Newman seemed justly proud of his achievement: 'I guess the biggest reward that I've ever had has been to take what I've got and be able to spread it around a little bit.' In 1992, Newman and Joanne Woodward were honoured by the Kennedy Center for the Hole-in-the-Wall venture, at a ceremony hosted by Robert Redford. The special guests included a group of children who'd benefited from the camp. Newman, not given to public displays of emotion, was moved to tears. There are now eight Hole-in-the-Wall Camps.

The Color of Money did reasonably well in the 1987 Academy Award nominations. Mary Elizabeth Mastrantonio was up for Best Supporting Actress, while Richard Price made the running for Best Screenplay. As expected, Newman received his seventh nomination for Best Actor, up against William Hurt (*Children of a Lesser God*), Bob Hoskins (*Mona Lisa*), James Woods (*Salvador*) and Dexter Gordon (*'Round Midnight*). While the competition lacked star power, there was no doubting the quality of the performances, though Newman's work on *The Color of Money* hardly compared with *The Hustler*, *Hud*, *Cool Hand Luke* or *The Verdict*. He could not depend on his performance alone to break the Oscar jinx. This time around, he needed luck to work for him. When Warren Cowan proposed an Oscar campaign, Newman vetoed the idea. Attending the ceremony was also out of the question, Newman being 'too busy' to make the trip.

In March 1987, Newman was in England to publicize *The Color of Money*'s UK release. He preferred not to discuss his 'honorary' Oscar, claiming, 'I don't really know what that means.' Having attended the London première, he returned to the US in time for the Academy Awards ceremony, held on 30 March. On the night, Newman was in New York, three thousand miles away. Officially, he was busy with post-production work on his new film, *The Glass Menagerie*. Director Robert Wise, an old friend, had agreed to accept the award on Newman's behalf, should the need arise. Both Wise and Newman felt he should have been nominated for *Somebody Up There Likes Me*, thirty years earlier. Maybe having that film's director on hand would win favour with the movie gods. The Best Actor award was presented by veteran star Bette Davis. On stage, Davis's advanced years and poor health were painfully evident, the actress confused and rambling. When Newman's name was announced, Wise came on stage to collect the trophy and give a prepared speech. Davis kept interrupting, feeling that Wise should be properly introduced to the audience. As the embarrassment level rose ever higher, the show's producers cut the presentation short, and Wise never got to finish the acceptance speech. Backstage, he explained to the press why Newman hadn't shown up. Apparently, the superstitious star feared that attending the ceremony in person would bring bad luck, losing him the trophy for the seventh time. As Wise pointed out, this hands-off approach had worked: 'Now the jinx is broken. He's in.' Newman and Joanne Woodward watched the ceremony on television. Interviewed shortly afterwards, Newman proved typically self-deprecating: 'I'm on a roll now. Maybe I can get a job.' He was also pleased 'to have evened the score with my wife', a reference to Woodward's 1958 win for *The Three Faces of Eve*.

Past history aside, Martin Scorsese felt the trophy was no more than Newman deserved for *The Color of Money*: 'Paul gave a performance that was controlled yet emotional. His Oscar was no consolation prize.' In public, Newman seemed genuinely pleased to have finally won. Interviewed on television, the star explained: 'When you look down the pike and see that your work is finite, these awards mean more than when you're a kid.' Newman received the Oscar statuette a month after the ceremony, during a private party held at Warren Cowan's house. The guests included Hollywood star Loretta Young, who asked Newman how he felt about the Academy Award. According to Young, Newman admitted to a sense of anti-climax: 'It's like chasing a beautiful woman for eighty years. Finally she relents, and you say, "I am terribly sorry, I'm tired."'

Twenty-five years on from *Sweet Bird of Youth*, Newman returned to Tennessee Williams country with *The Glass Menagerie* (1987), arguably the playwright's finest work. This time around, Newman directed the film, ensuring fidelity to Williams's original text. As Newman freely admitted, *The Glass Menagerie* was a showcase for Joanne Woodward.

In 1985, Woodward had been approached by Nikos Psacharopoulos, artistic director of the summer festival at the Williamstown Theater in Williamstown, Massachusetts. Psacharopoulos wanted her to play the lead role in his production of *The Glass Menagerie*. Woodward accepted the invitation. Her fellow cast members included Karen Allen, who'd studied at the Lee Strasberg Theatre Institute. The male roles went to James Naughton and John Sayles.[1] The Williamstown *Glass Menagerie* premièred in August 1985, and Woodward found the experience both rewarding and enjoyable: 'I love Williamstown . . . it creates a different atmosphere, a sense of camaraderie, living together and being together.' Woodward and Psacharopoulos transferred their production to the Long Wharf Theatre, in New Haven, Connecticut.

Both Woodward and Newman were interested in making a film version of *The Glass Menagerie*. According to Newman, their aim was to 'put Tennessee on the screen as he was written'. Having co-starred in the emasculated *Cat on a Hot Tin Roof* and *Sweet Bird of Youth*, Newman could now film one of the plays in uncensored form. He also wanted a record of Woodward's stage performance: 'I wanted to put it on film, even if it was only for the archives.' His erratic career as a director hadn't lived up to the promise of *Rachel, Rachel*. Though hardly a strong commercial prospect, *The Glass Menagerie* could restore Newman's reputation as a heavyweight film-maker.

The Glass Menagerie – Woodward as Amanda

Like Newman, Woodward had set herself a daunting task. The original 1945 stage production of *The Glass Menagerie* starred Laurette Taylor and, in the opinion of most critics, her portrayal of deluded matriarch Amanda Wingfield remained definitive. That said, Taylor's performance had never been recorded. When Warner Brothers turned *The Glass Menagerie* into a 1950 film, the studio cast Gertrude Lawrence, supported by Jane Wyman, Kirk Douglas and Arthur Kennedy. According to Douglas, Lawrence insisted on major rewrites, adding flashbacks that showed her aging, embittered character as a glamorous young woman. Despite its solid credentials, Warners' *Glass Menagerie* proved a critical and commercial failure. Katharine Hepburn later starred in an acclaimed 1973 television version, directed by Anthony Harvey.

Largely inactive in films, Woodward's television career continued to thrive. Her recent work included *Do You Remember Love* (1985), the moving story of a middle-aged academic who contracts Alzheimer's disease. Back in 1978, Woodward's own mother had been diagnosed with Alzheimer's, giving her painful first-hand experience of its debilitating effects. She received another Emmy Award for her strong performance.

Newman and Woodward made *The Glass Menagerie* in association with the Cineplex company. The film was produced by Burtt Harris, Sidney Lumet's regular assistant director since *The Pawnbroker* (1965). On *The Verdict*, Harris also served as an executive producer and bit-part actor, playing Frank Galvin's favourite bartender. Newman recruited cameraman Michael Ballhaus, who photographed *The Color of Money*. The production designer, Tony Walton, had once been married to Julie Andrews, Newman's co-star from *Torn Curtain*. Composer Henry Mancini provided his third score for a Newman-directed film.

Woodward's co-stars included Karen Allen and James Naughton, from the original Williamstown Theater production. When John Sayles proved unavailable, he was replaced by John Malkovich, who'd played the same role on stage. Everyone involved with the film took a reduced salary, the cast deferring their fees in favour of profit participation. Budgeted at $3 million, *The Glass Menagerie* was shot at the Kaufman-Astoria Studios in New York. Newman had a clear idea of his role on the film: 'A director's expertise is to give a really good actor the freedom to make their own decisions.'

Tennessee Williams receives top billing on *The Glass Menagerie*. As a record of a play, Newman's *Glass Menagerie* is undeniably well-crafted, if heavy on the red–orange colour schemes. Partial to a mobile camera, Newman also experiments with multiple exposures. His handling of the actors shows sensitivity, though much of the groundwork was done by stage director Nikos Psacharopoulos. As a piece of cinema, *The Glass Menagerie* is hard to appreciate. Perhaps Newman and

Woodward set themselves an impossible task. Reflecting the confused, conflicting intentions, Woodward explained: 'We wanted to record the play and yet still make it into a movie but not change it.' It's obvious that the drama is paced for the stage, not the big screen. Under the camera's scrutiny, the dialogue seems overwritten and overwrought.

The Glass Menagerie – Newman confers with John Malkovich, while Joanne Woodward looks on

While Karen Allen is touching as Laura, Woodward has problems balancing Amanda's character traits. Both selfish and sad, Amanda is lost in the past, obsessed with 'gentlemen callers'. Though Amanda clearly loves her children, she also suffocates them. Many fans of the play find Woodward's performance mannered and overbearing.

Interviewed during the run-up to the 1987 Academy Awards, Newman seemed pleased with *The Glass Menagerie*:

> It's a good piece of work, which I did really for Joanne, who had played in it two or three times on stage. And I think she is quite marvellous in it and it seemed a pity that it wasn't on record some-where. It would just drift away like a hiccup and be forgotten. So we filmed it and I'm happy with the result.

The film was launched as an official entry at the 1987 Cannes Film Festival, with Newman and Woodward in attendance. Their press conference focused entirely on the new film, Newman refusing to

276 PAUL NEWMAN

answer questions about his career or personal life. Discussing the appeal of Tennessee Williams's work, he claimed that *The Glass Menagerie* was the best play by America's greatest playwright. The film received its North American première at the Toronto Film Festival, on 19 September 1987, and Newman and Woodward took their film around the various festivals, always on hand for post-screening discussions. As the release dates drew near, the couple raised their media profile, becoming available for selected interviews. Despite the downbeat material, Newman believed the film could enjoy the same 'sleeper' success as *Rachel, Rachel*: 'I'm convinced it has a great commercial promise, considering what it cost.' *The Glass Menagerie* opened in New York in the late autumn of 1987, well placed for inclusion on critics' 'Films of the Year' lists. The reviews, however, were decidedly mixed. Overall, most critics felt that both Newman and Woodward were too reserved in their approach to the play. For all Newman's hopes, *The Glass Menagerie* grossed only $895,904 at the North American box office. The cast, who all owned one sixth of the film, found their profit points counted for little. When the major film awards were announced, *The Glass Menagerie* was conspicuously absent from the lists. By way of compensation, Kirk Douglas praised *The Glass Menagerie* as superior to the 1950 film version, rating Woodward's performance as 'wonderful'.

Given Newman's Oscar-anointed success with *The Color of Money*, he seemed in no rush to star in another film. He claimed this was not through choice: there just weren't many good scripts for an actor his age. As he explained, 'I used to do two movies a year. Now it's lucky if I can find a picture to do every two years.' Newman felt that Robert Redford and Dustin Hoffman, both a decade his junior, had the same problem. In 1987, John Huston offered him a leading role in *Benito Cereno*, one of the veteran director's personal projects. Based on a Herman Melville story, this nautical tale would be filmed in the Caribbean. However, Newman turned down the chance for a reunion, perhaps aware of Huston's failing health. In truth, Huston was now too frail to be insured for a film, let alone direct one. While filming *The Dead* (1987), he had needed constant medical supervision. John Huston died on 28 August 1987, aged eighty-one.

A reunion with director Martin Ritt seemed a possibility. Back in 1972, Ritt became involved with Warner Brothers' *First Blood* project. Based on an acclaimed novel by David Morrell, this harrowing drama pitted a disturbed Vietnam veteran against smalltown prejudice and aggression. Ritt worked on a script with Walter Newman, who co-wrote

Ace in the Hole (1951), *The Man with the Golden Arm* (1955) and *Cat Ballou* (1965). Ritt offered the starring role to Newman, who promptly declined. Like most of Hollywood, he wasn't ready to tackle the Vietnam experience head-on. Ritt and Warner Brothers soon followed his example. In 1982, *First Blood* emerged as a Sylvester Stallone vehicle, dumping most of Morrell's social comment in favour of action set pieces.

During the mid-1980s, Newman and Ritt discussed making another film together, their first since *Hombre* (1967). Ritt wanted to make a film about General Joseph Stilwell, best known for the American–Sino–Anglo campaign in Burma during World War II. Stilwell had turned up in Steven Spielberg's *1941* (1979), played by Robert Stack, Newman's old Navy Air Corps instructor. Despite *1941*'s disappointing box office, MGM/UA was interested in Ritt's project. The director felt that Newman would be ideal casting for Stilwell. Ritt assigned the screenplay to novelist George MacDonald Fraser, whose film credits included *The Three Musketeers* (1973). Unfortunately, there were major problems from the start. Ritt envisaged Stilwell as a heroic figure, while MacDonald Fraser, who served in Burma, saw him as amoral and self-serving. The writer also fell out with MGM/UA over the depiction of Madam Chiang Kai-shek, who was still alive at the time and quite capable of suing. Nicknamed 'Vinegar Joe', Stilwell hadn't got on with Chiang's late husband. Whatever Newman's interest, the project rapidly stalled.

Newman was also offered the starring role in *Taipan*, a nineteenth-century saga of big-business shenanigans in Hong Kong. Based on a novel by James Clavell, this ambitious epic had been adapted by MacDonald Fraser. While Newman liked the script, he still regarded himself as 'a twentieth-century man', ill-suited to period pieces. Westerns aside, MacDonald Fraser tended to agree.

Around the same time, producer Arnon Milchan announced plans to make *The Big Brass Ring*, one of Orson Welles's many unfilmed screenplays. Budgeted at $8 million, this political thriller looked promising in outline. Milchan, who'd been involved with *The King of Comedy* (1982), *Once Upon a Time in America* (1983) and *Brazil* (1985), seemed able to bring off ambitious, offbeat projects. Newman was among the big names offered $2 million to play the lead, corrupt senator Blake Pellarin. Unfortunately, the Orson Welles factor was no guarantee and *The Big Brass Ring* was never made. Newman turned the film down, as did Warren Beatty, Clint Eastwood, Jack Nicholson, Burt Reynolds and Robert Redford.

In the late 1980s, Redford announced that he'd love to make another film with his 'best friend' Paul Newman. Interviewed in the mid-1990s,

Newman joked about appearing in a sequel to the Redford hit *Indecent Proposal* (1994): 'I'd shack up with anyone for a million dollars. I'd shack up with a gorilla for a million, plus 10 per cent.' A few years later, he explained why the Redford reunion still hadn't happened:

> Robert and I have spent the past twenty years looking for another script as good as *Butch Cassidy* or *The Sting*. We want to work together again but we won't do just any old script and the sad truth is that kind of quality just isn't out there any more.

Jane Fonda offered Newman a co-starring role in the period drama *Old Gringo* (1989), based on a novel by Carlos Fuentes. Fonda, who owned the film rights, cast herself as a schoolteacher caught up in the 1913 Mexican revolution. Argentinian director Luis Puenzo, who co-wrote the script, had won international acclaim for *The Official Version* (1985), a harrowing account of state-sponsored murder in his native country. For *Old Gringo*, Fonda made a production deal with Columbia TriStar, who agreed to a $25-million budget. Newman would play the real-life figure of Ambrose Bierce, a noted American journalist and novelist who disappeared while covering Pancho Villa's revolution. However, shortly before the start of production, Newman resigned from the film, with no official explanation. Rumours spread that he felt overshadowed by producer–star Fonda. While Newman worked harmoniously with Fonda's father on *Sometimes a Great Notion*, he'd been the one calling the shots. Placed in Henry Fonda's position – a veteran star under the orders of a younger actor with more box-office appeal – Newman didn't feel comfortable. Burt Lancaster, Newman's co-star from *Buffalo Bill and the Indians*, stepped into the breach, only to withdraw soon afterwards. Running out of aging romantic leads, Fonda settled on Gregory Peck.

Newman hoped to star in the police drama *Man with a Gun*, based on a novel by Robert Daley. Though the book's main character was in his mid-thirties, the sixty-three-year-old star believed he could do the role justice. Thirty years earlier, Humphrey Bogart had played Newman's stage role in the film version of *The Desperate Hours* (1955), despite being too old for the character. Daley didn't share Newman's enthusiasm, feeling that, when it came to the character's crucial decisions, 'an older man would know better'. While Newman could comfortably play ten, maybe fifteen years younger than his actual age, audiences were not going to buy him as a thirtysomething. *Man with a Gun* soon joined the list of aborted Newman projects.

Long absent from the New York stage, Newman stayed loyal to the Actors Studio, serving as the organization's president during the mid-1980s. The Studio hit a rocky patch after the death of Lee Strasberg in 1982. There were persistent rumours of a rift between Newman and actress Ellen Burstyn, the Studio's artistic director. Best known for *The Exorcist* (1973), Burstyn wanted to accept singer–performer Madonna Ciccone into the Actor's Studio. If nothing else, star names would raise the organization's fading profile. Newman disagreed, preferring to nurture new, unknown acting talent. When it became clear that a compromise wasn't possible, Burstyn resigned her post. In the spring of 1988, Frank Corsaro took over as artistic director. An old friend of Newman and Joanne Woodward, Corsaro had worked on *Baby Want a Kiss?* (1964), an Actors Studio stage production, and the more successful *Rachel, Rachel* (1968). Few doubted that Corsaro was Newman's choice for the job, Burstyn having little say in the matter.

In August 1987, Newman and Woodward were allegedly involved in a scuffle with several New York paparazzi. The freelance photographers had followed the celebrity couple into the lobby of their 5th Avenue apartment building in East Side Manhattan. Still a force on the race track at sixty-two, Newman had few qualms about laying into the tabloid press, either figuratively or literally.

In 1988, Yale University made Newman an honorary Doctor of Humane Letters in recognition of his artistry and philanthropy. Newman also remained politically outspoken, making his convictions clear in the run-up to the 1988 presidential elections:

> I'll be supporting someone who is directly in favour of arms control, which I consider the single most important issue today. I don't mean that I support unilateral disarmament, but we have to halt the spread and possible use of nuclear weapons.

Nevertheless, Newman seemed resigned to disappointment: 'The big problem in the United States is that a candidate has to win the nomination, win the election and govern the country. These three things are not compatible.'

17 History Lessons

It's all about ass, isn't it? You kick it or you lick it.
  General Groves, *Fat Man and Little Boy*

Newman's first acting role after *The Color of Money* came in *Fat Man and Little Boy* (1989). Set between 1942 and 1945, this ambitious film chronicles the development of the atom bomb. While the theme of the morality of nuclear warfare held great importance for Newman, the end result proved disappointing. *Fat Man and Little Boy* originated with British producer David Puttnam, whose international hits included *Midnight Express* (1978) and *Chariots of Fire* (1980). The late 1980s were a turbulent period in Puttnam's career. In 1986, he became the new chairman of Columbia Pictures, only to quit after thirteen months. At odds with the Hollywood system, Puttnam wanted to make films that had depth and significance. Newman could sympathize with this goal, both men bearing the scars, critical and commercial, of creative ambition.

Fat Man and Little Boy was directed by Roland Joffe, who worked with Puttnam on *The Killing Fields* (1984) and *The Mission* (1986). Both films earned Joffe Academy Award nominations. Several years earlier, Puttnam had commissioned a script from Bruce Robinson. A former actor, Robinson made a notable screenwriting début with *The Killing Fields*, receiving his own Academy Award nomination. A few years later, he turned writer–director with the cult favourite *Withnail and I* (1987), a finely judged comedy of failure. The *Fat Man and Little Boy* script went through several drafts, Joffe taking a co-writing credit on the final version. The film would be produced by Tony Garnett, best known for his television work with director Ken Loach. Paramount's budget allowed Garnett to hire top-of-the-range camera-man Vilmos Zsigmond, whose credits included *Deliverance* (1972), *Close Encounters of the Third Kind* (1977) and *The Deer Hunter* (1978). Garnett and Joffe also secured the services of Italian composer Ennio Morricone, whose score for *The Mission* received an Academy Award nomination.

The pivotal role of scientist J. Robert Oppenheimer went to stage actor Dwight Schultz, best known as 'Howling Mad' Murdock in *The A Team* (1983–7). Newman would play General Leslie R. Groves, Oppenheimer's military superior.

Fat Man and Little Boy – General Leslie R. Groves and J. Robert Oppenheimer (Dwight Schultz)

As *Fat Man and Little Boy* opens, General Groves is recruiting the scientists needed for the atom-bomb project in Los Alamos, New Mexico. J. Robert Oppenheimer is the obvious choice for team leader, despite his controversial politics and questionable private life. The Allied forces believe they are racing against the Nazis to develop the atom bomb. When it becomes clear that the Los Alamos group is way ahead, other factors take over. While the outcome is well known, based-on-fact films can generate excitement and tension. However, *Fat Man and Little Boy* is weakened by a flawed script and awkward staging, with anachronistic dialogue and shaky period detail. At times, the film feels like a cut-down mini-series, subplots and characters barely sketched in. Even the doomed Michael Merriman (John Cusack), Oppenheimer's top scientist, is badly underwritten. The moral issues around the project are given cursory treatment. Speaking in a low growl, Newman can do little with his one-note character.

Released in the US on 20 October 1989, *Fat Man and Little Boy* flopped badly, taking only $3.56 million at the box office. Released in Britain as *Shadow Makers*, the film did no better. Co-star Dwight Schultz publicly criticized it, dismissing the film as a wasted opportunity.

Newman's deal with Touchstone Pictures finally bore fruit in the shape of *Blaze* (1989). Based on fact, this romantic drama detailed the 'scandalous' 1950s affair between Blaze Starr, a celebrity stripper, and Earl K. Long, Governor of Louisiana. A Touchstone–Warner Brothers co-production, *Blaze* was written and directed by Ron Shelton. A former baseball player, Shelton co-scripted *Under Fire* (1983), a potent drama about America's covert operations in Nicaragua in 1979. He had made a confident directing début with *Bull Durham* (1988), a well-handled tale of sex and baseball. His script for *Blaze* was based on Starr's autobiography. Starr agreed to serve as a production consultant, granting the film her seal of approval. She also secured a cameo appearance, cast as a rather elderly stripper. Shelton auditioned over six hundred actresses for the role of Blaze Starr, finally settling on Canadian actress Lolita Davidovich. Davidovich agreed to put on weight for the role, attempting to match Starr's voluptuous figure.

In 1950, Blaze Starr is a naive country girl from Twelvepole Creek, a rural idyll with sun-dappled postcard views. An aspiring singer–songwriter, she finds a different line of work, persuaded that stripping for soldiers is her patriotic duty. Nine years later, the seasoned entertainer encounters Earl Long, who takes an immediate shine to her. The breast-fixated governor praises Starr's act as a 'powerful expression of basic human needs'. Wary of Long's advances, Starr eventually falls for his charm and sincerity. While Starr becomes a liability during Long's re-election campaign, the outspoken Governor needs no assistance in stirring up controversy.

Blaze is well made but not very interesting. While the light-hearted approach keeps the sex scenes palatable, Shelton undermines the serious issues. Worse, the relationship at the heart of the film doesn't work. Davidovich has the screen presence for Blaze Starr, but not the experience. As scripted by Shelton, Starr is a superficial character, the stripper with sharp wits and a heart of gold. Newman offers an energetic portrayal of Earl Long, who, at times, resembles a hot-wired Deep South version of *The Verdict*'s Frank Galvin. Opening in the US on 13 December 1989, *Blaze* grossed a disappointing $19.13 million. There was some talk of Academy Award consideration. *Los Angeles Times* journalist Jack Matthews tipped Newman as a surefire Best

Actor nominee. In the event, the movie went unrecognized by the Academy. Newman's Touchstone deal expired, three movies short of the original agreement. On the plus side, Shelton and Davidovich later married.

Blaze – Earl Long and Blaze Starr (Lolita Davidovich)

Newman resumed his screen partnership with Joanne Woodward for *Mr and Mrs Bridge* (1990), a Depression-era tale of staid middle-class folk. During the late 1980s, Woodward was heavily involved in the theatre, directing actors' workshops and Off-Off-Broadway productions. She encouraged several talented newcomers, including actor Dylan McDermott, who subsequently appeared in *In the Line of Fire* (1993).

Newman and Woodward made *Mr and Mrs Bridge* with the Merchant–Ivory team: producer Ismail Merchant, director James Ivory and screenwriter Ruth Prawer Jhabvala. It was based on two acclaimed novels by Evan S. Connell, *Mrs Bridge* (1959) and *Mr Bridge* (1969). Ivory first read *Mrs Bridge* in 1963. While he believed the book had cinematic potential, Jhabvala felt a film adaptation would be difficult. Ivory was similarly impressed by *Mr Bridge*. The books' fans also included Woodward, who first met Ivory in 1987. At the time, she planned to adapt *Mrs Bridge* for television. Ivory suggested combining both books into a feature film, Jhabvala now happy to tackle Connell's work. According to Ivory, Newman offered a deal on the spot: '. . . if she comes up with a screenplay I like, I'll play Mr Bridge'. His interest secured a deal with Miramax.

Ivory, Newman and Woodward occasionally found it strange recreating a period they remembered vividly from their youths. Ivory described the experience as 'somewhat Proustian . . . frustrating . . . a little eerie'. The younger actors looked to their venerable co-stars for instruction in both dining and dancing etiquette.

Set during the 1930s, *Mr and Mrs Bridge* follows the lives of Walter and India Bridge, an affluent middle-class couple living in Kansas City, home town of author Evan S. Connell. Walter is a successful lawyer with a strong moral code. Emotionally distant, he has problems relating to people, whether family, friends or colleagues. The Bridges have three children, who all disappoint their parents, choosing the 'wrong' career or marriage. The son, Douglas (Robert Sean Leonard), is based on Connell himself. Ivory saw the film as a comment on 'the practical [and] the ethical spheres of life, which, with Americans like the Bridges, tend to be one and the same'.

As a vehicle for Newman and Woodward, *Mr and Mrs Bridge* is largely successful. Warm and kind, India Bridge seems clueless in most respects, showing little grasp of human nature. Dependent on Walter for support and guidance, she rarely questions his decisions. India's best friend, Grace (Blythe Danner), is more spirited, criticizing Walter's reactionary attitudes: 'You wouldn't give a communist the time of day.' Unfortunately, Grace's fragile mental state will soon overwhelm her. Newman supposedly based the stern, patrician Walter on his own father. A cool, humourless figure, Walter follows the Protestant work ethic, earning respect and admiration. At a party, one guest comments: 'In a crowd, you are the first person everybody sees. You have the gift of gods and hard work.' Walter likes his life to run along predictable lines. As he explains to India, 'In twenty years, I've always said when something will happen and when something won't happen. Have I on any significant occasion been proved wrong?' In contrast to the generous, outgoing India, Walter suppresses his emotions. Whatever love he feels for his family goes unexpressed, except in material terms.

Mr and Mrs Bridge – Mr

Mr and Mrs Bridge – and Mrs Bridge (Joanne Woodward)

Mr and Mrs Bridge premièred in New York City and Los Angeles on 23 November 1990. Veteran critic Judith Crist announced that 'Paul Newman and Joanne Woodward give the performances of their careers.' Woodward received an Academy Award nomination, prompting Miramax to expand the film's release from thirty-five to two hundred screens. She was up against Kathy Bates (*Misery*), Angelica Huston (*The Grifters*), Julia Roberts (*Pretty Woman*) and Meryl Streep (*Postcards from the Edge*). Bates proved the winner, wowing Academy voters with her performance as a psychotic fan of pulp romance. By way of consolation, Woodward completed her BA at Sarah Lawrence College, graduating alongside daughter Clea. Despite the Oscar hype and subsequent wider release, *Mr and Mrs Bridge* took only $7.69 million at the US box office. At least Newman had started the new decade with a critical success. All things considered, his Merchant–Ivory venture proved a worthwhile trip.

18 Harsh Realities

The Hudsucker Proxy – Mussburger finds his plans in jeopardy

Business is war, kid.
  Sidney J. Mussburger, *The Hudsucker Proxy*

By the time *Mr and Mrs Bridge* opened in American cinemas, Newman had reached retirement age. He appeared to take this milestone
seriously, shunning film work for the next few years. Absent from the
big screen, he maintained his Hollywood profile by other means. He
agreed to present the Best Picture Oscar at the 1992 Academy Awards
ceremony, alongside former co-star Elizabeth Taylor. The prize went
to the grisly thriller *The Silence of the Lambs* (1991).

  In November 1992, John Foreman, Newman's one-time co-producer,
died of a heart attack, aged sixty-seven. Six months younger than
Newman, Foreman had been around during a major period of the
star's career. He could take part credit for *Butch Cassidy and the Sundance Kid*, *Sometimes a Great Notion*, *They Might Be Giants*, *The
Effect of Gamma Rays on Man-in-the-Moon Marigolds* and *The Life
and Times of Judge Roy Bean*.

  Newman played a starring role, of sorts, in *La Classe américaine*
(1993), a French comedy that utilized clips from old Hollywood
movies. Co-produced by Dune and Canal+, this made-for-television
special was devised and scripted by Michel Hazanavicius and
Dominique Mezerette. Running a brisk seventy minutes, *La Classe
américaine* reworks *Citizen Kane* (1941), deciphering the last words
of Georges Abitbol (John Wayne), the world's classiest man. Newman
'plays' a journalist named Dave who investigates Abitbol's life with
fellow reporters Peter (Dustin Hoffman) and Steven (Robert Redford).
Distributed by Warner Brothers television (France), *La Classe américaine* premièred on 31 December 1993.

  On the acting front, Joanne Woodward seemed far busier than her
husband. Following her success with *Mr and Mrs Bridge*, she co-produced and starred in *Blind Spot* (1993), a harrowing television drama.
She played a hard-nosed congresswoman, forced to deal with drug
addiction in her family. Working from bitter personal experience,
Woodward gave another Emmy-nominated performance. On the big
screen, she served as the narrator for Martin Scorsese's *The Age of
Innocence* (1993) and took a supporting role in *Philadelphia* (1993),
playing Tom Hanks's mother. Woodward moved back to television for
Breathing Lessons (1994), based on Anne Tyler's Pulitzer Prize-winning

novel. She and James Garner starred as a middle-aged couple travelling to a friend's funeral.

In 1993, the Academy of Motion Picture Arts and Sciences gave Newman the Jean Hersholt Humanitarian Award in recognition of his charity work. Handed a second honorary Oscar, he chose to ignore the implication that it was time for him to retire.

The Hudsucker Proxy – Sidney J. Mussburger and Norville Barnes (Tim Robbins)

Newman returned to feature films with *The Hudsucker Proxy* (1994), an offbeat period comedy produced, written and directed by Ethan and Joel Coen. While the Coens were not mainstream film-makers, *The Hudsucker Proxy* was executive produced by Joel Silver, a specialist in blockbuster action movies. A fan of the Coens' work, Silver raised the $25-million budget through his own company, Silver Pictures, securing distribution deals with Warner Brothers and Polygram. The critical success of the Coens' *Barton Fink* (1991), a triple prize-winner at Cannes, probably helped. The brothers wrote the *Hudsucker Proxy* script in collaboration with director Sam Raimi, a friend and colleague best known for *The Evil Dead* (1983). The production team included British cameraman Roger Deakins and composer Carter Burwell, who'd scored all the Coens' films.

The Coens cast Tim Robbins as Norville Barnes, a naive country boy lost in New York. Newman agreed to play Sidney J. Mussburger, a villainous wheeler-dealer with no redeeming features. While Newman was one of the Coens' first choices for the role, the brothers couldn't explain why he seemed right for Mussburger, 'Which is kinda why we wanted him!' Nevertheless, Newman liked both the script and his character, describing Mussburger as 'a road company Machiavelli'. Once Newman came on board, he requested his own make-up artist, Monty Westmore of the renowned Westmore clan. Newman cited *The Hudsucker Proxy* as his most enjoyable shoot since *Slap Shot*: 'I'm not a comic actor by instinct, but I came to relish every moment of it . . . I had a ball.'

Set in 1958 New York, *The Hudsucker Proxy* is a homage to 1930s screwball comedy and directors Frank Capra and Preston Sturges. Newman does what he can with the underwritten Mussburger, who finishes a dead man's cigar rather than see it wasted. Growling out of the corner of his mouth, Mussburger has no time for sentiment. A massage scene shows that Newman is still in good physical shape. Released in the US on 11 March 1994, *The Hudsucker Proxy* earned mixed reviews. Interviewed in 1998, Newman dismissed his performance as a failure: 'The audience would much prefer to see me as an anti-hero. I've played villains and they haven't been very successful.'

Newman found a more rewarding role in *Nobody's Fool* (1994), a low-key character study written and directed by Robert Benton. A former writer, art director and editor for *Esquire* magazine, Benton got his big movie break co-scripting *Bonnie and Clyde* (1967). In partnership with fellow *Esquire* contributor David Newman, Benton had helped turn two dull-witted killers into glamorous, all-American folk heroes. *Nobody's Fool* was produced by Arlene Donovan and Scott Rudin, and was based on a novel by Richard Russo, published in 1994.

The *Nobody's Fool* script drew the interest of Bruce Willis, who was looking to consolidate his credentials as a serious actor. Since his fleeting appearance in *The Verdict*, he had become one of Hollywood's leading stars. An admirer of both Benton and Newman, Willis took a pay cut to appear in *Nobody's Fool*. According to Hollywood insider Peter Bart, Willis is one of the few big stars willing to do this. Willis also dropped his price tag to co-star in *Pulp Fiction* (1994), released the same year. His wife was played by Melanie Griffith, seen in *The Drowning Pool* two decades earlier. While Griffith looked set for stardom after *Something Wild* (1986) and *Working Girl* (1988), her career soon lost momentum.

Nobody's Fool began filming on 19 November 1993. Newman got on well with Benton, later commenting: 'There are a lot of directors who really don't like actors. They see them as puppets. Benton allows for a lot of experimentation.' Benton praised Newman as a meticulous actor who left nothing to chance.

Nobody's Fool – Sully and Miss Beryl (Jessica Tandy)

The film is set in North Bath, upstate New York, between Thanksgiving and Christmas. Newman plays Mike 'Sully' Sullivan, a good-natured loser with poor employment prospects and a bad knee. Injured on a job, Sully indulges in revenge fantasies against Carl Roebuck (Bruce Willis), his former boss. He flirts with Toby Roebuck (Melanie Griffith), Carl's estranged wife.

Nobody's Fool is the film that *Harry and Son* should have been. While the latter never brought its characters to life, *Nobody's Fool* is a well-crafted drama, with uniformly strong performances. If Benton's script is overwritten in places, the film avoids lapsing into schmaltz. Sully is a gambler, petty thief and dog doper, sustained by small triumphs against the establishment. Like Newman, Sully hates wearing a tie, the ultimate symbol of conformity. An outrageous flirt, he is disconcerted when Toby flashes her breasts at him. Compared to Griffith's teen nymphet in *The Drowning Pool*, Toby is both confident and comfortable with her sexuality. Sully, by contrast, seems lost for words.

Sully also contends with a cool ex-wife and an estranged son, Peter (Dylan Walsh). A poor husband and worse father, Sully feels guilty when Peter's own marriage falls apart. Thrown together by mutual misfortune, father and son start to close the vast distance between them. Inevitably, they have much to learn from each other. The strait-laced Peter is almost impressed when Sully punches petty-minded Officer Raymer (Philip Seymour Hoffman) in the face. By and large,

Nobody's Fool is about acceptance and reconciliation. Faced with the regrets and pain of old age, Sully must deal with the past, especially his late father, a violent drunk. He also accepts his responsibilities as a father and grandfather, turning down Toby's offer of a new life in Hawaii. For all his faults, Sully inspires genuine affection: 'I grow on people.'

Nobody's Fool went on limited release in the US on 23 December 1994, followed by a general release on 13 January 1995. The strategy paid off, the film picking up good reviews and favourable word of mouth. Never a candidate for blockbuster success, *Nobody's Fool* grossed a respectable $18 million at the North American box office. In Britain, the film was similarly well received. Reviewing it in *Time Out*, Gilbert Adair praised Newman's 'supremely easy playing'. Eva Marie Saint, Newman's co-star from *Our Town* and *Exodus*, saw a new quality in his acting: 'there was a certain dimension that surprised me . . . a kind of relaxation'. Worldwide, *Nobody's Fool* took $39.5 million. Newman's assured performance earned him an eighth Best Actor Academy Award nomination. Benton's screenplay was also nominated. Newman attended the 1995 Academy Awards, proving a gracious loser when Tom Hanks took the Oscar for *Forrest Gump* (1994), playing a loveable *idiot savant*. By way of compensation, the 1995 Berlin Film Festival awarded Newman the Silver Bear for Best Actor.

Newman's television work included *Baseball* (1994), an ambitious PBS documentary series directed and co-written by Ken Burns. Newman's voice-only contribution suggested a genuine passion for the game. First broadcast on 18 September 1994, *Baseball* proved popular with both sports fans and students of American history.

On the political front, Newman continued to support the Democrats, who returned to power in 1992 under Bill Clinton. In 1994, just before the mid-term elections, Newman, Joanne Woodward and Gore Vidal dined with President Clinton and First Lady Hillary Clinton. In 1998, when Clinton's affair with White House intern Monica Lewinsky became public, Newman criticized the media coverage: 'They validated rumours and reported [them] as truth.' In this instance, of course, the press had got it right, despite Clinton's initial denials. By the late 1990s, Newman had cut down on his political activism. While age may have played a part, he seemed disenchanted with the climate of timidity. Interviewed by John Urbancich, Newman put his feelings on the record:

. . . I would be much more prepared to get involved in politics if
the great political figures we have were taking huge, giant steps.
Both political parties are taking teeny steps, and I don't really
sense any great leadership there. Washington has a way of alienating people now, and I'm not just talking about the scandals.
Maybe when this crisis at the White House clears itself up, it will
invigorate people to take great steps.

Newman seemed equally disillusioned with the film business. Interviewed in 1994 for a documentary on *Butch Cassidy and the Sundance
Kid*, he was nostalgic for the old days: 'They made films. Now they
shoot budgets, they shoot schedules, they shoot somebody's bonus,
they shoot a release date . . .' This heartfelt lament suggested a star
ready to call it quits. In fact, Newman intended to follow *Nobody's
Fool* with a western drama, *The Homesman*. The project was scheduled to begin shooting in the spring of 1996. In May 1995, Newman
scouted locations in Alberta, Canada, where *Buffalo Bill and the Indians* was filmed. While he felt the Alberta landscape would be 'perfect',
he had doubts about the screenplay. The original start date came and
went, with Newman still insisting, 'It's a film I very much want to do.'
Interviewed in early 1998, Newman explained: 'The problem is we
just can't get the script into shape. We've had a couple of good writers
working on it over the years.' While Newman claimed that 'It's still a
priority for me,' *The Homesman* remained on hold. He turned down
a leading role in *Affliction* (1997), written and directed by Paul
Schrader. This bleak, depressing film centres on Wade Whitehouse
(Nick Nolte), a divorced, middle-aged cop with bad childhood memories and a severe drink problem. Schrader wanted Newman to play the
monstrous 'Pop' Whitehouse, Wade's sadistic, abusive father. The role
went to James Coburn, who subsequently won an Academy Award for
Best Supporting Actor.

With the *Homesman* project in limbo, Newman didn't make another
film until *Twilight* (1998). This downbeat private-eye drama reunited
Newman with Robert Benton, Arlene Donovan and Scott Rudin. Ben-
ton had explored similar territory in *The Late Show*, which starred Art
Carney as an aging PI, uncovering dark deeds in sunny Los Angeles.
Benton collaborated on the *Twilight* script, initially titled *The Magic
Hour*, with novelist Richard Russo, author of *Nobody's Fool*. From
the start, he had Newman in mind for the lead role.

Newman's co-stars were Susan Sarandon and Gene Hackman.

Sarandon and Hackman's teenage daughter was played by newcomer Reese Witherspoon. A professional actress from the age of fourteen, Witherspoon abandoned her studies at Stanford University to appear in *Twilight*. As she later explained, this was not a hard choice: 'Psych 101 or a movie with Paul Newman? My parents didn't quite understand my decision, but to me it was a no-brainer.'

Most of the interiors for *Twilight* were filmed at the Sunset-Gower Studios in Hollywood. The locations included a Santa Monica house formerly owned by actress Delores Del Rio and art director Cedric Gibbons. Based at Metro-Goldwyn-Mayer for most of his career, Gibbons also designed the Academy Award statuette, winning the trophy himself eleven times. Gibbons' 1,500 film credits included *The Rack* and *Somebody Up There Likes Me*, though it's doubtful he and Newman ever met. Sarandon found Newman a pleasure to work with, describing the star as 'just so enthusiastic about life'.

Newman described *Twilight*'s appeal as 'the allure of the guy on the outside looking in'. The film is well made, yet insubstantial, offering a conventional murder-mystery plot. It also explores the nostalgia and regrets of old age. In contrast to *Nobody's Fool*, the film treats these elements in cursory fashion.

Now in his early seventies, Newman promoted *Twilight* with a series of interviews. After forty-four years as a film actor, he seemed relaxed in his approach to the craft: 'When I was younger, I did a great deal of research for my characters. Now I make them become a part of me.' In an interview with John Urbancich, Newman talked about gradually losing the Method baggage:

> After a while, instead of working your way up every canyon and crevice, you know how to get rid of all this peripheral stuff you're not going to use anyway. You start going much more directly; you don't waste as much time working on it.

He also discussed his status as a Hollywood icon: 'I'm glad to be called a living legend, but I'll start worrying when they call me a dead legend.' Somewhat ironically, Newman had become nostalgic for the days of the studio system:

> When I started in the business, people were contract players. So you'd have a rehearsal for two weeks and you'd have every actor there. And at the end of two weeks, you'd have a run-through. That's a perfect rehearsal that you don't find anymore.

Newman seemed realistic about *Twilight*'s commercial prospects: 'I'm no longer a marquee star. I can't open a film any more the way

Tom Cruise can, but I can still get a good table in a restaurant.' He felt
his second collaboration with Benton had gone well:

> I'm proud of *Twilight* and I think it's an entertaining film. I just
> hope it will be given the time to build an audience . . . Maybe
> there's an audience out there for films that compel your attention
> simply by the human aspect.

Released in the US on 6 March 1998, *Twilight* took a modest $15
million at the North American box office.

Newman played his last starring role to date in *Where the Money Is*
(2000), a caper movie featuring the ever-popular One Last Job. This
misconceived comedy–thriller was produced by director brothers
Ridley and Tony Scott, through their Scott Free company. Busy with
other commitments, the Scotts hired fellow director Marek Kanievska,
whose only feature-film credit was the British-made *Another Country*
(1984). Newman's leading lady was Linda Fiorentino, who made a
strong impression in *The Last Seduction* (1993).

Budgeted at $18 million, *Where the Money Is* began shooting in
Canada on 7 January 1998. For Newman, the production offered a
return trip to Montreal, Quebec, where he'd filmed *Quintet* two
decades earlier. Newman got on well with Fiorentino, who had a
reputation for being difficult. The script called for several car chases,
Newman staying behind the wheel throughout the filming. As
Kanievska explained:

> Paul can drive better than most stunt drivers. It was just another
> day on the race track for him, but it proved to be a pretty harrowing
> experience for Linda Fiorentino, who was sitting next to him in
> those vehicles.

Boasting a total of ten producers, *Where the Money Is* scores a misfire, neither funny nor exciting. Transcending the script, Newman is a
charismatic presence as veteran crook Henry Manning, projecting a
tough authority. On the dance floor, Manning demonstrates natural
rhythm. His involuntary 'business' partnership with Carol Ann MacKay
(Linda Fiorentino) gradually turns into something deeper. To Newman
and Fiorentino's credit, Carol Ann's romantic interest in Manning
doesn't seem ludicrous. The plot builds to an armoured car heist, with
the expected twists and turns. It comes as no surprise when Carol Ann
chooses Manning over her weak, treacherous husband, and the upbeat
crime-does-pay finale is cheerfully amoral.

Where the Money Is went on limited release in the US on 14 April

2000, over two years after it was shot. Both Newman and Fiorentino did their share of media promotion. Interviewed by Bruce Kirkland, Fiorentino claimed to find her seventy-five-year-old leading man very attractive: 'He's about the only man I could think of that I would have sex with even if he were in his nineties. He is beautiful physically, but he has this internal beauty, too. It's endless. It's forever.' Informed of Fiorentino's generous offer, Newman played along: 'Holy smoke! What a compliment!' Kirkland shared Fiorentino's high opinion of Newman:' . . . his skin still looks soft and supple, his body is still trim and virile and those colour-blind, baby-blue eyes still pierce when people lock him in a gaze'.

With a nod to *Butch Cassidy and the Sundance Kid*, Newman joked about being cast as another career criminal: 'I would say larceny is always a very attractive and wonderful thing to play.' While *Where the Money Is* fell a long way short of *Butch Cassidy*, he seemed happy enough with the film:

> I like the fact that the actors had to carry the film and not the special-effects guys . . . No one got shot. No one got stabbed. There isn't any profanity in the film and it still, I think, is funny and suspenseful.

He talked about retirement, acknowledging the shortage of strong roles on offer:

> It's a young person's business. It's very dry out there for us older antiques . . . I would like to find a film I can bow out on, something that has some serious aspirations to it, something that has some exploration of the human condition.

The quest for the elusive great scripts continued. Asked about his reasons for retiring, Newman pointed to his advancing years: '. . . it's time . . . I don't want to go out on my knees'. For all Newman's public endorsement, *Where the Money Is* was not a worthy finish to his career. The film took only $5.65 million at the North American box office, less than a third of its production cost.

So, who's got a hug for a lonely old man?
  John Rooney, *Road to Perdition*

The first half of 1998 proved a busy time for Newman. Shortly after *Where the Money Is* wrapped, he played a supporting role in *Message in a Bottle* (1999), produced by Warner Brothers. This sappy romantic drama was a vehicle for Kevin Costner, who needed a hit to salvage his waning career.

Message in a Bottle was based on Nicholas Sparks's bestselling novel, adapted by Gerald DiPego. Warner agreed to a $30-million budget, with Costner serving as co-producer. The director was Luis Mandoki. Costner hired Newman to play his father. Busy promoting *Twilight*, Newman claimed he'd be 'playing the bottle'.

An old-style romance with contemporary trimmings, *Message in a Bottle* is utterly mediocre. Regrettably, Newman doesn't have enough screen time to salvage the movie. As Alan Rickman discovered on *Robin Hood: Prince of Thieves* (1991), Costner disliked competition. Even so, Newman's scenes in *Message in a Bottle* are by far the strongest.

The film opened in the US on 12 February 1999. Despite lukewarm reviews, it did reasonable box-office business, taking $52.8 million in the US and Canada. Released in Britain on 23 April, the film met with a similar response. *Time Out* reviewer Trevor Johnston appreciated Newman's scene-stealing turn: 'Clipped and wise, the old boy does ornery to perfection.' The film grossed another $51 million overseas, taking the final total to over $100 million.

Though Newman announced his retirement from acting in 2000, it came as no great surprise when he changed his mind. As he explained to journalist Chrissy Iley, 'I get restless, and the best thing that happens to be around at the time, I've just got to do it.' The same year, Newman returned to the stage, appearing alongside Joanne Woodward in *Ancestral Voices*. Written by A. R. Gurney, this gentle comedy concerned a young man coming to terms with his grandparents' divorce. It proved modestly successful, and Newman and Woodward reprised their performances in a 2002 revival of the play. Newman also contributed a brief vocal cameo to *The Simpsons* (1989–). While the show was produced for the Fox network, owned by Newman's old nemesis Rupert Murdoch, he liked the programme enough to swallow any objections. Joining a long list of celebrity guest stars, Newman supplied the voice of a salad bottle for 'The Blunder Years', first broadcast on 9 December 2001. If nothing else, the script gave Newman a joke at Robert Redford's expense.

Newman hadn't appeared in a major film since *Nobody's Fool*. While *Twilight* qualified as an interesting misfire, neither *Where the Money Is* nor *Message in a Bottle* were worthy of his talents. Looking for a more substantial project, Newman accepted a role in the gangster drama *Road to Perdition* (2002), a DreamWorks production distributed by Twentieth Century Fox. *Road to Perdition* was based on a 1998 graphic novel by writer Max Allan Collins and artist Richard Piers Rayner, who took their story from actual events. Two of the central figures, John and Connor Looney, were real-life father-and-son gangsters. For the film, their surname was changed to Rooney. Cast as John Rooney, Newman described the character as 'a marvellous part . . . of a size that is appropriate for a gentleman my age'. *Road to Perdition* was the second film by theatre director Sam Mendes, who had made a confident screen début with *American Beauty* (1999). According to the press releases, Newman was Mendes' first choice for *Road to Perdition*.

Road to Perdition starred Tom Hanks, cast as Michael Sullivan, a devoted family man who works for John Rooney. Newman took second billing to Hanks, who beat him to the 1995 Best Actor Oscar. Casting Newman as Hanks's surrogate father seemed appropriate, as Joanne Woodward had played his mother in *Philadelphia*.

The producers for *Road to Perdition* included Richard D. Zanuck, who worked with Newman on *Butch Cassidy and the Sundance Kid*, *The Sting* and *The Verdict*. The film also reunited Newman with Conrad Hall, who photographed *Harper*, *Cool Hand Luke* and *Butch Cassidy*.

Budgeted at $80 million, *Road to Perdition* began shooting on 5 March 2001. According to Mendes, Newman seemed nervous on his first day of shooting. Ironically, the rest of the cast and crew were in 'spasms of terror' at the prospect of working with Newman. Even Hanks treated Newman with wary respect. At a Berlin press conference, Hanks explained: 'I was in awe of him, and felt intimidated when we met. I worried he'd act me off the screen.' In the event, both Newman and Hanks were consummate professionals. Mendes praised his stars' exemplary behaviour:

> All they wanted to do was act, they didn't want to play at being movie stars. There was no stomping around or staying in their trailers. They didn't diss the crew or burst into tears. You don't know how rare that is.

Road to Perdition – A hollow man with no chance of redemption

As usual, Newman requested two weeks of rehearsal prior to filming. Mendes recalled Newman wanting his performance set before shooting began. Both Newman and Hanks were keen to pare down their dialogue, especially during the key Sullivan–Rooney scenes. As Newman explained to *New York Times* reporter Rick Lyman:

> There was a lot of duplication of language in the confrontations between the characters, and we worked hard to cut it down to the absolute minimum. Because it has more force that way, it just does.

Newman suggested a number of new touches, such as Rooney slamming his hand down on a table as he upbraids his son Connor (Daniel Craig). He also felt that Rooney would embrace Connor after striking him in anger. In one scene, Rooney and Sullivan perform a piano duet, 'Perdition', by John M. Williams. Newman and Hanks did their own playing, practising in church halls on an electronic keyboard. A J. S. Bach enthusiast, Newman had been a competent pianist for years.

Now seventy-six, he worked a nineteen-hour day to complete one difficult scene. By the end of filming, Mendes had no complaints about his veteran star: 'He was absolutely brilliant.' Newman returned the compliment, awarding the director his highest praise: 'He knows what he's doing.' Towards the end of production, Conrad Hall was lighting a close-up of Newman as he stared into a fire. According to Mendes, Hall cried at the sight of Newman's aged features, telling the director: 'He was so beautiful.'

Newman saw John Rooney as 'a good bad guy, a lovable killer'. Deploying a fair Irish accent, Newman portrays him as a sentimental, twinkly-eyed monster. Rooney's affection for Sullivan appears genuine. An orphan, Sullivan was raised by Rooney as his own, and it's clear that Rooney trusts Sullivan over Connor, his actual son. Their piano duet suggests a close, unbreakable bond. By contrast, Rooney treats Connor like a wayward child. Once Connor has forced Rooney's hand, however, Sullivan discovers the true worth of their friendship. Mendes describes Rooney as a 'black crow' and a 'harbinger of doom'. Rooney is a man with a corroded soul. In Mendes' view, Newman brought a sense of guilt and regret to the part. The script plays with a favourite Tennessee Williams theme: the decayed, corrupt family dynasty that devours the weak and destroys itself. A widower, Rooney won't turn against Connor, his only living flesh and blood. He laments that 'Sons are put on this earth to trouble their fathers', a sentiment Newman could appreciate. Both sad and sinister, Rooney is undone by his loyalty to Connor. Mendes wanted the final Sullivan–Rooney encounter to play as a 'love' scene. On a dark and rainy night, Sullivan corners Rooney in a lonely street. As he guns down Rooney's henchmen, the only sound is Thomas Newman's music. Rooney accepts his own death with equanimity: 'I'm glad it's you.' Sullivan kills his former employer, friend and surrogate father, machine-gun fire roaring on the soundtrack.

Twentieth Century Fox and DreamWorks launched *Road to Perdition* with a major media blitz. A select group of international journalists were invited to Chicago for a screening, followed by a press conference with Newman. Now hard of hearing, Newman made a strong impression on his audience. Chrissy Iley described him as 'the ultimate, the perfect, butch American beauty'. When the conference ended, he was surrounded by journalists, all clutching videos and DVDs for him to sign. Iley was impressed: 'I've never seen this fan-like behaviour at a press conference. He plays along, signing and smiling.' Iley found Newman a difficult interviewee, describing the star as 'a strange mixture of arrogance and modesty'. Asked about his reasons for making the film, Newman responded:

Sam Mendes, Tom Hanks, the struggle with father and son, the bonding with father and son, the loss of father and son, the dealing with moral people and incorrupt people who are living in a corrupt environment.

Interviewed by Rick Lyman, Newman praised *Road to Perdition* as 'a film of consequence'. Newman felt that Mendes' handling of the violence was neither sensational nor gratuitous:

> . . . the story is more about the impact of the violence on the person who commits it, or witnesses it, than it is about the actual effect of the violence on the person who is hurt or killed.

Inevitably, the film's preoccupation with father–son relationships prompted questions about Scott. Newman sidestepped the issue with his usual courtesy: 'That was a very long time ago. I didn't think about it . . .' The star's only son had been dead for nearly twenty-five years.

Commenting on the current state of Hollywood, Newman argued that 'Audiences for the most part prefer to be entertained than informed. They want explosions, brassieres, body parts, mindless violence.' Movies had become an 'endless appeal to the senses', leaving actors with little to do: 'People aren't challenged. They aren't asked to do better.' Newman also punctured the myth that he never watched his old films: '. . . I don't know, I let them go for a while. And then some mysterious mechanism clicks and I find that I'm ready to watch them.' In 1982, he claimed that it took him seven years or more to know if a film had worked. That said, Newman hadn't yet seen *Road to Perdition*, 'but I know it is extraordinary'.

Road to Perdition opened in the US on 12 July 2002. While the critical response proved mixed, some reviews were highly favourable. The *New York Times* praised the film as 'a truly majestic visual tone poem'. It went on limited release in Britain on 20 September 2002, followed by a wide release a week later. *Observer* critic Philip French described the film as 'a sombre cinematic poem', lacking 'human warmth, something to engage us emotionally, rather than just aesthetically and viscerally'. David Thomson – a harsh Newman critic – was impressed by his performance: '. . . all of a sudden, very late in life, Newman has become a wonderful actor'. *Road to Perdition* grossed $104 million in North America. The film did less well overseas, taking $57.3 million.

Two years after *Ancestral Voices*, Newman embarked on a major theatre 'comeback' in Thornton Wilder's *Our Town* (2002). His participation caused a minor sensation. Having quit the Broadway stage in 1964,

Newman seemed to give up on acting in the theatre. He was familiar with Wilder's play, having co-starred in the 1955 television version, with Frank Sinatra and Eva Marie Saint. Five decades on, Newman became involved in a revival through Joanne Woodward, now artistic director for the Westport Country Playhouse in Connecticut. The playhouse was established in 1931, a year after Woodward's birth. Woodward had long wanted to stage *Our Town*. Shaken by the 9/11 terrorist attack, she felt Wilder's celebration of human resilience was an appropriate response. *Our Town* would launch the Westport Country Playhouse's seventy-second summer season.

The play was directed by James Naughton, a friend of Newman and Woodward. As an actor, Naughton worked with Woodward on the 1985 Williamstown production of *The Glass Menagerie*, reprising his role as the Gentleman Caller in Newman's 1987 film version. Naughton and Woodward, who co-produced *Our Town*, persuaded Newman to play the Stage Manager. Interviewed by Steve Lawson, Naughton explained: 'Joanne and I had been scheming for fifteen years how to get Paul back onstage. I'd about given up.' Woodward felt Newman's decision to abandon stage work had been misguided: 'He was a *wonderful* theatre actor and I think it was a big mistake . . . film is film but for actors the stage is where it's at.' When Woodward told Newman about the *Our Town* production, he asked to see the text. After a brief read-through, he announced: 'I could do this.' According to Woodward, Newman could already recite the Stage Manager's first monologue, virtually word perfect.

Many of the *Our Town* cast were near neighbours of the couple. Naughton had the idea of using local actors: 'I thought it'd be neat if we cast as much as we could from this area, then Westport would be "our town".' The sets and costumes were designed by Tony Walton, who worked on *The Glass Menagerie*. The production came together quickly, with only two and a half weeks of rehearsal. Naughton turned up on set in a Newman's Own sweatshirt, a good-natured nod to his star. Newman jokingly compared the experience to 'just like sticking a rifle in your mouth'. While *Ancestral Voices* had eased him back into the theatre, he felt nervous on stage, telling Steve Lawson: 'I never really got . . . comfortable in the part until maybe a month before it was over. Lots of hand sweating.' Woodward had no reservations about her husband's performance: 'It's lovely to see Paul on the stage again.' In Newman's view, Wilder's play remained highly relevant:

> . . . in *Our Town*, the speeds at which people live and perform
> and rest are human . . . Today, the speeds are inhuman . . . Maybe

you can't go home again, but if there's some way to bring part of this play into your own life, sit down, look around . . .

Four months after the Westport run, *Our Town* transferred to Broadway's Booth Theater. The production marked Newman's first appearance on the New York stage since *Baby Want a Kiss?*, nearly forty years earlier. Newman wrote his own biography for the programme, claiming he was 'best known for his spectacularly successful food conglomerate'. His acting career came a poor second: 'Purely by accident, he has done 51 films and four Broadway plays.' *Our Town* opened at the Booth Theater in early December 2002, to mixed reviews. Critic Edward Karam felt James Naughton had mishandled the play, forsaking Wilder's specified 'empty stage, in half-light' for pointless backstage clutter. Karam was impressed with some of the cast, praising Jane Curtin's Myrtle Webb as 'vocally and physically on target, nailing the warmth and truth in her character'. He had mixed feelings about Newman's performance: 'It should have been easy for Newman to shine in these surroundings, but he has gone out of his way to dim his star wattage amid the ensemble.' Refusing to treat his role as a star turn, Newman seemed unnecessarily subdued: 'His Stage Manager has charm and occasional vinegar, but only once does he reach full throttle.' Explaining how fifty years of a man's life can pass in a flash, Newman brought an unexpected force and passion to the scene. Karam suggested that only here did Newman really connect with the material: 'Clearly, this is a sentiment felt by the actor as much as the character.' Newman finished his nine-week run in the play on Sunday 26 January 2003, his seventy-eighth birthday. His performance was nominated for a Tony Award, Broadway's equivalent to the Oscars.

During the New York run of *Our Town*, two of Newman's film colleagues passed on. Director George Roy Hill died at his Manhattan home on 27 December 2002 of complications from Parkinson's disease. Aged eighty, Hill was barely two years older than Newman. Since his retirement from film-making, he had taught drama at Yale University, one of Newman's *alma maters*. Newman paid a heartfelt, if idiosyncratic, tribute: 'He was the best friend that anyone could have: friend, mentor, enemy. He gave everyone a hell of a ride. Himself included.' Cameraman Conrad Hall died of cancer on 4 January 2003. Having lost touch after the late 1960s, Newman and Hall enjoyed a memorable reunion on *Road to Perdition*. For all its faults, the film proved a worthy conclusion to Hall's career.

At James Naughton's instigation, *Our Town* was recorded for television. Naughton worked with his cast to tone down their performances and adjust the blocking for the camera. Restricted to one set, Naughton could shoot over twenty minutes of footage a day, compared to the standard five and a half minutes for regular television shows. *Our Town* was first screened by Showtime in May 2003. Set between 1901 and 1913, it remains a filmed play, with perfunctory television 'presentation'. For all the adjustments, the pacing and performances are not geared for the small screen. Close up, leading man Ben Fox looks too old for the teenage George Gibbs, and Newman seems subdued and hesitant as the worldly Stage Manager, glasses perched on the end of his nose. The best performance comes from Frank Converse. Cast as Dr Gibbs, George's father, Converse has the telling line, 'The relation of father and son is the damndest, awkwardest . . .' On television, the most effective scene takes place in a cemetery, as Emily Gibbs (Maggie Lacey) is laid to rest. Emily's ghost watches the funeral, conversing with her fellow graveyard residents. The television version of *Our Town* proved popular with both audiences and critics. Overall, Newman's performance met with positive reviews. The *New York Daily News* described his work as subtle and superb. The *San Francisco Chronicle* credited him with 'a terrific performance, perhaps one of the best stage managers you'll ever see'. Newman received an Emmy nomination, the television industry's seal of approval.

The 2003 Academy Award nominations were announced on 11 February. Hotly tipped as an Oscar contender, *Road to Perdition* missed out on the major categories. As expected, Conrad Hall received a posthumous nomination for Best Cinematography. There were also nods for Best Score, Best Art Direction, Best Sound and Best Sound Editing. Newman found himself up for Best Supporting Actor, his first nomination in this category. His competition included Chris Cooper (*Adaptation*), Ed Harris (*The Hours*), John C. Reilly (*Chicago*) and Christopher Walken (*Catch Me If You Can*), with Cooper the favourite to take the prize. Interviewed by Chrissy Iley, Newman claimed he'd never taken the Oscar sweepstakes seriously:

> I've always had a problem with the idea of acting being a competitive profession . . . That's what's nice about racing, it's very clean. You cross the line in front of someone, then you're the winner. But this is so speculative.

Newman had no intention of attending the Academy Awards, as the ceremony clashed with a date on the Newman–Haas racing calendar. As he explained to Lawrence Donegan:

I burned my tuxedo five years ago and with that comes a certain resolution . . . I promised myself that I wasn't going to attend any of those functions. I've never been very comfortable at them and at my age a man is entitled to burn his tuxedo.

Newman used the inevitable media exposure for a little political comment. Never afraid of controversy, he spoke out against President George W. Bush, who was planning a military strike against Iraq without United Nations authorization. Newman lent his voice to the much-maligned anti-war movement: 'The concept of national defence and national security has somehow begun to justify the idea that debate is unpatriotic.' With America involved in an ongoing conflict, the Hollywood community became uneasy about the Oscars. A self-congratulatory showbiz bash could seem both irrelevant and disrespectful. A number of celebrities, including Will Smith, Cate Blanchett, Angelina Jolie, Jim Carrey and director Peter Jackson announced they would not be attending. While the ceremony went ahead as scheduled, on Sunday 23 March 2003, the usual glitz was toned down. As predicted, the Best Supporting Actor award went to Chris Cooper, despite strong competition from Christopher Walken. The late Conrad Hall took the Oscar for Best Cinematography, collected by his son, fellow cameraman Conrad Hall Jr.

Interviewed in 2002, Newman seemed relieved that his public profile had diminished over the years:

Twenty-five years ago I couldn't walk down the street without being recognized. Now I can put a cap on, walk anywhere and no one pays me any attention. They don't ask me about my movies and they don't ask me about my salad dressing because they don't know who I am. Am I happy about this? You bet.

Away from the media spotlight, Newman and Woodward's family have prospered. Melissa Newman is married with two children, while Elinor Newman now runs Newman's Own Organics. The company recently made a deal with the McDonald's fast food empire, supplying Newman's Own dressing for McDonald's premium salads. Given Newman's love of gourmet cooking, this unlikely alliance says a lot about hard commercial realities. At the start of 2004, Newman's Own had given over $150 million to charitable causes. Newman remains fiercely committed to his work as a philanthropist:

This is not about celebrity, this is a political issue. The concept that a person who has a lot holds his hand out to someone who has less is still a human trait. I am confounded by the stinginess of some institutions and some people. You can only put away so much stuff in your closet . . . I don't think there's anything odd about philanthropy. It's the other stance that confounds me.

Woodward also does her bit for good causes, appearing in a television commercial to promote recycling in 2003.

As with acting, Newman announced that he'd retired from motor racing, only to change his mind. Interviewed in 1998, he claimed his days on the track were coming to an end: 'I'm gradually retiring from racing. It's been difficult for me to give it up. It's been my one addiction.' If nothing else, Newman remained a hightly successful competitor. In 1995, just after he turned seventy, he took part in the Daytona twenty-four-hour race. His team went on to win, Newman citing this victory as a personal favourite. Whatever his intentions, his passion for the sport remained as strong as ever:

The allure is the grace . . . You know, at 240 mph, to put your left front tire that close to the apex, that's grace . . . the great drivers are really the ones who are smooth.

The Newman–Haas team continues to do well. In 2002, driver Cristiano da Matta won the team's fourth CART championship. According to one journalist, Newman–Haas's lasting success is hardly a matter of luck: 'They are the best organized and best-financed team on the grid. The surprise is they don't win the championship every year.'

On the downside, Newman received two harsh reminders of the sport's inherent risks. In January 2000, he was involved in a 185 mph crash while competing at the Daytona International Speedway. Though he escaped with a few bruised ribs, the seventy-five-year-old star couldn't shrug off this injury the way he did thirty years earlier. Interviewed a few months later, Newman still seemed troubled by the incident: 'I think if you think about that, there is no sense in getting in the car . . . Stupid, stupid.' Competing at Watkins Glen, New York, in the summer of 2002, he crashed at 100 mph. Shaken, he still believed that racing was good for him: 'It tests the level of your pulse, and I need to test my physical endurance once in a while.' Having endured Newman's hobby for thirty years, Joanne Woodward still tried to put him off the sport. In April 2003, the *National Enquirer* reported that Woodward had covered Newman's beer refrigerator with photographs of car wrecks. Wise to this scheming, Newman merely reached for his beer and went on his way. As he admitted to Lawrence Donegan, his passion for racing would always outweigh Woodward's concerns:

> She ain't exactly happy, that's for sure. But in the end she's supportive. In any case, why would I want to retire? I know I'm old but I can still get in and out of the car, and as long as I'm able to do that, I'll keep racing. What else am I going to do?

In early 2004, Newman secured an unusual deal with Pixar, a computer animation company best known for the hit films *Toy Story* (1995), *Monsters, Inc.* (2001) and *Finding Nemo* (2003). He agreed to voice a character for Pixar's new movie, *Cars* (2005), which follows the adventures of classic automobiles travelling down Route 66. In return, Pixar and parent company Disney would sponsor Newman's Porsche when he competed in the Rolex 24 race at Daytona, held over the weekend of 31 January and 1 February. Although Newman didn't triumph at Daytona 2004, he still holds the world record as the oldest man to win a professional motor racing event. It's a record he intends to continue breaking.

Over the past few years, Newman has talked about finding the right film to end his career on. In an interview with *TV Guide*, he stated that *Road to Perdition* would not be his last screen appearance:

> It's probably closer to a vulture than a swan song. I don't seem to be able to retire. I'd love to do another film with Joanne. There's still a little vinegar in the old dog yet.

In fact, Newman and Woodward were among the all-star cast of *Empire Falls* (2004), a dark comedy-drama. This Home Box Office television film marked the couple's first joint screen appearance since *Mr and Mrs Bridge*, fourteen years earlier. Woodward hadn't appeared in a film since *Philadelphia*, now a decade old. Set in a declining Maine town, *Empire Falls* was based on Richard Russo's Pulitzer Prize-winning novel, published in 2002. Newman approached HBO with the *Empire Falls* project, feeling Russo's novel couldn't be compressed to standard feature-film length. Impressed by Newman's commitment, HBO agreed to a three-hour running time. In addition to his acting duties, Newman served as an executive producer. He hoped *Empire Falls* would reunite him with Russo and director Robert Benton. While Russo agreed to adapt his novel, Benton had other commitments. Forced to look elsewhere, Newman and HBO settled on Fred Schepisi. A gifted film-maker, Schepisi came from the 1970s generation of Australian directors who relocated to the US.

Newman and Woodward's co-stars on *Empire Falls* were Ed Harris, a distinguished character actor, and Helen Hunt, who had won an Academy Award for her performance in *As Good As It Gets* (1997). *Empire Falls* began filming in September 2003. For the most part, the production proceeded smoothly. During the Maine shoot, in early November, co-star Aidan Quinn ran into problems with the local police. Pulled over for suspected drunk driving at two o'clock in the morning, Quinn was charged and bailed after failing a breath test.

On the big screen, Newman accepted a role in *Conspirator*, a thriller set during the aftermath of the American Civil War (1861–5). Newman, Robin Williams and Susan Sarandon starred as characters caught up in the assassination of President Abraham Lincoln. The film began production in 2004, with location filming in Liverpool, England.

Approaching eighty, Newman seems philosophical about his packed schedule:

> I keep trying to retire from everything and discover that I have retired from nothing. I was going to get out of racing, and I'm back in. And I'm back in spaghetti sauce.

Having exposed himself to audiences over six decades, with or without his pants on, Newman seems in no hurry to quit acting for good. The young hopeful ready to flee Hollywood after *The Silver Chalice* keeps coming back for more. He would probably argue that he has never given a definitive performance, crawling out of his skin to leave 'Paul Newman' behind. Distracted by racing and wary of *auteur* directors, he sometimes steered his career off course or simply let it drift. On form, Newman is one of the cinema's strongest leading men, a sensitive actor who became a star, whatever his reservations. As Eddie Felson and Hud Bannon, Newman delivered two of the finest performances ever seen on the big screen. *Road to Perdition's* John Rooney, a hollow man with no chance of redemption, is one of the most haunting character portraits of recent years. By and large, 'Newman's luck' has held as firm as the marriage to Joanne Woodward. His blue eyes never turned brown and, despite his father's worries, he will not die a failure. For the time being, Newman is content to be 'Maintaining a pulse, and still on the right side of the grass.'

Notes

Chapter 4

1. Thirty years later, Vidal attempted a definitive version of his original script with *Gore Vidal's Billy the Kid* (1989). Produced on the back of *Young Guns* (1988), a 'bratpack' take on the William Bonney myth, this made-for-cable effort starred Val Kilmer. Competently directed by television veteran William A. Graham, *Gore Vidal's Billy the Kid* is an intelligent, if unexciting treatment of the story. Kilmer's Method-style performance could be taken as a homage to Newman's interpretation of the character.
2. Trained at the Hal Roach Studios, McCarey directed the acclaimed comedies *Duck Soup* (1933), with the Marx Brothers, and *The Awful Truth* (1937), starring Cary Grant and Irene Dunne, before lapsing into the slushy sentiment of *Going My Way* (1944). McCarey's most recent film was the slick tearjerker *An Affair to Remember* (1957). A remake of the director's own *Love Affair* (1939), this new version starred Cary Grant and Deborah Kerr, who proved a winning combination at the box office.

Chapter 5

1. Active in Hollywood from 1936, Rossen made his name with *Body and Soul* (1947), a harsh examination of the boxing world. He went on to win the Best Picture Academy Award for *All the King's Men* (1949), a potent tale of political corruption. During the 1950s, Rossen was blacklisted after refusing to testify before HUAAC. Though he eventually gave in, admitting past membership of the Communist Party, his career remained in the doldrums. After a self-imposed exile in Europe, Rossen returned to the US, directing the mediocre dramas *Island in the Sun* (1957) and *They Came to Cordura* (1959).

Chapter 6

1. An experienced screenwriter for comics Bob Hope and Danny Kaye, Shavelson enjoyed one of his biggest hits with *Houseboat* (1958), a romantic comedy starring Cary Grant and Sophia Loren.

2. Kanin's film credits included the romantic comedies *Woman of the Year* (1942), which won him an Academy Award, and *Teacher's Pet* (1958).

3. There was also talk of Newman and Loren co-starring in a film version of Arthur Miller's play *After the Fall* (1963).

Chapter 7

1. Arthur Newman would work on *Cool Hand Luke*, *The Secret War of Harry Frigg*, *Rachel, Rachel*, *Winning*, *Sometimes a Great Notion*, *Pocket Money*, *The Life and Times of Judge Roy Bean*, *The Mackintosh Man*, *The Drowning Pool* and *Slap Shot*.

2. Frank Sinatra, who'd passed on *Harper*, starred in *Tony Rome* (1967) and its sequel, *Lady in Cement* (1968). Producer–director–writer Blake Edwards contributed *Gunn* (1967), based on his popular television series *Peter Gunn* (1958–60), with original star Craig Stevens. James Garner took on Raymond Chandler's archetypal private eye in *Marlowe* (1969), based on *The Little Sister* (1949). Elliott Kastner later produced two superior Chandler adaptations, Robert Altman's *The Long Goodbye* (1973) and Dick Richards' *Farewell My Lovely* (1975).

3. For the record, the surviving fragments of Herrmann's *Torn Curtain* score are perfectly serviceable, with elements of *Vertigo*, *North by Northwest* and even *Jason and the Argonauts*.

4. Ritt went on to make *The Brotherhood* (1968), starring Kirk Douglas, and *The Molly Maguires* (1969), with Sean Connery and Richard Harris. Both films proved box-office failures. While he regained some critical standing with *The Great White Hope* (1971) and *Sounder* (1972), his time as a major Hollywood player had passed. Even the Academy Award-winning *Norma Rae* (1979) proved a one-off.

Chapter 8

1. Gainfully employed in television, Rosenberg had worked on episodes of *Alfred Hitchcock Presents* (1955), *The Naked City* (1958), *Rawhide* (1959), *The Twilight Zone* (1959) and *The Untouchables* (1959). He had two feature films to his name, *Murder, Inc.* (1960) and *Question 7* (1961). These low-budget efforts made little impression and Rosenberg returned to the small screen, winning

an Emmy award for a 1963 episode of *The Defenders*, 'The Madman'. He later worked on such glossy television movies as *Fame Is the Name of the Game* (1966), starring Anthony Franciosa.

2. *Rachel, Rachel* was hardly breaking new ground with this credit arrangement. *The Outrage* opens with just the MGM name and the title, the production credits not appearing until the end.

3. Goldstone's small-screen work for Universal included the feature-length pilot for *Ironside* (1967) and *Jigsaw* (1968). He made his feature début with the western *A Man Called Gannon* (1969), a remake of *Man without a Star* (1955).

4. An Emmy Award-winning television director, Hill began his movie career with *Period of Adjustment* (1962), based on a Tennessee Williams play. He made more impression with *The World of Henry Orient* (1964), an offbeat comedy about two teenage girls fixated on a concert pianist. In need of a hit, Hill replaced Fred Zinnemann on the sprawling epic *Hawaii* (1966), starring Max Von Sydow, Julie Andrews and Richard Harris. Hill reunited with Andrews for *Thoroughly Modern Millie* (1967), a romantic comedy–musical set in the 1920s.

5. Other films in production at the Fox studios included the big-budget musical *Hello, Dolly!* (1969), set largely in 1890s New York. It was shooting on an adjacent soundstage to *Butch Cassidy*. George Roy Hill assumed that he would film *Butch Cassidy*'s New York scenes on the *Hello, Dolly!* sets, as the films' schedules didn't clash. However, Fox refused Hill permission, feeling that *Dolly*'s lavish production design should stay under wraps. Undeterred, Hill took Newman, Robert Redford and Katharine Ross over to the *Hello, Dolly!* stage, where they posed for a series of still photographs. These pictures were combined with authentic period photographs for the New York montage sequence seen in the finished film. Fox's protective attitude towards *Hello, Dolly!* was not unique. Stanley Kubrick destroyed the sets and costumes made for *2001: A Space Odyssey* (1968), feeling his film would be devalued if they turned up in other productions. Incidentally, the *Hello, Dolly!* sets were later recycled, heavily disguised, for *Beneath the Planet of the Apes* (1970).

6. A superior piece of entertainment, *Butch Cassidy* does not bear close analysis. The film never questions the outlaws' way of life, mourning the loss of their old world. Depicted as appealing free spirits, Butch and Sundance are the acceptable face of armed robbery. Cassidy sees himself as both a schemer and a dreamer, standing out from the herd. As he puts it: 'Boy, I've got vision and the rest of the world wears bifocals.' In fact, Cassidy's 'vision' is both blinkered

and short-sighted. Furthermore, he is not even a competent robber, using too much dynamite and struggling with basic Spanish. As Sheriff Bledsoe (Jeff Corey) points out, Butch and Sundance are just 'two-bit outlaws on the dodge'.

7. Etta needn't have worried: no one has to watch Butch and Sundance die. The outlaws are frozen in time, guns at the ready, mythical status intact.

Chapter 9

1. Malick had done uncredited rewrites on *Drive He Said* (1971) and *Dirty Harry* (1971). He also co-wrote *Deadhead Miles* (1971), a bizarre road movie that was barely released. Malick went on to write and direct the cult favourites *Badlands* (1973) and *Days of Heaven* (1978).

Chapter 10

1. Roy Bean had previously appeared on screen in *The Westerner* (1940), directed by William Wyler for Samuel Goldwyn. Here, Bean is played by character actor Walter Brennan. The sad-faced Bean is a childlike, psychopathic bully, utterly ruthless in his actions. Brennan won an Academy Award for his performance. During the early 1970s, Universal considered remaking *The Westerner*, with Jack Lemmon as Bean. When Newman–Foreman announced their *Judge Roy Bean* production, Universal cancelled the project.

2. Best known for *The Maltese Falcon* (1941), *The Treasure of the Sierra Madre* (1948) and *The African Queen* (1952), Huston remained a formidable, if erratic, talent. Following a string of flops in the 1960s, he returned to critical, if not commercial, favour with *Fat City* (1972), a compelling character study of two boxers.

3. The impressive, if eclectic, supporting cast included Roddy McDowall, Jacqueline Bisset, Victoria Principal, Anthony Perkins, Tab Hunter, Stacy Keach, Ava Gardner and John Huston himself.

4. Huston originally planned to make the film with his father, Walter Huston. The director later drew the interest of Clark Gable and Humphrey Bogart. After Bogart's death, Frank Sinatra became a possibility. During the 1960s, Huston discussed the project with Richard Burton and Peter O'Toole.

5. With Sean Connery and Michael Caine signed up, *The Man Who Would Be King* went into production, Huston recruiting cameraman Oswald Morris and composer Maurice Jarre. John Foreman stayed on the project as producer, reuniting with Huston a decade later for the critically acclaimed *Prizzi's Honor* (1985).

Chapter 11

1. A former advertising executive, Irwin Allen found a niche in disaster movies during the early 1970s. *The Poseidon Adventure* was the top-grossing film of 1973, taking $160 million worldwide. Interviewed at the time, Allen explained his formula for box-office success: 'Put a lot of people in jeopardy, preferably rich and famous people. See who makes it out, and who doesn't. Watch from the comfort and safety of your seat in the stalls. That's the appeal.'

2. Interviewed in the *Daily News*, Scott Newman seemed happy with his film career: 'I love it, and I'm good at it . . . And it has given me the opportunity to dispel some of the myths people have about me. I've made and paid my own way.'

3. Perhaps the biggest tribute to Newman's enduring charisma came from the French porn industry. In Just Jaeckin's softcore hit *Emmanuelle* (1974), Newman served as a masturbatory fantasy for one of Emmanuelle's girlfriends.

Chapter 13

1. In 1974, Scott Newman was charged with felonious assault after kicking a police officer in the head. Paul Newman supposedly used his influence to obtain leniency for his son. Whatever the case, the assault charge was reduced to a misdemeanour, the judge imposing a $1,000 fine and two years probation. (Paul) Newman paid the fine.

Chapter 16

1. The respected writer–director of *Return of the Secaucus Seven* (1979), *Lianna* (1982) and *The Brother from Another Planet* (1984).

Filmography

THE SILVER CHALICE
1954
Warner, 142 mins
Producer: Victor Saville; Associate producer: Lesser Samuels; Director: Victor Saville; Screenplay: Lesser Samuels (based on the novel by Thomas B. Costain); Director of photography: William V. Skall (Warnercolor/Cinemascope); Production design: Rolf Gerard; Editing: George White; Music: Franz Waxman.
Cast: Paul Newman (Basil), Pier Angeli (Deborra), Jack Palance (Simon the Magician), Virginia Mayo (Helena), Walter Hampden (Joseph of Arimathea), Joseph Wiseman (Mijamin), Alexander Scourby (Saint Luke), Lorne Greene (Saint Peter), Michael Pate (Aaron Ben Joseph), E. G. Marshall (Ignatius), David J. Stewart (Adam), Herbert Rudley (Linus), Jacques Aubuchon (Nero), Natalie Wood (Helena as a child), Donald Randolph (Selech).

THE RACK
1956
Metro-Goldwyn-Mayer, 100 mins
Producer: Arthur M. Loew Jr; Director: Arnold Laven; Screenplay: Stewart Stern (based on the teleplay by Rod Serling); Director of photography: Paul Vogel (b/w); Art direction: Cedric Gibbons, Merrill Pye; Editing: Harold F. Kress, Marshall Neilan Jr; Music: Adolph Deutsch.
Cast: Paul Newman (Captain Edward Worthington Hall Jr), Walter Pidgeon (Colonel Edward W. Hall Sr), Edmond O'Brien (Lieutenant Colonel Frank Wasnick), Anne Francis (Aggie Hall), Lee Marvin (Captain John R. Miller), Cloris Leachman (Caroline), Wendell Corey (Major Sam Moulton), Robert Burton (Colonel Ira Hansen), Robert Simon (Law Officer), Trevor Bardette (Court President), Adam Williams (Sergeant Otto Pahnke), James Best (Millard Chilson Cassidy), Fay Roope (Colonel Dudley Smith), Barry Atwater (Major Byron Phillips).

SOMEBODY UP THERE LIKES ME
1956
Metro-Goldwyn-Mayer, 112 mins
Producer: Charles Schnee; Director: Robert Wise; Screenplay: Ernest Lehman (based on the autobiography of Rocky Graziano, written with Rowland Barber); Director of photography: Joseph Ruttenberg (b/w); Art direction: Cedric Gibbons, Malcolm F. Brown; Editing: Albert Akst; Music: Bronislau Kaper.
Cast: Paul Newman (Rocco Barbella, a.k.a. Rocky Graziano), Pier Angeli (Norma Levine), Everett Sloane (Irving Cohen), Eileen Heckart (Ida Barbella), Sal Mineo (Romolo), Joseph Buloff (Benny), Harold J. Stone (Nick Barbella), Sammy White (Whitey Bimstein), Arch Johnson (Heldon), Robert P. Lieb (Questioner), Theodore Newton (Commissioner Edward Eagan), Robert Loggia (Frankie Peppo), Judson Pratt (Johnny Hyland), Matt Crowley (Lou Stillman), Harry Wismer (himself), Steven McQueen (Fidel) [uncredited].

THE HELEN MORGAN STORY (UK: *Both Ends of the Candle*)
1957
Warner, 118 mins
Producer: Martin Rackin; Director: Michael Curtiz; Screenplay: Oscar Saul, Dean Riesner, Stephen Longstreet, Nelson Gidding; Director of photography: Ted McCord (bw/Cinemascope); Art direction: John Beckman, Editing: Frank Bracht; Musical director: Ray Heindorf.
Cast: Ann Blyth (Helen Morgan), Paul Newman (Larry Maddux), Richard Carlson (Russell Wade), Gene Evans (Whitey Krause), Alan King (Benny Weaver), Cara Williams (Dolly), Walter Woolf King (Ziegfeld), Dorothy Green (Mrs Wade), Edward Platt (Haggerty), Warren Douglas (Mark Hellinger), Rudy Vallee (himself), Walter Winchell (himself), Joe Besser (bartender).

UNTIL THEY SAIL
1957
Metro-Goldwyn-Mayer, 95 mins
Producer: Charles Schnee; Director: Robert Wise; Screenplay: Robert Anderson (based on the story by James A. Michener); Director of photography: Joseph Ruttenberg (bw/Cinemascope); Art direction: Paul Groesse, William A. Horning; Editing: Harold F. Kress; Music: David Raksin.
Cast: Jean Simmons (Barbara Leslie Forbes), Joan Fontaine (Anne Leslie), Paul Newman (Captain Jack Harding), Piper Laurie (Delia Leslie), Charles Drake (Captain Richard Bates), Wally Cassell (Phil Friskett), Sandra Dee (Evelyn Leslie), Alan Napier (Prosecution Attorney), Ralph Votrian (Max Murphy), John Wilder (Tommy), Adam Kennedy (Andy), Mickey Shaunessy (US Marine), Dean Jones (US Marine) [uncredited], Patrick Macnee (Private Duff) [uncredited].

THE LEFT-HANDED GUN
1958
Warner/Haroll, 102 mins
Producer: Fred Coe; Director: Arthur Penn; Screenplay: Leslie Stevens (based on the teleplay *The Death of Billy the Kid*, by Gore Vidal); Director of photography: Peverell Marley (b/w); Art direction: Art Loel; Editing: Folmar Blangsted; Music: Alexander Courage.
Cast: Paul Newman (William Bonney, a.k.a. Billy the Kid), John Dehner (Pat Garrett), Lita Milan (Celsa), Hurd Hatfield (Moultrie), James Congdon (Charlie Boudre), James Best (Tom Folliard), Colin Keith-Johnston (Tunstall), John Dierkes (McSween), Bob Anderson (Hill), Wally Brown (Moon), Ainslie Pryor (Joe Grant), Martin Garralaga (Saval), Denver Pyle (Ollinger), Paul Smith (Smith), Nestor Paiva (Pete Maxwell), Robert Foulk (Sheriff Brady), Anne Barton (Mrs Hill).

THE LONG HOT SUMMER
1958
Twentieth Century Fox, 118 mins
Producer: Jerry Wald; Director: Martin Ritt; Screenplay: Irving Ravetch, Harriet Frank Jr (based on the stories 'Barn Burning' and 'The Spotted Horses', and the novel *The Hamlet*, by William Faulkner); Director of photography: Joseph LaShelle (Eastmancolor/Cinemascope); Art direction: Maurice Ransford, Lyle R.

Wheeler; Editing: Louis R. Loeffler; Music: Alex North.
Cast: Paul Newman (Ben Quick), Joanne Woodward (Clara Varner), Orson
Welles (Will Varner), Anthony Franciosa (Jody Varner), Lee Remick (Eula Varner),
Angela Lansbury (Minnie Littlejohn), Richard Anderson (Alan Stewart), George
Dunn (Peabody), Sarah Marshall (Agnes Stewart), Mabel Albertson (Mrs Stewart),
Jess Kirkpatrick (Armistead).

CAT ON A HOT TIN ROOF
1958
Metro-Goldwyn-Mayer/Avon, 108 mins
Producer: Laurence Weingarten; Director: Richard Brooks; Screenplay: Richard
Brooks, James Poe (based on the play by Tennessee Williams); Director of
photography: William Daniels (Metrocolor); Art direction: William A. Horning,
Urie McCleary; Editing: Ferris Webster.
Cast: Paul Newman (Brick Pollitt), Burl Ives (Big Daddy), Elizabeth Taylor
(Maggie 'The Cat' Pollitt), Jack Carson (Gooper), Judith Anderson (Big Mama),
Madeleine Sherwood (Mae), Larry Gates (Dr Baugh), Vaughn Taylor (Deacon
Davis), Zelda Cleaver (Sookey).

RALLY 'ROUND THE FLAG, BOYS!
1958
Twentieth Century Fox, 106 mins
Producer: Leo McCarey; Director: Leo McCarey; Screenplay: Claude Binyon,
Leo McCarey and George Axelrod [uncredited] (based on the novel by Max
Shulman); Director of photography: Leon Shamroy (DeLuxe/Cinemascope); Art
direction: Leland Fuller, Lyle R. Wheeler; Editing: Louis R. Loeffler; Music: Cyril
J. Mockridge.
Cast: Paul Newman (Harry Bannerman), Joanne Woodward (Grace Banner-
man), Joan Collins (Angela Hoffa), Jack Carson (Captain Hoxie), Dwayne
Hickman (Grady Metcalf), Tuesday Weld (Comfort Goodpasture), Gale Gordon
(Brigadier General W. A. Thorwold), Tom Gilson (Corporal Opie), O. Z. White-
head (Isaac Goodpasture), Tap Canutt (Soldier) [uncredited], Murvyn Vye
(Oscar Hoffa) [uncredited], David Hedison (Narrator) [uncredited], Sammy Ogg
(Delinquent) [uncredited], Ralph Osborn III (Danny Bannerman) [uncredited].

THE YOUNG PHILADELPHIANS (UK: *The City Jungle*)
1959
Warner, 136 mins
Producer: James Gunn [uncredited]; Director: Vincent Sherman; Screenplay:
James Gunn (based on the novel *The Philadelphian*, by Richard Powell);
Director of photography: Harry Stradling (b/w); Art direction: Malcolm Bert;
Editing: William Ziegler; Music: Ernest Gold.
Cast: Paul Newman (Anthony Judson Lawrence), Barbara Rush (Joan Dickin-
son), Alexis Smith (Carole Wharton), Brian Keith (Mike Flanagan), Billie Burke
(Mrs J. Arthur Allen), John Williams (Gilbert Dickinson), Otto Kruger (John
Marshall Wharton), Diane Brewster (Kate Lawrence), Robert Vaughn (Chester
A. Gwynn), Paul Picerni (Louis Donetti), Robert Douglas (Morton Stearnes),
Frank Conroy (Doctor Stearnes), Adam West (William Lawrence III), Anthony
Eisley (Carter Henry), Richard Deacon (George Archibald).

FROM THE TERRACE
1960

Twentieth Century Fox/Linebrook, 144 mins
Producer: Mark Robson; Director: Mark Robson; Screenplay: Ernest Lehman
(based on the novel by John O'Hara); Director of photography: Leo Tover
(DeLuxe/Cinemascope); Art direction: Maurice Ransford, Howard Richmond,
Lyle R. Wheeler; Editing: Dorothy Spencer; Music: Elmer Bernstein.
Cast: Paul Newman (David Alfred Eaton), Joanne Woodward (Mary St John),
Myrna Loy (Martha Eaton), Ina Balin (Natalie Benziger), Leon Ames (Samuel
Eaton), Felix Aylmer (James Duncan MacHardie), George Grizzard (Alexander
Porter), Patrick O'Neal (Dr Jim Roper), Elizabeth Allen (Sage Rimmington),
Barbara Eden (Clemmie Shreve), Marie Blake (Nellie), Howard Caine
(Creighton Duffy), Dorothy Adams (Mrs Benziger), Ted de Corsia (Ralph W.
Benziger), Lauren Gilbert (Charles Frolick), Elizabeth Russell (Frolick's Woman).

EXODUS
1960

United Artists/Carlyle/Alpha, 220 mins
Producer: Otto Preminger; Director: Otto Preminger; Screenplay: Dalton Trum-
bo (based on the novel by Leon Uris); Director of photography: Sam Leavitt
(Technicolor/Super Panavision 70); Art direction: Richard Day; Editing: Louis R.
Loeffler; Music: Ernest Gold; Title design: Saul Bass.
Cast: Paul Newman (Ari Ben Canaan), Eva Marie Saint (Kitty Fremont), Ralph
Richardson (General Sutherland), Peter Lawford (Major Caldwell), Lee J. Cobb
(Barak Ben Canaan), Sal Mineo (Dov Landau), John Derek (Taha), Hugh
Griffith (Mandria), Gregory Ratoff (Lakavitch), Felix Aylmer (Dr Lieberman),
David Opatoshu (Akiva Ban Canaan), Jill Haworth (Karen), Marius Goring
(Von Storch), Alexandra Stewart (Jordana), Michael Wager (David), Martin
Benson (Mordekai), Paul Stevens (Reuben), Betty Walker (Sarah), Martin Miller
(Dr Odenheim), Victor Maddern (Sergeant), George Maharis (Yaov), John
Crawford (Hank Schlosberg), Samuel Segal (Proprietor), Dahn Ben Amotz (Uzi),
Ralph Truman (Colonel), Peter Maddern (Dr Clement), Joseph Furst (Avidan),
Marc Burns (Lieutenant O'Hara), Esther Reichstadt (Mrs Hirschberg), Zipora
Peled (Mrs Frankel), Phil Hauser (Novak).

PARIS BLUES
1961

United Artists/Pennebaker/Diane/Jason/Monica/Monmouth, 98 mins
Executive producers: George Glass, Walter Seltzer; Producer: Sam Shaw;
Director: Martin Ritt; Screenplay: Jack Sher, Irene Kamp, Walter Bernstein;
Adaptation: Lulla Rosenfeld (based on the novel by Harold Flender); Director of
photography: Christian Matras (b/w); Art direction: Alexandre Trauner; Editing:
Roger Dwyre; Music: Duke Ellington.
Cast: Paul Newman (Ram Bowen), Joanne Woodward (Lillian Corning), Sidney
Poitier (Eddie Cook), Diahann Carroll (Connie Lampson), Louis Armstrong
(Wild Man Moore), Serge Reggiani (Michel Duvigne), Barbara Laage (Marie
Seoul), Andre Luguet (Rene Bernard), Marie Versini (Nicole), Moustache
(Drummer), Aaron Bridgers (Pianist), Guy Pederson (Bass player).

THE HUSTLER
1961
Twentieth Century Fox, 135 mins
Producer: Robert Rossen; Director: Robert Rossen; Screenplay: Robert Rossen, Sidney Carroll (based on the novel by Walter Tevis); Director of photography: Eugene Schufftan (bw/Cinemascope); Editing: Dede Allen; Production design: Harry Horner; Music: Kenyon Hopkins; Technical advisor: Willie Mosconi.
Cast: Paul Newman ('Fast' Eddie Felson), Jackie Gleason (Minnesota Fats), George C. Scott (Bert Gordon), Piper Laurie (Sarah Packard), Myron McCormick (Charlie Burns), Murray Hamilton (James Findley), Michael Constantine (Big John), Stefan Gierasch (Preacher), Clifford Pellow (Turk Baker), Jake LaMotta (Bartender), Gordon B. Clarke (Cashier), Alexander Rose (Score Keeper), Carolyn Coates (Waitress), Vincent Gardenia (Bartender), Willie Mosconi (Willie) [uncredited].

SWEET BIRD OF YOUTH
1962
Metro-Goldwyn-Mayer/Roxbury, 120 mins
Producer: Pandro S. Berman; Associate producer: Kathryn Hereford; Director: Richard Brooks; Screenplay: Richard Brooks (based on the play by Tennessee Williams); Director of photography: Milton Krasner (Metrocolor/Cinemascope); Art direction: George W. Davis, Urie McCleary; Editing: Henry Berman; Music: Harold Gelman [uncredited]; Music director: Robert Armbruster.
Cast: Paul Newman (Chance Wayne), Geraldine Page (Alexandra Del Lago), Ed Begley (Tom 'Boss' Finley), Mildred Dunnock (Aunt Nonnie), Rip Torn (Thomas J. Finlay Jr), Shirley Knight (Heavenly Finley), Madeleine Sherwood (Miss Lucy), Philip Abbott (Dr George Scudder), Corey Allen (Scotty), Barry Cahill (Bud), Dub Taylor (Dan Hatcher), James B. Douglas (Leroy), Barry Atwater (Ben Jackson), Charles Arnt (Mayor Henricks).

HEMINGWAY'S ADVENTURES OF A YOUNG MAN (a.k.a. *Adventures of a Young Man*)
1962
Twentieth Century Fox, 145 mins
Producer: Jerry Wald; Director: Martin Ritt; Screenplay: A. E. Hotchner (based on stories by Ernest Hemingway); Director of photography: Lee Garmes (DeLuxe/Cinemascope); Art direction: Paul Groesse, Jack Martin Smith; Editing: Hugh S. Fowler; Music: Franz Waxman.
Cast: Richard Beymer (Nick Adams), Diane Baker (Carolyn), Corinne Calvert (Contessa), Fred Clark (Mr Turner), Dan Dailey (Billy Campbell), James Dunn (Telegrapher), Juano Hernandez (Bugs), Arthur Kennedy (Doc Adams), Ricardo Montalban (Major Padula), Susan Strasberg (Rosanna), Paul Newman (Ad Francis), Jessica Tandy (Mrs Adams), Eli Wallach (John), Michael J. Pollard (George), Simon Oakland (Joe Boulton), Ed Binns (Brakeman), Whit Bissell (Ludstrum), Tullio Carminati (Rosanna's father), Pat Hogan (Billy Tabeshaw).

HUD
1963
Paramount/Salem/Dover, 112 mins
Producers: Martin Ritt, Irving Ravetch; Director: Martin Ritt; Screenplay: Irving
Ravetch, Harriet Frank Jr (based on the novel *Horseman, Pass By*, by Larry
McMurtry); Director of photography: James Wong Howe (bw/Panavision); Art
direction: Tambi Larsen, Hal Pereira; Editing: Frank Bracht; Music: Elmer Bern-
stein.
Cast: Paul Newman (Hud Bannon), Patricia Neal (Alma Brown), Melvyn Dou-
glas (Homer Bannon), Brandon De Wilde (Lonnie Bannon), Whit Bissell (Mr
Burris), Crahan Denton (Jesse), John Ashley (Hermy), Val Avery (Jose), George
Petrie (Joe Scanlon), Curt Conway (Truman Peters), Pitt Herbert (Mr Larker),
Yvette Vickers (Lily Peters), Richard Deacon (Pharmacist).

A NEW KIND OF LOVE
1963
Paramount/Llenroc, 110 mins
Producer: Melville Shavelson; Director Melville Shavelson; Screenplay: Melville
Shavelson; Director of photography: Daniel Fapp (Technicolor); Art direction:
Arthur Lonergan, Hal Pereira; Editing: Frank Bracht; Music: Leith Stevens,
Erroll Garner.
Cast: Paul Newman (Steve Sherman), Joanne Woodward (Samantha Blake),
Maurice Chevalier (Himself), Thelma Ritter (Leena), Eva Gabor (Felicienne
Courbeau), George Tobias (Joe Bergner), Marvin Kaplan (Harry), Robert F.
Simon (Bertram Chalmers).

THE PRIZE
1963
Metro-Goldwyn-Mayer/Roxbury, 135 mins
Producer: Pandro S. Berman; Director: Mark Robson; Screenplay: Ernest
Lehman (based on the novel by Irving Wallace); Director of photography:
William Daniels (Metrocolor/Panavision); Art direction: George W. Davis, Urie
McCleary; Editing: Adrienne Fazan; Music: Jerry Goldsmith.
Cast: Paul Newman (Andrew Craig), Elke Sommer (Inger Lisa), Edward G.
Robinson (Dr Max Stratman), Diane Baker (Emily Stratman), Kevin McCarthy
(Dr Garrett), Leo G. Carroll (Count Jacobson), Micheline Presle (Denise
Marceau), Gerard Oury (Claude Marceau), Sergio Fantoni (Dr Farelli), Sacha
Pitoeff (Daranyi), Don Dubbins (Ivar), Jacqueline Beer (Monique), John Wengraf
(Eckart).

WHAT A WAY TO GO!
1964
Twentieth Century Fox/APJAC/Orchard, 111 mins
Producer: Arthur P. Jacobs; Director: J. Lee Thompson; Screenplay: Betty
Comden, Adolph Green (based on a story by Gwen Davis); Director of photog-
raphy: Leon Shamroy (DeLuxe/Cinemascope); Art direction: Ted Haworth, Jack
Martin Smith; Editing: Marjorie Fowler; Musical director: Nelson Riddle;
Music: Jule Styne; Lyrics: Betty Comden, Adolph Green.
Cast: Shirley MacLaine (Louisa Foster), Robert Cummings (Dr Stephanson),

Dick Van Dyke (Edgar Hopper), Robert Mitchum (Rod Anderson), Gene Kelly
(Pinky Benson), Dean Martin (Leonard Crawley), Paul Newman (Larry Flint),
Reginald Gardiner (Painter), Margaret Dumont (Mrs Foster), Lou Nova
(Trentino), Fifi D'Orsay (Baroness), Maurice Marsac (Rene), Wally Vernon
(Agent), Jane Wald (Polly), Lenny Kent (Hollywood Lawyer), Tom Conway
(Lord Kensington) [uncredited], Queenie Leonard (Lady Kensington)
[uncredited].

THE OUTRAGE
1964
Metro-Goldwyn-Mayer/Harvest/February/Ritt/Kayos, 97 mins
Producer: A. Ronald Lubin; Associate producer: Michael Kanin; Director:
Martin Ritt; Screenplay: Michael Kanin (from the play *Rashomon*, by Fay and
Michael Kanin, based on Akira Kurosawa's film script); Director of
photography: James Wong Howe (bw/Panavision); Art direction: George W.
Davis, Tambi Larsen; Editing: Frank Santillo; Music: Alex North.
Cast: Paul Newman (Juan Carrasco), Edward G. Robinson (Con Man),
Laurence Harvey (Husband), Claire Bloom (Wife), William Shatner (Preacher),
Albert Salmi (Sheriff), Howard Da Silva (Prospector), Thomas Chalmers (Judge),
Paul Fix (Indian).

LADY L
1965
Metro-Goldwyn-Mayer/Concordia/Champion, 124 mins
Producer: Carlo Ponti; Director: Peter Ustinov; Screenplay: Peter Ustinov (based
on the novel by Romain Gary); Director of photography: Henri Alekan
(Eastmancolor/Panavision); Art direction: Jean D'Eaubonne, Auguste Capelier;
Editing: Roger Dwyre; Music: Jean Francaix.
Cast: Sophia Loren (Louise, a.k.a. Lady L), Paul Newman (Armand), David
Niven (Lord Lendale), Claude Dauphin (Inspector Mercier), Philippe Noiret
(Gerome), Michel Piccoli (Lecoeur), Marcel Dalio (Sapper), Cecil Parker (Sir
Percy), Eugene Deckers (Koenigstein), Jacques Dufilho (Beala), Daniel Emilfork
(Kobeleff), Hella Petri (Madam), Jean Wiener (Krajewski), Sacha Pitoeff
(Revolutionary), Arthur Howard (Butler), Peter Ustinov (Prince Otto of Bavaria)
[uncredited].

HARPER (UK: *The Moving Target*)
1966
Warner, 121 mins
Producers: Jerry Gershwin, Elliott Kastner; Director: Jack Smight; Screenplay:
William Goldman (based on the novel *The Moving Target*, by John Ross
Macdonald); Director of photography: Conrad Hall (Technicolor/Panavision);
Art direction: Alfred Sweeney; Editing: Stefan Arnsten; Music: Johnny Mandel;
Song 'Livin' Alone' by Andre Previn.
Cast: Paul Newman (Lew Harper), Lauren Bacall (Elaine Sampson), Pamela
Tiffin (Miranda Sampson), Robert Wagner (Allan Taggert), Arthur Hill (Albert
Graves), Janet Leigh (Susan Harper), Shelley Winters (Fay Estabrook), Julie
Harris (Betty Fraley), Robert Webber (Dwight Troy), Strother Martin (Claude),
Harold Gould (Sheriff Spanner), Roy Jenson (Puddler), Martin West (Deputy

Sheriff), Jacqueline deWit* (Mrs Kronberg), Eugene Iglesias (Felix), Richard
Carlyle (Fred Platt).

TORN CURTAIN
1966
Universal, 119 mins
Producer: Alfred Hitchcock [uncredited]; Director: Alfred Hitchcock; Screen-
play: Brian Moore, and Keith Waterhouse, Willis Hall [uncredited]; Director of
photography: John F. Warren (Technicolor); Production design: Hein Heckroth;
Editing: Bud Hoffman; Music: John Addison.
Cast: Paul Newman (Michael Armstrong), Julie Andrews (Sarah Sherman),
Wolfgang Kieling (Hermann Gromek), Ludwig Donath (Professor Gustav Lindt),
Lila Kedrova (Countess Kuchinska), Hansjoerg Felmy (Heinrich Gerhard),
Tamara Toumanova (Ballerina), Gunter Strack (Professor Karl Manfred), David
Opatoshu (Mr Jakobi), Gisela Fischer (Dr Koska), Mort Mills (Farmer), Carolyn
Conwell (Farmer's Wife), Arthur Gould-Porter (Freddy), Gloria Gorvin
(Fraulein).

HOMBRE
1967
Twentieth Century Fox/Hombre Productions, 111 mins
Producers: Martin Ritt, Irving Ravetch; Director: Martin Ritt; Screenplay: Irving
Ravetch, Harriet Frank Jr (based on the novel by Elmore Leonard); Director of
photography: James Wong Howe (DeLuxe/Panavision); Art direction: Jack
Martin Smith, Robert Emmet Smith; Editing: Frank Bracht; Music: David Rose.
Cast: Paul Newman (John Russell), Diane Cilento (Jessie), Fredric March
(Faver), Richard Boone (Grimes), Martin Balsam (Henry Mendez), Barbara
Rush (Audra Faver), Cameron Mitchell (Braden), Peter Lazer (Billy Lee Blake),
Margaret Blye (Doris Blake), Skip Ward (Steve Early), Frank Silvera (Mexican
Bandit), David Canary (Lamar Dean), Val Avery (Delgado), Larry Ward
(Soldier), Linda Cordova (Mrs Delgado) [uncredited], Pete Hernandez (Apache)
[uncredited], Merrill C. Isbell (Apache) [uncredited].

COOL HAND LUKE
1967
Warner/Jalem, 126 mins
Producer: Gordon Carroll; Associate producer: Carter DeHaven Jr; Director:
Stuart Rosenberg; Screenplay: Donn Pearce, Frank R. Pierson (based on the
novel by Donn Pearce); Director of photography: Conrad Hall
(Technicolor/Panavision); Art direction: Cary Odell; Editing: Sam O'Steen;
Music: Lalo Schifrin.
Cast: Paul Newman (Lucas 'Cool Hand' Jackson), George Kennedy (Dragline),
Jo Van Fleet (Arletta Jackson), J. D. Cannon (Society Red), Lou Antonio (Koko),
Robert Drivas (Loudmouth Steve), Strother Martin (Captain), Clifton James
(Carr), Morgan Woodward (Boss Geoffrey), Luke Askew (Boss Paul Hunnicut),
Marc Cavell (Rabbitt), Richard Davalos (Blind Dick), Robert Donner (Boss
Shorty), Warren Finnerty (Tattoo), Dennis Hopper (Babalugats), John McLiam

---

* Contrary to some accounts, Jacqueline deWit is not Jacqueline Witte, Newman's first
wife.

(Boss Kean), Wayne Rogers (Gambler), Harry Dean Stanton (Edgar 'Tramp' Potter), Charles Tyner (Boss Higgins), Ralph Waite (Alibi Gibson), Anthony Zerbe (Dog Boy), Buck Kartalian (Dynamite), Joy Harmon (Car Washing Girl), Joe Don Baker (Fixer) [uncredited], Rance Howard (Sheriff) [uncredited], Donn Pearce (Sailor) [uncredited].

THE SECRET WAR OF HARRY FRIGG
1968
Universal/Albion, 109 mins
Executive producer: Leo L. Fuchs; Producer: Hal E. Chester; Director: Jack Smight; Screenplay: Peter Stone, Frank Tarloff (based on a story by Frank Tarloff); Director of photography: Russell Metty (Technicolor/Techniscope); Art direction: Henry Bumstead, Alexander Golitzen; Editing: J. Terry Williams; Music: Carlo Rustichelli.
Cast: Paul Newman (Private Harry Frigg), John Williams (General Mayhew), Sylva Koscina (Countess De Montefiore), Andrew Duggan (General Armstrong), Tom Bosley (General Pennypacker), Charles D. Gray (General Cox-Roberts), Vito Scotti (Colonel Ferrucci), Jacques Roux (General Rochambeau), Werner Peters (Major von Steignitz), James Gregory (General Prentiss), Fabrizio Mioni (Lieutenant Rossano), Johnny Haymer (Sergeant Pozzallo), Norman Fell (Captain Stanley), Buck Henry (Stockade Commandant).

RACHEL, RACHEL
1968
Warner/Kayos, 101 mins
Producer: Paul Newman; Associate producers: Harrison Starr, Arthur Newman; Director: Paul Newman; Screenplay: Stewart Stern (based on the novel *A Jest of God*, by Margaret Laurence); Director of photography: Gayne Rescher (Eastmancolor); Art direction: Robert Gundlach; Editing: Dede Allen; Music: Jerome Moross.
Cast: Joanne Woodward (Rachel Cameron), Estelle Parsons (Calla Mackie), James Olsen (Nick Kazlik), Kate Harrington (Mrs Cameron), Donald Moffat (Niall Cameron), Geraldine Fitzgerald (Reverend Wood), Bernard Barrow (Leighton Siddley), Terry Kiser (Preacher), Frank Corsaro (Hector Jonas), Nell Potts [Elinor Newman] (Rachel as a child), Shawn Campbell (James), Violet Dunn (Verla), Izzy Singer (Lee Shabab), Tod Engle (Nick as a child), Bruno Engler (Bartender).

WINNING
1969
Universal/Newman-Foreman, 123 mins
Executive producers: Jennings Lang, Paul Newman [uncredited]; Producer: John Foreman; Associate producer: George Santoro; Director: James Goldstone; Screenplay: Howard Rodman; Director of photography: Richard Moore (Technicolor/Panavision 70); Production design: Alexander Golitzen, John J. Lloyd, Joe Alves [uncredited]; Editing: Edward A. Biery; Music: Dave Grusin.
Cast: Paul Newman (Frank Capua), Joanne Woodward (Elora Capua), Richard Thomas (Charley), Robert Wagner (Luther Erding), David Sheiner (Crawford), Clu Gulager (Larry), Barry Ford (Bottineau), Karen Arthur (Miss Dairy Queen),

Bobby Unser (Himself), Tony Hulman (Himself), Bobby Grim (Himself), Dan
Gurney (Himself), Roger McCluskey (Himself), Robert Quarry (Sam Jagin)
[uncredited].

BUTCH CASSIDY AND THE SUNDANCE KID
1969
Twentieth Century Fox/Campanile, 110 mins
Executive producers: Paul Monash, Paul Newman [uncredited]; Producer: John
Foreman; Director: George Roy Hill; Screenplay: William Goldman; Director of
photography: Conrad Hall (DeLuxe/Panavision); Art direction: Philip M.
Jefferies, Jack Martin Smith; Editing: John C. Howard, Richard C. Meyer;
Music: Burt Bacharach.
Cast: Paul Newman (Robert Leroy Parker, a.k.a. Butch Cassidy), Robert Red-
ford (Harry Longbaugh, a.k.a. The Sundance Kid), Katharine Ross (Etta Place),
Strother Martin (Percy Garris), Henry Jones (Bike Salesman), Jeff Corey (Sheriff
Steve Bledsoe), Cloris Leachman (Agnes), Ted Cassidy (Harvey Logan), Kenneth
Mars (Marshal), Donnelly Rhodes (Macon), Jody Gilbert (Large Woman),
Timothy Scott (News Carver), Don Keefer (Fireman), Charles Dierkop (Flat
Nose Curry), Francisco Cordova (Bank Manager), Nelson Olmsted (Photographer),
Paul Bryar (Card Player 1), Sam Elliott (Card Player 2), Charles Akins (Bank
Teller), Eric Sinclair (Tiffany's Salesman), Percy Helton (Sweetface) [uncredited].

WUSA
1970
Paramount/Mirror/Coleytown/Stuart Rosenberg, 117 mins
Producers: Paul Newman, John Foreman; Director: Stuart Rosenberg;
Screenplay: Robert Stone (based on his novel, *A Hall of Mirrors*); Director of
photography: Richard Moore (Technicolor/Panavision); Production design:
Philip Jefferies; Editing: Bob Wyman; Music: Lalo Schifrin.
Cast: Paul Newman (Rheinhardt), Joanne Woodward (Geraldine), Laurence
Harvey (Farley), Anthony Perkins (Rainey), Pat Hingle (Bingamon), Cloris
Leachman (Philomene), Michael Anderson Jr (Marvin), Don Gordon
(Bogdanovich), Robert Quarry (Noonan), Bruce Cabot (King Wolyoe), Moses
Gunn (Clotho), Wayne Rogers (Calvin Minter), Susan Batson (Teenaged Girl),
Hal Baylor (Shorty), Lucille Benson (Matron), Jim Boles (Hot Dog Vendor),
Jerry Catron (Sidewinder Bates), Zara Cully (White-Haired Woman), Geoffrey
Edwards (Irving), Leigh French (Girl), Paul Hampton (Rusty Fargo), David
Huddleston (Heavy Man), Clifton James (Speed), Diane Ladd (Barmaid at
Railroad Station), B. J. Mason (Roosevelt Berry), Laird Stuart (Bobby), Jesse
Vint (Young Doctor), Geraldine West (Matron), Skip Young (Jimmy Snipe).

PUZZLE OF A DOWNFALL CHILD
1970
Universal/Newman-Foreman, 104 minutes
Producer: John Foreman; Director: Jerry Schatzberg; Screenplay: 'Adrien Joyce'
(Carole Eastman); Director of photography: Adam Holender (Technicolor); Art
direction: Richard Bianchi; Editing: Evan Lottman; Music: Michael Small.
Cast: Faye Dunaway (Lou Andreas Sand), Barry Primus (Aaron Reinhardt),
Viveca Lindfors (Paula Galba), Barry Morse (Dr Galba), Roy Scheider (Mark),

Barbara Carrera (T. J. Brady).

THEY MIGHT BE GIANTS
1971
Universal, 88 mins (theatrical version)/91 mins (television/video/DVD version)
Executive producers: Paul Newman, Jennings Lang; Producer: John Foreman;
Associate producer: Frank Caffey; Director: Anthony Harvey; Screenplay: James
Goldman (based on his play); Director of photography: Victor Kemper (Techni-
color); Production design: John Robert Lloyd; Editing: Gerald B. Greenberg;
Music: John Barry.
Cast: George C. Scott (Justin Playfair), Joanne Woodward (Dr Mildred Watson),
Jack Gilford (Wilbur Peabody), Lester Rawlins (Blevins Playfair), Al Lewis (Mes-
senger), Rue McClanahan (Daisy Playfair), Ron Weyland (Dr Strauss), Oliver
Clark (Mr Small), Theresa Merritt (Peggy), Jenny Egan (Miss Finch), Jane
Hoffman (2nd Telephone Operator), Michael McGuire (Telephone Guard),
Eugene Roche (Policeman), James Tolkan (Mr Brown), Kitty Winn (Grace),
Sudie Bond (Maud), F. Murray Abraham (Clyde), M. Emmet Walsh
(1st Sanitation Man), Louis Zorich (2nd Sanitation Man).

SOMETIMES A GREAT NOTION (UK: *Never Give an Inch*)
1971
Universal, 114 mins
Executive producer: Paul Newman; Producer: John Foreman; Associate producer:
Frank Caffey; Directors: Paul Newman, Richard A. Colla (uncredited);
Screenplay: John Gay (based on the novel by Ken Kesey); Director of
photography: Richard Moore (Technicolor/Panavision); Art direction: Philip
Jefferies; Editing: Bob Wyman; Music: Henry Mancini; Lyrics: Alan Bergman,
Marilyn Bergman.
Cast: Paul Newman (Hank Stamper), Henry Fonda (Henry Stamper), Lee
Remick (Viv Stamper), Michael Sarrazin (Leland Stamper), Richard Jaeckel (Joe
Ben Stamper), Linda Lawson (Jan Stamper), Cliff Potts (Andy Stamper), Sam
Gilman (John Stamper), Lee de Broux (Willard Eggleston), Jim Burk (Biggy
Newton), Roy Jenson (Howie Elwood), Joe Maross (Floyd Evenwrite), Roy
Poole (Jonathan Stamper), Charles Tyner (Les Gibbons).

POCKET MONEY
1972
Warner/First Artists/Coleytown, 100 mins
Producer: John Foreman; Associate producer: Frank Caffey; Director: Stuart
Rosenberg; Screenplay: Terrence Malick, John Gay [uncredited] (based on the
novel *Jim Kane*, by J. P. S. Brown); Director of photography: Laszlo Kovacs
(Technicolor); Art direction: Tambi Larsen; Editing: Bob Wyman; Music: Alex
North; Title song: Carole King.
Cast: Paul Newman (Jim Kane), Lee Marvin (Leonard), Strother Martin (Bill
Garrett), Kelly Jean Peters (Sharon), Wayne Rogers (Stretch Russell), Hector
Elizondo (Juan), Christine Belford (Adelita), Gregory Sierra (Guerro Chavarin),
Fred Graham (Uncle Herb), Matt Clark (American prisoner), Claudio Miranda
(Manisterio Publico), Richard Farnsworth (Man), Terrence Malick (Workman)
[uncredited].

THE EFFECT OF GAMMA RAYS ON MAN-IN-THE-MOON MARIGOLDS
1972

Twentieth Century Fox/Newman-Foreman, 101 mins

Producer: Paul Newman; Director: Paul Newman; Screenplay: Alvin Sargent (based on the play by Paul Zindel); Director of photography: Adam Holender (DeLuxe); Production design: Gene Callahan; Editing: Evan A. Lottman; Music: Maurice Jarre.

Cast: Joanne Woodward (Beatrice), Nell Potts [Elinor Newman] (Matilda), Roberta Wallach (Ruth), Judith Lowry (Nanny), David Spielberg (Mr Goodman), Richard Venture (Floyd), Carolyn Coates (Mrs McKay), Will Hare (Junk Man), Estelle Omens (Caroline), Jess Osuna (Sonny), Ellen Dano (Janice Vickery), Lynne Rogers (Miss Hanley), Roger Serbagi (Charlie), John Lehne (Apartment Manager), Michael Kearney (Chris Burns), Dee Victor (Miss Wyant).

THE LIFE AND TIMES OF JUDGE ROY BEAN
1972

Warner Brothers/First Artists/National General, 124 mins

Executive producer: Paul Newman [uncredited]; Producer: John Foreman; Associate producer: Frank Caffey; Director: John Huston; Screenplay: John Milius; Director of photography: Richard Moore (Technicolor); Art direction: Tambi Larsen; Editing: Hugh S. Fowler; Music: Maurice Jarre; Lyrics: Alan and Marilyn Bergman.

Cast: Paul Newman (Judge Roy Bean), Roddy McDowall (Frank Gass), Victoria Principal (Maria Elena), Ned Beatty (Tector Crites), Anthony Perkins (Reverend Mr LaSalle), Tab Hunter (Sam Dodd), Stacy Keach (Original Bad Bob), John Huston (Grizzly Adams), Jacqueline Bisset (Rose Bean), Ava Gardner (Lillie Langtry), Frank Soto (Mexican leader), Jim Burk (Big Bart Jackson), Matt Clark (Nick the Grub), Bill McKinney (Fermel Parlee), Steve Kanaly (Whorehouse Lucky Jim), Billy Pearson (Stationmaster Billy), Neil Summers (Snake River Rufus Krile), Jack Colvin (Pimp), Francesca Jarvis (Mrs Jackson), Karen Carr (Mrs Grub), Lee Meza (Mrs Parlee), Dolores Clark (Mrs Whorehouse Jim), Howard Morton (Photographer), David Sharpe (Doctor), Anthony Zerbe (Opera House Hustler), Michael Sarrazin (Rose's husband), Roy Jenson (Outlaw), Richard Farnsworth (Outlaw), Terry Leonard (Outlaw), Barbara J. Longo (Fat Whore).

THE MACKINTOSH MAN
1973

Warner/Newman-Foreman/John Huston, 99 mins

Producer: John Foreman; Associate producer: William Hill; Director: John Huston; Screenplay: Walter Hill, William Fairchild [uncredited] (based on the novel *The Freedom Trap*, by Desmond Bagley); Director of photography: Oswald Morris (Technicolor); Production design: Terence Marsh; Editing: Russell Lloyd; Music: Maurice Jarre.

Cast: Paul Newman (Joseph Rearden), James Mason (Sir George Wheeler), Dominique Sanda (Mrs Smith), Nigel Patrick (Soames-Trevelyan), Harry Andrews (Mackintosh), Michael Hordern (Brown), Ian Bannen (Slade), Peter Vaughan (Brunskill), Roland Culver (Judge), Percy Herbert (Taafe), Robert Lang (Jack Summers), Jenny Runacre (Gerda), John Bindon (Buster), Hugh Manning

(Prosecutor), Wolfe Morris (Malta Police Commissioner), Noel Purcell (O'Donovan), Niall MacGinnis (Warder), Eddie Byrne (Fisherman), Shane Briant (Cox), Eric Mason (Postman), Nosher Powell (Army Guard), Donal McCann (1st Fireman), Leo Genn (Rollins), Clarissa Kaye-Mason (Guest at reception) [uncredited].

THE STING
1973
Universal, 129 mins
Executive producers: Richard Zanuck, David Brown; Producers: Tony Bill, Michael Phillips, Julia Phillips; Associate producer: Robert L. Crawford; Director: George Roy Hill; Screenplay: David S. Ward; Director of photography: Robert Surtees (Technicolor); Art direction: Henry Bumstead; Editing: William Reynolds; Music: Scott Joplin; Musical director: Marvin Hamlisch.
Cast: Paul Newman (Henry Gondorff), Robert Redford (Johnny Hooker), Robert Shaw (Doyle Lonnegan), Charles Durning (Lieutenant William Snyder), Ray Walston (J. J. Singleton), Eileen Brennan (Billie), Harold Gould (Kid Twist), John Heffernan (Eddie Niles), Dana Elcar (Special Agent Polk), Jack Kehoe (Joe Erie), Dimitra Arliss (Loretta), Robert Earl Jones (Luther Coleman), James Sloyan (Mattola), Charles Dierkop (Floyd), Sally Kirkland (Crystal), Avon Long (Benny Garfield), Arch Johnson (Combs), Ed Bakey (Granger), John Quade (Riley), Leonard Barr (Burlesque House Comedian), Paulene Myers (Alva Coleman), William Benedict (Roulette Dealer).

THE TOWERING INFERNO
1974
Twentieth Century Fox/Warner, 165 mins
Producer: Irwin Allen; Directors: John Guillermin, Irwin Allen; Screenplay: Stirling Silliphant (based on the novels *The Tower*, by Richard Martin Stern, and *The Glass Inferno*, by Thomas M. Scortia and Frank M. Robinson); Directors of photography: Fred Koenekamp, Joseph Biroc (DeLuxe/Panavision); Production design: William Creber; Editing: Harold F. Kress, Carl Kress; Music: John Williams; Special effects: L. B. Abbott, A. D. Flowers, Frank Van der Veer [uncredited], Douglas Trumball [uncredited] .
Cast: Paul Newman (Doug Roberts), Steve McQueen (Chief O'Halloran), William Holden (Jim Duncan), Faye Dunaway (Susan), Fred Astaire (Harlee Claiborne), Susan Blakely (Patty), Richard Chamberlain (Simmons), Robert Vaughn (Senator Parker), Jennifer Jones (Lisolette), O. J. Simpson (Jernigan), Robert Wagner (Bigelow), Susan Flannery (Lorrie), Sheila Mathews (Paula Ramsay), Norman Burton (Giddings), Jack Collins (Mayor Ramsay), Don Gordon (Kappy), Felton Perry (Scott), Gregory Sierra (Carlos), Dabney Coleman (Deputy Chief), Scott Newman (Young Fireman), John Crawford (Callahan).

THE DROWNING POOL
1975
Warner/Coleytown/Turman-Foster, 108 mins
Producers: Lawrence Turman, David Foster; Associate producer: Howard W. Koch; Director: Stuart Rosenberg; Screenplay: Walter Hill, Lorenzo Semple Jr, Tracy Keenan Wynn, Eric Roth [uncredited] (based on the novel by John Ross MacDonald); Director of photography: Gordon Willis (Technicolor/Panavision);

Production design: Paul Sylbert; Editing: John C. Howard; Music: Michael Small.

Cast: Paul Newman (Lew Harper), Joanne Woodward (Iris Devereaux), Coral Browne (Olivia Devereaux), Tony Franciosa (Chief Broussard), Murray Hamilton (Kilbourne), Gail Strickland (Mavis Kilbourne), Melanie Griffith (Schuyler Devereaux), Linda Haynes (Gretchen), Richard Jaeckel (Lieutenant Franks), Paul Koslo (Candy), Joe Canutt (Glo), Andrew Robinson (Pat Reavis), Helena Kallianiotes (Elaine Reavis).

SILENT MOVIE

1976

Twentieth Century Fox/Crossbow, 87 mins

Producer: Michael Hertzberg; Director: Mel Brooks; Screenplay: Mel Brooks, Ron Clark, Rudy DeLuca, Barry Levinson; Director of photography: Paul Lohmann (DeLuxe); Production design: Albert Brenner; Editing: John C. Howard, Stanford C. Allen; Music: John Morris.

Cast: Mel Brooks (Mel Funn), Marty Feldman (Marty Eggs), Dom DeLuise (Dom Bell), Bernadette Peters (Vilma Kaplan), Sid Caesar (Studio Chief), Harold Gould (Engulf), Fritz Feld (Maitre d'), Henny Youngman (Fly-in-Soup Man), Ron Carey (Devour), Carol DeLuise (Pregnant Lady), Liam Dunn (News Vendor), Chuck McCann (Studio Gate Guard), Valerie Curtin (Intensive Care Nurse), Harry Ritz (Man in Tailor Shop), Arnold Soboloff (Acupunture Man), Rudy DeLuca (Executive), Barry Levinson (Executive), Howard Hesseman (Executive); Guest stars: Anne Bancroft, Paul Newman, Burt Reynolds, James Caan, Liza Minnelli, Marcel Marceau (Themselves).

BUFFALO BILL AND THE INDIANS, OR SITTING BULL'S HISTORY LESSON

1976

United Artists/Dino De Laurentiis, 123 mins/105 mins

Executive producer: David Susskind; Producer: Robert Altman; Associate producers: Scott Bushnell, Jac Cashin, Robert Eggenweiler; Director: Robert Altman; Screenplay: Robert Altman, Alan Rudolph (based on the play *Indians*, by Arthur Kopit); Director of photography: Paul Lohmann (Panavision); Production design: Tony Masters; Editing: Peter Appleton, Dennis M. Hill; Music: Richard Baskin.

Cast: Paul Newman (William F. Cody, a.k.a. Buffalo Bill), Burt Lancaster (Ned Buntline), Joel Grey (Nate Salisbury), Kevin McCarthy (Major John M. Burke), Geraldine Chaplin (Annie Oakley), Harvey Keitel (Ed Goodman), Allan Nicholls (Prentiss Ingraham), John Considine (Frank Butler), Denver Pyle (McLaughlin), Frank Kaquitts (Sitting Bull), Will Sampson (William Halsey), Robert DoQui (Oswald Dart), Mike Kaplan (Jules Keen), Bert Remsen (Crutch), Pat McCormick (President Grover Cleveland), Shelley Duvall (Mrs Cleveland), Bonnie Leaders (Margaret), Noelle Rogers (Lucille DuCharme), Evelyn Lear (Nina Cavalini).

SLAP SHOT

1977

Universal, 124 mins

Producers: Robert J. Wunsch, Stephen Friedman; Director: George Roy Hill; Screenplay: Nancy Dowd; Directors of photography: Victor Kemper, Wallace Worsley (Technicolor); Production design: Henry Bumstead; Editing: Dede Allen; Musical director: Elmer Bernstein.

Cast: Paul Newman (Reggie Dunlop), Michael Ontkean (Ned Braden), Lindsay Crouse (Lily), Jennifer Warren (Francine), Strother Martin (McGrath), Melinda Dillon (Suzanne), Jerry Houser (Killer Carlson), Andrew Duncan (Jim Carr), Jeff Carlson (Jeff Hanson), Steve Carlson (Steve Hanson), David Hanson (Jack Hanson), Yvon Barrette (Denis), Allan Nicholls (Upton), Brad Sullivan (Wanchuk), M. Emmet Walsh (Dickie Dunn), Swoosie Kurtz (Shirley), Ned Dowd (Ogilthorpe), Nancy Dowd (Andrea), Paul Dooley (Hyannisport Announcer), Susan Newman (Pharmacist) [uncredited].

QUINTET

1979

Twentieth Century Fox/Lions Gate, 118 mins

Executive producer: Tommy Thompson; Producer: Robert Altman; Associate producer: Allan Nicholls; Director: Robert Altman; Screenplay: Robert Altman, Frank Barhydt, Patricia Resnick (based on a story by Altman, Lionel Chetwynd and Resnick); Director of photography: Jean Boffety (DeLuxe); Production design: Leon Ericksen; Art direction: Wolf Kroeger; Editing: Dennis M. Hill; Music: Tom Pierson; Costumes: Scott Bushnell.

Cast: Paul Newman (Essex), Vittorio Gassman (Saint Christopher), Fernando Rey (Grigor), Bibi Andersson (Ambrosia), Brigitte Fossey (Vivia), Nina Van Pallandt (Deuca), David Langton (Goldstar), Tom Hill (Francha), Craig Richard Nelson (Redstone), Monique Mercure (Redstone's Mate), Maruska Stankova (Jaspera), Anne Gerety (Aeon), Michel Maillot (Obelus), Max Fleck (Wood Supplier), Francoise Berd (Charity House Woman).

WHEN TIME RAN OUT

1980

Warner, 121 mins (US)/109 mins (UK)

Producer: Irwin Allen; Associate producers: Al Gail, George E. Swink; Director: James Goldstone; Screenplay: Carl Foreman, Stirling Silliphant (based on the novel *The Day the World Ended*, by Max Morgan Witts and Gordon Thomas); Director of photography: Fred Koenekamp (Technicolor/Panavision); Production design: Philip M. Jefferies; Editing: Edward Biery, Freeman A. Davies; Music: Lalo Schifrin.

Cast: Paul Newman (Hank Anderson), Jacqueline Bisset (Kay Kirby), William Holden (Shelby Gilmore), Edward Albert (Brian), Burgess Meredith (Rene Valdez), Valentina Cortesa (Rose Valdez), Red Buttons (Francis Fendly), Alex Karras (Tiny Baker), Ernest Borgnine (Tom Conti), Barbara Carrera (Iolani), Veronica Hamel (Nikki Spangler), James Franciscus (Bob Spangler), John Considine (John Webster), Sheila Allen (Mona), Pat Morita (Sam), Gayle Kananiokalapontigay (Waitress).

FORT APACHE, THE BRONX
1981
Time Life/Producer Circle, 123 mins
Producers: Martin Richards, Thomas Fiorello, David Susskind; Director: Daniel
Petrie; Screenplay: Heywood Gould; Director of photography: John Alcott
(DeLuxe); Production design: Ben Edwards; Editing: Rita Roland; Music:
Jonathan Tunick.
Cast: Paul Newman (Murphy), Edward Asner (Connolly), Ken Wahl (Corelli),
Danny Aiello (Morgan), Rachel Ticotin (Isabella), Pam Grier (Charlotte),
Kathleen Beller (Theresa), Tito Goya (Jumper), Miguel Pinero (Hernando),
Jaime Tirelli (Jose), Lance Guecia (Track Star), Ronnie Clanton (Pimp), Clifford
David (Dacey), Sully Boyar (Dugan), Dominic Chianese (Corelli's Father),
Thomas Fiorello (Fence).

ABSENCE OF MALICE
1981
Columbia/Mirage, 116 mins
Executive producer: Ronald L. Schwary; Producer: Sydney Pollack; Director;
Sydney Pollack; Screenplay: Kurt Luedtke, David Rayfiel [uncredited]; Director
of photography: Owen Roizman (DeLuxe); Production design: Terence Marsh;
Editing: Sheldon Kahn; Music: Dave Grusin.
Cast: Paul Newman (Michael Colin Gallagher), Sally Field (Megan Carter), Bob
Balaban (Elliot Rosen), Melinda Dillon (Teresa Perrone), Luther Adler (Santos
Malderone), Barry Primus (Bob Waddell), Josef Sommer (McAdam), John
Harkins (Davidek), Don Hood (District Attorney James A. Quinn), Wilford
Brimley (James A. Wells).

THE VERDICT
1982
Twentieth Century Fox, 128 mins
Executive producer: Burtt Harris; Producers: Richard Zanuck, David Brown;
Director: Sidney Lumet; Screenplay: David Mamet (based on the novel by Barry
Reed); Director of photography: Andrzej Bartkowiak (Technicolor); Production
design: Edward Pisoni; Editing: Peter C. Frank; Music: Johnny Mandel.
Cast: Paul Newman (Frank Galvin), James Mason (Edward J. Concannon),
Charlotte Rampling (Laura Fischer), Jack Warden (Mickey Morrissey), Milo
O'Shea (Judge Hoyle), Lindsay Crouse (Kaitlin Costello Price), Edward Binns
(Bishop Brophy), Julie Bovasso (Maureen Rooney), Roxanne Hart (Sally
Doneghy), James Handy (Kevin Doneghy), Wesley Addy (Dr Robert Towler), Joe
Seneca (Dr Lionel Thompson).

HARRY AND SON
1984
Orion, 117 mins
Producers: Paul Newman, Ronald L. Buck; Director: Paul Newman; Screenplay:
Paul Newman, Ronald L. Buck (based on the novel *A Lost King*, by Raymond
DeCapite); Director of photography: Donald McAlpine (Technicolor); Produc-
tion design: Henry Bumstead; Editing: Dede Allen; Music: Henry Mancini.
Cast: Paul Newman (Harry Keach), Robby Benson (Howard Keach), Ellen

Barkin (Katie), Wilford Brimley (Tom Keach), Judith Ivey (Sally), Ossie Davis (Raymond), Morgan Freeman (Siemanowski), Joanne Woodward (Lilly), Katherine Borowitz (Nina), Maury Chaykin (Lawrence), Michael Brockman (Driver), Cathy Cahill (Waitress), Robert Goodman (Andy), Tom Nowicki (Tommy), Claudia Robinson (Nurse), Russ Wheeler (Doctor).

THE COLOR OF MONEY
1986
Touchstone/Silver Screen Partners, 119 mins
Producers: Irving Axelrad, Barbara de Fina; Associate producer: Dodie Foster; Director: Martin Scorsese; Screenplay: Richard Price (based on characters created by Walter Tevis); Director of photography: Michael Ballhaus (DuArt); Production design: Boris Leven; Editing: Thelma Schoonmaker; Music: Robbie Robertson.
Cast: Paul Newman (Eddie), Tom Cruise (Vincent), Mary Elizabeth Mastrantonio (Carmen), Helen Shaver (Janelle), Bill Cobbs (Orvis), John Turturro (Julian), Robert Agins (Earl), Alvin Anastasia (Kennedy), Elizabeth Bracco (Diane), Joe Guastaferro (Chuck), Keith McCready (Grady Seasons), Grady Mathews (Dud), Iggy Pop (Skinny Player), Forest Whitaker (Amos).

THE GLASS MENAGERIE
1987
Cineplex, 135 mins
Producer: Burtt Harris; Director: Paul Newman; Screenplay: Tennessee Williams's original text; Director of photography: Michael Ballhaus (DuArt); Production design: Tony Walton; Editing: David Ray; Music: Henry Mancini, Paul Bowles.
Cast: Joanne Woodward (Amanda Wingfield), John Malkovich (Tom Wingfield), Karen Allen (Laura Wingfield), James Naughton (Jim O'Connor).

FAT MAN AND LITTLE BOY (UK: *The Shadow Makers*)
1989
Paramount, 127 mins
Executive producer: John Calley; Producer: Tony Garnett; Associate producer: Kimberly Cooper; Director: Roland Joffe; Screenplay: Roland Joffe, Bruce Robinson; Director of photography: Vilmos Zsigmond (Technicolor); Production design: Gregg Fonseca; Editing: Françoise Bonnot; Music: Ennio Morricone.
Cast: Paul Newman (General Leslie R. Groves), Dwight Schultz (J. Robert Oppenheimer), Bonnie Bedelia (Kitty Oppenheimer), John Cusack (Michael Merriman), Laura Dern (Kathleen Robinson), Ron Frazier (Peter de Silva), John C. McGinley (Captain Richard Schoenfield, MD), Natasha Richardson (Jean Tatlock), Ron Vawter (Jamie Latrobe), Michael Brockman (William Parsons), Del Close (Dr Kenneth Whiteside), John Considine (Robert Tuckson), Ed Lauter (Whitney Ashbridge), Fred Dalton Thompson (Major General Melrose Hayden Barry).

332

BLAZE
1989

Warner/Touchstone/Silver Screen Partners IV/A&M, 117 mins
Executive producers: David V. Lester, Don Miller; Producers: Gil Friesen, Dale Pollock; Director: Ron Shelton; Screenplay: Ron Shelton (based on the auto-biography *Blaze Starr: My Life as Told to Huey Perry*, by Blaze Starr and Huey Perry); Director of photography: Haskell Wexler (DuArt); Production design: Armin Ganz; Editing: Robert Leighton, Adam Weiss; Music: Bennie Wallace.
Cast: Paul Newman (Earl Long), Lolita Davidovich (Blaze Starr), Jerry Hardin (Thibodeaux), Gailard Sartain (LaGrange), Jeffrey DeMunn (Tuck), Garland Bunting (Doc Ferriday), Richard Jenkins (Picayune), Brandon Smith (Arvin Deeter), Jay Chevalier (Wiley Braden), Robert Wuhl (Red Snyder), Michael Brockman (Bobby), Eloy Casados (Antoine), James Harper (Willie Rainach), Teresa Gilmore (Tamara Knight), Dianne Brill (Delilah Dough), Blaze Starr (Lily).

MR AND MRS BRIDGE
1990

Miramax Films/Merchant Ivory/Cineplex Odeon/Robert Halmi, 125 mins
Executive producer: Robert Halmi; Producer: Ismail Merchant; Associate producers: Mary Kane, Humbert Balsan (France); Director: James Ivory; Screenplay: Ruth Prawer Jhabvala (based on the novels *Mr Bridge* and *Mrs Bridge*, by Evan S. Connell); Director of photography: Tony Pierce-Roberts (Technicolor); Production design: David Gropman; Editing: Humphrey Dixon; Music: Richard Robbins.
Cast: Paul Newman (Walter Bridge), Joanne Woodward (India Bridge), Robert Sean Leonard (Douglas Bridge), Margaret Welsh (Carolyn Bridge), Kyra Sedgwick (Ruth Bridge), Blythe Danner (Grace Barron), Simon Callow (Dr Alex Sauer), Austin Pendleton (Mr Gadbury), Saundra McClain (Harriet), Diane Kagan (Julia), Gale Garnett (Mabel Ong), Remak Ramsay (Virgil Barron), John Bell (Douglas Bridge as a boy), Marcus Giamatti (Gil Davis), Melissa Newman (Young India Bridge).

THE HUDSUCKER PROXY
1994

Warner/Polygram/Silver/Working Title, 111 mins
Executive producers: Tim Bevan, Eric Fellner; Producer: Ethan Coen; Co-producer: Graham Place; Directors: Joel Coen, Ethan Coen [uncredited]; Screenplay: Ethan Coen, Joel Coen, Sam Raimi; Director of photography: Roger Deakins; Production design: Dennis Gassner; Editing: Thom Noble; Music: Carter Burwell.
Cast: Tim Robbins (Norville Barnes), Jennifer Jason Leigh (Amy Archer), Paul Newman (Sidney J. Mussburger), Charles Durning (Waring Hudsucker), Jim True (Buzz), John Mahoney (Chief), Bill Cobbs (Moses), Bruce Campbell (Smitty), Harry Bugin (Aloysius), John Seitz (Benny), Joe Grifasi (Lou), David Byrd (Dr Hugo Bronfenbrenner), Peter Gallagher (Vic Tenetta), Thom Noble (Thorstenson Finlandson), Steve Buscemi (Beatnik Barman), Anna Nicole Smith (Za-Za), Sam Raimi (Hudsucker Brainstormer).

NOBODY'S FOOL

1994

Twentieth Century Fox/Paramount/Capella/Scott Rudin/Cinehaus, 110 mins
Executive producer: Michael Hausman; Producers: Scott Rudin, Arlene
Donovan; Associate producer: Scott Ferguson; Director: Robert Benton;
Screenplay: Robert Benton (based on the novel by Richard Russo); Director
of photography: John Bailey; Production design: David Gropman; Editing: John
Bloom; Music: Howard Shore.
Cast: Paul Newman (Don 'Sully' Sullivan), Jessica Tandy (Miss Beryl), Bruce
Willis (Carl Roebuck), Melanie Griffith (Toby Roebuck), Dylan Walsh (Peter),
Pruitt Taylor Vince (Rub Squeers), Gene Saks (Wirf), Josef Sommer (Clive
Peoples, Jr), Philip Seymour Hoffman (Officer Raymer), Philip Bosco (Judge
Flatt), Catherine Dent (Charlotte), Alexander Goodwin (Will), Carl John
Matusovich (Wacker), Jay Patterson (Jocko), Jerry Mayer (Ollie Quinn), Angela
Pietropinto (Cass).

TWILIGHT

1998

Paramount/Cinehaus, 94 mins
Executive producer: Michael Hausman; Producers: Arlene Donovan, Scott
Rudin; Associate producers: Scott Ferguson, David McGiffert; Director: Robert
Benton; Screenplay: Robert Benton, Richard Russo; Director of photography:
Piotr Sobocinski (DeLuxe); Production design: David Gropman; Editing: Carol
Littleton; Music: Elmer Bernstein.
Cast: Paul Newman (Harry Ross), Susan Sarandon (Catherine Ames), Gene
Hackman (Jack Ames), Reese Witherspoon (Mel Ames), Stockard Channing
(Lieutenant Verna Hollander), James Garner (Raymond Hope), Giancarlo
Esposito (Reuben Escobar), Liev Schreiber (Jeff Willis), Margo Martindale
(Gloria Lamar), John Spencer (Captain Phil Egan), M. Emmet Walsh (Lester
Ivar), Peter Gregory (Verna's Partner), Lewis Arquette (Water Pistol Man),
Michael Brockman (Garvey's Bartender), Clint Howard (EMS Worker).

MESSAGE IN A BOTTLE

1999

Warner/Bel-Air/Tig, 132 mins
Producers: Denise Di Novi, Jim Wilson, Kevin Costner; Associate producer:
Leslie Weisberg; Director: Luis Mandoki; Screenplay: Gerald DiPego (based on
the novel by Nicholas Sparks); Director of photography: Caleb Deschanel
(Technicolor/Panavision); Production design: Jeffrey Beecroft; Editing: Steven
Weisberg; Music: Gabriel Yared.
Cast: Kevin Costner (Garret Blake), Robin Wright Penn (Theresa Osborne), John
Savage (Johnny Land), Illeana Douglas (Lina Paul), Robbie Coltrane (Charlie
Toschi), Paul Newman (Dodge Blake), Jesse James (Jason Osborne), Bethel Leslie
(Marta Land), Tom Aldredge (Hank Land), Viveka Davis (Alva), Raphael Sbarge
(Andy), Richard Hamilton (Chet), Rosemary Murphy (Helen), Steven Eckholdt
(David), Justin DiPego (Typewriter Repairman).

WHERE THE MONEY IS
2000

Intermedia Films/Pacifica Film Dist/Scott Free/IMF-Warner, 88 mins
Executive producers: Tony Scott, Guy East, Nigel Sinclair, Chris Sievernich,
Moritz Borman; Producers: Ridley Scott, Charles Weinstock, Chris Zarpas,
Christopher Dorr; Co-producer: Beau E. L. Marks; Director: Marek Kanievska;
Screenplay: E. Max Frye, Topper Lilien, Carroll Cartwright; Director of pho-
tography: Thomas Burstyn; Production designer: Andre Chamberland; Editing:
Garth Craven, Samuel Craven, Dan Lebental; Music: Mark Isham.
Cast: Paul Newman (Henry Manning), Linda Fiorentino (Carol Ann McKay),
Dermot Mulroney (Wayne McKay), Bruce MacVittie (Karl).

ROAD TO PERDITION
2002

Twentieth Century Fox/DreamWorks, 117 minutes
Executive producers: Joan Bradshaw, Walter F. Parkes; Producers: Sam Mendes,
Dean Zanuck, Richard D. Zanuck; Associate producers: Tara B. Cook, Cherylanne
Martin; Director: Sam Mendes; Screenplay: David Self (based on the graphic
novel by Max Allan Collins and Richard Piers Rayner); Director of photography:
Conrad L. Hall; Production design: Dennis Gassner; Editing: Jill Bilcock; Music:
Thomas Newman.
Cast: Tom Hanks (Michael Sullivan), Paul Newman (John Rooney), Tyler
Hoechlin (Michael Sullivan Jr), Liam Aiken (Peter Sullivan), Daniel Craig (Connor
Rooney), Jude Law (Maguire), Jennifer Jason Leigh (Annie Sullivan), Ciaran
Hinds (Finn McGovern), Dylan Baker (Alexander Rance), Stanley Tucci (Frank
Nitti), Rob Maxey (Drugstore Owner).

Bibliography

Alexander, Paul, *James Dean. Boulevard of Broken Dreams*, London, Warner Books 1995.

Armstrong, Vic, 'The 10 Best Stunts Ever Pulled', *Guardian*, 22 November 2002.

Bacall, Lauren, *By Myself*, London, Coronet, 1979.

Baker, Carroll, *Baby Doll*, London, W. H. Allen, 1984.

Bart, Peter and Guber, Peter, *Shoot Out*, London, Faber and Faber, 2003.

Base, Ron, *Starring Roles*, London, Little, Brown, 1994.

Baxter, Brian, 'Paul Newman', *Films and Filming*, March 1987, no. 390.

Baxter, John, *Steven Spielberg. The Unauthorised Biography*, London, Harper-Collins, 1996.

Biskind, Peter, *Easy Riders, Raging Bulls*, London, Bloomsbury, 1999.

Bloom, Claire, *Limelight and After*, London, Weidenfeld & Nicolson, 1982.

Bona, Damien, *Opening Shots*, New York, Workman Publishing, 1994.

Brady, Frank, *Citizen Welles*, London, Hodder & Stoughton, 1990.

Braun, Eric, *Deborah Kerr*, London, W. H. Allen, 1977.

Braun, Liz, 'Paul Newman still going strong', *Toronto Sun*, 7 July 2002.

Brosnan, John, *Movie Magic*, London, Abacus, 1977.

Brownlow, Kevin, *David Lean. A Biography*, New York, St Martin's Press, 1996.

Clinch, Minty, *Clint Eastwood*, London, Hodder & Stoughton, 1994.

Collins, Joan, *Second Act*, London, Boxtree, 1996.

Curtis, Tony with Paris, Barry, *Tony Curtis. The Autobiography*, London, Mandarin, 1995.

Donegan, Lawrence, 'The Newman Factor', *Observer Sport Monthly*, May 2003, no. 39.

Douglas, Kirk, *The Ragman's Son*, London, Pan, 1989.

Dunaway, Faye with Sharkey, Betsy, *Looking for Gatsby. My Life*, London, HarperCollins, 1995.

Engel, Joel, *Rod Serling: The Dreams and Nightmares of Life in the Twilight Zone*, Chicago, Contemporary Books, 1989.

Epstein, Edward Z. and Morella, Joe, *Paul and Joanne*, London, W. H. Allen, 1989.

Falk, Quentin, *Cinema's Strangest Moments*, London, Robson Books, 2003.

Feeney Callan, Michael, *Sean Connery. His Life and Films*, London, W. H. Allen, 1983.

Fishgall, Gary, *Against Type. The Biography of Burt Lancaster*, New York, Scribner, 1995.

Fraser-Cavassoni, Natasha, *Sam Spiegel. The Biography of a Hollywood Legend*, London, Little, Brown, 2003.

French, John, *Robert Shaw: The Price of Success*, London, Nick Hern Books, 1993.

Frischauer, Willi, *Behind the Scenes of Otto Preminger*, London, Michael Joseph, 1973.

Galbraith IV, Stuart, *The Emperor and the Wolf*, London, Faber and Faber, 2002.

Gansberg, Alan L., *Little Caesar: A Biography of Edward G. Robinson*, London, New English Library, 1983.

Gelmis, Joseph, *The Film Director as Superstar*, London, Secker & Warburg, 1971.

Goldman, William, *Adventures in the Screen Trade*, London, Futura, 1985.

Goring, Rosemary (ed), *Larousse Dictionary of Writers*, Edinburgh, Larousse, 1994.

Gow, Gordon, 'Cool It' (Lee Remick interview), *Films and Filming*, February 1971, vol. 17, no. 5.

Grobel, Lawrence, *The Hustons*, New York, Avon, 1989.

Hay, Peter, *Hollywood Anecdotes*, Oxford, Oxford University Press, 1990.

Herman, Jan, *A Talent for Trouble*, New York, Putnam, 1995.

Heston, Charlton, *In the Arena: The Autobiography*, London, HarperCollins, 1995.

Hickey, Des and Smith, Gus, *The Prince. The Public and Private Life of Laurence Harvey*, London, Leslie Frewin, 1975.

Higham, Charles, *Brando. The Unauthorised Biography*, London, Grafton Books, 1989.

Hobson, Louis B., 'Fast times with Newman', *Calgary Sun*, 24 April 2000.

Hobson, Louis B., 'Living legend', *Calgary Sun*, 22 February 1998.

Hobson, Louis B., 'Newman finds a match in Alberta', *Calgary Sun,* 3 February 1998.

Hogan, Ron, 'It's Not Just for the Money', *Publishers Weekly*, 13 October 2003.

Holden, Anthony, *The Oscars: The Secret History of Hollywood's Academy Awards*, London, Little, Brown and Company, 1993.

Hordern, Michael, *A World Elsewhere*, London, Michael O'Mara Books Ltd, 1994.

Hunter, Allan, *Faye Dunaway*, London, W. H. Allen, 1986.

Huston, John, *An Open Book*, London, Macmillan, 1981.

Iley, Chrissy, 'Bright-Eyed and Ageless', *Sunday Times*, 15 September 2002.

Kaminsky, Stuart, *John Huston. Maker of Magic*, London, Angus & Robertson, 1978.

Kaplan, Fred, *Gore Vidal*, London, Bloomsbury, 1999.

Karam, Edward, 'Adventures of an old man', *Guardian*, 9 December 2002.

Katz, Ephraim, *The Macmillan International Film Encyclopaedia*, London, Macmillan, 1994.

Kazan, Elia, *A Life*, London, Andre Deutsch, 1988.

Kim, Erwin, *Franklin J. Schaffner*, London, Scarecrow, 1985.

Kirkland, Bruce, 'Paul Newman as sexy as ever', *Toronto Sun*, 9 April 2000.

Kolker, Robert Phillip, *A Cinema of Loneliness*, Oxford, Oxford University Press, 1988.

Levy, Emanuel, *George Cukor. Master of Elegance*, New York, Morrow, 1994.

Lyman, Rick, 'So, as Paul said to Tom . . . ', *Observer*, 15 September 2002.

MacDonald Fraser, George, *The Light's on at Signpost*, London, HarperCollins, 2003.

Madsen, Axel, *John Huston*, London, Robson Books, 1979.

Malden, Karl and Malden, Carla, *When Do I Start?* New York, Simon & Schuster, 1997.

Maltin, Leonard (ed), *Leonard Maltin's Movie and Video Guide, 1995*, London, Signet, 1994.

Mamet, David, 'Victims and Villains', *Guardian*, 24 January 2003.

Manso, Peter, *Brando*, London, Weidenfeld & Nicolson, 1994.

Margulies, Edward and Rebello, Stephen, *Bad Movies We Love*, New York, Plume, 1993.

Marvin, Pamela, *Lee*, London, Faber and Faber, 1997.

McGilligan, Patrick, *Jack's Life. A Biography of Jack Nicholson*, London, Harper-Collins, 1995.

McGilligan, Patrick, *Robert Altman. Jumping Off the Cliff*, New York, St Martin's Press, 1989.

Medved, Harry and Medved, Michael, *The Golden Turkey Awards*, London, Angus & Robertson, 1980.

Medved, Harry and Medved, Michael, *The Hollywood Hall of Shame*, London, Angus & Robertson, 1984.

Meltsir, Aljean, 'The "Dignity Explosion"', *Photoplay*, November 1963, vol. 64, no. 5.

Mendes, Sam, 'One of the Few Genuine Artists I Have Known', *Guardian*, 17 January 2003.

Milius, John, *The Life and Times of Judge Roy Bean*, New York, Bantam, 1973.

Miller, John, *Peter Ustinov. The Gift of Laughter*, London, Weidenfeld & Nicolson, 2002.

Mordden, Ethan, *Medium Cool. The Movies of the 1960s*, New York, Alfred A. Knopf, 1990.

Neal, Patricia, *As I Am*, London, Century, 1988.

Netter, Susan, *Paul Newman and Joanne Woodward*, London, Piatkus, 1989.

Niven, David, *Bring on the Empty Horses*, London, Coronet, 1976.

Norman, Barry, *Talking Pictures*, London, Arrow, 1991.

Peary, Danny, *Guide for the Film Fanatic*, New York, Fireside/Simon & Schuster, 1986.

Peer, Robert, 'The Nightmare that Haunts Paul Newman', *Photoplay Film Monthly*, October 1969, vol. 20, no. 10.

Phillips, Julia, *You'll Never Eat Lunch in this Town Again*, London, Mandarin, 1992.

Poitier, Sidney, *This Life*, London, Hodder and Stoughton, 1980.

Powell, Dilys, *The Golden Screen*, London, Headline, 1990.

Pym, John (ed), *Time Out Film Guide, Ninth Edition*, London, Penguin, 2000.

Reed, Rex, *Do You Sleep in the Nude?* London, W. H. Allen, 1969.

Robinson, Edward G. with Spigelgass, Leonard, *All My Yesterdays. An Auto biography*, London, W. H. Allen, 1974.

Robson, Eddie, *Coen Brothers*, London, Virgin, 2003.

Roman, Shari, 'Tales of Hoffman', *Neon*, issue 20, August 1998.

Rosso, Diana de, *James Mason. A Personal Biography*, Oxford, Lennard, 1989.

Sandford, Christopher, *McQueen*, London, HarperCollins, 2001.

Sangster, Jim, *Scorsese*, London, Virgin, 2002.

Schroeder, Maria with Preston, Whit, 'Paul Newman's 2 Days in a Nudist Colony!', *Photoplay*, November 1963, vol. 64, no. 5.

Server, Lee, *Robert Mitchum. 'Baby, I Don't Care'*, London, Faber and Faber, 2001.

Siegel, Joel E., *Val Lewton: The Reality of Terror*, London, Secker & Warberg, 1972.

Silvester, Christopher (ed), *The Penguin Book of Hollywood*, London, Viking, 1998.

Skow, John, 'Verdict on a Superstar', *Time*, 6 December 1982.

Spoto, Donald, *The Art of Alfred Hitchcock*, London, Fourth Estate, 1992.

Spoto, Donald, *The Dark Side of Genius. The Life of Alfred Hitchcock*, London, Plexus, 1983.

Spoto, Donald, *Rebel. The Life and Legend of James Dean*, London, Harper-Collins, 1996.

Stoynoff, Natasha, 'An age of reason', *Toronto Sun*, 15 February 1998.

Taylor, John Russell, *Hitch. The Life and Work of Alfred Hitchcock*, London, Faber and Faber, 1978.

Thomas, Bob, *Golden Boy. The Untold Story of William Holden*, London, Weidenfeld & Nicolson, 1983.

Thompson, David and Christie, Ian (eds), *Scorsese on Scorsese*, London, Faber and Faber, 1989.

Thompson, Douglas, *Clint Eastwood. Sexual Cowboy*, London, Warner Books, 1993.

Thompson, Richard, 'Stoked' (John Milius interview), *Film Comment*, July–August 1976.

Thomson, David, *A Biographical Dictionary of the Cinema*, London, Secker & Warburg, 1980.

Thomson, David, 'Going for a gong', *Independent*, 20 January 2003.

Urbancich, John, '*Twilight* falls on Paul Newman', *Sun News*, 26 February 1998.

Ustinov, Peter, *Dear Me*, London, Penguin, 1977.

Vidal, Gore, *Palimpsest. A Memoir*, London, Andre Deutsch, 1995.

Walker, Alexander, *Elizabeth*, London, Weidenfeld & Nicolson, 1990.

Walker, John (ed), *Halliwell's Film & Video Guide 2001*, London, HarperCollins, 2000.

Walker, John (ed), *Halliwell's Filmgoer's Companion, 10th Edition*, London, HarperCollins, 1993.

Weddle, David, *If They Move . . . Kill 'Em!* New York, Grove Press, 1994.

Welles, Orson and Bogdanovich, Peter, *This Is Orson Welles*, London, Harper-Collins, 1993.

Windeler, Robert, *Burt Lancaster*, London, W. H. Allen, 1984.

Winecoff, Charles, *Split Image. The Life of Anthony Perkins*, New York, Plume, 1997.

Winters, Shelley, *Shelley II. The Middle of My Century*, New York, Simon & Schuster, 1989.

Wood, Robin, *Arthur Penn*, London, Studio Vista, 1968.

Young, Jeff, *Kazan on Kazan*, London, Faber and Faber, 1999.

Zec, Donald, *Marvin. The Story of Lee Marvin*, London, New English Library, 1979.

Internet

imdb.com
italianstudies.org
pbs.org
tiscali.co.uk

DVD commentaries/interviews/documentaries/production notes

The Long Hot Summer (Twentieth Century Fox)
The Hustler (Fox)
Torn Curtain (Universal)
Cool Hand Luke (Warner)
Butch Cassidy and the Sundance Kid (Fox)
They Might Be Giants (Universal / Anchor Bay)
The Sting (Universal)
Slap Shot (Universal)
Absence of Malice (Columbia)
The Verdict (Fox)
Road to Perdition (Fox/DreamWorks)

Index